AF608250

BEYOND THE WELFARE STATE

Postwar Social Settlement and Public Pension Policy in Canada and Australia

Studies in Comparative Political Economy and Public Policy

Editors: MICHAEL HOWLETT, DAVID LAYCOCK (Simon Fraser University), and STEPHEN MCBRIDE (McMaster University)

Studies in Comparative Political Economy and Public Policy is designed to showcase innovative approaches to political economy and public policy from a comparative perspective. While originating in Canada, the series will provide attractive offerings to a wide international audience, featuring studies with local, subnational, cross-national, and international empirical bases and theoretical frameworks.

For a list of books published in the series, see page 339.

Beyond the Welfare State

Postwar Social Settlement and Public Pension Policy in Canada and Australia

SIRVAN KARIMI

UNIVERSITY OF TORONTO PRESS
Toronto Buffalo London

Toronto Buffalo London
www.utppublishing.com

ISBN 978-1-4875-0041-2

Library and Archives Canada Cataloguing in Publication

Karimi, Sirvan, 1966–, author
Beyond the welfare state: postwar social settlement and public pension policy in Canada and Australia / Sirvan Karimi.

(Series: Studies in Comparative Political Economy and Public Policy; 51)
Includes bibliographical references and index.
ISBN 978-1-4875-0041-2 (cloth)

1. Pensions – Government policy – Canada. 2. Pensions – Government policy – Australia. 3. Welfare state – Canada. 4. Welfare state – Australia. 5. Canada – Social policy. 6. Australia – Social policy. I. Title. II. Series: Studies in Comparative Political Economy and Public Policy; 51.

HD7129.K37 2017 331.25'20971 C2016-905669-4

This book has been published with the help of a grant from the Federation for the Humanities and Social Sciences, through the Awards to Scholarly Publications Program, using funds provided by the Social Sciences and Humanities Research Council of Canada.

University of Toronto Press acknowledges the financial assistance to its publishing program of the Canada Council for the Arts and the Ontario Arts Council, an agency of the Government of Ontario.

Canada Council for the Arts
Conseil des Arts du Canada

Funded by the Government of Canada
Financé par le gouvernement du Canada
Canada

Contents

List of Tables

Foreword

With his comparative study of the retirement income systems in Australia and Canada, Sirvan Karimi makes a valuable contribution to our understanding of an important and increasingly contested area of social policy. And what is so essentially important about this book is that it reminds us that this vital area of public policy, like all public policy, is not a given, something that flows naturally from the good intentions of well-meaning individuals occupying important positions within the state. Instead, Karimi coherently and comprehensively excavates the factors and forces that gave rise to two rather different pension systems despite the apparent institutional similarities of Canada and Australia.

And this work identifies the social, political, and ideological variables explaining the different trajectories of old age pension policy in these two federal states. The patterns of economic and political development in Canada and Australia provide significant variables for a comparative analysis of welfare states. The two states have similar attributes, including being "white settler societies," former British colonies that gradually gained independence without a revolutionary rupture. Also, both are affluent liberal democracies with federal systems, and both economies are to a large degree based on resource exploitation and a relatively weak industrial sector. In addition, both countries have been subject to the same or similar forces of neoliberal restructuring over the past four decades.

But despite these institutional and economic similarities, the two countries differ rather markedly in terms of class-based politics and ethno-racial/linguistic characteristics. Here is the material basis for the central question posed by Karimi: the Australian pension system moved rather sharply towards privatization, with only a residual universal and public component; whereas in Canada, old age pension policy moved in precisely the opposite direction, as a universal public program based ideologically on a pan-Canadian idea of social solidarity. What variables explain this divergence within a structure of general institutional similarity? As Karimi notes, these divergent approaches to the same policy field are not adequately explained by mainstream welfare studies perspectives. Karimi seeks to remedy this gap by combing elements of Marxist class analysis and the power resources model. But as his research reveals, even this is not fully adequate: the unity of the Australian working class and the success of labourism in the electoral field in Australia did not result in a more solidaristic pension policy; yet in Canada, a fragmented working class and weak social democratic parties at the national level seem not to have been essential variables in the emergence of a much more public and universal Canadian pension regime. The solution to this conundrum is to be found in the particular national characteristics within the postwar class compromise forged within each state. In Australia, this compromise was based on the industrial relations regime governing labour–capital relations. That relationship was shaped much more strongly by the exigencies of competitiveness and the logic of capital. In Canada, the overarching concern was national unity, given the presence of competing nationalisms and the role of social policy in creating and cementing a pan-Canadian identity. Such a concern was entirely absent in Australia. And while the postwar labour–capital compromises in Canada were not dramatically different in general, the highly uneven and fractured nature of working-class political mobilization in Canada and the fact that much of the work of managing labour relations was assigned to the provinces meant that pension policy was driven to some greater extent by forces other than those of the unionized working class.

Karimi engages with the debates within the welfare state studies literature and makes a contribution in his own right, especially in formulating several unique conceptual frameworks that can be readily applied to future analyses. His work is nothing less than rich and revealing.

Bryan Evans, PhD
Associate Professor
Department of Politics and Public Administration
Ryerson University
Toronto, Canada

Acknowledgments

Rarely does a book result from the time and effort of a single individual, and this one is no exception. Many people have directly or indirectly contributed to the completion of this project.

I wish to express my deepest appreciation for those who have supported me during this arduous but amazing journey.

Though the roots of some ideas in this book can be traced back to my undergraduate studies at the University of Winnipeg, its central ideas were developed in the Department of Political Science at York University, an environment that fosters creativity and intellectual engagement.

I would like to express my profound and sincere gratitude to Professor Gregory Albo, Professor Leo Panitch, and Professor Thomas Klassen, each of whom played a crucial role in shaping the ideas developed in this book. My project would not have been completed without the guidance and invaluable assistance I have received from these three scholars. Their constructive criticisms and suggestions enriched my ideas enormously.

I would like to express my special thanks to the School of Public Policy and Administration at York University for hiring me as sessional assistant professor in 2013. This full-time position provided me with a golden opportunity to complete this book.

The faculty and administrative staff at the school have all been kind and supportive.

I would like to take this opportunity to thank the University of Toronto Press for its commitment to this book, particularly Daniel Quinlan, acquisitions editor there, who saw the potential of my book at the first stage of its submission. Daniel's patience, clear thinking, and guidance are remarkable.

Finally, I beg forgiveness of all those who have been with me over the course of the years and whose names I have failed to mention.

Acronyms

ACTU	Australian Confederation of Trade Unions
ALP	Australian Labor Party
BCA	Business Council of Australia
BQ	Bloc Québécois
CCF	Co-operative Commonwealth Federation
CCL	Canadian Congress of Labour
CHST	Canada Health and Social Transfer
CLC	Canadian Labour Congress
CPP	Canada Pension Plan
GIS	Guaranteed Income Supplement
IMF	International Monetary Fund
IPA	Institute for Public Affairs
NDP	New Democratic Party
OAS	Old Age Security
OECD	Organisation for Economic Co-operation and Development
PAYG	pay-as-you-go
PRPPs	Pooled Registered Pension Plans
QPP	Quebec Pension Plan
RPPs	Registered Pension Plans
RRSPs	Registered Retirement Saving Plans
SPC	Socialist Party of Canada
TLC	Trades and Labor Congress
UN	United Nations
YMPE	Year's Maximum Pensionable Earnings

BEYOND THE WELFARE STATE

Postwar Social Settlement and Public Pension Policy in Canada and Australia

Introduction

The welfare state has established itself as one of the defining institutions of liberal democratic societies. In the social sciences, the welfare state has attracted theoreticians and analysts of various ideological and political persuasions. The appeal of welfare state studies lies not only in the broad nature of social policy (which encompasses almost three-quarters of state activities in advanced capitalist societies) but also in its role in modifying living conditions so as to promote human welfare.[1] For the purposes of this study, "welfare state" refers to a set of political, social, and economic interventions designed to modify market forces in a capitalist economy so as to secure stable societal reproduction. Asa Briggs characterizes the welfare state as one in which "organized power is deliberately used (through politics and administration) in an effort to modify the interplay of market forces."[2] Thus the overall aim of the welfare state is to create and maintain living conditions conducive to the enhancement of human welfare.

Throughout human history, societies have developed mechanisms for protecting social welfare that are specific to their respective socioeconomic conditions. Social welfare programs can be traced back to the nineteenth century; however, the modern welfare state is tied to the triumph of Keynesian macroeconomic theory over classical liberal theory in the post–Second World War era. Keynesianism provided the grounds for public intervention in the economic cycle to counter the instability of market forces. Keynesianism was adopted as a technical solution to problems relating to capital accumulation; but as it turned out, it was also conducive to expanding the welfare state and thereby strengthening the social position of the working class.

During the economic crisis of the 1970s, however, Keynesian tools of economic management proved inadequate in tackling the phenomenon of stagflation. The inability of Keynesianism to solve the economic crisis created an opportunity for neoliberal doctrines of political economy to launch a successful theoretical battle against the Keynesian macroeconomic policy that had dominated the governmental agenda for three consecutive decades in the advanced capitalist countries.

Since the ascendancy of neoliberalism in the 1980s, welfare states in liberal democratic societies have undergone restructuring and retrenchment. Restructuring does not necessarily involve reducing social welfare expenditures, but it is synonymous with "recalibration," which entails modifying or reconfiguring certain social programs.[3] Retrenchment, by contrast, entails reducing social benefits and tightening eligibility criteria for specific social welfare programs.

With the eclipse of Keynesian demand management and the rise of neoliberalism, the pressure for welfare state reconfiguration has become universal. Welfare state restructuring has been advocated by supranational organizations such as the Organisation for Economic Cooperation and Development (OECD), the World Bank, the International Monetary Fund (IMF), and the United Nations (UN). To bring social welfare programs into line with market forces, the OECD has been calling on its member countries to shift their emphasis from income support programs to employment-friendly social policies geared towards reintegrating the unemployed into the labour market.[4]

The World Bank has emerged as the most passionate promoter of pension reforms. In its 1994 report on old age pensions, it warned countries about an "aging crisis" and called on governments to adopt social welfare policies that would link the protection of elderly people to economic growth. The World Bank explicitly encourages countries around the world to diversify their pension programs by establishing multi-pillar pension systems and placing greater emphasis on privately managed mandatory retirement savings and personal voluntary savings than on public pension plans.[5] The central thrust of the World Bank's recommendations has been to present high levels of expenditure on public pensions as an unsustainable burden on welfare states. It has endorsed privately managed mandatory saving schemes as a safer road to securing retirement income. The World Bank's loud calls for pension reform amount to a tacit endorsement of an individualistic approach to retirement income provision; in fact, that approach is a cornerstone of the neoliberal enterprise. In its 2001 report on globalization and the public sector, the UN emphasized that the reform of that sector "would give states a better opportunity to globalize."[6] Even the International Labour Organization (ILO), while calling for a greater degree of protection for elderly people, has endorsed raising the average age of retirement (or the age of eligibility for a public pension) and is advocating multi-tier pension systems.[7]

But despite all the calls for welfare state reform, especially with regard to public pensions, states have varied with regard to the pace, degree, and form of retrenchment. These variations in welfare state restructuring and retrenchment are reflected in differences in how advanced capitalist countries are reconfiguring retirement income. Old age pension systems were the most dramatic development in the public sector in the twentieth century and have become a hallmark of developed countries.[8] Several welfare state scholars have noted the centrality of old age pensions to analyses of welfare states (and the variations between them). According to John Myles, "an understanding of old age is central to the enterprise of those political theorists who are engaged in explaining the welfare state. This is simply because, the contemporary welfare state in capitalist democracies is largely a welfare state for the elderly ... Expenditures on the elderly are now the largest component of the welfare state budget."[9] In the same vein as Myles, Gøsta Esping-Andersen has suggested that "if an analysis of pensions appears somewhat narrow and pedestrian, keep in mind two circumstances. First, pensions account for more than 10 percent of GDP in many contemporary nations. Second, pensions constitute a central link between work and leisure, between earned income and redistribution, between individualism and solidarity, between the cash nexus and social rights. Pensions therefore, help elucidate a set of perennially conflictual principles of capitalism."[10] The impact of ageing populations on the public purse has become a pressing issue in welfare state policy; so have responses to the growing population of elderly.[11] As Sheila Shaver has pointed out, the old age pension is "the paradigm setter for welfare politics."[12]

The rise of welfare state restructuring has set the stage for competing theoretical and analytical endeavours to unravel and explain the variations in welfare state restructuring and retrenchment in advanced capitalist societies. Competing arguments about welfare state expansion and restructuring revolve around three linked questions. What are the determinants of the welfare state? What are the forces behind the parallel but divergent patterns of welfare state restructuring in advanced industrial countries? And can theories of welfare state expansion also explain the politics of welfare state contraction during this era of neoliberalism?

The Welfare State Debate

The main theoretical accounts of welfare state expansion and subsequent processes of welfare state retrenchment revolve around three lines of interpretation, each of which focuses on a different set of variables. The first approach emphasizes the impact of economic growth and its demographic corollaries.[13] The second emphasizes the roles played by political institutions in shaping social welfare policy.[14] The third emphasizes the centrality of sociological and political forces in moulding the direction of social programs.[15] These three lines of interpretation frame the main theoretical debates on the development, expansion, and restructuring of the welfare state in advanced capitalist countries.

Although the analytical line of demarcation between economic and non-economic factors is difficult to draw, diverse explanatory perspectives on the welfare state can nonetheless be distinguished from one another by the varying degrees of emphasis they place on structures, institutions, and agency. Welfare state literatures can therefore be respectively classified along liberal, Weberian, and Marxian lines of analysis, posing as rival theoretical paradigms.

While each of the main theoretical perspectives might explain particular aspects of the welfare state, none of them provide a comprehensive picture of the variations in welfare state retrenchment. The existing comparative welfare state studies have focused mainly on factors such as economic development levels, demographic composition, institutional structures, and the power of labour as the chief explanatory variables for variation in welfare state reconfiguration in liberal democratic societies. Less attention has been paid to nationalism's impact on postwar social class compromises, even though this is key to understanding welfare state expansion as well as the tide of welfare state retrenchment driven by neoliberalism.

The inadequacy of mainstream theoretical approaches in providing a clear picture of welfare state expansion and subsequent processes of restructuring can be largely accounted for by their failure to explain the differences in postwar political strategies built around class, nationhood, and social alternatives. More specifically, prevailing theoretical perspectives fail to integrate the interplay of national settings, social classes, and the state's role in shaping the postwar social class settlement, which not only structured the postwar welfare state expansion but also has shaped welfare state restructuring and retrenchment.

Retirement Income Systems in Canada and Australia

Economic and political developments in Canada and Australia provide a useful set of variables for a comparative inquiry into welfare states. Canada and Australia are appropriate for a "most similar systems" research design because they share many attributes.[16] Both are "white settler societies," having been settled by waves of immigrants who marginalized the original inhabitants. Both colonies refrained from pursuing a revolutionary break with Britain, instead gaining their independence gradually, and both have remained constitutional monarchies. Canada and Australia are both affluent liberal democracies whose staple-led economies have long been marked by resource exportation and a relatively weak industrial base.[17] Having been assembled from fragmented colonies, both countries combine a federal structure with a Westminster-style parliamentary system. Although Canada and Australia employ different electoral methods, both countries have multi-party systems, and during the era of postwar economic growth, they were run by single-party governments.[18] There is a greater fiscal centralization in Australia; that said, both countries are marked by a similar pattern of federal–provincial (or federal–state in the case of Australia) jurisdictional division of powers with regard to the arrangement, provision, and delivery of social services.

But with respect to national composition, Canada and Australia diverge. Quebec's historical quest for political independence, which has touched all aspects of Canadian politics, distinguishes Canada from Australia and accounts for differences in working-class politics between the two countries. In Australia, the labour movement has historically been united and the Australian Labor Party has periodically exercised governmental power at the national and sub-national levels; in Canada, by contrast, the working class has long been fragmented and there has never been a social democratic government at the federal level.

Despite their striking similarities at the institutional and economic levels, the Australian and Canadian welfare states have taken different routes. The divergent patterns of welfare state expansion and subsequent variations in welfare state retrenchment in Australia and Canada reveal the explanatory weaknesses of the mainstream theoretical paradigms. The Canadian and Australian welfare states (along with their counterparts in the United States and Britain) are usually characterized as liberal regimes that rely heavily on means-tested social assistance as the primary mechanism of social protection.[19] Yet Canada and Australia not only were marked by variations in postwar welfare state expansion but also have been distinguished by differences in their responses to welfare state restructuring and retrenchment.

Australia has made several attempts to establish a publicly administered pension plan, but its retirement income system continues to rely on private occupational plans. Furthermore, during the era of welfare state expansion, Australia's old age security system could not extricate itself from means-testing mechanisms. In Canada, by contrast, old age pension policy moved gradually towards the principles of universality and collectivity as a basis for social solidarity. Even in this neoliberal era of welfare state restructuring, Canada's retirement income system has largely retained its universal and collectivistic characteristics. The Australian retirement income system, meanwhile, has drifted sharply towards more residualism and privatization.

These divergent patterns of retirement income expansion and restructuring in Canada and Australia raise significant research questions that have not been answered adequately by mainstream theoretical perspectives. Australia is more politically centralized than Canada and has a stronger labour movement. The Canadian labour movement is more fragmented, and Canada has never had a social democratic government at the federal level. How then, did Canada's retirement income system come to acquire a universal character, while its Australian counterpart came to be marked so strongly by selectivity? Why, despite the neoliberal economic restructuring in both countries, has the direction of retirement income retrenchment in Australia been so sharply different from that of Canada?

An Approach to the Study of Welfare State Variation

Clearly, no single theoretical framework can provide a comprehensive explanation for variations in welfare state expansion and retrenchment. So it is useful to rely on "a combination of explanations drawn from a variety of different theoretical perspectives."[20] An analytical framework that can explain the interplay of national settings, the role of the state, and the specific form of the welfare state requires us to combine elements of Marxian class analysis and the power resources model. By grounding the analysis of variations in welfare state expansion and of divergent patterns of welfare state retrenchment within this integrated approach, we can formulate the main arguments of this book as follows:

In both Canada and Australia the welfare state, as the political manifestation of the postwar social class compromise, was harnessed to deflect the threat that radicalism posed to the existing socio-political order and thereby preserve the hegemony of capitalist social relations. Contrary to prevailing assumptions held by mainstream theoretical perspectives on the welfare state, the presence of a single nationalism within a given social formation in Australia was not sufficient to guarantee the emergence there of a comprehensive and generous welfare state. Conversely, the clash of competing nationalisms within the Canadian social formation did not result in the pursuit of a residual social welfare policy.

All postwar social class compromises were politically constructed, but they also all acquired different characteristics. A politically constructed market-oriented social class compromise manifested itself in the adoption of market-oriented regulatory measures as a surrogate for a redistributive social policy designed to secure the welfare of the working class. Such a social pact was able to take root in Australia, where relative ethnic homogeneity and the presence of one nationalism strengthened the unity of the labour movement. That movement's aspirations, however, did not exceed the purview of capital–labour relations. A politically constructed redistributive-oriented social settlement did emerge in Canada, where politicized national heterogeneity had heightened the fragmentation of the working class. Within Canada's particular social environment, the management of national unity required the adoption of a progressive and comprehensive social welfare policy.

Under a politically constructed market-centred postwar social class settlement in Australia, the welfarist goals of social income security were to be accomplished through market-regulated measures that left less room for social spending and that marginalized the principle of universality. In Canada, redistribution and universality, not labour market regulation, became the primary mechanisms of social protection. In contrast to the politically constructed redistributive-oriented postwar social settlement in Canada that was conducive to strengthening the links between the welfare state, social citizenship, and universalism, the Australian social settlement was geared more towards promoting "market citizenship." Under the Australian social class settlement, the notion of social citizenship entitlement was embedded in market forces that encouraged the pursuit of means-tested income security provisions.

In both Canada and Australia, the responses to neoliberal pressures for welfare state restructuring were shaped largely by the nature of the postwar social settlement that had structured postwar patterns of welfare state expansion. The market-centred postwar social settlement was vulnerable to the turbulent market forces in the 1970s; the redistributive-oriented social settlement was less susceptible to alteration by the balance of class forces that followed a wave of economic restructuring. With the shift in the balance of class forces accompanying the economic crisis, the market-centred social class settlement in Australia was destined to readjust itself to the demands of market forces. Under a redistributive-oriented social settlement in Canada, the decline in the bargaining power of labour was compensated for by the discourse of national unity, which had the potential to partly shield the welfare state from the retrenchment process.

Under the market-centred postwar social pact, the direction of Australian welfare state restructuring was governed by the discourse of economic rationalism, which was amenable to the process of retrenchment. In other words, the seeds for targeting, retrenchment, and marketization were already contained within the structure of the Australian social settlement. Under a postwar social compromise that had acquired a redistributive-oriented character in Canada, the discourse of national unity had the potential to decelerate welfare state retrenchment and privatization.

This book's analytical approach focuses on the nature and character of postwar social settlements as the main explanatory variable behind welfare state variations. The same approach will be used to explain the divergent patterns of old age pension systems in Canada and Australia. In both countries, the postwar social settlement not only structured the postwar expansion of pension systems but also came to shape the social policy responses to the economic crisis of the 1970s. More specifically, the nature and structure of the postwar expansion of the welfare state locked in the early choices that would later mould the processes of restructuring and retrenchment.

The market-centred postwar social compromise in Australia was vulnerable to the drastic measures deemed imperative to tackle the economic crisis, which had destabilized the foundations of the postwar social settlement. The Australian social class compromise was vulnerable to the post-1970s economic turbulence; in contrast, the redistributive-oriented postwar social settlement in Canada came to function as a brake on the wheels of neoliberal inroads into the domain of pension policy.

A Methodological Note

A comparative investigation of the welfare state expansion and contraction in Canada and Australia requires a historical approach. A comparative study over this long period provides a basis for assessing the linkage between the politics of welfare state expansion and those of retrenchment. This specific approach to investigating welfare state expansion and restructuring entails three levels of analysis. At the first level, the focus is on the relations between state, society, and structural exigencies that required the adoption of social welfare policies. At the second, the balance of social forces is examined for each country, including the specific national settings within each social formation that structured the postwar social class settlement, which in turn shaped the contours of the welfare state. At the third, the influence of social forces and national factors on changes to each country's retirement income systems is traced. This approach meets the fundamental criterion of a comparative study: it allows a simultaneous analysis "at the level of systems (or macrosocial level) and at the within-system level."[21]

The focus here is on political discourse as a crucial factor in shaping the postwar social class settlement.[22] Both primary and secondary sources have been used. Attention will be paid to the analysis of relevant parliamentary debates, political speeches, official statements, and relevant government documents to shed light on how of postwar class compromise shaped welfare state expansion and the ensuing welfare state contraction.

To compare and evaluate changes in different countries' welfare states, the prevailing methodological approaches focus on both quantitative measurements (of public social expenditures as a percentage of GDP) and qualitative assessments (of the degree of comprehensiveness, the rate of replacement, and eligibility criteria).[23] The use of public social expenditures to measure the generosity of welfare states has been questioned on the grounds that it does not fully reflect the nature and dynamics of social welfare policy.[24] Furthermore, it is argued that relying on public expenditures as a tool for comparing welfare states ignores the structural relationship between public spending and changing social needs.[25] Yet as Gregg Olsen has pointed out, it is public social expenditure as a proportion of GDP, not total government expenditure, that signals the relative generosity of welfare states.[26] Public social expenditure as a proportion of the GDP indicates the degree of welfare state generosity and is also directly related to the welfare state goal of income inequality reduction. Several analysts have pointed out that the level of public social expenditures is closely linked to income inequality reduction and poverty amelioration.[27] Levels of social spending cannot be dissociated from levels of taxation; the reduction of income inequality and poverty is positively correlated with higher levels of social welfare spending.[28]

The assessment of the distributional outcomes of policy instruments that are designed to ameliorate poverty and diminish income inequality is another method widely used by analysts to compare and evaluate variations among welfare states.[29] According to the proponents of this methodological approach, despite a statistically significant relationship between public expenditure and the alleviation of social inequalities, expenditure alone is not an appropriate measure of the success of the state's protective activities.[30] In this method, there is an assertion that selective targeting through either transfer or taxation might also accomplish the aims of poverty alleviation and income inequality reduction.[31] In other words, targeting is much more effective than high social expenditures or universal provision at reducing both income inequality and poverty.

Another method that has recently been employed to examine welfare state support involves measuring levels of decommodification and degrees of universality that affect the quality of citizenship.[32] This approach has become a point of reference for many cross-national studies of welfare states. It shifts the focus to the decommodifying effects of social programs and to how the welfare state is designed to structure the quality of citizenship. Using the level of decommodification and the degree of universality as criteria for measuring the comprehensiveness of welfare states also points to the ideological orientations underlying welfare states. On the basis of this approach, welfare states have been classified variously as social democratic, corporatist-conservative, or liberal.[33] This approach has been deployed as a counter to the above-mentioned ones; even so, it cannot extricate itself from the analysis of public social expenditure and the welfare goals of income inequality reduction and poverty alleviation.

The entire theoretical edifice of the welfare state typology rests on Esping-Andersen's insight that "not all spending counts equally." Yet "his classifications rest on composite indices which are heavily influenced by expenditure considerations."[34] The social wage or replacement rate that signals the degree of decommodification is intrinsically related to public social expenditures. The intrinsic relationship between decommodification and social welfare expenditures is reinforced by the fact that the least decommodifying welfare states exist in Anglo-Saxon countries that have relatively low levels of social expenditures. The poverty rate and the magnitude of income inequality are lowest in those societies where the level of social welfare spending as a percentage of GDP is relatively high.[35] The classification of welfare states based on the principles of decommodification and universalism must also reflect the structural relationship between public social expenditures and the qualitative nature of decommodification and universalism.

An adequate methodological approach to account for welfare state variation requires combining the above-mentioned quantitative and qualitative measurements of the welfare state. This approach is able to relate social spending, policy instruments, and distributional outcomes to one another; it is also conducive to shedding light on the ideological orientations lurking beneath the edifice of welfare states.

The Plan of the Book

This book has begun by introducing crucial research questions, outlining case studies, and formulating an alternative analytical framework for the comparative study of welfare state. The main arguments are divided into 9 chapters. Chapter 1 assesses the main theoretical perspectives on the welfare state, highlighting the strengths and weaknesses of mainstream theoretical explanations of welfare state development, expansion, and contraction. An analytical framework that combines elements of Marxian class analysis and the power resources model for the analysis of the welfare states in Canada and Australia is introduced. Chapter 2 discusses the theoretical explanations for variations in pension systems and pension reforms. It also reflects on the welfare state and pension policy literature related to Canada and Australia. It will be argued that comparative studies of welfare state and pension policy in these countries have been conducted within the parameters of institutional perspectives and the power resources model, which fail to explain variations in the historical trajectory of their pension systems. Chapter 3 examines the historical trajectory of the power resources of labour and the development of Keynesian policies in Canada and Australia. The interplay of historical and national settings on the organizational structure of labour, the role of the state, and emerging industrial relations in both countries are examined. It is demonstrated how differences in national settings and their impact on national policy-making paved the way for variations in Keynesianism between these two countries.

Chapter 4 discusses the postwar expansion of the old age income security system in Australia. It is demonstrated that the Australian pension system was unable to embrace universalism largely because of the nature of the postwar social class compromise, which reflected the labourist ideology of the Australian labour movement, which emphasized full employment and a centralized wage-setting system as surrogates for social welfare protection. The full employment focus of the Australian labour movement emphasized industrial citizenship and undermined the consolidation of a conception of social citizenship in Australia that might have encouraged the adoption of universality and collectivity as guiding principles of social income security.

Chapter 5 describes and analyses the variables underpinning the postwar trajectory of the retirement income system in Canada. The decisive influence of the politically constructed redistributive-oriented postwar social settlement in Canada on the old age pension system is outlined. This chapter elaborates on the links between the generosity, collectivity, and universality of the old age pension system and the political exigencies for maintaining national unity.

Chapter 6 reflects on the economic crisis of the 1970s and highlights its general impact on welfare states. It describes how, despite parallel commitments by the federal governments in Canada and Australia to deal with burgeoning deficits and debts and to foster stronger economic growth, neoliberalism took different forms in these two countries. More specifically, neoliberal pressures for social security retrenchment were accompanied by divergent responses to these pressures.

Chapter 7 demonstrates how the shift of Australia's old age pension system towards greater residualism and privatization was shaped by that country's politically constructed market-centred postwar social compromise. It demonstrates how the seeds for the restructuring and retrenchment of Australia's social welfare programs were in fact contained within the womb of its postwar social settlement. Chapter 8 shows that the politically constructed redistributive-oriented nature of Canada's postwar social settlement functioned as a brake on neoliberal inroads into the domain of old age pension policy. This chapter establishes the structural affinity between the discourse of national unity and the mitigation of neoliberal-motivated pressures for income security retrenchment in Canada.

In the conclusion of this book, its main findings are recapitulated. I reflect on the implications of this book for the prevailing theoretical perspectives on the welfare state. I also discuss the scope for extending my formulated analytical approach to other case studies. The future direction of pension reforms and their ramifications for policy-makers are highlighted.

1 Theoretical Perspectives on the Welfare State: Towards a New Synthetic Approach

Since the collapse of Keynesianism in the 1970s and the ascendancy of neoliberalism in the 1980s, the welfare state has faced restructuring. That restructuring has been marked by variations in the degree of welfare state retrenchment among advanced liberal democratic societies. Many theoretical and analytical studies have attempted to explain the process of welfare state restructuring as well as differences in the pace and degree of retrenchment. The existing comparative welfare state studies have focused mainly on factors such as the levels of economic development, demographic composition, institutional structures, and the level of power resources of labour as the chief explanatory variables for variations in welfare state expansion and retrenchment. These comparative welfare studies have paid less attention to the roles played by national settings – roles that underpin the variations in postwar social class compromises. These national settings not only have structured the postwar welfare state expansion but also have shaped the responses to welfare state retrenchment.

A comprehensive explanation of variations in welfare state expansion and contraction requires a framework that accounts for the interplay of class, nationalism, and the state in moulding the postwar social class settlement. Such an approach requires us to integrate elements of Marxian class analysis and the power resources model.

Before presenting the proposed analytical framework to explain differences in welfare state expansion and restructuring, it is essential to outline the strengths and weaknesses of the main theoretical approaches to welfare state studies. Reflecting the degree of emphasis placed on the significance of structures, institutions, and agency, these theoretical explanations of the welfare state variation can be classified as liberal, Weberian or Marxian.

The Liberal Approach

The liberal explanation of welfare state expansion identifies differences in levels of economic development and its demographic corollaries as the main factors underlying the divergence in patterns of welfare state expansion. Contemporary liberal theorizations of welfare state development are influenced by the school of structural-functionalism. In the 1950s and 1960s, structural-functionalism achieved theoretical hegemony within the sociological discourse, establishing itself as a granite slab upon which various theoretical explanations were erected.[1] A leading proponent of structural-functionalism, Talcott Parsons, contended that the social disequilibrium that accompanied the historical transformation of traditional societies into modern ones created structural imperatives to adopt societal measures that were indispensable to bringing about a new equilibrium.[2] The impact of structural-functionalism's main assumption as it relates to the logic or dynamic of adaptation to changes in the environment of the living system can be traced in various liberal explanations of social welfare policy in advanced industrial societies. Within the liberal narrative of welfare state development, the adoption of social policies is attributed largely to the "logic of industrialism," according to which the level of economic development is the overriding factor behind welfare state expansion.[3] Within this "agentless" liberal paradigm, irrespective of ideological factors, historical circumstances, or differences in political structures, welfare state activity "operationalized as the percentage of GDP spent on social security" is determined solely by the degree of economic development, the age of the social security system, and the age structure of the population.[4] The central claim of liberal explanations of welfare state development is that the level of economic growth and its related processes are more significant than ideological, institutional, and structural differences as predictors of welfare state expenditures.[5] Variations in the trajectory of welfare state expansion are reflected in the levels of public expenditures. In turn, variations in levels of public expenditures are determined by differences in economic growth and demographics.[6]

Lurking beneath the "logic of industrialism" is an explicit assumption that the levelling forces of technological development will bring about a convergence of social structures and social policies as nations move towards the industrialization.[7] The liberal claim that welfare states are converging towards parallel patterns of development assumes that as countries approach similar levels of economic growth, welfare state variations lose their significance. Since the liberal explanation of welfare state development focuses entirely on the transition from pre-industrial socio-economic relations to an industrialized economy, it is geared towards "emphasiz[ing] cross-national similarities rather than differences; being industrialized or capitalist over-determines cultural variations or differences in power relations."[8]

As an obverse of the industrialization thesis, the modernization thesis attributes the emergence of the welfare state to the social, political, demographic, and bureaucratic accompaniments of industrialization and urbanization. Industrialization and the ensuing urbanization exacerbated the problems of social integration, which manifested themselves in the destruction of pre-industrial modes of social reproduction.[9]

The emergence of the welfare state has also been interpreted as an outcome of a nation-building project launched by state officials and elites to integrate the working class into the capitalist order and thereby secure the state's legitimacy.[10] Although the modernization thesis explains welfare state development as a societal remedy for economic dislocation and the political mobilization accompanying economic growth and structural differentiation, socio-political factors are nonetheless "treated as epiphenomenal of structural variables."[11]

In line with its identification of economic growth levels, demographic composition, and the structure of the elderly population as the main variables behind welfare state expansion, the liberal perspective identifies the political backlash against taxation as the principal driver of welfare state retrenchment. Variations in welfare state restructuring are thus attributed to differences in taxation levels and in the intensity of the political backlash against taxation.[12] The backlash against the welfare state is overwhelmingly intense in countries where taxation is direct and visible.[13]

Liberal theorists generally pay little attention to the role of agency and ideology in shaping the development and expansion of old age pension programs. And whenever they do attempt to bring the role of social agency into their analyses of social welfare policy, they emphasize the role of non-class actors. This is conspicuous in the works of neo-pluralists, who emphasize the role of interest groups in shaping social income security policy.[14] In his analysis of public pensions in Canada, Britain, and the United States, Henry Pratt has argued that the gradual expansion of governments' role in the field of aging provided incentives for the formation and proliferation of interest groups, which then became active participants in the reform and restructuring of pension programs.[15]

When we shift socio-political conflicts from the centre of theoretical explanations of welfare state expansion, we end up with a distorted picture of the emergence of welfare states in capitalist societies. The liberal perspective on the welfare state hinges on socio-economic development as the primary unit of analysis; thus it downplays the roles of human agency, societal upheavals, and political mobilization in shaping social welfare programs. As Göran Therborn has pointed out, "the universal development of welfare states has not been consensual and non-political."[16] By theorizing social policy as impersonal, administrative, and procedural responses to socio-economic development and its structural correlates, the liberal approach depoliticizes the adoption of social welfare policies in liberal democratic societies.[17] The liberal depiction of welfare state configuration as a mechanical response to the practical problems of economic development delinks the inherent contradictions of capitalist social relations from their ramifications, which are identified as societal problems. The liberal perspective on the welfare state thus tends to confuse "function with cause, and needs with origins."[18]

The liberal conceptualization of the state tends to conceal the conflictual nature of social relations in capitalist societies. Liberal approaches to theorizing welfare state retrenchment do not square with the actual processes of social program curtailment in liberal democratic societies. The liberal assertion is that the backlash against social welfare expenditures is intense in societies with higher levels of taxation; but in fact the neoliberal assault on social programs has been more widespread in societies where levels of taxation are relatively low.[19] Indeed, public support for the welfare state is strong in Scandinavian countries, where levels of taxation have historically been high.[20] Moreover, the pace and degree of welfare state retrenchment has been more intense in countries where taxation levels have historically been low.[21]

Empirical investigations of welfare state expansion during the late nineteenth century and through to the 1960s and 1970s demonstrate that there is no direct correlation between levels of economic growth and patterns of social expenditures.[22] Indeed, some of the wealthiest countries were late in adopting social insurance institutions.[23] The divergent pattern of social expenditures in advanced industrial countries during the era of welfare state expansion contradicts the convergence thesis of liberal theory. Social welfare effort, as reflected in public social expenditures as a percentage of GDP, is not necessarily determined by wealth or by the proportion of the aged population, as the liberal approach has asserted.[24] Empirical evidence demonstrates that high economic growth can, in fact, go hand in hand with higher income inequality and rising poverty.[25] Even though a certain level of wealth is indispensable to the provision of old age pensions, many studies have questioned whether there is any direct correlation between the level of economic development and the institutionalization of the welfare state. These comparative welfare state studies have found no positive relationship between the level of economic development and the timing of the adoption of social security programs such as old age pensions.[26]

Another methodological shortcoming of the liberal approach stems from its use of public social expenditures as a dependent variable when measuring the size and quality of welfare states in advanced industrial societies. Even though the relevance of public social expenditures to the analysis of welfare states is beyond dispute, the use of public expenditures as a unit of analysis for comparing welfare states requires further elaboration. First, the employment of public social expenditures as a criterion for gauging the quantitative and qualitative dimensions of welfare states requires dissecting the relationship between public expenditures and changes in societal needs. Increases in the level of social spending might simply be a function of an increase in the magnitude of societal needs.[27] Second, despite a statistically positive correlation between state expenditures and the amelioration of social ills, public expenditures alone are not an adequate measure of the success of the state's socially protective activities. The positive linkage between social welfare expenditures and the "quality" of the welfare state requires us to investigate the recognition of the social right to protection from social risks. As well, the impact of social transfers on income inequality needs to be examined by comparing the relative generosity and comprehensiveness of welfare states.

The Weberian Approach

The Weberian approach, like the liberal one, de-emphasizes the role of societal forces; it stresses institutional settings and the state's organizational structures as the overriding determinants of social welfare policy. The influence of Weberian analysis on welfare state studies is visible in the state-centred approach in political science derived from comparative historiography's emphasis on specific historical analysis.[28] The emphasis on state structures as the key variable for explaining social welfare policy is also a rebuttal to "society-centred" perspectives," with their emphasis on social conflict and societal pressures as shapers of social welfare policy.

In the 1970s, society-centred explanations for the welfare state, epitomized by Marxian analysis, sparked a competing explanation among Weberian analysts, who attempted to bring the state back to the centre of their analyses. Marxians conceptualized the state as a political crystallization of class forces; Weberians responded by emphasizing the autonomous impacts of state structures and institutions in shaping the direction of the welfare state.[29] Proponents of the state-centred approach did not ignore the significance of economic development and societal pressures. However, they attributed social welfare policies – that is, the forms those policies took – mainly to the society-shaping activities of state organizations, including the state officials who pursued, implemented, and administered the state's national interests. In their view, such interests could not be reduced to the interests of societal forces.[30]

The state-centred approach has several theoretical and empirical shortcomings. State-centred theoreticians – somewhat like Marxian ones – identify the state as system manager and as the reproducer of social relations; but they also conceptualize authority relations particularized in the state as separate from power relations entrenched in the economic system of surplus expropriation. Because they dissociate state power from power relations within the overall social relations of production and conceptualize the state as an institutional complex rather than a product of class struggles, statist theoreticians have difficulty identifying the relationship between state and social forces and the former's degree of autonomy from the latter.

Weberians would contend that a state's capacity to accomplish the "general interest" depends on state autonomy (the insulation of the bureaucracy from private interests) and state embeddedness (the linkage between the state's internal structure and private organizations, mainly in the business community). These two variables determine the state's capacity to manoeuvre.[31] "Embedded autonomy" means that the state is autonomous from societal forces, but to be effective, it requires the cooperation of the private sector. Weberian institutionalists focus on cooperation between the state and the business community and largely ignore the inherently conflictual nature of capitalist social relations.

In challenging Marxian conceptualizations of the state, state-centred theoreticians have strived to depict "state and society as separate polar opposites, denying in practice the presence of classes and class struggle within the state."[32] For them, the state does not exist outside of social relations and state officials do not operate in a vacuum. Social welfare policy proposals may be implemented by state agents, but those proposals are formulated "not only by administrative structures and capacity, but also by large social forces."[33] It is social pressures that spur state managers to embark on a specific course of action. But as Linda Gordon has convincingly argued, state-centred analysts habitually replace social classes with politicians and allow political conflict among state officials to supersede social struggle in explaining welfare state development.[34] The state-centred perspective has difficulty explicating the paradigmatic shift from Keynesianism to neoliberalism – a shift that triggered a corresponding process of restructuring across welfare states in advanced industrial nations as a result of state-centred processes.[35]

As theoretical developments of the Weberian perspective, institutional approaches have attempted to explain the divergent patterns of welfare state expansion and restructuring among advanced industrial societies. Despite their methodological differences, institutional perspectives generally use institutional and organizational structures of the state as the primary units when analysing social welfare policy. Institutionalists generally concur that political institutions and the state's organizational structures play a decisive role in framing the patterns of welfare state expansion *and* restructuring.[36]

At least two streams of institutionalism are relevant to the study of welfare state expansion and restructuring. The first stresses the institutional and organizational characteristics of the state as determining factors that mould decision-making on social welfare policy.[37] Formal and informal decision-making processes are thus key to explaining welfare state expansion and subsequent contraction. In unitary states, political power is centralized and formal decision-making channels facilitate both the extension of the welfare state frontiers and unilateral processes of welfare state reform geared towards greater retrenchment. Conversely, the dispersion of political power provides multiple access points for dominant societal actors to influence the policy processes that govern both the development of welfare states and their ongoing restructuring.[38] It follows that higher social expenditures and universal retirement income systems have been easier to achieve in unitary political systems than in decentralized ones.[39]

In this line of institutional analysis, state structures and institutions not only frame the rules of the game but also constrain or enhance the capacity of societal organizations to pursue their social goals. Although this reflects an attempt to bring social forces into their analyses, the emphasis is still on the centrality of state structures and the national configuration of political institutions as key explanatory variables. This obsession prevents institutionalists from moving beyond the parameters of state institutions as an explanation. As one keen institutionalist puts it: "The focus on political institutions as an independent variable, however, can still have some predictive validity, if looked at in the long term. The impact of political institutions is affected by its interaction with other factors, particularly electoral dynamics which can either enhance or reduce executive power concentration and its effects on policy outcomes."[40]

The other "societal" factors, such as electoral systems, that institutionalists bring into their analyses of welfare states are just a different set of institutions and can hardly be equated with actual societal forces. The concentration of political authority and the fragmentation of political power are crucial elements in shaping the rules of the game. But within these political arrangements, social policy outcomes are decisively determined by the social power of the interacting actors. Regardless of the organizational structure of political authority, the capacity of pro-welfare forces to convert their sentiments into political goods is determined by the amount of social pressure and power they can exert on state institutions. Concentration of political authority in the national arena has often been conducive to enlarging the size of the state. However, decentralization of political power does not in itself prevent the emergence of a comprehensive welfare state. Indeed, in situations where political confrontation and a drift towards decentralized political authority reflect a political attempt to accommodate ethnic cleavages, the fragmentation of political power can foster growth in public social expenditures as a surrogate for political reconciliation. Welfare state studies have found no negative correlation between decentralized political power and social public expenditures.[41]

A second line of institutional analysis of the welfare state uses differences in production regimes to explain variations in welfare state expansion and retrenchment.[42] For these analysts, "production regime" refers to an overarching complex web of institutionalized societal and industrial relations that govern the overall performance of the national economy.[43]

Employing the organizational character of production regimes as the basis for analysing welfare expansion and social program restructuring parallels the approach taken by corporatist theory, which views the welfare state as a negotiated trade-off between capital, labour, and the state.[44] Corporatism has supposedly functioned as "a bridge from working class and social insurance reformism of the first half of the twentieth century to the welfare state in the second half."[45] Corporatism explicitly assumes that welfare states in strongly corporatist societies are more resistant to cuts than those in weakly corporatist ones.[46] Furthermore, it is a corollary of corporatist explanations of welfare states that in strongly corporatist countries, there should exist a broad gap in social provision between insiders (organized workers) and outsiders (non-unionized workers).

Despite its prevalence in the welfare state literature, corporatism has acquired an ambiguous status. That ambiguity reflects a lack of consistency in its definition and operationalization.[47] Corporatism purports to equalize the negotiating power of labour and capital on the basis of co-operation and interdependence, when actually it is an institutional arrangement that cements the structural subordination of labour and that places sectoral bargaining above the collective interests of the working class.[48] Several empirical findings have contradicted the central assertions of corporatist theory: neither the level of social spending nor the extent of social protection squares with the theoretical underpinnings of corporatism.[49] Furthermore, corporatist theories of social protection do not explain why, in some countries that rank low on any corporatist scale, the percentage of beneficiaries of unemployment benefits is higher than in highly corporatist countries.[50]

It has always been hard to corral welfare states into corporatist arrangements.[51] Instead, with some exceptions (such as specific social programs, like unemployment insurance, that are run by trade unions in Scandinavian countries), even in strongly corporatist societies, welfare state institutions are run by state administrators. As Therborn has pointed out, tripartite welfare state institutions do not exist, and bipartite institutions are in fact the result of collective bargaining between labour and capital.[52]

As a significant component of coordinated production regimes, centralized wage setting may be crucial for preventing wage differentials, but it does not go hand in hand with either greater scope for bargaining or higher social security expenditures.[53] Indeed, when labour market policy is confined to market regulation without any expansion of social income security, the welfare state is bound to remain small and exclusive, which runs counter to the principle of comprehensiveness that signals the relative generosity of welfare states.[54]

The Weberian and institutional approaches to the study of differences in welfare state reconfiguration face several theoretical, methodological, and empirical problems. First, they too often implicitly dismiss the role of societal forces in shaping social welfare policy. Instead, for the main explanatory variables, they focus on how labour, capital, and the state are structured. But this line of explanation fails to clarify why coordinated production regimes, which are seen as helping consolidate comprehensive social welfare programs, are formed mainly in societies where labour movements are strong. Second, they fail to explain why welfare state retrenchment has made decisive inroads in societies in which coordinated production regimes are prevalent. Institutions and organizational structures are not the result of independent developments that can be analysed in isolation from the societal forces that shape social, political, and economic institutions. To emphasize organizational structures as the primary unit of analysis is to risk ignoring that institutional and organizational settings are rooted in class relations and class dynamics.[55] Institutions may function as "grammatical rules of world politics," as Rothstein and Steinmo have suggested.[56] But institutional structures cannot be analysed independent of the specific socio-political configuration within each social formation. As Pontusson has noted, institutionalists have developed the habit of explaining variations in dependent variables such as governmental policies in terms of differences in political institutions, without paying attention to other non-institutional variables that interact with political institutions.[57]

What institutionalists have ignored is that institutions themselves have no particular policy content, and in the long run they are vulnerable to change if they encounter sufficient social and political pressures. Clearly, institutional settings are crucial in shaping "political games," but "homo politicus cannot be considered as structural-cum-institutional dope."[58] Institutional structures that are the congealed outcomes of past struggles play a vital role in channelling socio-political pressures. But those structures cannot be diagnosed independent of specific historical and national settings within different social formations.

In the institutional literature on the welfare state, a new approach has emerged that points to a rupture between welfare state expansion and retrenchment. In these analyses of welfare state reconfiguration, analysts have argued that the new politics of welfare state retrenchment and resilience are markedly different from the politics of welfare state expansion. The latter had been shaped by the organizational unity of the labour movement and by the political strength of social democratic parties, and both have lost their power.[59] Underscoring this line of interpretation is the explicit assumption that partisanship and class politics are less relevant to analyses of welfare state restructuring. For these analysts, the social forces behind welfare state resilience emanate from fear of the electoral repercussions if a frontal onslaught is made on social programs as a result of the mobilization of groups such as retirees and public service employees. Also, the transformation of the welfare state into a status quo institution conferring political advantages on various layers of the social order seems to slow the pace of welfare state retrenchment.[60]

The new politics of the welfare state hinge on the discovery that social welfare programs give rise to interest groups that vehemently defend these programs. Pierson characterizes this as the "positive policy feedback" of the welfare state.[61] In his attempt to draw the line between the politics of welfare state retrenchment and the political constellation behind welfare state expansion, Pierson asserts that "retrenchment is not simply the mirror image of welfare state expansion."[62] For Pierson, a comprehensive analysis of welfare state reconfiguration has to move beyond the boundaries of existing theories of welfare state expansion, since factors such as the power resources of labour are no longer crucial in shaping social welfare policy.

Yet the proponents of the new politics of the welfare state such as Pierson have not demonstrated that the diverse theories of welfare state expansion are incapable of explaining the political constellation behind welfare state restructuring. The assertion that the politics of welfare state reconfiguration cannot be explained by theories of welfare state expansion has been questioned by other analysts as well.[63] These analysts assert that the politics surrounding welfare state reconfiguration are linked to the politics that propelled welfare state expansion. Shifts in societal interests and coalitional alignments do not require the invention of "a new set of analytical categories in order to explain current patterns of welfare state retrenchment and restructuring."[64] Social democratic parties have not been eclipsed on the political scene, and labour unions remain a potential bulwark against welfare state retrenchment.[65] In other words, there has been continuity rather than disjuncture between the politics of welfare state expansion and the policy atmosphere of welfare state restructuring. The practitioners of the new politics of the welfare state have encountered formidable difficulties in explaining why welfare state–friendly institutions generally exist in societies where labour movements are strong. As Virpi Timonen has pointed out, the root causes of social policy strength or weakness may not lie in the structure of social welfare policy alone as Pierson has asserted, but rather in power resources and the organizational capacities of its recipients.[66]

The Marxian Approach

Broadly speaking, Marxian class analysts view the development of the welfare state as the political manifestation of the state's socio-economic response to the inherent contradictions of capitalist social relations.[67] A central theme of Marxism is that to reduce the contradictions of capitalism and its class antagonisms, social welfare policy must be adopted as a mechanism for upholding the rule of capital. In other words, social welfare programs are political prescriptions for mitigating the inherent tendency of capitalist social relations to breed socio-economic inequalities that threaten the capitalist order.[68] A common thread running through various Marxian approaches is an emphasis on entrenched power imbalances and the susceptibility of capitalism to crises that can only be alleviated through social welfare programs.[69]

According to the structuralist version of the Marxian concept of the state, the state is not an intrinsic entity with absolute autonomy, but neither is it an instrument that can be manipulated by one class or class faction.[70] The capitalist state is a specific "material condensation" of class forces and is, therefore, the strategic terrain for social struggle. From this, we can extrapolate that the dominant classes are vulnerable to fragmentation owing to their myopic pursuit of immediate interests and that the exploited working class is a threat to bourgeois hegemony. It follows that defusing working-class power is integral to bourgeois domination as well as to maintenance of the long-term interests of the dominant classes – maintenance that can only be carried out by the state. The state operates as the guardian of the nation and as the guarantor of national cohesion.[71] But it can perform this complex task of securing the ruling power bloc only if it is relatively autonomous from the dominant classes and factions.[72] The autonomy of the state is not absolute, for it is subject to change arising from the "concrete relation between social forces in the field of the political class struggle, in particular ... on the political struggles of the dominated classes."[73] Under certain circumstances, such as pressures emanating from the working class, the state may implement social measures that will harm the short-term interests of the bourgeois classes.[74] Shifts in underlying social relations generate corresponding oscillations in the relative autonomy of the state.

In line with Marxian class analysis, social welfare policy fulfils the legitimation function of the state. The welfare state is heralded as an instrument of income redistribution, when in fact it is employed as a mechanism of social control and working-class neutralization, aimed at converting organized labour into an integral element of capitalist hegemony.[75] The state's legitimation and accumulation functions (maintaining social harmony and securing the profitability of capital, respectively) are complementary; the former is a functional requirement to the latter. However, these functions of the state can collide when social expenditures rise so high as to become a drag on capital accumulation. This can manifest itself in a fiscal crisis of the state.[76] Stated more baldly, under capitalist social relations, the welfare state is bound to acquire a contradictory character. The welfare state is essential to mitigate the inadequacy of market forces and propitiate the working class; but at the same time, it has the potential to disturb the rhythms of capital profitability. As Offe pointed out, "capitalism cannot exist with, neither can it exist without the welfare state."[77]

Within the framework of Marxian class analysis, welfare state restructuring and retrenchment is a manifestation of a change in the regime of accumulation; it represents a shift in class power to capital that has reduced the relative autonomy of the state.[78] The decline in the state's relative autonomy serves to limit its capacity to carry out its legitimation function. This is then reflected in social welfare cutbacks.

With the shift in class power towards capital, Keynesian demand management gave way to monetarism and supply-side economics as a means to address the economic crisis of the 1970s. Monetarism and supply-side economics have the potential to thwart further social reforms and to identify previously acquired social gains as drags on competitiveness. The pursuit of market-centred policies, such as promoting financial mobility, spatially dispersing manufacturing facilities, privatizing public services, and encouraging labour market flexibility, reflected the structural subjugation of the state to the exigencies of capital accumulation. These policies were geared towards fragmenting the working classes so that capital could acquire an upper hand in its political struggle.[79] This change in the relations between class forces triggered corresponding changes in the qualitative and quantitative characteristics of social programs. This linkage between the balance of class forces and social welfare policy was cogently highlighted by Poulantzas:

> In the long run, the State can serve class hegemony by itself granting certain material demands of the popular masses – demands which, at the moment of their imposition, may assume a quite radical significance (free and universal public education, social security, unemployment benefits, etc.). Once the relationship of forces has changed, these popular gains can be

> progressively stripped of their initial content and character in a covert and mediate fashion.[80]

Marxian class analysis offers a plausible account of the structural links between social class struggle, the welfare state, and the rhythms of capital accumulation. It also explains the structural limitations to the welfare state's frontiers, which beyond a certain threshold cannot be tolerated by the imperatives of market forces. The Marxian explanation of the welfare state also sheds light on the class and immanent power imbalances on which capitalist social relations are founded, which have been strongly denied by liberal theorists of the welfare state.[81] Finally, Marxist theorizations of the welfare state not only clarify the limits of redistributive social welfare policy within capitalist social relations, but also expose the volatility of social welfare programs, which are held hostage to capital accumulation.

Despite its application to the study of individual social programs in specific countries, Marxism's theoretical claims have rarely been subjected to the empirical test of cross-national studies on welfare state restructuring.[82] Marxian analysts of the welfare state have often been criticized for dismissing significant qualitative differences between welfare states in liberal democratic societies.[83] The principal line of criticism against Marxian class analysis revolves around the significance of structure or agency as the predominant explanatory variable. It has been argued that Marxists, especially structuralist Marxists, in their analyses, subordinate social agency to the structural pressures that mould social welfare policies.[84] This contention is based on the assertion that in Marxism, societal pressures play crucial roles in shaping social welfare programs but social struggles are still determined by the structural matrix of capitalist social relations.[85] What seems to have escaped the attention of these critics is that structured power relations are congealed outcomes of past struggles and form the basis for social struggles aimed at altering entrenched structural settings. As Evelyn Huber and John Stephens have pointed out, structural constraints are formed by the balance of class power between capital, labour, and other social forces.[86] Structural relations have the potential to restrict the manoeuvrability of social agency, but their configuration is contingent on the balance of social forces and the intensity of social struggles, which determine the relative autonomy of the state.[87] The theoretical proposition of Marxism is simply that structural power relations and the role of social agency cannot be analysed independent of each other.

The Social Democratic Class Mobilization Thesis

The social democratic class mobilization perspective has its roots in Marxism and combines class and institutional factors. The shift in emphasis away from structures towards agency is the central feature of the social democratic class mobilization thesis that emerged in reaction to the Marxian class analysis. The social democratic class mobilization thesis gradually transformed itself into the "power resources model," which combines the impact of social agency with that of institutional structures in shaping social welfare policy. Although the social democratic class mobilization thesis dominated explanations of the welfare state in the 1970s and 1980s, it is in fact a theoretical legacy of revisionist social democracy, whose visions of social welfare reforms were reflected in the 1891 Erfurt Program of the German Social Democratic Party (SPD).[88] The principles of the Erfurt Program became a source of inspiration for social democratic parties across Europe and were endorsed by Vladimir Ilyich Lenin, Karl Kautsky, and Eduard Bernstein, who as the leading socialist theoreticians saw immediate social reforms as a precondition for expanding the social power of the working class. Despite this historical affinity with Marxism, and its emphasis on class structure and class conflict, the social democratic class mobilization explanation of the welfare state is fundamentally different from the Marxian interpretation. As a theoretical framework for welfare state analysis, the social democratic class mobilization thesis gained popularity during the ascendancy of Keynesianism, which also bolstered the position of social democratic parties.

The entire theoretical edifice of revisionist socialism hinged on the assumption that capturing governmental power through the ballot box would turn the power of the state against the privileged classes and pave the way for a bloodless seizure of political power.[89] The belief in social welfare reforms as a succession of small steps towards socialism was at odds with Marx's prophetic warning that socialists needed to eschew taking "over from the bourgeois economists the consideration of distribution as independent of the mode of production and hence present socialism as turning principally on distribution."[90] Social democratic theoreticians failed to realize that to rely on redistributive policy without socialization of investment was to tacitly endorse the transformation of social democracy from an oppositional position into a relation of dependence on the economic dynamism of capitalism.

Revisionist social democracy's vision of a sequential order of social transformation (beginning with working-class mobilization, followed by electoral politics, the welfare state, and socialism) was bolstered by the institutionalization of Keynesian demand management and the expansion of welfare states. It was during the postwar expansion of social programs that Anthony Crosland emerged as the ideologue for reformist social democracy; he interpreted welfare state expansion as signalling the advance of social democrats into the realm of socialism. In his response to M. Raymond Aron's remark that socialism had ceased to be a myth in the West because it was now part of reality, Crosland declared that this was "not, of course, a complete reality, but sufficiently so to be no longer a myth."[91] Crosland contended that the growth of the welfare state led by the electoral success of working-class social democratic parties had established a balance of power between capital and labour. It was Crosland's central conviction that the ascension of social democratic parties to governmental power would counterbalance the economic power of the dominant classes.[92]

The social democratic class mobilization thesis popularized by Walter Korpi and Gøsta Esping-Andersen in the 1980s also assumed a division between economic power exercised by those who held the means of production and political power flowing from strength of numbers through the democratic process. Electoral politics is geared to favour numerically larger collectivities such as the working classes. According to this line of interpretation, the institutionalized class struggle in capitalist societies is reflected in tensions between the logic of accumulation and the logic of democratic politics. This tension is resolved through the development and consolidation of the welfare state in favour of working-class movements.[93] Accordingly, the degree of reliance on market allocation and the inclusiveness of the welfare state depend on the strength of the organized working class and on the political domination of social democracy within each national formation. The social democratic class mobilization thesis does not ignore the significance of structural relations; nonetheless, it assumes that when the working class captures parliament, it can use legislative power as an effective means for translating social demands into political goods that are bound to weaken ruling-class hegemony.[94]

The class mobilization thesis tends to exaggerate the separation of the economic and political spheres. This separation blurs the real locus of power, which is entrenched in social relations of production to which the political sphere must be receptive. As Ralph Miliband observed, "a capitalist economy has its own rationality to which any government and state must sooner or later submit, and usually sooner."[95] But persuaded by the expansion of the Keynesian welfare state, proponents of the social democratic class mobilization thesis such as Przeworski assumed that "the state can turn capitalists into private functionaries of the public without altering the judicial status of private property."[96]

Since the exercise of governmental power by the political parties of the working classes has generally depended on class alignment with other political forces, the social democratic class mobilization thesis has given way to the class coalition or "power resources model," which has acquired tremendous momentum in the realm of comparative studies on welfare states. The class coalition approach blends the class mobilization thesis with class alignment as the overriding determinant of both welfare state expansion and the degree of resistance to the forces of welfare state retrenchment.

According to the power resources model, social democratic and labour parties were in a better position to strike a coalition with farmers wherever the rural economy was dominated by small, capital-intensive family farms. Conversely, where farming was based on large pools of cheap labour there was less potential for a labour–farmer class coalition, and conservative forces were in a better strategic position to incorporate farmers "into reactionary alliances" designed to politically isolate labour.[97]

Where there existed political conditions for a coalition of farmers and the working class – for example, in Scandinavian countries – welfare states were shaped by the socialist principles of generosity, equality, and universalism. Conversely, in continental Europe, where a hostile political environment thwarted the political alignment of labour and farmers, welfare states were structured by occupationally based status stratification. The liberal principles of class dualism as manifested in means-tested social assistance became the defining characteristic of welfare in those states – mainly the Anglo-Saxon countries – where the political significance of farmers had already been eroded and where the emerging new middle classes had not been wooed from the market to the state.[98]

This line of analysis classifies welfare states as social democratic (in Scandinavian countries, where socialism is the dominant ideology), conservative-corporatist (in continental Europe, where conservatism has held its ideological grip), or liberal (in Anglo-Saxon countries, where liberalism has eclipsed both socialism and conservatism).[99] In accordance with the degree of decommodification (i.e., the ability of individuals to have access to acceptable standards of living without direct reliance on market forces) and the principles of social stratification (the manner in which social services are tailored to the population), these three welfare state "clusters" are distinguished by the universal provision of social programs, the vertical stratification of social benefits, and means-tested social assistance, respectively.[100]

The power resources model identifies the welfare state as a political manifestation of a social class compromise. But unlike the Marxist model, which perceives social welfare policies as a capitalist safety valve to control the working class, the power resources model theorizes social welfare programs as an accumulation of capital's concessions geared towards ameliorating the social conditions of labour and as a precondition for generating labour solidarity, which strengthens the social position of the working class. Whatever its differences from Marxian class analysis, the power resources model highlights the centrality of social class struggle in determining the nature of social welfare policy in liberal democratic societies.

With its emphasis on social classes as the main agent of change, and with its identification of the balance of power as a crucial determinant of distributional outcomes, the power resources model moves beyond both liberal and institutional analyses of the welfare state. However, the power resources model has several theoretical and methodological shortcomings. Many cross-national studies on welfare states have found a positive correlation between the exercise of political power by social democratic governments and a high level of social security expenditures.[101] But it has also been shown that in some societies where the assumption of political power by social democracy has remained an unrealized goal, social security expenditures are higher than social expenditures in some nations where social democrats have formed the government.[102] Furthermore, the power resources model leaves unexplained why the degree of decommodification and universality in some countries where class is fragmented and social democracy has never exercised governmental power at the national level is, in fact, greater than in some societies where the labour movement has retained its unity and a pro-labour party has held governmental power. In other words, the exercise of political power by social democratic governments do not necessarily go hand in hand with higher levels of public social expenditures.

In terms of methodology, the power resources model places greater emphasis on the rate of decommodification and universalism as opposed to public social expenditure, as the basis for measuring the progressiveness of welfare states. Yet studies have found a positive correlation between decommodification and universalism, and public social expenditure.[103] The strength of the power resources model lies in its typology of welfare states as developed by Esping-Andersen: liberal, conservative-corporatist, and social democratic. Esping-Andersen's welfare state typology is a more elaborate and refined version of Richard Titmuss's earlier categorization of welfare states along residual, industrial achievement/performance, and institutional-redistributive lines.[104] This classification of welfare states emphasizes the path-dependent historical persistence of the institutional settings of welfare states. In other words, the variations among welfare states reflect differences in the outcomes of working-class struggle and class coalitions. These variations become institutionalized, since the balance of class power shifts over time. However, this welfare state typology tends to conceal differences within each regime cluster.[105] Furthermore, like other theoretical approaches to the study of welfare states, the power resources model fails to take into account the postwar variations in political strategies and social class settlement built around the specifics of national settings – something that is key to understanding variations in welfare state expansion and retrenchment.

An Approach to the Study of the Welfare State Variation

In the literature on the welfare state, there has been no serious attempt to analyse the interface of class, nationalism, and social welfare policy in advanced liberal democratic societies.[106] In explaining the divergent pattern of welfare state expansion among advanced industrial countries, the mainstream welfare state literature has largely disregarded national context as a unit of analysis. As Will Kymlicka has pointed out, "many of the most influential models for explaining comparative welfare state development have not included ethnic/racial diversity as one of the variables."[107] The failure of the main theoretical perspectives to take into account the centrality of national settings to postwar welfare state expansion has significantly reduced their capacity to explain the divergent patterns of welfare state expansion and subsequent retrenchment. There have been a few case studies about the interaction between nationalism and postwar welfare state expansion.[108] But these case studies have generally discussed the interplay of regionally based nationalist movements and welfare states in liberal democratic societies *without* formulating a comprehensive theoretical basis for their analyses. These case studies have found that the pressures emanating from sub-state nationalism not only affect the structure of welfare state expansion but also trigger the decentralization of social welfare provisions. But none of these studies attempt to explain the interactions among class, nationalism, and the role of state in shaping the postwar social settlement.

The influence of "national settings" on the state's redistributive role – a role that itself is shaped by the relative homogeneity or heterogeneity of a given society – has remained underresearched.[109] The interplay of nationalist movements and social welfare policy has been discussed by only a few authors,[110] none of whom have attempted to explain the interactions among class, national settings, and the role of the state in shaping the postwar social class settlements that laid the foundation for welfare state expansion. Nor have they examined the subsequent period of welfare state retrenchment.

More specifically, within the major theoretical perspectives on the welfare state, little attention has been paid to the impact of class and nationalism on the role of the state. Yet the influence of ethnic composition on class structures not only affects the power resources of labour but also structures the terrain of political discourse, which in turn affects the nature and form of social welfare programs. Depending on the degree of politicization, the relative homogeneity or heterogeneity of a given society affects the organizational and political strength of the labour movement and influences the terrain of social welfare policy discourse.

The existing comparative literature on the welfare state emphasizes the postwar social class compromise in advanced industrial societies. There is a lack of a consensus on the precise definition of class compromise; generally, though, the postwar social settlement has been described as a political-economic project that employs Keynesian and redistributive policies to sustain the hegemony of dominant classes by gaining the active consent of the subordinated classes.[111] The postwar social class compromise in advanced industrial societies is often depicted as a uniform phenomenon.[112] Yet despite the universality of postwar social class compromise among capitalist societies, postwar social pacts have been embedded in different institutional constellations across nations.[113]

Furthermore, less attention has been paid to how variations between social pacts have shaped responses to neoliberal pressures for welfare state retrenchment. Theorizing the variations in welfare state restructuring requires taking into account the historical and national settings that led to the postwar consolidation of the welfare state. The centrality of national historical context in shaping social income security today cannot be ignored.[114] The particulars of national settings shaped the political discourse governing the interplay of the state, societal forces, political institutions, and structural relations within each social formation, all of which cumulatively shaped the postwar social compromise within each country. As David Johnson and Roger Johnson have pointed out, "political discourse is the formal exchange of reasoned views as to which of several alternative courses of action should be taken to solve a societal problem."[115] Political discourse might be conducive to praising individual rights and their protection from governmental incursion, or it might be framed to encourage the use of state power to regulate the market and protect individuals and communities from the vagaries of market forces.[116] The national setting shapes political discourse, and this in turn sets the parameters for policy-making and thereby affects the direction of social welfare policy.[117]

A synthesis of the power resources model and Marxian class analysis can provide an analytical template for explaining the variations in welfare state expansion as well as variations in the degree of resistance to welfare state retrenchment. Integrating the role of national settings into this analytical framework requires a brief discussion of nationalism. On the surface there seem to be strong similarities between the liberal and Marxian views on nationalism, but in fact they differ significantly. The conflict-free liberal theory of the welfare state assumes that within a given society, a shared common heritage is a precondition for resource redistribution.[118] Accordingly, national sentiment cultivates concern for the common good and is indispensable to the legitimacy of redistributive policy.[119] It follows that ethnic heterogeneity would tend to damper calls for social welfare redistribution. A key assumption of liberalism is that ethnic fragmentation weakens the trust that is essential to encourage collective actions within a community.[120]

The insignificance of nationalism to the working-class struggle runs through the thought of major Marxist thinkers. According to Marx, capitalist development – manifested as the universalization of commerce and the market economy – together with the rise of the proletariat, will eventually erase national differences as a source of social conflict. According to *The Communist Manifesto*, "national differences and antagonism between peoples are daily vanishing more and more with the development of bourgeoisie, with freedom of trade, the world market, uniformity in industrial production ... The supremacy of the proletariat will cause them to vanish still more."[121] Marx and Engels endorsed or withheld their support for national movements "on the basis of a political assessment of each nation in the international context."[122] Lenin appreciated nationalism as long as it could function as a means of colonial emancipation. His position on national questions was largely in line with Marx and Engels's pragmatic one.

Rosa Luxemburg endorsed Polish national autonomy; nevertheless, she repudiated nationalism and identified self-determination as irrelevant to working-class struggles. She viewed nationalism and the nation-state as empty husks into which all historical epochs and class relations poured material content.[123] Lenin and Luxemburg disagreed regarding the relevance of nationalism to working-class emancipation; they agreed, however, that ethnic diversity and nationalism fragmented working-class struggle.[124] In Marxian class analysis it is a recurring theme that racial and ethnic divisions tend to undermine the capacity of progressive forces to bring about meaningful social reforms.[125] It is due to this historical relegation of nationalism to an insignificant position that the latter has failed to find a prominent place in Marxian class analysis.[126]

Parallel to Marxian class analysis, the power resources model regards national fragmentation as an obstacle to working-class struggle for a comprehensive welfare state. Accordingly, cultural accommodation may eclipse class compromises that hinge on redistributive policy. Similarly, the power resources model identifies ethnic differences within a given social formation as an obstacle to the adoption of progressive social welfare policies. According to the power resources model, ethno-linguistic divisions adversely affect the organization of labour and thus interfere with working-class unity.[127] On the terrain of political discourse, ethno-linguistic divisions marginalize class and thereby impede the adoption of progressive social welfare policies. A central theme among power resources model analysts is that ethnic diversity weakens support for welfare state expenditures.[128] However, the assertion that multicultural policies corrode the interethnic trust and solidarity needed to sustain the welfare state is debatable.[129]

Contrary to the liberal view that a common heritage is a precondition for the legitimacy of redistributive policy in a given community, states have in fact employed social welfare policy to generate national cohesion. T.H. Marshall's interpretation of welfare state expansion as the logical extension of the nation-building project, designed to incorporate the marginalized into the social order, has become a common theme within the welfare state literature.[130] It was Marshall's conviction that besides reducing risk and insecurity, the welfare state would function as a symbol for the nurturing of shared experiences among citizens. According to this line of interpretation, the entrenchment of citizenship rights embodied in the welfare state would transcend the social differences generated by market forces and thereby foster common bonds among citizens. The expansion of social welfare policy was geared not only to reinforce the bonds of nationhood among members of the community but also to mitigate class antagonisms by the equalizing the status of members of the political community.[131] According to Reinhard Bendix, the extension of political rights and the institutionalization of social rights together neutralized the transformation of social discontent into socialist revolution. He saw this as a "clue to the decline of socialism."[132]

As a centralizing and universalizing force, the welfare state helped strengthen solidarity and cohesion within nation-states.[133] In countries where entrenched ethnic cleavages prevented the development of national unity, the extension of social citizenship rights became a tool for cultivating national integration.[134]

The centrality of national settings to the shaping of postwar social class compromise can in fact be explained within Marxian class analysis. An assumption of Marxian analysis is that the state and the political organizations of capital always attempt to shift the political discourse towards non-class issues and that the state is structurally organized to act as an instrument of national cohesion.[135] The state, as the principal factor of national integration, constantly strives to channel class struggles into non-class forms as part of managing its structural dependence on capital accumulation and hence the reproduction of unequal power relations. However, the transformation of class antagonisms into non-class forms is contingent on whether non-economic sources of divisions and fragmentation are politicized.[136] In relatively homogenous societies, there is greater opportunity for class politics to prevail on the terrain of political discourse; conversely, the presence of politicized non-economic issues in ethnically divided societies provides a favourable atmosphere for the state and right-wing parties to marginalize class in the national political discourse. But at the same time, the clash of nationalisms paradoxically increases the state's relative autonomy to translate social welfare policy into a nation-building project. National fragmentation may facilitate the erasure of class from political discourse; redistributive social welfare policy may be an effective tool for accommodating and reconciling national fragmentation.

In accordance with Marxian class analysis, the relative autonomy of the state is determined by the "concrete relation between social forces in the field of the political class struggle; in particular ... on the political struggle of the dominated classes."[137] But class analysis must add the state's central role in preserving national unity as a factor determining the relative autonomy of the state. The pursuit of social welfare policy that may do short-term harm to the dominant classes is a manifestation of increasing the state's relative autonomy. In other words, the exigency of preserving national unity within a relatively heterogeneous society increases the state's capacity to employ social welfare policy as a mechanism of national integration. Paradoxically, this may counterbalance the relative weakness of a fragmented working class within an ethnically divided society. In contrast, within a given social formation with one nationalism, the absence or low levels of ethnic division tends to enhance working-class solidarity.[138] Under such conditions, the unity of the working class increases the relative autonomy of the state. However, the comprehensiveness of social welfare policy is contingent on both the social vision of the labour movement and the political project formed by the social democratic or labour party that acts as the political arm of the labour movement.

The main shortcomings of the power resources model are these two assumptions that it makes: that there is ideological uniformity among labour movements across countries; and that ethnic differences within a social formation reduce working-class unity and therefore threaten the progressive nature of the welfare state.[139] These theoretical assumptions need to be reconsidered. Ethnic homogeneity might have facilitated working-class unity during the postwar era, but it was not enough to spur the adoption of a universal and comprehensive social welfare policy. Similarly, ethnic diversity might have contributed to the fragmentation of the working class, but it did not necessarily prevent the adoption of universal and generous social welfare programs.

Postwar social class settlements were designed to enhance economic performance as well as to deal with distributive issues. So when the pressures mount on economic productivity and changes occur in the balance of class forces, social pacts are bound to undergo alteration.[140] The character of the postwar social class compromise has also shaped responses to the forces of economic restructuring. A politically constructed market-centred postwar social settlement is vulnerable to the vicissitudes of market forces; whereas a politically constructed redistributive-oriented social settlement is less susceptible to changes in the balance of class forces that ensue as a result of economic contraction. With a shift in the balance of class forces accompanying economic crisis, a market-centred postwar social class settlement will adjust to the demands of market forces. Under a redistributive-oriented social settlement, a weakening of the bargaining leverage of labour will be compensated for by the political discourse of national unity, and this has a potential to partly shield the welfare state from retrenchment.

Conclusion

The divergent patterns of retirement income program expansion and subsequent restructuring and retrenchment in Canada and Australia can be explained within the proposed analytical framework, which combines elements of Marxian class analysis and the power resources model. As the following chapters will demonstrate, the postwar direction of old age pension policy in Canada and Australia came to be shaped by the nature and character of their respective postwar social class settlements. Variations in the process had direct ramifications for the levels of social expenditures and the relations between social citizenship and social welfare programs. In Canada, the presence of two nationalisms facilitated the erasure of class from political discourse; also, the political management of national fragmentation led to the development of a social settlement that required social welfare redistribution. The social class settlement in Canada functioned as a glue that bonded social citizenship entitlements to national identity and the principles of universality and collectivity. The postwar social class compromise in Canada was thus conducive to the adoption of universality and collectivity as defining dimensions of the Canadian retirement income system.

A market-centred social class compromise emerged in Australia, where relative ethnic homogeneity and the presence of a single nationalism galvanized the labour movement. But that movement's political aspirations and expectations did not extend beyond market relations between capital and labour. Under the social class settlement in Australia, where labourist ideology had become the guiding principle of the labour movement, the social class compromise came to hinge on labour market regulations designed to provide social protection through full employment and national wage-setting institutions. A market-centred social class compromise in Australia thus helped prevent the move towards progressive social welfare principles such as universalism and collectivity.

Similarly, the restructuring of retirement income systems in Canada and Australia was shaped by postwar social class compromises. In Australia, the direction of welfare state restructuring came to be influenced by the discourse of "economic rationalism," which was conducive to rationalizing selectivity and privatization in pension programs. In other words, the seeds for the targeting, retrenchment, and privatization of the retirement income system had already been planted in the postwar social class compromise in Australia. In Canada, the ongoing national unity discourse was a manifestation of a redistributive-oriented postwar social settlement and slowed down the neoliberal forces of welfare state retrenchment.

An analysis of the impact of the postwar social settlement on the retirement income systems in Canada and Australia requires us to outline the theoretical perspectives on pensions and evaluate the comparative literature on pensions. The following chapter does this.

2 Pension Systems: Canadian and Australian Cases

Although the Canadian and Australian welfare states are characterized as liberal regimes, their public pension systems are starkly different. During the era of welfare state expansion, the retirement income systems in Australia and Canada took different directions. The distinguishing feature of Australia's pension system was reliance on private occupational plans and the principle of selectivity; in Canada, the retirement income system came to be characterized by the principles of universality and collectivity. Reflecting these differences in postwar retirement income expansion, restructuring in Canada and Australia has also taken divergent routes: the Canadian retirement income system has largely retained its universal and collectivistic character; the Australian one has drifted towards greater residualism and privatization. These patterns cannot be explained adequately by mainstream theoretical perspectives, as is clear from the existing welfare state literature on these two countries, which falls mainly within mainstream theoretical perspectives. Neither individual case studies nor the handful of comparative inquiries plausibly explain the divergent patterns of old age pension expansion and restructuring in these two countries.

Welfare state studies on Canada and Australia have focused mainly on factors such as level of economic development, demographic composition, institutional structures, and the levels of power resources of labour as the principal explanations for variation in retirement income restructuring. However, these studies have paid scant attention to differences in the nature of the postwar social class settlement, which structured the postwar welfare state expansion and shaped the responses to retrenchment.

Before evaluating the literature on Canadian and Australian welfare states and their pension systems, it is essential to outline the historical development of retirement income systems and elaborate on how prevailing theoretical perspectives explain the politics of pension reform and retrenchment in advanced industrial societies.

Pension System Development

Throughout history, protective and paternalistic measures for maintaining social equilibrium have always been indispensable to the social vision guiding societies.[1] As historical legacies of feudal social relations, charity and philanthropy were the main mechanisms of social stabilization throughout the eighteenth and nineteenth centuries. The ruling classes harnessed the charitable and philanthropic societies of the bourgeoisie to pacify social resentment and thereby secure private property.[2] Given the potential of social conflict to disrupt the existing political order, charitable organizations were, in John Stuart Mill's words, "an important saviour of upper class necks."[3] Municipal and church authorities, which provided allowances to the elderly poor, were the forerunners of today's national social income security provisions. During this era, only the wealthiest layers of the population could secure their old age income by buying public bonds or entering into an annuity with a private insurance company.[4] The main sources of social income security for the marginalized strata were family care, thrift, private charity, or poor relief in the public sector.[5] Local relief directed at the marginalized was based on discretionary and moralistic principles that differentiated between the deserving and undeserving poor. Public relief based on character evaluation stigmatized its recipients – a characteristic of all early social income security programs.

The seeds of today's retirement income maintenance were sown by the transformation of pre-industrial social arrangements into capitalist ones. The social transformation accompanying industrialization triggered a tumultuous surge of social dislodgement and class reorganization that necessitated political accommodation. The rise of industrial social relations and its demographic and employment consequences required a new approach to social income security that entailed extending state power to mitigate conflict with the existing social order.[6] Pressures from labour and the destabilizing ramifications of the emerging market economy were the main impetus for public intervention in the market distribution of income and opportunities. State intervention in the market distribution of income was deemed indispensable to sustaining marginalized sections of society and thereby integrating the subordinate classes into the existing social order. The emergence of capitalist social relations led to "the paradox of plenty within the midst of misery"; social income security came to be associated with the national deployment of resources to address the disruptive effects of market forces.[7]

The early state interventions intended to alter the market distribution of income in the late nineteenth century and the early decades of the twentieth constituted the "experimentation phase" of the welfare state. This initial stage of the welfare state was characterized by residual provision of social services.[8] Whatever the degree of economic development and institutional (including political) differences in Western societies, initial national experiments with income security were pursued in countries where an emerging labour movement had come to be seen as a threat to the status quo. The relationship between the rise of modern labour movements and the first major welfare initiatives in Western societies point to a casual linkage between the "experimentation phase" of the income security system and the emergence of the working class on the political scene.[9]

The consolidation and expansion phases of the welfare state were reinforced by the triumph of Keynesianism over the classical theory of free markets. The ascendancy of Keynesianism provided a logical justification for regulating capital and intervening in the economic sphere in ways that were conducive to fostering social harmony.[10] With the adoption of Keynesian measures justifying state intervention in business cycles, social welfare policy broke radically with past practices of poor relief.[11] It was in fact after the great crash of the 1930s and the Keynesian revolution at the centre of political-economic thought that the term "welfare state" found its place in political discourse.[12] Indeed, it was under Keynesianism that social security provision came to be associated with social entitlements.[13] Under Keynesianism, social solidarity as a public reflection of social welfare provision was elevated as a public good to counter the insecurities of the capitalist market economy, which was envisaged as a threat to the existing political order.[14] Although the roots of pension systems can be traced back to the nineteenth century, the consolidation of the modern pension systems has been associated with the ascendancy of Keynesianism.[15]

Pension systems are established in order to provide an income for those who incur a loss in earning capacity due to aging, disability, or the death of a wage earner in the family.[16] More specifically, retirement pensions are a means to provide for a period of time (retirement) where individuals do not draw income from paid employment. Thus, retirement pensions are state designed and a regulated social right. Allowing for

Table 2.1 Different types of retirement income provisions

First tier: Mandatory adequacy	Second tier: Mandatory savings		Third tier: Voluntary savings
Basic	Public	Private	Employer-sponsored pension plans
Resource-tested social assistance	Defined benefit	Defined benefit	Life insurance
Minimum pension	Points	Defined contribution	Individual accounts
	Notional accounts		

Source: Edward Whitehouse, *Canada's Retirement Income Provision: An International Perspective* (Ottawa: Department of Finance, 2009). http://www.fin.gc.ca/activty/pubs/pension/ref-bib/whitehouse-eng.asp.

variation across nations, retirement income systems generally have three pillars.[17] Table 2.1 illustrates different types of retirement pension plans.

The first pillar consists of a non-contributory flat rate pension payment funded through general government taxation and not linked to past contributions. This is the bedrock of the old age pension and is a redistributive component of the retirement income system. Pension payments funded from general taxation may operate on the basis of universal or income/asset test principles. Different countries have different first tiers. Under the basic pension, the benefit is a flat rate and the same amount is paid to everyone who is eligible. With resource-based schemes, higher benefits are paid to poorer pensioners and lower benefits (or none) to wealthier retirees. Under minimum pension schemes, which share many features with resource-based schemes, the amount of the pension payment is determined by taking account of only pension income.[18]

The second pillar of pension systems is an earnings-related pension insurance plan, which may be a publicly administered compulsory pension scheme or a state-mandated privately arranged pension plan. A contributory publicly administered earnings-related pension plan generally operates in line with the principles of a defined benefit plan. Under a defined benefit plan, there is a guarantee for a certain payment during retirement that is related to the member's salary and number of years of membership in the plan. In addition to a defined benefit under the publicly administered pension plan, there are two other variants. First, there can be a points scheme (as found in France and Germany) whereby workers earn pension points based on their individual earnings for each year of contribution. At retirement, the sum of pension points is multiplied by a pension point value to convert them into a regular pension payment stream.[19] Second, there are notional accounts schemes (as found in Italy and Sweden). Under these plans, each worker's contribution is recorded in an individual account, and a rate of return is applied to the account. A notional plan is designed to parallel the defined-contribution plan. Notional schemes are often called notional defined contribution plans.[20] In contrast, state-mandated privately managed occupational pension schemes operate on the principles of defined contribution plans or defined benefit plans. Under a defined contribution plan, the payment during retirement depends on the contribution amount and the performance of the investments. Defined contribution plans have become widespread, and most pension plans in the private sector are moving in this direction.[21] A defined benefit plan can be funded or unfunded. Under an unfunded defined benefit plan, benefits are paid out from current workers' contributions and payroll taxes, which are also known as pay-as-you-go (PAYG). The financial sustainability of unfunded defined benefit plans depends on high wage growth, demographic factors, and high rates of labour force participation.[22] Under a funded plan, the payment during retirement is contingent on the future return on investment. Benefits to be paid in the future are not known, so there is no guarantee that a certain amount of contribution will be enough to generate the required benefits. Publicly administered defined benefits do have some of the risk features associated with defined contribution plans. However, those risks are born in a different way, such as by future generations.

The third pillar of pension systems consists of private savings set aside by individuals over their lifetime.[23] This pillar includes employer-sponsored voluntary private pension plans, individual accounts, and private savings that are encouraged through favourable tax treatment. The establishment of employer-sponsored voluntary private pension plans is to a significant degree contingent on the bargaining leverage of labour unions in eliciting concessions from employers.[24] The inclination of individuals to utilize favourable tax treatment in order to save for their own retirement is directly tied to levels of income. High-income individuals are in a better position to utilize this tax break.[25]

Pension systems that were put in place and expanded during the Keynesian era have come under pressure since the 1980s. With the ascendancy of neoliberalism, pension systems in many countries have been subject to varying degrees of restructuring and retrenchment.[26] Pension reforms across nations have taken four pathways: from a PAYG plan to a funded plan; from defined benefits to defined contribution; from a publicly managed pension system to a privately managed one; and from a singular scheme to a multi-pillar one. Pension retrenchment has variously taken the form of reduced pension benefits, a raised retirement age, and an increasing role for privately managed retirement plans.[27] Variations in the pace and the degree of restructuring and retrenchment have been the subject of debate among mainstream theoretical paradigms.

Pensions and Mainstream Theoretical Perspectives

The liberal explanation of the welfare state attributes the development and expansion of retirement income programs to the technological, social, and economic ramifications of industrialization. The establishment of old age pension programs and other welfare state programs has been interpreted by liberal theory as a response to the forces of industrialization. Accordingly, industrialization and urbanization broke down the system of social supports based on kinship and sharpened the distinction between employed and unemployed, between the wealthy and the poor.[28] With the undermining of traditional forms of social support by industrialization and urbanization, there emerged an imperative for the state to respond to these changes by establishing social welfare programs such as old age pensions.[29] According to the liberal explanation, the creation of wealth associated with industrialization provided a logical ground for governments to establish social income security programs in order to alleviate poverty.[30] The age structure of the population to a great extent determines the level of public expenditure on the elderly; the degree of industrialization shapes the level of private expenditure on retirement income.[31] The restructuring and reform of pension systems is shaped by the design of the existing pension system, the special reform needs, and the environment; these in turn are tied to a country's levels of development and income.[32] It is obvious that a certain level of wealth is indispensable for the provision of old age pensions. But a direct correlation between the level of economic development and the institutionalization of welfare states has been questioned by many studies. These welfare state studies have found no positive relationship between level of economic development and the timing of the adoption of social security programs such as old age pensions.[33]

Liberal theorists generally dismiss the role of agency and ideology in shaping the development and expansion of old age pension programs.

Whenever the proponents of the liberal theory attempt to bring the role of social agency into their analyses of social welfare policy, they emphasize the role of non-class factors. This is evident in the works of neo-pluralists, who emphasize the role of interest groups in shaping income security policies.[34] Neo-pluralists interpret social income security as an outcome of competition among various groups that attempt to influence decision-making.[35] In his analysis of public pensions in Canada, Britain, and the United States, Henry Pratt has argued that the gradual expansion of governments' role in the pension policy field provided incentives for the formation and proliferation of interest groups, which subsequently became active participants in the reform and restructuring of pension programs.[36] Pampel and Williamson also argue that the aged, as a demographic *and* political force, play a crucial role in determining the level of public expenditure on pensions.[37] However, they admit that they "lack direct evidence" to corroborate their assertion. Accordingly, a comprehensive pension reform should include provisions that would increase the incentives to work and reduce inequities across demographic groups.[38]

The institutional perspective on the welfare state identifies state structures and political institutions as explanatory variables that shape old age pension programs. Under a centralized political structure, countries pursued generous and universal pension policies.[39] Conversely, under a decentralized political structure, the fragmentation of decision-making power functioned as a bulwark against the establishment of universal and generous pension programs.[40] As Weaver and Pierson have argued, "the centralization of legislative power and the absence of veto points that characterize majority governments in parliamentary systems" provide a golden opportunity for such governments to impose public pension retrenchment.[41] However, studies have also found no negative correlation between the decentralization of political power and public social expenditures.[42]

High levels of political fragmentation can make it a challenge for the central government to achieve consensus on pension reform, especially if it entails an unpopular retrenchment.[43] In such circumstances, implementing unpopular reforms requires *quid pro quo* in the austerity package in order to appease opposing groups and thereby neutralize their opposition.[44] Some institutionalists identify intermediary entities such as corporatist arrangements as a crucial factor shaping social income security programs.[45] Accordingly, variations in pension reforms across countries reflect differences in political institutions and the policy legacies.[46]

The resistance of old age pension programs to the pressure for curtailment is largely due to the nature of state structures and the design of the pension system. Past policy legacies shape subsequent policy development,[47] as well as the policy ideas and the political weight of the aged population, which as a non-class group can influence electoral outcomes.[48] Institutionalists emphasize the centrality of political institutions in framing old age income policy in Western societies, but they have also highlighted the role of non-institutional factors. According to institutionalists, non-institutional factors such as economic pressures, the policy legacy, and the balance of resources between opponents and proponents of retrenchment all have the potential to mediate the institutional effects on the establishment of pension systems.[49]

The power resources model highlights institutional structures, the power resources of labour, and patterns of class coalitions as the main determinants of old age pension programs.[50] Public spending on pensions and other social programs is a function of the strength of labour and the characteristics of the national class coalition.[51] Working-class mobilization was crucial to the development of pension programs. However, the class effects on pension expenditures are conditioned by political institutions.[52] Accordingly, a generous and universal pension system tends to exist in a society where labour is centralized and its political wing exercises governmental power.

For the power resources model, public pension systems across countries correspond to the three types of welfare state. Social democratic welfare regimes provide a generous and universal public pension. Under liberal welfare regimes, public expenditures target needy sections of the aged population and the rest of the population is encouraged to make private provision for their retirement. Conservative or corporatist welfare regimes provide a strongly stratified insurance-based old age support system.[53] The restructuring and reform of these different types of pension systems are shaped by the design of the programs, the power resources of labour, and the nature of the class coalition.[54] Partisan political competition and the structure of the pension system over time shape the age orientation of the welfare state.[55] Pension reforms across countries have been marked by shifts from defined benefits to defined contribution and by the raising of the retirement age.[56] However, these changes are shaped by the institutional features of the existing systems. Under Bismarckian pension systems, defined benefits are replaced by defined contributions. Similarly, the shift from universality to targeting has become a hallmark of Beveridgean models.[57]

Despite its growing currency in the realm of comparative welfare studies, the power resources model cannot answer a significant question that emerges from its own theorization: Why is the degree of decommodification and universality in some countries where class is fragmented and social democracy has never exercised governmental power at the national level greater than in some countries where the labour movement has retained its unity and social democracy has held governmental power?

In Marxian class analysis, old age pension systems were a systemic response to the problems of capitalism and an attempt to maintain social peace.[58] The establishment of the first modern state pension in Germany in the 1880s was an effort to "preempt revolutionary sentiments."[59] In this regard, Wonik established a direct relation between the expansion of social insurance and the threat of social revolution in Europe between 1880 and 1945.[60] Accordingly, the retrenchment of publicly provided old age pensions and the drift towards the privatization of retirement income provisions is a manifestation of the shift of class power to capital. In terms of policy, neoliberal assaults on non-contributory flat rate pensions are intended to replace universalism with selectivity. The return to targeting the most needy of the aged population is a return to the era of residualism that prevailed in the nineteenth century and the early twentieth. Moreover, the privatization of retirement income provisions is intended to open up a new frontier for capital accumulation.[61] In consequence, the privatization of retirement income tends to eclipse the claim of citizenship as the basis for public pension benefits.

In the realm of private occupational pension schemes, the shift from defined benefit to defined contribution schemes requires employees bear the market risk since benefits to be paid are not predetermined.[62] Pension funds not only have given new scope to the operation of capitalism but also have become critical to the processes of globalization.[63] Private pension saving accounts are meant to increase overall savings, reduce the role of the state in pension provisions, and provide more choices to individuals that are consistent with neoliberal economic policy.[64] In the world of "grey capitalism," pension funds have become chips in the hands of highly paid corporate executives and fund managers.[65] Some argue that workers' savings are being manipulated through pension fund investment practices that serve aggrandize corporations at the expense of workers' welfare.[66] Pension privatization benefits wealthy individuals who have more disposable income to invest, increases income inequality, and exposes individuals to social risk.[67] For Marxists, collective ownership and control of massive pension funds is indispensable to diminishing the anti-social power of financial capital in a globalized world.[68] The widespread ownership of companies by pension funds has the potential to democratize the capitalist economy.[69] Some argue that it is only through the transfer of ownership and control to workers that pension funds can be directed towards socially responsible investment.[70] According to Blackburn,[71] the growing needs of the world's aged people must be addressed by a universal pension system financed by taxes on global financial transactions and corporate wealth.[72]

In the social program restructuring literature, the impact of neoliberalism on the welfare state is found in comparative as well as individual case studies in Canada and Australia. As with the comparative welfare state literature, welfare studies of Canada and Australia have relied mainly on the institutional structures and power resources of labour as explanatory variables.

The Welfare State Literature on Canada and Australia

The literature on welfare state contraction in Canada is dominated by descriptions of neoliberal ascendancy and its negative impacts on national income security.[73] This welfare state explanation identifies free trade and continental economic integration as the primary causes of welfare state curtailment.[74] This echoes Kari Levitt's argument that continental economic integration "is fundamentally destructive of Canadian unity because it rejects the maintenance of a national community as an end in itself."[75] However, as James Rice and Michael Prince have pointed out, although economic pressures and globalization have adversely affected the redistributive role of the federal government, the Canadian welfare state has not lost its relevance.[76]

Similarly, the recent Australian welfare state literature identifies economic globalization as the underlying force that has weakened the foundations of the welfare state.[77] Accordingly, financial deregulation, the decline in the appeal of protectionism, and labour market readjustment to emerging global economic forces generated compelling pressures for welfare state retrenchment.[78] The imperatives of economic restructuring and the ascendancy of neoliberalism are identified as the main drivers of social welfare austerity and intrusive eligibility criteria for receiving social welfare benefits.[79]

No welfare state has emerged unscathed from neoliberalism.[80] Economic restructuring and a shift in the balance of social forces have dragged labour and social democratic parties into "the magnetic field of their opponents."[81] As Piven has pointed out, all social democratic parties have internalized "the necessity of adapting to international markets and of the austerity policies capital has demanded," and they have attempted to rationalize their own technical capacity to "administer the neo-liberal policies that matches market imperatives."[82]

The boundary between the restructuring and the retrenchment of welfare states has been blurred. Restructuring and retrenchment are not synonymous, and welfare state transformation does not necessarily imply the dismantling or obliteration of welfare state programs. John Shields and Brian Evans have pointed out that welfare state restructuring has manifested itself in various forms. Changes in the provisions and the substance of the welfare state can be detected along three dimensions: "recommodification" (tightening eligibility and qualification for receiving social wages); "cost curtailment" (reducing social expenditures for certain social programs); and "recalibration" (the modification and reconfiguration of certain social programs justified as a historical necessity to adjust to changing circumstances).[83]

Comparative welfare state studies about Canada and Australia have been grounded mainly in either the power resources model or institutional approaches. But within the debate on welfare state classification, scant attention has been paid to the Canadian welfare state. As Haddow and Klassen have pointed out, of ten major comparative studies on welfare state typology, only one devoted a full page to the theoretical details of the Canadian welfare state.[84]

In his comparative studies on old age pensions in developed industrial societies, Myles attributes variation in the dependent variables (such as differences in the qualitative and qualitative expansion of old age pensions) to variation in power resources of labour.[85] Myles's work is a theoretical advance beyond individual case studies of social income security in Canada. However, Myles's analysis does not adequately explain the divergent paths of the postwar old age expansion in Canada and Australia. A critical question left unanswered by Myles is: Why, despite higher levels of power resources of labour in Australia, did the Australian old age pension remain within the bounds of residualism and private occupational pension schemes even while old age pension in Canada moved towards universalism?

In recent work on old age pension restructuring in advanced industrial countries, Myles and Pierson emphasize institutional differences and interest group politics as independent variables that explain the differences in old age pension restructuring across developed nations.[86] For

Myles and Pierson, "the new politics of the welfare state" governing old age pension restructuring are different from the postwar politics of welfare states that shaped the postwar expansion of old age pensions. Thus, Myles and Pierson fail to establish a systemic connection between the expansion and the restructuring of old age security income, although they are related to each other. Parallel to Myles and Pierson's attempt to reduce old age pension policy to an outcome of interest group politics, Alexander Gash's main thesis on the comparative study of pension systems in Canada, Australia, and Sweden hinges on an interest group explanation.[87] According to Gash, political elites in these countries have employed pensions as political leverage to appease voting constituencies and secure electoral victories. But this interpretation does not provide a plausible explanation for the divergent patterns of old age pension systems in Canada and Australia. In the 1990s, senior citizens in Canada and Australia respectively constituted 11.4 and 11.5 per cent of the overall population.[88] Due to this demographic similarity, variations in retirement income systems in Canada and Australia can hardly be attributed to differences in the political weight of the elderly population in these countries.

Several analysts have employed the power resources model to explain the overall national configuration of income security in Canada and Australia. Proponents of the power resources model have catapulted the Australian welfare state to a higher position relative to its counterpart in Canada, based on the organizational character of the labour movement and the exercise of political power by the working class.[89] Yet empirical findings presented by studies using the power resources model as an explanatory framework have demonstrated that the degree of decommodification and universality for income security in Australia during the era of welfare state expansion was lower than in Canada.[90] If universalism and decommodification are criteria for measuring the comprehensiveness of social income security, then the ranking order of Canada and Australia within the parameters of the power resources model is questionable.

Employing the same theoretical framework but using a different methodology, Castles and Mitchell have added another world to the three worlds of welfare capitalism of Esping-Andersen.[91] According to Castles and Mitchell, a fourth world of welfare capitalism is distinguished by the welfare goals of poverty amelioration and income inequality reduction; these are accomplished through redistributive instruments rather than high levels of social expenditures. In accordance with the criteria they use to construct the fourth world of the welfare state, Australia is at the centre of this fourth world and Canada has been pushed to its periphery. Castles and Mitchell attempt to rationalize the principles of selectivity and targeting entrenched in the foundations of old age income security in Australia. However, due to its intrusive means test, which tends to demean personal dignity, the Australian welfare state can hardly be identified as comprehensive. Furthermore, levels of social security expenditures have a direct impact on the welfare goal of income inequality reduction.[92] Finally, the trajectory of income distribution and rates of poverty in Canada and Australia bring into question the alleged superiority of the Australian welfare state over its Canadian counterpart.[93] Since the postwar recovery, Australia has been one of the richest countries in the OECD in terms of per capita GDP. Yet in terms of social welfare expenditures, it has come to be regarded as a welfare laggard.[94] Furthermore, Castles and Mitchell fail to consider the significant contribution of universalism to social stability. As Rothstein has pointed out, the universal character of the welfare state may have two crucial implications for social trust.[95] The first implication is that people receiving support from government cannot be portrayed as "the others." Second, compared to means-tested social security programs, universal programs are far less likely to generate suspicion that people are cheating the system.

Institutional approaches to the study of welfare states in Canada and Australia have emphasized either centralization/decentralization of collective bargaining or centralization/decentralization of the political system as explanatory variables. With respect to the former, it is argued that the greater centralization of the labour movement in Australia played a crucial role in the ascendancy of full employment in Australia. Conversely, the greater decentralization of the labour movement in Canada contributed to the Canadian state's tolerance for higher levels of unemployment.[96] Several authors have identified the absence of a coordinated production regime in Canada as reason for the underdevelopment of the Canadian welfare state.[97] These studies fail to consider that full employment is not the only indicator of welfare state comprehensiveness. Furthermore, without a simultaneous expansion of the frontiers of the welfare state, centralized wage bargaining can in fact coexist with a residual welfare state. In other words, centralization of wage setting alone does not signal the comprehensiveness of the welfare state. Compulsory state arbitration ostensibly provides a legal avenue for workers to participate in the productivity of the economy. However, it is correspondingly geared to diminish the threat of a strike on economic production.

Furthermore, the centralization of wage setting is not necessarily opposed by the dominant classes. A centralized wage determination system can in fact be used by employers to check the increase in wage levels, as studies of corporatism have shown.

The second institutional approach to welfare state restructuring in Canada and Australia, the one that emphasizes the degree of political centralization, can be found in the comparative studies of federalism. These analysts argue that the centrally coordinated intergovernmental relations in Australia have allowed the swift adjustment of Australian national social policy to global economic restructuring. Conversely, the adversarial nature of intergovernmental relations in Canada has impeded social policy adjustment.[98] These analysts do not explain why universalism became a reality under a decentralized political system in Canada, while under the centralized federal system in Australia, residualism remained a defining dimension of old age pensions. These analysts also remain silent on the adverse impact of unilateral adjustment of the Australian welfare state to the demands of market forces. Furthermore, they fail to unravel the underlying forces beneath the conflictual dimension of intergovernmental relations in Canada.

Several analysts of Canadian politics have attempted to address what is left unexplained by Brown and Courchene. According to these analysts, the fundamental force behind the conflictual process of social policy adaptation in Canada is the institutionalization of regionalism, which has functioned as a brake on welfare state restructuring.[99] What seems to have not been taken into account by these analysts is that regionalism is socially constructed.[100] Regional variations are not confined to Canada; they have asserted themselves in all countries, including Australia.[101] In other words, these analysts fail to account for why, despite the ubiquity of regional variations within most countries, those interests have acquired a political character in Canada.

As a political phenomenon, regionalism in Canada must be comprehended in the context of the historical relations between Canada and Quebec and the clash of nationalisms from which no aspect of Canadian politics has escaped unaffected. The clash of nationalisms in Canada has generated a political atmosphere in which social class conflicts often manifest themselves as regional ones. By casting socio-economic cleavages as regional conflicts, the Canadian elites have found a golden opportunity to popularize national unity as a means to surmount the mystified territorial conflict.[102]

The historical trajectory of intergovernmental relations in Canada and Australia cannot be analysed independent of the historical and national specificity of each country. Canada commenced its federal life with a concentration of political power at the national level; the Australian federation emerged with greater decentralization. In Canada, the federal evolution has been marked by progressive decentralization of governmental jurisdiction; in Australia, governmental power has firmly swung to the national level. These patterns of intergovernmental evolution in Canada and Australia have been shaped by each country's particular national setting.[103]

Even though the national governments in Australia and Canada were hobbled by constitutional limits on their power, the imperative of national involvement in socio-economic reconstruction prepared the ground for greater central intervention in both countries. It was indeed under the aegis of Keynesianism that national governments in both countries acquired a higher degree of fiscal centralization, although the magnitude of fiscal centralization was higher in Australia, reflecting both the relative homogeneity of Australian society and the political weight of labour. As part of socio-economic reconstruction, the Australian federal government acquired a virtual monopoly and permanent ascendancy over taxation power by consenting to provide grants for the states in return for vacating the taxation field. In contrast, the taxation and spending powers of the Canadian federal government were subject to challenges waged by Quebec and then imitated by other provinces.[104]

The relative homogeneity of Australian society and the discourse of Australian nationhood, as opposed to the binary character of Canadian society compounded by the protracted quest for national unity, drove the evolution of intergovernmental relations in each country.[105] As Watts has suggested, in the absence of "the Quebec question," the Canadian federation might have retained its centralized character.[106] Despite the continuing determination by both countries to retain their British heritage as constitutional monarchies, differences in their linguistic and ethnic make-up influenced their tempo and pace towards adding national citizenship to British heritage. It was in fact due to the differences in their national settings and ethnic composition that Canada preceded Australia in integrating the concept of citizenship into its official discourse. This would play a crucial role in shaping the Canadian welfare state.[107]

The same lines of analysis have dominated the literature on pension systems in these countries. The central theme of the literature on retirement income systems in Canada and Australia revolves around the significance of institutional structures and the degree of power resources of labour as explanatory variables, and how pension systems have been subject to neoliberal-motivated forces of economic restructuring.

The Welfare State Literature on Pension Systems in Canada and Australia

Dennis Guest's *The Emergence of Social Security in Canada* has been identified as the first and most detailed study of income security development in Canada.[108] It might be regarded as a Canadian counterpart to T.H. Kewley's *Social Security in Australia*,[109] which details the evolution of the welfare state in Australia. But as Woodsworth pointed out, Guest's study "does not provide a theoretical framework for even its own descriptive detail."[110] Despite the breath of his study as reflected in his attempt to trace modern Canadian social welfare policy to the colonial era in the eighteenth and nineteenth centuries, Guest fails to explain why, among many alternatives, Canada embraced the universal principle for old age pensions.[111] Similarly, Bryden's case study of old age pension policy in Canada can be regarded as the most comprehensive account of the expansion of pensions in Canada.[112] Yet he fails to establish a link between numerous independent variables and old age pension expansion. As Simeon has observed, Bryden's theoretical framework "does bear little relationship to the detailed historical reconstruction of a set of events which takes up the bulk of the book."[113]

Within the literature on social welfare policy, the effectiveness of retirement income policy in keeping retired Canadians out of poverty has been highlighted by many analysts.[114] The income gap between rich and poor Canadians in the late 1950s and early 1960s tends to disappear as pension income kicks in and stabilizes income. Due to its stabilizing effect, public pension income sources tend to reduce income instability among all age groups.[115]

Furthermore, the centrality of retirement income programs in the Canadian welfare state has been acknowledged. As Banting and Boadway have pointed out, "retired Canadians are the biggest winners from the introduction of the welfare state."[116] Banting and Boadway have attributed the high place of the Canadian pension system within the Canadian welfare state to public sympathy for the aged and the electoral weight of the elderly population.

With regard to retirement income restructuring since the 1980s, Canadian studies have emphasized the crumbling of the Canadian welfare state and its shift from an institutionalized welfare state to a residual one. These analysts have mainly highlighted the neoliberal inroads into the retirement income system.[117] Even though demographic pressures and the rising cost of retirement programs were used by federal governments in the 1980s and 1990s to justify retrenchment, the pressures for restructuring and retrenchment of the income retirement system during these eras are attributed to the reassertion of market power and the penetration of neoliberal principles into the governmental agenda.[118] Changes in the Canadian Pension Plan's investment policy and increasing contribution rates in order to move the system towards a hybrid PAYG funding plan are interpreted as manifestations of the "marketization" of the public pension system.[119]

According to Ken Battle, the success of both Progressive Conservative and Liberal administrations in the restructuring and retrenchment of the retirement income system in the 1980s and 1990s was due to the dexterity of these administrations in pursuing incremental changes rather than embarking on "Big Bang" change.[120] The changes that were made to the public pension plan (CPP), the second pillar of the Canadian retirement income system, kept the administrative and decision-making powers in the hands of governments and did not provide for a broad "participation of social partners."[121] However, the involvement of labour unions in the investment policy of pension funds related to employer-sponsored private pension schemes has been growing.[122] The growing involvement of labour organizations in the investment policies of pension funds is construed by some as a new weapon in the arsenal of labour that has the potential to replace the collapsed collective bargaining system.[123]

Pro-market think tanks such as the C.D. Howe Institute and the Fraser Institute have advocated reshaping the Canadian pension plan along market lines and expanding the realm of private arrangements for retirement saving as a safe road to securing retirement incomes for Canadians.[124] Some argue that the long-term sustainability of the Canadian retirement income system necessitates the establishment of a "Super RRSP"[125] and the transformation of the third pillar of the Canadian pension system into a fully funded privately managed mandatory system. According to Estelle, a privately managed pension scheme is not only the best way to allocate capital based on economic rather than political objectives, but also more efficient than the publicly managed pension system in linking benefits to contributions.[126] These studies pay less attention to the comparative ability of the Canadian retirement income system to retain its progressive and collectivist dimensions. Wherever there has been an acknowledgment of the relative success of the Canadian income retirement system in withstanding the forces of welfare state retrenchment, it has been attributed to the design of the system in the 1950s and 1960s that shaped the politics of reform.[127] However, this path-dependent explanation requires us to establish a clear linkage between welfare state expansion and welfare state contraction. The retention of mandatory retirement until the mid-2000s, which is often interpreted as a sign of welfare state comprehensiveness, is also imputed to the strength of the labour movement. Yet Klassen and Forgione have found that the elimination of forced retirement in Quebec has not been accompanied by the degeneration of the income security system in that province.[128] As Béland has pointed out, these analysts have not clarified why, despite the presence of a relatively strong labour movement in Quebec, mandatory retirement was abolished in that province.[129]

Indeed, the standard power resources model cannot adequately account for variations in old age income restructuring in Canada and Australia. There has been a progressive decline in union density in Australia, yet restructuring of the Australian welfare state was in fact consolidated under the auspices of the Labor administration. In Canada, restructuring of the welfare state was initiated and consolidated under Conservative and Liberal administrations, both of which enjoyed majority governments that left no latitude for the NDP to flex any coalition leverage.

Castles's earlier description of social income security in Australia as a "wage earners' welfare state" has become a point of reference for the majority of welfare state studies in Australia.[130] Castles's theoretical study of the Australian welfare state surpasses Kewley's detailed evaluation of social income security in Australia, which "implicitly leans to the view that the Australian welfare state has evolved and progressed as the result of rational (or liberal and compassionate) notions capturing the imagination of the electorate or of key figures in Government."[131] According to Castles, "the wage earners welfare state" was sustained mainly through the Australian pattern of centralized wage determination and labour market regulations designed to accomplish full employment as a substitute for the social wage.[132] In his work on welfare state restructuring, Castles identifies globalization as the main culprit behind the crumbling of the postwar social settlement, which in turn rationalized retrenchment of social income security in Australia.[133] Despite the importance of his analysis within the Australian welfare state literature, Castles does not establish a linkage between welfare state expansion and contraction in Australia.

The failure of the Australian retirement income system to embrace universalism during the era of welfare state expansion is attributed to the lack of political will by political parties.[134] The revival of intrusive means testing (asset and tight income tests) as governing principles to access old age pension payments in 1980s is often interpreted as the ascendancy of neoliberalism in Australia and the eclipse of social citizenship.[135] The intensification of selectivity has been hailed for its effectiveness in tackling poverty among the aged Australians, but also criticized for generating disincentives for saving.[136]

The successive waves of reform in economic and social welfare policy in Australia have been heralded as the birth of a "new economic model."[137] The reform of the retirement income system manifested in the establishment of a state-mandated privately managed superannuation scheme in 1992 was hailed by some as a successful model that deserves to become an example for the reform of retirement income systems in other countries.[138] In contrast, it is argued that the privately managed superannuation plans in Australia cannot be regarded as a comprehensive international model since their regulatory measures are weak and ambiguous in protecting the interests of their members.[139] Furthermore, the national superannuation scheme fails to cover part-time workers, whose numbers have been on the rise since 1980s.[140] By linking income in old age to employment-based earnings during working life, superannuation schemes tend to adversely affect those with intermittent work patterns, who most likely happen to be women.[141]

The expansion of mandatory private arrangements for retirement income in Australia is interpreted as reflecting an ingrained philosophical belief in individualism and market forces that has marked Australia's political culture.[142] Furthermore, the consolidation of privately managed pension schemes is viewed as a long-term plan to substitute the non-contributory flat rate old age pension with private pension arrangements.[143] The national superannuation in Australia is intended to promote the moral and economic virtues of thrift and "is a part of an economic and social culture that embraces individualistic paths to security in old age."[144]

What seems to have escaped the attention of these analysts of the Australian pension system is that the direction of income security retrenchment in Australia may already have been enabled by the structure of the postwar social class compromise in Australia. In other words, the intensification of selectivity and the expansion of the privatization of retirement income provisions since 1980s were to a significant extent shaped by the way in which the Australian postwar social class settlement had been arranged.

Conclusion

The existing comparative literature and individual case studies on welfare states in Canada and Australia do not provide a convincing explanation for divergent patterns of old age retirement income policy in these countries. As explained earlier, these comparative and individual case studies emphasize levels of economic development, differences in institutional structures, and differences in the power resources of labour. The significance of levels of economic development, with its demographic corollaries, political institutions, and power resources of labour as units of analysis, cannot be refuted. But these variables cannot be analysed independent of a wider historical and national context within which social forces and political institutions interact with one another. The existing welfare state literature does not provide a clear picture of retirement income expansion and subsequent restructuring. This is due to the failure to integrate the intersection of national settings, social classes, and the role of the state in shaping the postwar social class settlement. Explaining variations in old age pension expansion and restructuring in Canada and Australia requires us to consider differences in the nature of the postwar social class settlement in these two countries, which not only structured the postwar trajectory of retirement income systems but also shaped the responses to neoliberal pressures for old age income restructuring. As will be demonstrated in the following chapters, variations in the postwar social class settlements in Canada and Australia to a great extent shaped the divergent patterns of pension systems in these two countries.

3 National Settings, Class Forces, and Keynesianism

With the seismic shift in the political landscape that accompanied the economic slump of the 1930s in the advanced industrial countries, greater state intervention in the economy became imperative. That intervention came to be justified by Keynesian economics, which triumphed over the classical liberalism of free market economics. By 1930, laissez-faire was identified as having contributed to the Great Crash. Keynesian and Beveridgean welfare state ideas prevailed in the official discourse in Canada and Australia, whose social welfare policies were marked by variations in the official adoption of these ideas. That adoption was in turn influenced by the distinct socio-political forces within each country.

The homogeneity of Australian society strengthened the unity of the labour movement in that country. In Canada, by contrast, national fragmentation accentuated working-class disunity. Australia's homogeneity helped consolidate a centralized corporatist industrial relations system; Canada's fragmented national setting contributed to the emergence of adecentralized and localized industrial relations system. The social vision of the Australian labour movement emphasized market regulation and industrial bargaining as surrogates for social welfare protection. In Canada, disunity within the labour movement reinforced by national fragmentation led to a form of Keynesianism that placed less emphasis on market regulation in the workplace and more on income redistribution as the main mechanism of social welfare protection.

To understand how economic and political factors shaped postwar social settlements in Canada and Australia, we need to assess the historical interplay of class, state, and national settings in each country. Although their political institutions were roughly similar, as were their patterns of staples-led economic development, Australia and Canada took different directions in terms of how their labour movements emerged and organized politically. The power resources of labour in Canada and Australia were greatly shaped by differences in their national settings.

Canada: State, Class, and National Settings

The uneven industrial development in pre-Confederation Canada was intensified by a long-standing clash of nationalisms. After Confederation, that clash impeded the formation of a working class. The absence of feudal or semi-feudal structures at least in Upper Canada and the West, and the availability of cheap land on which even the poorest immigrants could support themselves without relying on wage labour, did not foster proletarianization.[1] The sheer number of small independent producers, and their persistence, slowed down the pace of proletarianization in the nineteenth century, which in turn delayed the development of a Canadian labour movement.[2] The domination of Canadian agriculture by small farmers impeded the growth of the labour movement. It also complicated the class alignments between workers and farmers during the major socio-economic shifts of the 1930s and the 1940s. All of this generated the conditions for the social class settlement that formed the basis for the Canadian welfare state.[3] By the time the Canadian labour movement began to assert itself in the early decades of the twentieth century, the petty bourgeoisie had already emerged as a significant force on the political scene.[4] As far as electoral politics were concerned, "in no other democratic society was the result so unfavorable to the spokesman for socialism and independent labour actions as it was in Canada."[5] The political weakness of the Canadian labour movement in the early decades of the twentieth century was a clear manifestation of division, rivalry, internecine battles, and procrastination among trade unions. This disunity prevented the Canadian labour movement from flexing its political muscle.

The organization of Canadian workers can be traced back to pre-Confederation times. Long before then, some workers were expressing their collective desire to organize in order to improve their wages and working conditions.[6] By the second half of the nineteenth century, the intensification of labour exploitation in the early factories had led to the proliferation of fragmented local unions as the principal mechanisms of working-class struggle.[7] The need to confront the dominant classes led a number of local, scattered trade unions to form a national organization, which in turn led to the founding of the Trades and Labor Congress

(TLC) in 1886. As a national umbrella organization for unions and the main vehicle of class leadership, the TLC attempted to embrace both purely Canadian and international craft unions.[8] The TLC's ideological disposition was, however, influenced by the anti-party and anti-socialist orientation of American union leaders.[9] Pressured by the American Federation of Labor (AFL), the TLC expelled national and international unions that did not embrace the political position of the American labour leaders. The expelled national and international unions eventually formed the Canadian Congress of Labour (CCL) as a rival to the TLC.

Simultaneously, industrial and craft unions in Quebec formed the Canadian Catholic Confederation of Labour (CCCL) in 1921, later renamed the Confederation of National Trade Unions (CNTU). From the outset, the labour movement in Quebec was subject to the decrees of Roman Catholic Church. Thus, Quebec's labour movement was deeply rooted in French Canadian nationalism and sought to express the national identity and cultural traits of francophone workers.[10] As a result of this amalgam of working-class solidarity and national identity, class collaboration between the labour movement and Quebec's business elites was the order of the day into the 1960s.[11]

The socio-economic upheavals of the early decades of the twentieth century led to industrial militancy in Canada, the epicentre of which was Winnipeg, where (famously) a general strike was launched in 1919. But organized labour was unable to forge a united political front. As the main centre of labour, the TLC took a murky position on political action. At its 1917 convention, it called for the formation of an independent labour party and encouraged the founding of provincial labour parties. Yet at its 1927 convention, the TLC recanted on this and vowed to remain the mouthpiece for organized labour, independent of any political party.[12]

The political fragmentation of the organized working class, exemplified by the rivalry between the main centres of labour, complicated the formation of a working-class party. In the early decades of the twentieth century, working-class fragmentation was evident in the sheer number of small socialist organizations and parties, which were often torn by petty ideological differences. The most significant of these early socialist parties was the Socialist Party of Canada (SPC), which declared its existence in 1904. The SPC was confined mainly to British Columbia, where it expressed its unequivocal commitment to consigning capitalism to the dustbin of history.[13] The SPC's radical stance eventually caused the moderate elements within the party to desert it and form the Social Democratic

Party of Canada in 1911.[14] The remaining radical figures within the SPC converted the party into the Workers Party of Canada, which became the Communist Party of Canada in 1921.[15]

There were also independent labour parties, some of which strove to bring about a wide range of labour and social reforms in their respective provinces. These parties were dominated by British immigrants who were already acquainted with parliamentary labour politics.[16] These provincial labour parties served as buffers between the revolutionary socialists who saw violent destruction of capitalism as the most appropriate road to socialism and those who were comfortable with the status quo.[17]

The momentum that allowed the Co-operative Commonwealth Federation (CCF) to emerge as a third political force in 1932 was generated by ideologically diverse radical forces. The economic turbulence of the 1930s facilitated the political convergence of labour, farmers, Christian evangelists, and urban intellectuals.[18] Notwithstanding its diverse components and their discordant voices, the CCF proclaimed its arrival on the political scene with a radical commitment: it would limit corporate power by democratic means and establish a social order in which "the domination and exploitation of one class by another will be eliminated."[19] The CCF's statement of principles came to be known as the Regina Manifesto.[20]

A Gallup poll taken in September 1943 found the CCF to be the most popular political party in Canada.[21] Its presence on the political scene compelled the established parties to overhaul their political platforms. James Macdonald, a conservative figure, declared that the Conservative Party would have to change its orientation in order to win election "rather than ... the country has a red government."[22] William Lyon Mackenzie King, the leader of the Liberal Party, was concerned with the "danger of the Liberal party being eliminated all together in Canada."[23] In his view, social reforms were required that "might save the country from falling into the hands of inexperienced men who also might head its affairs in the direction of a socialistic state."[24]

In 1944, in farmer-dominated Saskatchewan, the CCF succeeded in forming the first social democratic government in North America, but it was unable to forge an enduring national coalition of farmers and workers. With the postwar economic recovery, farmers began to move away from the radicalism of the 1930s towards political reforms that would stabilize markets. Many farmers' groups now defected from the CCF.[25]

In Quebec, the CCF encountered a hostile political atmosphere that the party was unable to overcome. It was branded as godless by the

Catholic Church, and it was perceived by nationalists as a centralizing force that threatened the Quebec's historical aspirations for greater political autonomy. As McKay has pointed out, the Catholic authorities regarded socialism as "an atheism in disguise, a Bolshevik conspiracy, and a rival power."[26]

Farmers' defection, electoral barriers in Quebec, the refusal of many labour unions to accept the CCF as the political expression of the working class, and moves by established parties to implement social welfare measures, all placed enormous pressure on the CCF to overhaul its ideological principles. For the sake of expanding, the CCF was compelled to modify the radical language of the Regina Manifesto and move towards a general call for peace, justice, and cooperation in the Winnipeg Declaration in 1965.[27] By then, the CCL and the TLC had merged to form the Canadian Labour Congress (CLC) in 1956. In 1961, after long discussions among the ranks of the CCF and the CLC, the CCF transformed itself into the NDP as the political arm of the labour movement.

The disunity among working-class organizations had created a friendly atmosphere for the business sector. Capitalist organizations felt no pressure to develop a strong, unified organization to challenge labour and defend the interests of the business community.[28] The main centres of the business community, such as the Canadian Chamber of Commerce and the Canadian Manufacturers' Association, "tended to be spokespeople for narrow sectoral interests ... [and] appeared capable only of reacting negatively ... to government policies and programs."[29]

In studies about working-class politics in Canada, the historical fragmentation of the labour movement and the failure to form a class-based party have been attributed to factors such as the conservative leanings of labour unions, the federal structure of the Canadian political system, and uneven patterns of economic development.[30] Academic observers have often observed that the CCF/NDP has gradually moved to the centre of the ideological spectrum. It is obvious that organized labour was reluctant to endorse the CCF/NDP as the political arm of the working class and in some cases refused to do so. But attributing the CCF/NDP's classless image of Canadian society to the conservative attitude of organized labour appears to be controversial. Despite the factionalism within the labour movement, Canadian labour centres were in the early twentieth century calling loudly for universal and progressive social income security programs.[31] Furthermore, if the CCF/NDP deradicalized its ideological orientation because of the conservative leanings of trade unions, then the latter should have logically supported the former, which had ostensibly adjusted itself to the conservatism of organized labour. But in fact, the vast majority of unionized workers have historically refrained from voting for the NDP.[32]

Also, it is often noted that the absence of class in national political dialogue is due to Canada's federal structure. Federalism by its nature tends to conceal class issues and conduct political struggles along territorial, regional, and ethnic lines.[33] Accordingly, federalism tends to institutionalize territorial divisions and to blur class cleavages. This leads to a politics preoccupied with regional, linguistic, and religious conflicts. Federalism is based on a territorial dispersion of political power between two levels of government, and the federal structure multiplies the points of access and political spaces for social forces to champion their own interests. Federalism may provide opportunities to replace social conflicts with non-economic ones. But this does not in itself preclude the penetration of class politics into popular language. Class-based politics, for example, has historically been salient in Australia, which also operates under a federal system.[34]

There is no doubt that unequal patterns of economic development have had divisive implications for the Canadian labour movement, but unequal levels of economic development are not confined to Canada alone. Uneven patterns of economic development can be traced in other societies where labour movements have shown more unity. Attributing working-class fragmentation in Canada to regional variations in economic development implies an automatic transformation of objective class relations into subjective class formation that does not take into account that political struggle precedes class formation.

Objective economic locations do not necessarily give rise to class consciousness and class politics. As Panitch has pointed out, class mobilization is a necessary "organizational and ideological condition" to the formation of working-class identity.[35] Segmentation and stratification within the working class is an inevitable implication of the centrifugal propensities of market forces. The articulation and aggregation of the interests of the working class into a unified whole can only be accomplished by a workers' political party.[36]

To counteract the disintegrative power of capital, the political organization of workers must devise strategies that can offset differences within the working class and overcome the subjective differences emanating from the objective location of workers within the social relations of production. As Przeworski has asserted, the party of the working class functions as "glue," and "without glue, class is a house of cards."[37] The impacts of uneven economic development on working-class unity in Canada have also to be seen in relation to the inability of the CCF/NDP to operate along class lines and bring class issues to the centre of political struggle.[38]

It is regional particularism that has most often been invoked as the reason for the fragmentation of the working-class identity in Canada. Regional diversity within Canada allows religious and ethnic identities to transcend those of class.[39] Ethnic, religious, and linguistic characteristics affect individuals' comprehension of their class position within overall social relations. Political conflicts along any dimension tend to be expressed at least partly in terms of territorial identity, but regional particularism can in fact be depicted as the crystallization of class struggles. Regionalism, which has been the main axis of Canadian politics, is in fact a spatial manifestation of political reaction to unequal power relations. The rise of farmers in the West, for example, was not a petty bourgeois effort to preserve Alberta's regional identity. It was spurred by farmers' comprehension of their "quasi-colonial" position and their subjugation to the dominant class, which was predominantly located in eastern Canada.[40]

The historical transformation of Quebec nationalism from a defensive posture to an assertive and offensive one was also motivated by a class reaction to the domination of the Quebec economy by anglophone capitalists.[41] In Quebec, even internal class cleavages have been clouded by the national aim of "decolonization"; in English-speaking regions, by contrast, class differences have continued to be more pronounced than any supposed cultural particularism. It was this academic obsession with cultural particularism that provoked John Porter to construe the emphasis on the cultural particularity of English Canadian analysis as a "hollowed nonsense."[42]

By portraying socio-economic cleavages as regional conflicts, the politico-ideological apparatuses of the business classes found a golden opportunity to herald national unity as significant means to overcome territorial conflict. Almost fifty years ago, Porter articulated how national unity became a strategic weapon in the arsenal of the two business-oriented political parties to circumvent class division:

> The major themes in Canadian political thought emphasize those characteristics, mainly regional and provincial loyalties, which divide the Canadian population. Consequently, integration and national unity must be a constantly reiterated goal to counter such divisive sentiments. The dialogue is between unity and discord rather than progressive and conservative forces. The question which arises is whether the discord-unity dialogue has any real

meaning on the lives of Canadians or whether it has become, in the middle of the twentieth century, a political technique of conservatism.[43]

As a political phenomenon, regionalism in Canada must be understood in the context of the historical relations between Canada and Quebec and the ensuing clash of nationalisms from which no aspect of Canadian politics has escaped unaffected. In conjunction with the dual character of the Canadian labour movement, the historical chasm between Canada and Quebec provided the opportunity to establish political parties that would marginalize class within the political discourse. This in turn constrained the political space for the CCF/NDP to adopt the language of class. According to Porter, long before the emergence of the CCF on the political scene, the pro-business parties were using used the national duality of Canada to shape a particular definition of politics that revolved around the axis of ethnic and religious divisions.[44] During the gestation period of party politics in the late nineteenth century, the Liberal Party astutely structured itself as the party of national reconciliation by attempting to accommodate the ethnic and religious grievances of French Canadians.[45] With the heightened period of class confrontation in the early decades of the twentieth century, the Liberals, who had already acquired an inherent advantage by anchoring themselves as the party of accommodation, were able to cement themselves as the linchpin of national integration. Although the rise of the CCF during the economic downturn in the 1930s compelled the established political parties to modify their political outlooks, its political manoeuvrability was constrained by the ideological flexibility of the Liberal Party. The Liberals slowed down the CCF's political advance and even forced it to moderate its orientation on class and adopt a moderate stance on socio-economic conflict.

From the 1940s on, demands by Quebec for greater autonomy provided a pretext for other provinces to advance their own interests.[46] As a result of this confrontation between Canada and Quebec, the English provinces were able to play "the game of riding on Quebec's coat tails."[47]

The national conflict between Canada and Quebec has given paramountcy to Canadian national unity. Consequently, the national political parties of business have found ample opportunity to obfuscate their position on class divisions and consolidate a territorial definition of politics. The territorialization of politics has meant that the official discourse of Canadian politics is dominated by reified collective actors such as "Canada," "Quebec," "Ontario," and "Alberta" that displace other politically relevant socio-economic cleavages.[48]

The national imperative of Canadian unity has encouraged the establishment parties to shun the political issues of class. The adverse implications of ethnic-national division for working-class politics did not escape the attention of the early leaders of social democracy in Canada. Frank Scott, a leading member of the League for Social Reconstruction (LSR) which functioned as the intellectual arm of the early CCF, captured the centrality of the Quebec question for the fate of social democracy in Canada. In a letter to David Lewis in 1948, he wrote: "I have often said to you that the CCF has scarcely begun to realize the importance of Quebec in the total picture. The more we grow in strength elsewhere the more this problem emerges as of a crucial significance in our long-range plans."[49]

The centrality of the Quebec question to the fate of social democracy in Canada was also captured by Audrey McLaughlin, the NDP leader during the mid-1990s. McLaughlin asserted that "the NDP will never become a party of national significance without a presence in Quebec."[50] The national dualism of Canadian society reproduced itself within the labour movement, and this was bound to neutralize aspirations for a united working-class movement across Canada. Early on, ethnic divisions became a prominent bulwark against working-class unity.[51] As Palmer has pointed out, ethnic conflict and the marginalization of ethnic workers within the Canadian labour movement became a serious barrier to working-class solidarity.[52] This early ethnic antagonism within the working class was later followed by the subordination of trade unions in Quebec to the Catholic Church, which refrained from endorsing the CCF as the political arm of labour. Social upheavals in the 1940s led to the Quiet Revolution of the 1960s, which culminated in the transformation of Quebec nationalism. Socialist and social democratic sentiments among unions came to be subordinated to the goals of national liberation from English hegemony.[53] The subordination of social democracy to nationalism in Quebec dashed any hope of a social democratic alliance across Canada. The complexities of mobilizing social democratic forces across Canada have manifested themselves in the historical inability of the CCF/NDP to make inroads in Quebec. Unless it gained electoral ground there, the NDP would need a miracle to capture governmental power at the national level.

Australia: State, Class, and National Settings

The ethnic homogeneity of Australian society facilitated the emergence of "one nationalism," which became a key framework for labour politics.

The Canadian labour movement had procrastinated in forming its own political party; by contrast, the Australian Labor Party (ALP) made an early entry into Australian politics as the representative of the Australian labour movement. The ALP can be traced back to the second half of the nineteenth century, a time when class warfare was a prominent feature of Australian society. By the 1870s, trade union activity and the search for a united organization at the national level had acquired considerable momentum. In 1888, during the fifth Intercolonial Trade Union Congress (ITUC) held in Brisbane, Queensland, the delegates expressed their aspiration to unify trade unions across Australia.[54] The growing force of unionization and labour's engagement in electoral politics were spurred by the pre-manufacturing character of the Australian economy and by successive defeats of labour on the economic front, which drove organized labour to displace industrial conflict into the political arena.

During the nineteenth century, the power of capital was centred on the mining, grazing, and shipping industries. It was in these sectors that militant unionism began to emerge as a countervailing force against the business classes. At the same time, the domination of the Australian economy by the pastoral and agricultural sectors encouraged proletarianization.[55] Australian society was initially characterized by "a pastoral upper class intent on emulating the English gentry and served by a class of propertyless men who furnished the labor supply."[56] The proletarian component of economic production and the predominance of large-scale pastoral and agricultural centres in Australia encouraged shearers and some small landholders to organize and join the Australian labour movement.[57] Indeed, one of the early major labour confrontations with the dominant classes was conducted by shearers in 1890. However, this labour confrontation ended with the employers' victory.[58]

The concentration of pastoral and agricultural units of production, which required a corresponding concentration of labour, was bound to lead to class conflict. This fostered an auspicious climate for labour movement organization. The rapid growth of unionization in the pastoral and agricultural sectors intensified the hostility of big farmers towards labour. Growing business hostility led to the emergence of the National Country Party in the early decades of the twentieth century.[59]

The setback suffered by the labour movement during the shearers' strike was followed by the defeat of the maritime workers' strike in 1891, which "was perhaps the most gigantic strike ever organized within the Empire."[60] These successive industrial defeats of labour at the economic level left a trail of bitterness and an awareness of class interests among

Australian workers. Defeat on the industrial front fomented resentment among trade unions, which now challenged capital on the electoral front. Although trade unions had engaged in sporadic electoral politics before this, it was after these major industrial defeats that the embattled leaders of the labour movement called on workers to "sweep monopolists and class representatives from parliament."[61]

The politicization of the Australian labour movement led to the political ascendancy of the ALP on the national scene. The Australian labour movement's inclination to enter electoral politics signaled labour's intention to convert parliament into a battleground for countering the political hegemony of the ruling classes. With the formation of the Australian federation in 1901, the ALP emerged as the national voice of the working class, which was depicted by its conservative opponents as "a socialist tiger about to burst from its cage and wreak havoc."[62]

To the astonishment of socialists around the globe, whose focus was on the march of social democracy in the continental Europe, the ALP was the first working-class party in the world to challenge for parliamentary power. In 1899 the growing momentum towards an electoral breakthrough permitted the ALP to form the first labour government in history in Queensland.[63] In 1905 the force of the ballot box catapulted the ALP onto the national scene, where it captured governmental power at the federal level. In the federal election of 1910, in a spectacular display of political power, the ALP was the first working-class party in the world to form a majority labour government. By 1914, all six states in Australia had elected labour governments.[64] The ALP reached its political apogee in 1915 when it gained absolute majorities both at the federal level and in five of the six states.[65] The ALP was now seen by both its supporters and its opponents as a dominant factor in the political life of Australians.

The ALP's electoral triumph reflected the determination of organized labour to confront capital in both economic and political terms. Australia's ethnic homogeneity facilitated the unity of labour movement at the national level, despite sectoral and occupational divisions within the Australian working class (a hallmark of all capitalist societies).[66] Since 1927, the unity of Australian trade unions has been secured under the leadership of the Australian Council of Trade Unions (ACTU). The ACTU has been the economic and industrial voice of the labour movement in the political arena.[67]

The growth of the labour movement in Australia affected the strategic position of the dominant classes. The threat of the emerging labour movement, accompanied by the ALP's capacity to flex its electoral muscle, led to calls for a political alliance among the various factions of Australian capital.[68] Despite the absence of an umbrella business organization at the national level until 1977, heightened periods of class confrontation compelled Australian business factions to coordinate their resources to deflect the perceived political threat of labour.[69] The relative unity of the working class frightened the dominant classes. In the words of one leader of the Employers Association, labour unity had to be countered by "the unity of employers."[70]

With the ALP's arrival on the national scene, *The Worker*, the mouthpiece of the labour movement in Brisbane, spoke of the spectre of socialism on the political horizon and depicted the federal parliament as the site of confrontation between capitalism and socialism: "In the wide domain of federal affairs, the forces of progress and reaction have already ranged their rival hosts for the new struggle, and Socialism is openly named on the one side and accepted on the other as the *casus belli*."[71]

For the ALP, parliamentary politics became a weapon of social struggle – a means to translate the interests of the working class into political demands. The ALP envisioned parliamentary politics, not class confrontation, as the means by which Australian society would be propelled towards a just social order. Andrew Fisher, the ALP leader during the first decades of the twentieth century, was convinced that the effectiveness of parliamentary politics had diminished the political importance of industrial struggle. During the ALP federal conference in 1908, Fisher declared that "we [labour leaders] have reached the stage in Australia, where, with universal suffrage and educated democracy, we [labour leaders] can do in parliament for the workers what we could not accomplish by a universal strike."[72] The success of the Australian labour movement in gaining industrial legislation (factory acts) and democratic reforms (abolishing plural voting and expanding the boundaries of the voting franchise) generated a wave of hope and jubilation among socialists and labour leaders throughout the world.[73]

By the turn of the twentieth century, the ALP's progressive legislation had given Australia the reputation of a "workers' paradise" and an exciting "social laboratory." Australia became a Mecca for socialist pilgrims.[74] The political march of the ALP caused socialists such as Tom Mann to travel to Australia to "gaze on its wondrous achievements."[75] Even the members of the German Social Democratic Party (SPD), the icon of socialism in continental Europe, hoped that "the Australian Labor's successes … will spur SPD comrades to match … the Australian achievements."[76] In the early 1900s, the ALP found itself in a position to school even its counterpart in Britain. British Labour leaders such as Keir Hardie and Ramsay MacDonald after their visit to Australia asked the ALP's leadership to pass a resolution in favour of women's suffrage, which was universal in Australia but was still denied to British women.[77] In its 1912 federal conference, the ALP boasted of the international notice taken of its remarkable accomplishments: "The eyes of all reformers throughout the civilized world are upon us, watching with sympathy and interest our unequalled progress."[78]

The grandiose proclamations of the ALP leadership in depicting the party as the fount of inspiration for social democrats beyond Australia, and the legendary image it had created abroad, proved to be cosmetic. Indeed, the continuity of capitalist hegemony, despite domination of both houses by the ALP in the first decade of the twentieth century, made it clear that the governmental power was not the same as state power. Far from ending the hegemony of the ruling class, the ALP led the working class through the tunnel of electoral politics into a social settlement that came to be predicated mainly on the universal commodification of labour. This, of course, ran counter to the spirit of socialism.

Despite making frequent references to socialism, class confrontation, and social justice, the ALP adopted an idiosyncratic social vision stripped of inspiring socialist principles. The ALP's political standing came to rest on three related planks: the preservation of a "White Australia"; protection for national industrialization; and a centralized wage-setting system as a means to secure the social welfare of the working class.[79] Although these policy measures were largely formulated by the dominant elements of the non-working classes, the ALP embraced them as the basis of a plan for defending workers' interests.[80]

Building on Australians' general antipathy towards Asian workers, the ALP presented itself as a champion of nationalism. This had a strong appeal for different classes in Australia. As guardian of "White Australia," the ALP established its dominance in defending Australian nationalism.[81] During the parliamentary debate on the immigration restriction bill in 1901, J.C. Watson, the ALP leader, declared that the party would exhaust all means for "preventing them [Asians] from coming to this land which we have made our own."[82] In late nineteenth century and the early decades of the twentieth, a firm commitment to "the cultivation of an Australian sentiment based upon the maintenance of racial purity" became a dominant theme in the ALP's electoral platform.[83] "White Australia" would be preserved by imposing harsh restrictions on non-European immigrants.[84] Asians were demonized, and "Asian hordes" were invoked as a threat to the racially superior white Australians. Within the ALP, class solidarity was forged by harnessing these and similar sentiments. The ALP would not delete the "White Australia" concept from its political agenda until the 1970s.

"White Australia" was also used to justify tariffs that would shield domestic industry from foreign competition. Long before the Australian federation emerged, sectional interests such as manufacturers, pastoralists, and large-scale farmers were pressuring the colonial authorities to adopt protectionist measures to insulate them from international competition.[85] When it entered the federal parliament, the ALP allied itself with the protectionists on the promise that the tariff wall would secure jobs, increase wages, and improve working conditions.[86]

Related to protectionism and to the building of national industry was the founding of the Commonwealth Court of Conciliation and Arbitration in 1904. This court was intended as a rational solution to the large-scale strikes in the late nineteenth century that had disrupted economic production.[87] As a surrogate for collective bargaining, compulsory state arbitration gradually evolved into a mechanism for centralized wage fixing. The transformation of the Australian Court of Conciliation and Arbitration into a mechanism for determining "a fair and reasonable living wage" was consolidated by the famous *Harvester Judgment* of 1907, where Justice Higgins set a minimum wage for unskilled workers that was to ensure that a worker could look after his wife and children in comfort and health.[88] The determination of a living wage institutionalized the conception of the male as breadwinner; it also consolidated gender inequality by setting the wages of women at half the basic wage paid to men.[89] Since state tribunal decisions were to follow the verdict of the Commonwealth Conciliation and Arbitration Commission, a substantial degree of uniformity in award wages prevailed throughout Australia. The Court of Conciliation and Arbitration directly encouraged unionization since only registered unions could have access to the court; it also subjected the internal affairs of unions to direct state scrutiny.

Compulsory state arbitration provided a legal avenue for workers to gain from the productivity of the economy. However, centralized wage arbitration had been designed to maintain an adequate minimum wage and prevent wage differentiation, "thereby reducing reliance on the social security system to redistribute income."[90] Furthermore, centralized wage setting correspondingly diminished the threat posed by strikes to economic production. This was rationalized as substituting force with reason and the employment of "the might of the state to enforce peace between industrial combatants."[91] Centralized wage setting was not, therefore, opposed by Australian capital. A centralized wage determination system was also used by employers to check increases in wage levels. In the words of one Australian business leader, "there is a fairly fixed feeling amongst Employers' association ... that they have a better chance of holding wage increase to a minimum by having them dealt with on a national basis."[92]

The determination of a living wage was linked to employers' capacity to pay wages and salaries. Despite the entrenchment of a living wage as the primary mechanism of wage settlement, the inclusion of capacity to pay when determining the basic wage equipped employers with a weapon for challenging labour's push for wage increases. During the first part of the twentieth century, the living wage was gradually detached from the standards of the community.[93]

Analysts of labour politics in Australia have long characterized these various components of the ALP's social vision as "labourism."[94] This conventional interpretation of the ALP requires further elaboration, for Australian labourism acquired peculiar features. Labourism is generally interpreted as unions' acceptance of the market as the primary distributive mechanism of income; this is coupled with recourse to state regulatory measures designed to protect wage earners. This has historically been an ingredient of the industrial platforms of unions in other Western countries.[95] But unlike some European countries where labourism went hand in hand with broader notions of social solidarity and with loosening the bonds between citizens' entitlement and labour market employment, the Australian brand of labourism directly linked citizens' entitlement to collective bargaining. This peculiarity of Australian labourism was noticed by Lenin, who, while he regarded European labourism as "moderate and capital-serving," characterized its counterpart in Australia as "peaceful and purely liberal." According to Lenin, the ALP "is a liberal-bourgeois party and the so called Liberals in Australia are really Conservatives ... The leaders of the Australian Labor Party are trade union officials, an element which is everywhere most moderate and capital-serving but in Australia is altogether peaceful and purely liberal."[96]

The unique features of the ALP's labourist ideology had been moulded by the class structure and by the balance of class interests within the Australian labour movement in the nineteenth century. In the period of its ideological development, the social vision of the Australian labour movement was profoundly influenced by the populism of small farmers and the idealism of utopian socialists. The Australian labour movement's ideology thus transformed the notion of class into folk sentiment, which in turn was gradually submerged into industrial and economic reformism.[97] The confluence of these two streams of thought, which left a lasting imprint on the labour movement's ideology, was located in New South Wales. There, the political platform of labour became the basis on which the ALP formulated its national plan of political action.[98] The ideological imprint of populism and utopian socialism was plain as day in the political orientation of the Australian Workers' Union, the dominant labour centre, which encompassed shearers, bush workers, and small farmers. These occupationally diverse elements of Australian society were guided by a narrow and specific aspiration to build a "petty bourgeois" community immune from the dominance of the larger pastoral and agricultural sectors.[99]

The ALP's limited ideological horizon meant that its political platforms were permeated with demands for a "restriction of public borrowing" (which was equivalent to contemporary demands for fiscal austerity) and for "self-reliance" (which amounted to tacit support for the privatization of income security). The ALP was also averse to taxation except for taxes on unproductive land.[100] Even though the ALP occasionally inserted more socialist planks into its electoral platform, the party leadership never emphasized translating these socialist slogans into practical results. After two decades of political existence, at its federal conference of 1921, the ALP reluctantly adopted "the socialization of industry, production, distribution and exchange" as one of its objectives.[101] At the same federal conference, the ALP leadership rejected a radical plank proposed by socialist elements within the party that called for "the emancipation of labour from all forms of capitalistic exploitation [through] (a) the nationalization of those agencies of production, distribution and exchange which are used under capitalism to despoil community; and (b) cooperative action in financing, marketing and distributing primary products."[102] The quest for industrial cooperation, and a preoccupation with immediate gains, led successive federal leaders of the ALP to gradually play down "socialization to extinction."[103]

The forces of populism and utopian socialism shaped the social vision of Australian labourism towards supply-side social democracy (to use a modern term). The emerging labour radicalism in Australia emphasized the imperatives of cooperation between capital and labour; the employment of the state as a mechanism for maintaining market output at high levels to forestall the need for social programs; and support for those who involuntarily fell outside the realm of market relations. All of this emphasized that the state's primary role was to facilitate socio-economic conditions under which individuals could sustain their livelihoods. By removing the main socialist principle of decommodification from its social vision, this quintessentially Australian version of labourism came to identify the market as the main locus of welfare state provision. The ALP's reliance on a regulated market as the chief provider of income security implicitly anchored the notion of social citizenship entitlement within the parameters of market employment. This particular vision of social citizenship became conspicuous during the era of Keynesianism in Australia. It formed the basis for a social class compromise that stressed high employment as a surrogate for a comprehensive welfare state.

National Specificity and Variations in Keynesianism

The mass unemployment of the 1930s, and the ensuing socio-political conflict during and after the Second World War, propelled Keynesianism to the centre of the economic and governmental agenda. State intervention to stabilize markets became a universal trend in advanced industrial countries, including Canada and Australia.[104] The central point of Keynesianism was that the state should stabilize the chronic cycle of economic boom and bust, as well as commit itself to full employment and the expansion of social security programs.[105] The need to respond to working-class mobilization, and the successful economic recovery with state planning during the Second World War, gave both urgency and plausibility to the primacy of state intervention in shaping postwar social and economic reconstruction.

Even though the national governments in Australia and Canada were restrained by constitutional limits on their power, the imperative of national involvement in socio-economic reconstruction generated a greater degree of central government intervention in both countries. Under Keynesian economic doctrines, both national governments grew more fiscally centralized. But there was greater federal fiscal supremacy in Australia, which reflected the relative ethnic homogeneity of Australian society as well as the political weight of labour. During the years of postwar reconstruction, the Australian federal government acquired control over taxation power by consenting to provide grants to the states in return for their vacating some taxation fields. In contrast, the taxation and spending powers of the Canadian federal government were subjected to challenges during the postwar period launched first by Quebec and then by other provinces.[106]

Within the limits of postwar social relations, industrial and social peace was to be maintained through a "social pact" designed to enhance economic performance and address the negative implications of income distribution.[107] State intervention in the business cycle was rationalized by Keynesian demand management, and this helped reconcile capital accumulation with the welfare functions of the state. The legitimation role of the state was indispensable to containing social disruption and any encroachment on business hegemony.[108] Indeed, social security protection and state intervention in the business cycle were geared to overcome obstacles to economic growth.[109] As Yargin and Stanislaw have concluded, Keynesianism was a deliberately contrived politico-economic formula to sustain a "managed capitalism – capitalism saved from both socialism and from itself."[110]

Postwar reconstruction in Canada and Australia was profoundly influenced by William Beveridge's plan of attack on the "five giant evils" (squalor, ignorance, want, idleness, and disease), a plan that became "the Magna Carta of the British welfare state."[111] In terms of social policy history, Beveridge's social blueprint linked full employment to the provision of social welfare benefits. The same logic behind Beveridge's plan was to contain political radicalization among the working class. Social programs such as unemployment insurance, provisions for full employment, and pensions for elderly people were geared to limit the social stigmas associated with means-tested benefits. These social welfare programs underpinned the emergence of a social citizenship model of the welfare state. Beveridge's compulsory social insurance paradigm generated a shift from means-tested income security to a rights-based entitlement to social benefits earned through employment contributions.[112]

Under the influence of Keynes and Beveridge, Canada and Australia committed themselves to the pursuit of full employment and social welfare security, each expounded in 1945 White Papers. Although both countries made high employment an intended social target, their commitments took on different characteristics. In its 1945 White Paper, titled *Full Employment,* the ALP government declared full employment "a fundamental aim of the Commonwealth Government" and pledged "responsibility for stimulating spending on goods and services to the extent necessary to sustain full employment."[113] The ALP government also assumed the duty of maintaining conditions essential to the realization of full employment as "an obligation owed to the people of Australia by Commonwealth and State governments."[114]

Given the ALP government's position in the 1940s and its vision of full employment as a means to protect the social welfare of the working class, Keynesian demand management became linked to a centralized wage-setting system and to stronger state intervention in labour market policy. Keynesian prescriptions for sustaining full employment became a hallmark of party politics in Australia. As Gough Whitlam, the Labor prime minister from 1972 to 1975, pointed out, "during the post-war economic boom, questions of economic management were scarcely deemed to require original answers ... The broad principles, and indeed objectives of Keynesian economics held sway over the major parties."[115]

In contrast to the strong commitment of the Australian federal government to pursue full employment as its overriding social security goal, the Canadian federal government adopted a more ambiguous commitment to full employment. Despite the pervasiveness of the concept of full employment within the Canadian official discourse on social reconstruction, the term full employment was gradually superseded by "high levels" of employment.[116] In its 1945 White Paper, the Canadian government declared the "adoption of a high and stable level of employment and income as a major aim of employment policy."[117] But despite federal finance ministers' references to Keynesian principles in their budget speeches, the pursued macroeconomic policy initiatives did not reflect a strong adherence to Keynesian ideas.[118]

The Canadian government eschewed planning and intensive public investment as a substitute for encouraging investment in private enterprises. Instead of embarking on state investment and regulating labour market relations, Canada adopted a "technocratic version of Keynesianism" that emphasized maintaining a stable environment for private sector investment as well as strong export performance by Canadian resources.[119] Placing its faith in the market economy, the Canadian government envisioned the private sector as key to job and wealth creation: "The government does not believe it to be either desirable or practical to look for the expansion of government enterprise to provide, to any large degree the additional employment required. It follows that a major and early task of reconstruction is to facilitate and encourage an expansion of private industry."[120]

In stark contrast to the Australian state's strong commitment to intervene in labour market relations in order to achieve full employment as a surrogate for social income security, the Canadian state granted a prominent role to the private sector and restricted its scope of intervention in labour markets.[121] Unlike Australia, the Canadian state placed greater emphasis on social security programs as the basis for postwar social reconstruction.[122]

Until the early 1940s, the Canadian federal government had avoided the compulsory recognition of unions' right to collective bargaining.[123] Then in 1944, Order in Council P.C. 1003 incorporated the principles of compulsory collective bargaining. Decentralized collective bargaining was ultimately legitimized in Canada, but it was a strikingly different system from the one that had been granted to Australian workers in the 1900s. This difference in the degree of recognition of union rights reflected variations in the unity, strength, and organizational structure of labour movements between these two countries. This had a profound impact on market regulation and on the formation of the welfare states of the two countries.[124]

Throughout the decades of Keynesian macroeconomic policies from the 1940s to the mid-1970s, the differences in the degree of commitment to full employment policies in Australia and Canada translated into variations in the actual achievement of high employment. As can be observed from tables 3.1, 3.2, and 3.3, Canada tolerated a certain degree of unemployment despite a higher rate of average growth. Furthermore, throughout the 1960s and early 1970s, Australia retained a higher degree of market control, which reflected greater state involvement in labour market regulation in Australia.

Conclusion

National settings played crucial roles in shaping the power resources of labour in Canada and Australia. Differences in national conditions shaped the interplay of class, party, and nation in Canada and Australia, which in turn paved the way for variations in Keynesianism across these two countries. Conditions in Australia were conducive to the emergence of a united labour movement that did much to consolidate a centralized industrial relations system that facilitated cooperation between labour and capital. Yet the Australian labour movement's social vision was often restricted to the relationship between capital and labour. Consequently, the social vision of the Australian labour movement supported a residual conception of the welfare state. Due to the Australian labour movement's vision of social protection, social citizenship rights were directly

Table 3.1 Average rates of unemployment (%) in Canada and Australia, 1950–1979

	1950–9	1960–7	1968–73	1974–9
Australia	1.8	1.9	2.0	5.0
Canada	4.9	4.8	5.4	7.2

Sources: Adopted from Ramesh Mishra, *The Welfare State in Capitalist Society: Policy of Retrenchment and Maintenance in Europe, North America, and Australia* (Toronto: University of Toronto Press, 1990); and Robert Malcolm Campbell, *The Full Employment Objectives in Canada, 1945–85: Historical, Conceptual, and Comparative Perspectives* (Ottawa: Economic Council of Canada, 1991).

Table 3.2 Average rates of real GDP growth (per cent per annum)

	1914–39	1939–60	1960–80
Australia	3.2	2.9	4.2
Canada	2.4	5.1	4.8

Source: Adopted from Boris Schedvin, "Staples and Regions of Pax Britannica," *Economic History Review* 4 (1990): 533–59.

Table 3.3 Indicators of market controls, 1960–1973

	Degree of liberalization of capital controls	Trade openness
Australia	2.3	30
Canada	3.8	40

Sources: Adopted from Evelyne Huber and John Stephens, "Welfare States and Production Regimes in the Era of Retrenchment," in *The New Politics of the Welfare State*, edited by Paul Pierson, 107–45 (New York: Oxford University Press, 2001); and Boris Schedvin, "Staples and Regions of Pax Britannica," *Economic History Review* 4 (1990): 533–59.

linked to industrial rights to work and decent wages. It was due to this ingrained conviction that full employment was the road to prosperity for the working class that in Australia less emphasis was placed on the social insurance dimension of Beveridgean welfare state plans.

In Canada, the fragmentation of unions and the weakness of working-class political organizations were decisive factors in the development of a weak and decentralized industrial relations system. The fragmentation of the labour movement in Canada contributed to the pursuit of a type of Keynesianism that put less emphasis on market regulation and full employment as the policy means to provide social income security.

But full employment and stronger market control are not adequate yardsticks to measure the generosity and comprehensiveness of the Canadian and Australian welfare states. A commitment to full employment does not in itself make for a comprehensive and generous welfare state. Full employment policies might be a key issue in social welfare policy arrangements, since they remove the drag of the reserve army of unemployed on labour's bargaining power. But the welfare state cannot be reduced to employment alone. The right to work associated with full employment has no direct decommodifying impact. A welfare state's generosity and comprehensiveness is measured by its universality and level of decommodification and by the distributional outcomes of social welfare expenditures in reducing poverty and income inequality.

Based on these criteria, the postwar retirement income systems in Canada and Australia took different directions. Despite relatively higher levels of power resources of labour in Australia, that country's retirement income system remained within the bounds of residualism and selectivity. Paradoxically, the relatively low levels of power resources of labour and the fragmentation of the working class in Canada did not prevent the emergence of a universal and comprehensive old age pension system.

4 Postwar Expansion of the Pension System in Australia

The national state in Australia became involved in old age pension provisions during the early years of the twentieth century; the expansion and consolidation of the retirement income system there was then reinforced by Keynesian principles. Keynesian-inspired postwar reconstruction provided justification for the regulation of capital, and the expansion of public intervention was geared to the expansion of the welfare state. State intervention in the economy and the establishment of social welfare programs helped enhance class harmony. Despite greater state involvement in old age pension provisions and the progressive liberalization of eligibility criteria, universalization of the non-contributory flat rate old age pension in Australia remained an unrealizable goal. The postwar pension system in Australia came to be characterized by selectivity in coverage and the encouragement of private occupational pension plans as a complement to the non-contributory flat rate pension.

The postwar Australian retirement income system was shaped by the political class settlement and the particularities of national context. As with Canada, the Australian welfare state evolved to accommodate working-class demands and thereby diminish the threat of political radicalism. But the postwar social class settlement in Australia depended on market forces to achieve full employment. This dependence on market forces anchored the principle of "residualism" as a core parameter of social protection. The market-led postwar social class compromise reflected the Australian labour movement's social vision of the welfare state. This was conducive to retaining the targeting mechanism for benefits. This frustrated the quest to collectivize retirement income through establishing a publicly administered earnings-related social insurance plan; it also encouraged reliance on private occupational pension plans.

This chapter has three sections. In the first, the postwar development of the old age pension policy in Australia is outlined. The main changes that were made to the pillars of the retirement income system in Australia are discussed. In the second, the link between the postwar social class settlement and the retirement income system in Australia is clarified. In the third, the main points are recapitulated and the vulnerability of a politically constructed market-centred welfare state to neoliberal retrenchment will be explained.

The Postwar Expansion of the Australian Retirement Income System

As historical relics of feudal social relations, charity and philanthropy were the main mechanisms of social stabilization throughout the eighteenth and nineteenth centuries. Charitable and philanthropic societies were deployed by the ruling classes as means to contain social resentment against private property.[1] Despite the ingrained liberal values of self-help, self-reliance, and outdoor relief as the primary mechanisms of income security provisions for elderly people throughout the nineteenth century, the national state in Australia gradually became involved in directly providing income security in the first decade of the twentieth century. With the birth of the Australian federation in 1901, the responsibility for a non-contributory flat rate old age pension was allotted to the federal government. Pensions payable by the national government were introduced through the Invalid and Old-Age Pensions Act of 1908.[2] This was a national extension of pension schemes that had been legislated in the states of Victoria and New South Wales in 1900.[3] The Commonwealth invalid pension scheme was based mainly on the New South Wales Invalid and Accident Pension Act, which was the first invalid pension plan in the world established on a non-contributory basis.[4] The implementation of a national retirement income in Australia heralded the first major entry of national governments into the field of social welfare policy. The first national plan for providing income security for elderly people in Australia was a radical departure from the past practice of outdoor relief run by municipal and charitable organizations.

Prior to the establishment of the first national program in 1908, the delivery of local relief was directed at marginalized sections of the population and was based on discretionary and moralistic principles that drew a line between the deserving and the undeserving poor.[5] The main objective of the initial old age pension was to supplement relief to the deserving destitute. However, it was not designed "to replace the normal social mechanism assistance which was seen to be the primary family and voluntary sector responsibilities."[6] The distribution of public relief based on character evaluation meant that recipients of income assistance were stigmatized. Such pejorative connotations marked the early history of social income security provision. The provisions for old age income in nineteenth-century Australia reflected the reluctance of state governments to involve themselves directly in welfare state provision. This underscored the ideological legacy of the minimal state that had been bequeathed from classical liberalism.[7]

With the assumption of responsibility for the payments of old age pension by the Australian government – payments that were to be financed through general government revenues – state-based pension laws ceased operating. The replacement of the diverse state-based old age pension schemes by an Australian-wide pension plan led to uniform old age pension provisions throughout Australia.[8] The Australian retirement income system gradually came to be characterized by a two-tier system. Table 4.1 summarizes the Australian pension system during the era of welfare state expansion.

First Tier

The early experiment with the payment of the old age pension in Australia highlighted the distribution of state charity in a selective and judgmental fashion. Despite this shift with past practices and change in attitudes towards charity, the initial provisions for old age income in Australia were governed by exclusionary principles.[9] Still, even with the eligibility requirement for old age pensions requiring proof of need, statutory entitlement was nonetheless conducive to removing the stain of charity. The strict eligibility criteria attached to the first national plan to provide income security for elderly Australians ran counter to the paradigm of social citizenship rights entitlements.[10] In accordance with the initial provisions of the 1908 Invalid and Old-Age Pensions Act, the Commonwealth old age payments were restricted to those who had attained the age of sixty-five years (for females, sixty years of age after 1910) and had continuously lived in Australia for at least twenty-five years.[11] At its inception, the Australian act contained racist provisions; it also subjected pension recipients to a means–income test and a character evaluation. The same act also excluded aliens, whom it referred to as "Asiatics (except those born in Australia), and aboriginal natives of Australia,

Table 4.1 Pension system in Australia during the postwar welfare expansion

First Tier: Old Age Pension (renamed Age Pension in 1947)	
Pre–Second World War era	
Funding	General tax revenue
Eligibility	Age (65 for men, 60 for women), residency, race, and character. Racial barriers and character evaluation prevented many people from receiving Age Pension benefits.
Benefits	Means test
Postwar welfare state expansion	
Funding	General tax revenue
Eligibility	Age (65 for men, 60 for women) and residency. Gradual elimination of specific racial disqualifications. Elimination of character evaluation. Easing of residency requirements.
Benefits	Means tested. Gradual increase in the levels of permissible income and property limits. In 1943, Wife's Allowance (assistance to wife of pensioner) was introduced. Supplementary Assistance (assistance to those pensioners who lived on Age Pension only) was introduced in 1958. In 1973, the means test was removed for people over 75. In 1975, the means test was removed for people aged 70 to 74 years. In 1976, any consideration of assets was removed from the means test calculation. The means test became an income test only.
Second Tier: Tax-assisted voluntary private occupational superannuation plans	
Voluntary savings	
Funding	Employer/employee contribution and individual savings
Eligibility	By contribution
Benefits	Defined contribution: Cumulation of assets plus interest from investments Defined benefits: Specified monthly benefits after retirement

Africa, the Islands of the Pacific, or New Zealand."[12] The maximum rate of pension was set at $52 per annum ($1 or 10 shillings per week) and was subject to reduction by the amount of non-pension income above $52, which was the level established for permissible income.[13] Payable pension was one-quarter of the amount that the Arbitration Court had established as an adequate minimum wage for a family of four.[14] In line with the criteria of the means–income test, the pension was not payable to any aged individual whose income exceeded $104 per year or whose property was valued at $620.[15] In the calculation of property, the 1908 act also included any increase in the capital value of a home "in which the pensioner was permanently resident and which produced no income."[16] Due to harsh eligibility criteria, many aged people were deprived of old age pension benefits. In 1910, only 33 per cent of the aged received the age pension; by 1940, still only 42 per cent.[17]

Despite gradual increases in the maximum rates of pension and the relaxation of income and property limitations on pension eligibility during the early decades of the twentieth century, the exclusionary nature of the non-contributory flat rate old age pension remained prominent. The gradual loosening of the eligibility criteria governing the state-run old age pension in Australia came at a time of postwar welfare state expansion in other advanced industrial societies.[18] In the context of postwar Keynesian policies, the expansion and improvement of income security for elderly people became a significant component of the class compromise.[19] In this regard, there had been comparatively few (and mostly minor) changes to rules governing the means-tested pension until 1946, when the Labor government extended the property exemptions to include furniture and personal effects and gifts, and raised the ceiling of the capital value of life insurance and annuities held by pensioners.[20] In 1941, the administration of Australia's 1908 act, which had been a prerogative of the treasury department, was transferred to the Department of Social Services, which began to function as a separate organization. In 1947, the Old Age Pension was renamed the Age Pension.[21]

Throughout the 1950s, eligibility for the old age pension underwent significant changes. During this period, the upper limits of property and permissible income and the ceiling limits on the total amount a pensioner could receive in the way of war and service pension plus civil pensions were raised.[22] In 1952, blind people eligible for pension were exempted from the means test mechanism to half their pension payment. In 1954, the means test for age and invalid pensions for permanently blind individuals was removed and a pensioner's income from property (rents, dividends, and interest from investment) became exempt from the calculation of permissible income.[23]

During the postwar expansion of the welfare state, the liberalization of income and property limits was extended to remove the restriction on pensioners' mobility within Australia. Pensioners who left Australia in order to reside in an external territory of the Commonwealth of Australia were able to receive their pensions, which had previously been cancelled.

Pensioners' access to medical services was also improved. While the pensioner medical service scheme was extended to include the supply of medicines prescribed by medical practitioners to pensioners and their dependents, the extension of benefits was nonetheless subject to the means test mechanism.[24] In 1955, provisions were put in place to exclude pensioners with incomes of more than $4 per week from receiving benefits of medical services.[25] In 1958, Supplementary Assistance (equivalent to the Guaranteed Income Supplement in Canada) was introduced to assist those pensioners who were solely dependent on age pension income.[26] Supplementary Assistance was available to those pensioners who "paid rent or board and lodging, whose income was not more than 10 Shillings per week, and whose property under means test was not sufficient to affect the rate of pension."[27]

Progressive relaxation of the means test during the 1950s continued throughout the 1960s. In 1961, a merged means test was introduced to supersede the separate tests on income and property. Under the newly adopted means test, the value of property was converted into a notional income equivalent and was added to other earned incomes. However, income from property was disregarded.[28] In 1962, a major change was made to the residency requirement for the age pension. Any individual could qualify for old age pension on residency grounds if he or she had completed ten years of continuous residence in Australia at any time.[29] More specifically, the residency requirement for the age pension was reduced from twenty years to ten.[30] In 1963, eligibility for children's allowance and additional pension for children was extended to include children who were full-time students at school or university and who were wholly dependent on a pensioner. In 1965, the Guardian Allowance was introduced for widowed and other non-married pensioners with children in their care.[31] The same year, the rate of Supplementary Assistance to aged people was increased.[32] In 1966, pensioners were no longer subjected to a special means test for the Pensioner Medical Service. Those who met the pension's means test criteria for payment of full or part pension automatically became eligible for that service.[33] Until 1969, means-tested age pensions were exempt from income taxation but were subject to a 100 per cent withdrawal rate.

In a further attempt to liberalize the restrictions on pension eligibility, the "tapered" means test was introduced in 1969. In accordance with this test, the maximum annual rate of pension was reduced by "only half of the amount of means as assessed in the excess of the permissible income."[34] Following the introduction of the tapered means test, which reduced the withdrawal rate from 100 to 50 per cent, the permissible income for both single and married pensioners was doubled in 1972.[35] The pensioner medical service and fringe benefits also became subject to the tapered means test mechanism. In 1972 the Wife's Allowance was superseded by the Wife's Pension, which became payable to the wife of an aged or invalid pensioner if she was otherwise ineligible for an old age pension in her own right.[36]

In tandem with the gradual liberalization of the means test during the 1960s, the racist dimension of pension eligibility was discarded. However, the removal of the restriction on Aboriginals' eligibility for pension in 1960 did not apply to those Aboriginals who had chosen to pursue a "nomadic life" – not until 1966, when these disqualifying provisions were repealed.[37] In a further attempt to expunge the racial connotations associated with pension eligibility, the provision disqualifying aliens from an age or invalid pension was repealed in 1966.[38] Until 1974, the Commonwealth Age Pension Act retained provisions that disqualified elderly people from receiving an age pension if they were:

(a) not of good character;
(b) not deserving of pension;
(c) if a husband had deserted his wife without a just cause;
(d) if being a husband, he has [during six months prior to grant]:
    1. Failed without just cause to provide his wife with adequate means of maintenance; or
    2. Neglected to maintain any of his children under the age of sixteen years.[39]

In 1974, Age Pension benefits were made payable to Australians who lived overseas. To receive age pension benefits, they were required to have lived in Australia for an aggregate of thirty years, to be of pension age or within five years of that age at the time of departure from Australia, or to have been permanently incapacitated or blind while in Australia.[40]

Parallel to progressive increases in the rate of pension and extending the scope of permissible income, two negative and subjective components of the eligibility criteria were also discarded in the 1970s. In 1974, character evaluation as a ground for pension eligibility was removed. Previous provisions had required a pensioner to be of good character and deserving in order to receive an age pension.[41] In 1976, the provision was repealed that disqualified an individual from receiving pension on the grounds that he or she had directly or indirectly deprived himself or herself of income and property in order to receive the pension. Under the new provisions, if responsible authorities in the Department of Social Services "considered that a claimant or pensioner or spouse had directly or indirectly deprived himself of income in order to qualify for a pension or for higher rate of pension, the income disposed of could be deemed to be income of the claimant or pensioner."[42]

During the 1970s, significant qualitative and quantitative improvements were made to the Age Pension. Despite these progressive strides in the direction of improving the income security of elderly people, the universalization of the Age Pension remained unrealizable.[43] The maximum rate of pension was progressively increased, and the ceilings on earned income and property income were raised; in addition to these steps, the means test for individuals seventy-five and over was removed in 1973.[44] That same year, the Guardian's Allowance and the additional pension for full-time dependent students of a pensioner became payable irrespective of the student's age. Effective 1 July 1973, payable age pension benefits became subject to income tax calculation.[45] However, Supplementary Assistance and additional payments remained exempt from the income tax mechanism. In 1975, the removal of the means test on the Age Pension was extended to cover those between seventy and seventy-four.[46] However, the elimination of the means test on the Age Pension for those older than seventy did not extend to the Wife's Pension, Guardian's Allowance, Supplementary Assistance, and additional pension for children, all of which continued to be subject to the appropriate means test.[47]

In 1976, the means test for Age Pension payments was superseded by an income test that considered only earned income. Under the new income test, the value of property was disregarded but the income derived from property was included.[48] In 1978, the trend towards eliminating the means test on Age Pension payments for people over seventy was reversed by the introduction of the partial income test. In accordance with the 1978 act, the rate of pension payable to those over seventy was fixed at a specific amount ($51.45 for a single pensioner; $89.90 for a married individual), but any indexation increase in the age pension became subject to the income test.[49] That same year, the maximum rate of pension benefits became subject to indexation once a year; previously, it had been indexed twice a year.[50]

Overall, even though the relaxation of the limits on old age pension eligibility permitted a greater number of aged Australians to receive the non-contributory flat rate old age pension, the removal of the means test was confined to people over seventy. The payment of the Age Pension to people between sixty-five and sixty-nine continued to be subject to an income test mechanism. Despite progressive increases in the level of maximum pension payments throughout the 1960s and 1970s, the rate of replacement remained below average weekly earnings.[51] As table 4.2 indicates, despite progressive improvements and the liberalization of the eligibility criteria, the continued application of the income test mechanism to the payment of Age Pension in Australia to people between sixty-five and sixty-nine deprived a significant percentage of Australians of Age Pension payments.

Second Tier

Before the 1970s, several attempts were made in Australia to complement the non-contributory flat rate old age pension with a compulsory earnings-related contributory pension plan based on the principles of social insurance. Attempts to expunge the taint of pauperism and charity associated with non-contributory old age pension culminated in the appointment of a Royal Commission in 1923 to investigate and report on the National Insurance as a governing mechanism to provide retirement benefits.[52] After several reports were submitted by the commission between 1925 and 1927, the National Insurance Bill was tabled in the Parliament in 1928. The bill, though, was "allowed to lie on the table."[53] By 1929, interest in implementing a National Insurance plan had begun to weaken and the political commitment to install a compulsory earnings-related pension scheme had largely disappeared.[54]

In 1935, politicians' interest in a compulsory pension plan began to resurface. Three years later, in 1938, the National Health and Pensions Insurance Act was introduced in Parliament.[55] The new national insurance scheme broadly followed the 1928 proposal but encompassed a wider range of social benefits.[56] The 1938 act provided that "all employed person[s] who have attained the age of sixteen years, and have not attained the maximum age ... were to be insured and insured persons" were entitled to receive old age pension, widow's pension, orphan's pension, and medical, sickness, and disablement benefits.[57]

In the 1938 act, the costs of social insurance were to be shouldered by employers, the employed, and government. The act as proposed was progressive in the sense that payments of earning-related benefits would have no effect on those who were eligible for the non-contributory flat rate old age pension.[58] Under the 1938 act, "any benefits payable to a person under this Act shall not be taken into account in the calculation of the income of that person or the spouse of that person, for the purpose of the ... Old Age Pensions Act 1908–1937."[59] The implementation

Table 4.2 Proportion of aged Australians receiving non-contributory flat rate old age pension, 1930–1980

Year	%
1930	32
1940	40
1950	42
1962	53
1972	62
1977–80	77

Source: Adapted from Michael Anthony Jones, *The Australian Welfare State: Evaluating Social Policy* (4th ed.) (Sydney: Allen and Unwin, 1996), 119.

of the 1938 act "was twice postponed and finally legislation was introduced in 1939 which provided for its indefinite postponement" – which was tantamount to its death.[60] Opposition to the contributory pension plan was too strong within the labour movement.[61]

After two failed attempts by the Liberal government to collectivize income security along the principles of social insurance, the debate on implementing a compulsory earnings–related pension scheme began to re-emerge in the early 1970s. In 1973, under the Labor government, a National Superannuation Committee of Inquiry headed by Professor K.J. Hancock was established to make recommendations to government on the feasibility of a publicly administered national plan for income retirement.[62] In its interim report, the Hancock Inquiry recommended two complementary programs: "a universal flat-rate scheme with pensions financed from general revenue ... [and] a non-funded contributory scheme, with pensions bearing some relation to past contribution."[63] The commission recommended that the contributory component of the proposed system have the following features:

1 Contributions related to income would be required. These would be levied on individuals within a specific age range. The collection of contributions would be integrated with the collection of personal income tax.
2 Benefits would have two components: a flat rate component, and an additional component related to past contributions. For the purpose of payment of pensions, the two components would be aggregated.

Payment would be the responsibility of the Department of Social Security.

3 The pensions of individuals who had made small contributory benefits would be supplemented.
4 The scheme would be run on a pay-as-you-go basis – that is, there would be no fund requiring investment management, and current contributions would be absorbed into current pensions paid from general revenue.
5 Contributions would be tax-free, but pensions would be fully taxable.[64]

In tandem with the Superannuation Committee of Inquiry, the Labor government assigned another committee in 1973 to investigate the effectiveness of the fragmented compensation and rehabilitation schemes. The principal aim of a Committee of Inquiry into Compensation and Rehabilitation was to integrate the disability and sickness benefits into a publicly administered compulsory pension plan. After submitting its report in 1974, the committee recommended replacing the fragmented protection offered by a combination of workers' compensation and social security with earnings-related injury and sickness benefits.[65]

The recommendations of these commissions of inquiry on the national retirement income system had the potential to radically reorient Australian social income security, which had been characterized by an inexorable expansion of publicly subsidized private occupational pension schemes that disproportionably benefited those in higher-paid occupations. The growth of tax-subsidized private occupational schemes had been marked by low coverage, inequality in the distribution and the extent of occupational arrangements, gender inequality, lack of portability (provisions for preserving benefits when a person changed his or her job prior to retirement), and taxation incentives that encouraged the payment of benefits by way of lump-sum rather than monthly pension benefits after retirement.[66] In the end, the recommendations of the Superannuation Committee that the means test mechanism governing the payment of non-contributory flat rate age pensions be abolished as the first tier of income security, and that a publicly administered earnings-related compulsory pension plan be implemented as the second tier, were rejected by the Labor government.[67]

During the era of welfare state expansion, private occupational pension schemes in Australia were growing more quickly than their counterparts in Canada.[68] As Michael Jones has pointed out, the expansion of occupational pension plans became "a milestone in Australian welfare history."[69] The roots of occupational superannuation plans can be traced back to the nineteenth century. Tax concessions for voluntary superannuation savings were introduced in 1915 and strengthened in 1936.[70] After the Second World War, as a result of claims lodged in the industrial relations arena, occupational superannuation schemes grew rapidly in public sector but slowly in the private sector.[71] Despite the massive expansion of private occupational pension plans in Australia, most workers were not covered by them.[72] Occupational superannuation coverage was confined mainly to highly paid white-collar workers in large corporations, employees in the financial sector, and public servants.[73] In the postwar era, private occupational superannuation came to function as a fringe benefit mainly for professionals, managers, administrators, public sector employees, and the financial sector.[74]

With the failure of the Labor government to implement a publicly administered compulsory pension plan, and the complete abandonment of the plan by the non-Labor coalition government of the Liberal and Australian National Parties, private occupational pension plans remained the hallmark of retirement income policy in Australia. The objective of superannuation pension plans was to reduce the number of the aged on the non-contributory flat rate pension.[75] The reliance on private occupational plans for securing old age income pointed to the weakness of the principles of collectivity and solidarity – principles that were essential to universalism and direct state involvement in retirement income. The consolidation of the Australian retirement income system was shaped by the postwar social class settlement and its economic characteristics.

A Market-Centred Social Class Settlement and Old Age Pensions

During and after the Second World War, social welfare policy gained a prominent place in Australian national politics, as it did in other Western societies. While the country's non-Labor political parties eschewed associating the welfare state with class reconciliation, the Labor Party passionately advocated the welfare state as the most effective bulwark against radical socialism. Ben Chifley, the postwar Labor prime minister and the architect of postwar Australian reconstruction, pointed out that the ALP took "great pride in the fact that it has always been closely associated, sometimes as the partner, in introducing and at other times as the originator of various social services."[76] For the postwar Labor government, political regimentation and physical force were not effective weapons to combat working-class radicalism. Instead, the Labor government praised the welfare state as the most effective mechanism for safeguarding the social order from radicalism. Chifley glorified the ALP as the champion of the Australian welfare state, identifying it as the political manifestation of social class compromise. In his view, it was conducive to deflecting the threat posed by radical socialism to the political order:

> Unfortunately, a flood of communism has swept Europe. Communism, rife not only in countries that are under communist domination, but also in the countries that are still democratic. That is the fruit of hundreds and hundreds of years in which eighty per cent of the people lived in the direst poverty ... With the help and advice of my colleagues in the Australian Labor movement, I launched the system of social security that we enjoy today. In the previous forty years, when for most of the time the anti-Labor parties were in power – the Labor Party had few years in office, not one piece of legislation was passed by the Australian parliament. I mention that because the only way ... to defeat communism is for the democracies of the world to be really democratic.[77]

The postwar expansion of the retirement income system in Australia reflected the social class compromise, which itself had been shaped by historical and national features specific to Australian society. As explained in chapter 3, the class structure and the homogeneous character of Australian society fostered unity in the labour movement. Yet that unity was also marked by a peculiar ideological disposition towards universalizing and maintaining wage labour. This was accomplished through state-sponsored regulatory measures such as compulsory state arbitration for wage setting, as well as protectionism to secure the employability of workers. In accordance with this particular vision, the ALP employed regulatory measures to maintain full employment and adequate wages that would preserve and enhance the welfare interests of the working class. Australian labourism emphasized that political power and national resources must be harnessed to create economic conditions in which Australians could stand on their own feet at all times. Thus the state's role was solely to facilitate socio-economic conditions within which individuals could maintain their living standards.

The ALP envisioned itself as "a movement bringing something better to the people, better standards of living, and greater happiness to the mass of the people."[78] These calls for utilitarian liberalism lurking beneath the ALP's faith in individual self-reliance, and the ALP's liberal conceptualizations of the state as an enabling entity, were strongly expressed by

Chifley, who held that "no government can do great things unless the people have the spirit and heart to move on and help themselves and one another. The most a Government can do is to make plans to assist the people."[79] The ALP's emphasis on self-help and self-reliance, and on the state as an enabling force, was not radically different from the stance taken by the non-Labor political parties. Robert Gordon Menzies, who headed the Liberal-Country coalition government of 1949–66, described the principles of government as follows: "To achieve the highest possible measure of self help and self reliance before asking somebody else to carry the burden… Government, the mystical creature which has come to be regarded as universal and provide, may well be the part of ultimate resort. But it should not be the first port of call."[80]

By identifying a regulated market as the chief distributor of income security and the locus of welfare state provision, this Australian labourist vision anchored the notion of social citizenship entitlement within the parameters of market employment, supplemented by a notion of "industrial citizenship," which was to be secured through full employment. Within the ALP's social vision, citizens' rights were identified with the market rights of labour to share the "fruits" of industry. Chifley, who was the prime mover of the postwar social welfare expansion, and who commanded respect within the Australian labour movement, alluded to this industrial conception of citizenship, which had been legally entrenched in the *Harvester Judgment*, when he stated that "we affirm for every man the right to receive a fair return for labour, enterprise and initiative."[81] Since the labour movement's horizon of aspirations did not extend much beyond the bounds of industrial relations, citizenship rights were implicitly restricted to relationships between capital and labour. The identification of citizenship with community (i.e., with something outside the market) was largely absent from the ALP's vision of the welfare state. The labourist vision of the welfare state had thus marginalized the principle of universalism and supported the liberal notions of selectivity and targeting.

During the postwar reconstruction years under the Curtin–Chifley Labor administration (1942–9), this vision held by the ALP affected the structure of postwar social welfare programs in Australia. It was under the ALP during this era that major new social programs were launched and existing ones were consolidated.[82] In 1945, Chifley, as the ALP treasurer and the minister for the new Department of Postwar Reconstruction, articulated the long-standing vision of full employment as indispensable to social welfare security:

> The modern idea is that there should be social security provisions to protect every citizen in his emergencies from the cradle to the grave. In the nation's economic life, of course, our objective is not primarily social security, but rather the much higher aim of full employment of manpower and resources in raising living standards. In other words, the main function of reconstruction will be positive to create conditions in which palliatives will become less and less necessary.[83]

The ALP's social vision as elucidated by Chifley subordinated social security to economic growth and full employment, both of which would by key to government measures to prevent poverty and social distress. In the ALP's program, social security had been identified as a prime objective. However, the ALP believed that sustaining full employment would allow Australians to retain self-reliance and also would forestall the need to expand social welfare programs. Accordingly, a regulated market would deliver the goods, and there would be no imperative to provide for the needs of citizens except for residual categories such as disabled and elderly people who had fallen outside the market. The ALP government contended that full employment would limit the need to expand social welfare programs beyond targeting "those people who have to spend the greatest part of their income on necessaries."[84]

The Labor administration reiterated this particular vision of the welfare state in its 1945 White Paper on Full Employment, which emphasized "work for all" and the maintenance of full employment as "an obligation owed to the people of Australia by the Commonwealth government."[85] The 1945 White Paper reflected the ALP's adherence to Keynesian principles of economic management. The application of public power to regulate the economy in order to bring about a more equitable share of claims to the national wealth became a defining creed of the ALP. During his address to the New South Wales Annual Conference on 12 June 1948, Chifley declared that the fundamental aim of the ALP was to sustain high production as the means to achieve social welfare security: "If workers did not produce as well they might, they were only cheating the government and their fellow citizens … I do not delude myself that complete and utmost production is the solution of the needs of the people."[86]

The Labor government's commitment to full employment did not challenge business interests. Notwithstanding their frequent references to Keynesian management of the economy as "tyrannical regimentation" and their successful mobilization to challenge the nationalization of the banking system, the business community and their political supporters in the Liberal Party maintained an official commitment to full employment. For all its political rhetoric, the Liberal Party accepted centralized wage setting, a mixed economy, and the goal of full employment, all of which had long been espoused by the ALP.[87] During the expansionary phase of the welfare state from 1950 to the late 1970s, these policies provided a broad framework for both Liberal and Labor governments.

The ALP's focus on full employment profoundly shaped its position on postwar income retirement. The political struggles over old age retirement in Australia revolved around two competing positions, which gradually became indistinguishable from each other. While the Liberal Party advocated a contributory social insurance scheme that, in its view, would end the taint associated with the means-tested pension, the ALP fiercely opposed a contributory social insurance plan.[88] The ALP endorsed the principles of social assistance directed only at those who could not make their way in the market. The ALP's endorsement of social assistance principles reflected its focus on selectivity and targeting; this in turn restricted the universalization of the old age pension.

The ALP's postwar stance on retirement income was in fact a continuation of its earlier position on the contributory social insurance program. Opposition to compulsory social insurance for unemployment and old age, and for invalids, came from different elements, such as farmers and the self-employed who had not been included in the proposed insurance plan. However, the ALP was the main opposing force to a contributory pension plan. When in 1938 the Liberal government introduced the National Insurance Bill (which was passed but not implemented), John Curtin, the leader of the federal ALP, outlined the ALP's opposition to a contributory social insurance plan:

> I decline to delude myself with the idea that a contribution is not a tax. We are taxing the employers and we are taxing employees ... The Labor Party expresses its utter condemnation of individual contributions a principle in regard to invalidity, old age and widows' pensions these services should be a charge on consolidated revenue of the Commonwealth. To impose special levies, either on workers or employers is unjust. The greater numbers of workers that a business employs the greater will be the tax on the enterprise ... The principle is bad on from two aspects. On the one hand, it imposes sectional taxation regardless of individual capacity to pay, while excluding many sections from their just obligation to pay. On the other hand, it

confines eligibility for benefits to the insurance status of the contributors, and, as this status depends on contingencies which cannot be foreseen, either in point of time or in character.[89]

The ALP's opposition to a compulsory scheme of contributory social insurance for the old age pension was a logical corollary of its overall vision of the welfare state. Sustaining full employment and enhancing the basic wage calculated under the *Harvester* principles would enable workers to maintain an adequate standard of living and also to make provisions for their own retirement. Only labour market "residual" categories, such as the disabled and elderly people who were in need of assistance, would be provided social benefits financed from consolidated national revenues. In 1943, Arthur Caldwell, an important Labor MP, who became the leader of the federal ALP in the 1960s, shed light on his party's long-standing stance on social income security provisions:

> The Labor Party objected to the scheme of national insurance, because basically, it provided that the worker should pay for his own old age pension. The Labor Party does not stand for that. I believe that the workers are entitled to a certain basic wage, which is sufficient to enable them to maintain life and have a reasonable standard of comfort; but in addition, it wants benefits in the way of social services which are paid for out of the national income.[90]

During the Second World War, the governing Labor Party launched an early outline of general principles of the postwar social reconstruction while the non-Labor parties renewed their call for a contributory scheme of social insurance for unemployment, disability, and old age. Promoting self-respect and self-reliance and overcoming the stigma associated with means-tested old age pension payments were the principles embraced by the Liberal Party as justification for installing a contributory scheme of social insurance. During a parliamentary debate in 1944, Robert Menzies, the opposition leader, reiterated the Liberals' position on contributory social insurance: "Every person living in a country like Australia should be a contributor to social insurance, and should be a beneficiary as of right, with no means test and no questions to ask. The sooner we decide whole-heartedly to adopt the principle of contribution, in which the contribution and benefits are indissolubly linked, the sooner we shall have a permanent, just and solvent scheme of social insurance."[91]

The ALP continued to hold that contributory principles would diminish the effectiveness of income redistribution and would force workers to fund their own old age income. A non-contributory scheme financed from general revenues was thus seen as the most effective measure to finance social security. Under principles of progressive taxation, higher-income individuals would then pay more of their income to financing the welfare system. After uniform taxation was introduced in 1942 that gave the federal government fiscal dominance within the Australian federal system, the Labor administration introduced a National Welfare Fund in 1943 as the basis for financing social security. Under the National Welfare Fund legislation of 1943, one-quarter of the total collections of consolidated revenue were to be devoted to this fund.[92] To provide a solid basis for financing the fund and to give it a contributory character, the Labor government introduced Social Services Contribution legislation in 1945. This bill provided that the direct income taxes paid by individuals be divided into two parts: general income taxation, and a social services contribution that adjusted the principle of contribution to the capacity to pay. By introducing this legislation, the Labor government broadened the tax base (which was partly geared to reduce the burden on higher-income individuals). On introducing the bill in Parliament, Chifley stated:

> This bill is one of several designed to give effect to the Government's taxation proposal ... I indicated to honorable members the intention [of] the Government to effect a reduction of the present weigh[t] of income tax on individual taxpayers ... [T]his course follows the lines of the recommendations of the Social Security Committee which expressed the view that social services should be financed by the imposition of graduated rates of tax on every income earner in the community, except those on the lowest scale ... As social services are available to individuals only, companies are not required to make social service contribution, except as regards the undistributed profits to private companies. Private companies will be obliged to pay the social services contribution that their shareholders would pay if the undistributed profits were released to the shareholders by way of dividend.[93]

With the broadening of the taxation base to justify the National Welfare Fund as an egalitarian counter to the compulsory social insurance scheme advocated by the Liberal Party, the Labor government made a tacit shift from its long-standing position that social services should be financed exclusively from taxes on higher-income and wealthy individuals. Under the 1945 Social Services Contribution legislation, the threshold for tax exemption for a single individual was set at £104; for an individual with dependents, £156.[94] Except for criticizing the proposed flat rate taxes on companies on the grounds that those rates would ignore the size of shareholders within each company and also hamstring economic growth and employment, the non-Labor opposition parties praised the expansion of the tax base as a positive step. Despite his attack on the company tax, Robert Menzies, the opposition leader, could not conceal his satisfaction with the ALP's move to shift the burden of taxation to middle- and low-income groups:

> [E]ach shareholder in a company with a large income from it ought to pay at a much higher rate of tax than the shareholder with a small income from it. But the company tax being in its nature a flat-rate tax on all shareholders in the first instance ignores whether they are great or small. Therefore, personal income tax is immediately more an instrument of justice than is the company tax. The chief effects of a heavy tax company are found upon expansion and employment ... [T]o the extent that there is a movement towards a true contributor system of social security; the opposition welcomes it.[95]

In his presentation to Parliament of the Labor government's budgetary proposal for 1948–9, Chifley as the prime minister and treasury minister stated that "it is an illusion that social welfare benefits can be had by some easy method of finance. They must be paid from taxation, either direct or indirect."[96] By lowering the threshold of income taxation and thereby sharply increasing the number of taxpayers, the Labor government paved the way for shifting the burden of financing social services to low- and middle-income groups. This pushed the Labor government closer to the position of other political parties. Radical elements within the labour movement and the Labor Party resented the taxation initiative launched by the Labor government and became disillusioned with the party's historical emphasis on income taxation as a redistribution mechanism. The labour movement did not stop to consider that, as long as there was no contributory plan, the fund would have to be defrayed through taxation. In a capitalist economy, such taxation could not be imposed solely on higher income brackets; it would have to be extended to all wage earners. Chifley's opponents within the Labor movement and the ALP wanted social welfare services such as pensions to be financed by heavy taxes on wealthy individuals, including on capital gains. Chifley justified the extension of taxation into low- and middle-income levels on the grounds that if there was to be a universal right to all benefits, there should be a universal contribution.

The extension of taxation to low- and middle-income individuals greatly diminished the intensity of political disputes over the merits of compulsory social insurance. By extending the tax base to low- and middle-income groups, the Labor government also found room to reduce the level of taxation, which was bound to trigger derisory compliments from its political opponents. After commending the Labor government for its bold stride, Senator John William Leckie, the acting leader of the opposition in the Senate, declared that "step by step the [Labor] government is adopting the policy of Opposition."[97] By espousing a tax-based scheme of social security as an alternative to a compulsory scheme of social insurance, the Labor government complicated any future move towards adopting a universal old age pension; it also provided effective electoral ammunition for other political parties. Non-Labor political parties found a golden opportunity to use the abolition of the means test on the Age Pension as a weapon of electoral competition, but at the same time they found grounds for retaining it. The elimination of the means test required further social expenditure, which in turn required an increase in the taxation level, and this was politically explosive. In reply to calls for the abolition of the means test on the old age pension during the debate over the 1945 budget, Chifley outlined the justification for retaining it, while at the same time signalling the ALP's adherence to fiscal conservatism:

> Although some members of Parliament talked about abolishing of means test, they did not put forward any financial proposals as to how it should be done ... I inferred from the remarks of the Leader of Opposition who was not specific, that whatever contributions are to be made to social services they ought to cover the whole field of those entitled to social services ... But he did not say how the £35 million a year, which it would cost to abolish the means test would be raised ... I should like any honourable member who advocates the abolition of the means test to tintack, and show me a method by which his objective could be achieved ... [P]ensions and other social service must be paid from revenue. They cannot be paid from bank credit ... The government will continue to do its utmost to avoid waste and guard the national economy.[98]

The postwar Labor government's refusal to abolish the means test for non-contributory flat rate pension payments was not a complete rejection of the ALP's ideological position. Nor was it a random attack on the general attitude within the Australian labour movement towards old age pensions. While both Labor and non-Labor political parties condemned the means test as a penalty on thrift and as an impediment to saving, the ALP never included the universal old age pension as a plank in its electoral platforms.[99] The ALP and the unions wanted to keep the means-tested non-contributory flat rate old age pension. They felt that the contributory principle would minimize redistribution and would force workers to fund their own social security. A non-contributory system financed through general revenues was seen as in keeping with Labor ideas. Under the principle of progressive taxation, those in higher brackets would contribute proportionally more of their income to finance the welfare state. This was especially so since only a fraction of the population paid income tax at the time. Although some Labor members called for the means test to be abolished, a substantial number of ALP members supported retaining it for the sake of higher rates of pension for people with no income. Within the labour movement, trade unions were mainly preoccupied with full employment and higher wages and therefore did not generally display a concern for the social wage.[100] Only well-paid workers, especially public servants who were already contributing to superannuation, sometimes opposed the means test.[101] In fact, the means test was not a concern for the Labor Party until 1953, when a "progressive easing of means test applicable to social services with a view to its ultimate abolition" became a plank in the ALP's electoral campaigns.[102]

Chifley's insistence on retaining the means test was in line with the outcome of a Parliamentary Labor Committee of Inquiry into the practicality of abolishing it. The committee did not call for a complete elimination of targeting; rather, it proposed a gradual liberalization of the means test. Having resigned itself to maintaining the means test, the postwar Labor government proceeded to loosen the stringent criteria attached to eligibility for old age pensions. Under the postwar Labor administration, improvements to old age pensions were restricted to raising the level of permissible income, increasing the limit of property, increasing maximum pension payments, and subjecting further liberalization of the old age pension to "the financial position of government."[103]

With the introduction of social services contributions and the ensuing weakening in the intensity of rival political arguments with respect to compulsory social insurance, the means test remained a key point of political debate during the non-Labor governments in power from 1949 to 1972. The introduction of social services contributions enabled the non-Labor government in 1950 to amalgamate the two components of taxes into a single levy.[104] This allowed the Menzies government to impose a taxation system that reached as far down the income scale as did the social services contribution.[105] The Labor administration had paved the way for the shifting of the tax burden to low- and middle-income individuals. In the end, the Labor government espoused an arrangement in which taxes levied on low- and middle-income earners would largely fund the new postwar welfare measures for the same income groups.[106] Since an increase in the number of taxpayers reduced the electoral appeal and political efficacy of an electoral pledge to abolish the means test, the Liberal Party under Menzies ultimately discarded its slogan of abolishing the means test: "Apart from indirect taxes, there are now 3 1/2 million income taxpayers. Tax includes the cost of social services. We therefore have, broadly a contributory system ... [W]ithout increased production the earning groups just cannot go on carrying the enormous burden of age benefits which accrue to an increasing proportion of our population every year ... [W]e have therefore decided that it is not practical completely to abolish the Means Test."[107]

By the time the Liberal Party abandoned its pledge to abolish the means test contingent on the adoption of a compulsory scheme of social insurance in the 1950s, the Labor Party had begun to place greater emphasis on eliminating the means test. In response to the ALP's electoral promise to eliminate the means test within the lifetime of its elected government, and Allan Fraser's (a Labor MP) passionate argument for the abolition of the means test as a matter of "justice," Freeth, a member of the Liberal-led coalition government, reminded the ALP's parliamentary members that "Mr. Chifley did not want to abolish the means test."[108] In fact, the coalition government was correct in pointing out that the ALP had never displayed a strong desire to end the means test. Even when in opposition as Labor Party leader, Chifley did not conceal his lack of interest in discarding the means test principle: "I am not greatly concerned about abolishing the means test so that everybody in the community above the prescribed age limit may receive an age pension ... I am concerned about people on the lowest rung of the economic ladder, who suffer great hardship under present living conditions."[109]

With an increase in the number of taxpayers, the Liberals did not see the need to establish a compulsory scheme of social insurance. The Liberal–Country coalition government thus did not contemplate implementing national social insurance. In 1961, Hugh Roberton, the social services minister in the Menzies government, conveyed the coalition government's ultimate decision to discard consideration of installing a scheme of social insurance for the old age pension – a scheme that had long been advocated by the Liberal Party. Having abandoned its demand that compulsory social insurance be implemented, the coalition government restricted its old age pension policy to the progressive easing of both income and means tests in order to promote self-help and self-reliance. The means test, which had been interpreted especially by the Liberal Party as an attack on human dignity that could only be overcome by compulsory social insurance, came to be defended by the coalition government as the most effective policy mechanism for the social protection of the elderly. In 1964, Roberton maintained that the Australian system of targeting and selectivity had been an attractive policy around the world:

> I am in a position to say with some authority that the Australian scheme of social services is envied by a great many countries where there are social security, national insurance and contributory superannuation scheme of every description ... I have been asked [by his counterparts in other countries]: what should a country do to adopt the Australian system of pensions and to apply the means test in a such a way as to enable the resources provided by the contribution to a scheme to be applied to the best advantage, giving the greatest possible assistance to those in greatest need?[110]

Notwithstanding Roberton's praise for what he viewed as an effective and generous Australian system of income provision for the aged, debate continued regarding the desirability of the means test and whether a contributory scheme of social insurance should be adopted. The late 1960s saw a resurgence of debates in Australia on the merits of the contributory principle; these centred on the adoption of a scheme of national superannuation to overcome the lack of pension portability within private superannuation plans that inhibited labour mobility.[111] As in the past, both Labor and non-Labor political parties presented the adoption of national superannuation as a missing link between the status quo and the abolition of the means test, which despite extensive modifications had remained a focal point of political debates.

The parliamentary debates about the desirability of abolishing the means test became more intense during the Whitlam Labor government. That government rested its social welfare agenda on justice, equality of opportunity in access to social services, and enabling communities. Whitlam's ALP government concluded that Australian "social services are not comparable to that of other advanced countries administering such services."[112] Whitlam emerged as the first Labor prime minister to embark on a serious initiative to tackle the stigma of means tests and the inadequacy of the Australian welfare state, which in his view lagged behind that of comparable countries. William Hayden, the social security minister in the Whitlam government, declared that the "policies of this government are aimed at converting the 'quality of life' from a slogan into a reality achieved."[113] Australia had long bragged that its system of retirement income was the envy of other countries; Hayden considered this an exaggeration, and painted a disparaging picture of the Australian system of social protection. According to him, "Australia is a long way short of being too generous either in the provision of benefits or welfare services or in the philosophy that motivates the development of these things."[114]

The Whitlam government declared that it would end the last vestiges of residualism that tarnished the image of the Australian welfare state; but the abolition of the means test would still be tied to the establishment of a national superannuation plan. In 1973, during his submission to Parliament on proposed modifications to the Social Security Act, Hayden proclaimed the Labor government's determination to introduce a national superannuation scheme (a policy reminiscent of the Liberal Party's earlier electoral promise): "We intend to abolish the means test within the term of this Parliament for people of 65 years and above. We aim to introduce[a] system of national superannuation. The 2 things which we hope to mesh but not mate are, the abolishing of the means test and the introducing of national superannuation, upon which the former is dependent."[115]

The Liberal Party until 1950 had advocated a compulsory scheme of social insurance as a precondition for abolishing the means test. Whitlam's Labor government now came to envision a scheme of national superannuation as a prerequisite for the ultimate abolition of the means test. Indeed, during the Whitlam government's tenure, the Liberal Party once again reclaimed its status as rightful crusader for the abolition of the means test and began attacking the Labor Party for its intention to retain it. Having rejected the abolition of the means test while social security minister in the Liberal–Country coalition government of 1971–2, William Wentworth emerged as an ardent advocate of its abolition in opposition to the Whitlam government. In 1973, Wentworth outlined the Liberals' argument for eliminating the means test:

> Because it eliminates or reduces the advantages which people obtain from their own effort or thrift, the means test is a socialistic device, whereas (presuming that some basic Government pension is given) the universal availability of the age pension would seem to be more compatible with the free enterprise system ... The abolition of the means test is fundamentally in line with Liberal Party philosophy and fundamentally opposes to Australian Labor Party philosophy ... The means test is a socialistic device and its abolition is therefore fundamentally out of line with Labor philosophy.[116]

Wentworth's call to abolish the means test was repeated by several members of the opposition, who pressed the Whitlam government to keep its electoral promise to eliminate it.[117] Even though the Whitlam government succeeded in abolishing the means test for residentially qualified people aged seventy-five and over in 1973, and for people aged seventy and over in 1975, the complete eradication of the means test for people aged sixty-five to sixty-nine remained unrealizable. In tandem with a partial elimination of the means test and a generous increase in the rates of maximum pension geared to average weekly earnings, the Whitlam government subjected Age Pension payments to income taxation. But despite its own electoral pledge to establish a national superannuation scheme as a prelude to eradicating the means test, the Whitlam government refrained from following the suggestions of the report of the National Superannuation Committee of Inquiry that had been set up by the previous Liberal–Country coalition government.

In Australian social policy history, the Whitlam era was the only time that a Labor government considered universalizing pensions (although this did not come about). Whitlam was the first Labor prime minister to tackle the means test and the inadequate social protection that characterized the Australian welfare state. The Whitlam government's failure to accomplish the welfare goal of universalism was largely a consequence of the ALP's historically entrenched vision of the Australian welfare state, which was devoid of universal principles and consideration for the social wage. It was an arduous task to shift the discourse on social welfare policy beyond the postwar social class compromise and its market-regulated character, which emphasized selectivity and targeting. As Hayden pointed out, "gauging the performances of past Australian governments, it is clear the promotion of social welfare programs was guided by a philosophy that social welfare was for the deserving poor."[118] The ALP's vision of the welfare state, which was quite compatible with non-Labor notions of welfare state provisions, formed an obstacle to the universalization of the old age pension.

By the time the Whitlam government began taking modest steps towards universalizing the Age Pension in the 1970s, structural changes in socio-economic conditions manifested in a looming economic contraction were more hostile to the discourse of universalism. Changes in economic conditions in the mid-1970s had begun to undermine the pillars of the postwar social settlement, which rested solely on regulatory measures that came to be identified as impediments to economic growth. No one put it better than Whitlam himself. The Labor Party had become enthralled with its own past vision of social income security:

> From the ALP itself, little was produced in the way of creative or innovative thinking on a matter which after all goes to the very heart of its mission and meaning. In a very real sense the ALP was a prisoner of its own past. Its perceptions of the real needs of its special constituency, the poor, was limited by its past pride in its own achievements. It was difficult to push ALP thinking beyond the basic concept of the provision of cash payments ... The problems of destitution and squalor were perceived in terms of financial deprivation. Hence, remedial action was framed almost entirely in terms of financial compensation.[119]

With the defeat of the Whitlam government and the ascendancy of a Liberal-led coalition government in 1975, the partial elimination of the means test for people aged seventy and over was subject to regressive measures. Once in power, the Liberal coalition government of John Malcolm Fraser threw its pledge to abolish the means test to the side and began to focus on structural responses to economic recession. This meant reversing the modest steps towards eliminating the means test on the Age Pension. For people aged sixty-five to sixty-nine, the means test was replaced by an income test. In 1978, after non–means tested Age Pension payments were fixed for people over seventy, the receipt of further assistance was subjected to a partial income test mechanism.[120]

Conclusion

Australia's postwar retirement income system came to be characterized by the selectivity principle governing the non-contributory flat rate old age pension, and the encouragement of non-compulsory private occupational pension plans. Despite the protracted political rhetoric by Labor and the other political parties on the need to eradicate the means test, the non-contributory flat rate old age pension remained intact, and a universal pension policy never materialized. The postwar expansion and consolidation of Australia's retirement income system was shaped decisively by the nature of the postwar social settlement, which manifested itself in a politically constructed market-centred welfare state. The Australian welfare state reflected the Australian labour movement's vision of social protection, which rested on a national wage-setting system and harnessed market forces to achieve full employment as a surrogate for the social wage. As a result, in Australia, the principle of residualism was etched into the foundation of the retirement income system. Within the Australian postwar political discourse on social welfare provision, social citizenship was tacitly superseded by industrial citizenship. This in turn reinforced the continuity of the targeting mechanism, encouraged private arrangements for old age income, and blocked the collectivization of retirement income by installing a publicly administered compulsory earnings–related social insurance plan.

The failure to establish a universal pension plan over the course of the postwar boom in Australia, during which Australian social democracy enjoyed some of its periods of greatest political strength, stands in sharp contrast to Canada, where labour was fragmented and social democracy was not in power, yet universality became a hallmark of the Canadian pension system.

5 Postwar Expansion of the Pension System in Canada

Despite a parallel liberalization of pension eligibility during the postwar years in Australia and Canada, variations in their pension systems became a striking feature of welfare state expansion in the two countries. In Canada, as in Australia, the postwar expansion and consolidation of the retirement income system was reinforced by the Keynesian-inspired postwar reconstruction that was integral to the social class settlement. Even though both countries encouraged private occupational pension plans as a means to secure retirement income, Canada and Australia differed in the degree of state involvement in the public provision of old age income. In contrast to Australia, where selectivity mechanisms and private arrangements predominated in the pension system, the Canadian retirement income system came to be characterized by the principles of universality and collectivity. The differences between the two countries' pension systems were not a result of robust actuarial calculation. Rather, variations were shaped by the national context within each country that determined the social income security objectives and the priorities attached to those objectives.

The postwar welfare state in Canada was harnessed largely as a mechanism for accommodating the working class and for deflecting the threat to the political order posed by radicalism. Unlike in Australia, where the postwar social class compromise assumed a politically constructed market-centred character, the social settlement in Canada acquired a politically constructed redistributive-oriented character that became an instrument of national integration. Whereas the market-regulated social class compromise in Australia was conducive to the retention of the selectivity mechanism and the proliferation of private occupational plans for old age income, the postwar social settlement in Canada reinforced the links between the welfare state, national unity, and social citizenship.

This chapter has three sections. In the first, the postwar evolution of old age policy in Canada is described and the main changes that were made to the pillars of the retirement income system are outlined. In the second, the decisive role of the postwar social class settlement in shaping the direction of the retirement income system in Canada is discussed. In the third, the main points are restated and the implications of Canada's particular type of welfare state are explained.

The Postwar Expansion of Old Age Pensions in Canada

Throughout the eighteenth and nineteenth centuries in Canada, charity and philanthropy were the main mechanisms of social reproduction. Charitable societies and public poor relief were used by the ruling classes as tools to ease social resentment.[1] Elderly people who had no family support were to rely on public poor relief to survive.[2] The federal government was not receptive to persistent calls for public pensions by organized labour, including the Trades and Labor Congress (TLC), and by the Moral and Social Reform Council of Canada.[3] Between 1906 and 1914 the issue of public pensions was mentioned only twice in the House of Commons, and on both occasions the federal government was not sympathetic to the idea.[4] During the late nineteenth century and the first decade of the twentieth, the federal government promoted self-reliance by encouraging Canadians to save for their retirement in post office and government savings banks.[5] In 1908, in response to growing societal problems and demands on government to provide social protection for elderly Canadians, the federal government introduced a system of government annuities. This program was not social assistance or a pension but rather a private savings account. It was designed to encourage Canadians to prepare for their own retirement by purchasing government-administered annuities.[6] Although the federal government guaranteed the benefits, this system of private arrangement for retirement income was not effective in enhancing the living conditions of elderly Canadians. Only well-off Canadians could benefit from the program. Between the introduction of government annuities in 1908 and the introduction of the Old Age Pension Act in 1927, only 7,713 annuities were issued, which left most aged Canadians relying on family support and organized charity in the form of indoor relief.[7]

Despite the prevalence of the liberal ethos of self-help, self-reliance, and relief work as the principal mechanisms of income security provision for elderly people, the national state in Canada gradually became involved in the direct provision of income security in the early decades of the twentieth century. In 1924, Parliament finally appointed a committee to investigate implementing a government-administered public pension.[8] The parliamentary committee proposed a non-contributory means-tested flat rate monthly pension of $20 for those aged seventy or older.[9] The Liberal government of Prime Minister William Lyon Mackenzie King was reluctant to implement this proposal. It was partly due to the pressure exerted by two independent labour members of parliament, J.S. Woodsworth and A.A. Heaps, and the government's need for their votes in order to escape a defeat in the House of Commons, that the Liberals relented and introduced the Pensions Bill in 1927.[10] The first national experiment with old age pensions in Canada came in the form of the passage of the Old Age Pension Act in 1927. Under this act, the federal government agreed to enter into an arrangement with any province to reimburse half the cost of pensions paid by that province that met the requirements of the Old Age Act and its regulations.[11]

The first national step towards providing income security for elderly people in Canada was a radical departure from the past practice of outdoor relief run by municipal and charitable organizations.[12] Even though the eligibility requirements for old age pensions in Canada required proof of need, statutory entitlement was nonetheless geared towards removing the stain of charity. Despite this shift with past practices and changes in public attitudes towards charity, the initial provisions for income security maintenance for aged people in Canada were marked by exclusionary principles. State adherence to means-test principles meant that old age pension payments maintained the appearance of public handouts for the improvident poor. Exclusionary mechanisms in Canada's state-run old age pension plan reflected the state's reluctance to involve itself in welfare. The lack of state interest in providing social protection reflected the philosophical legacy of the minimal state bequeathed by classical liberalism.[13]

Early experiments with old age pensions in Canada highlighted the distribution of state charity in a conspicuously selective and judgmental fashion. The strict eligibility criteria attached to the first national plan to provide income security for elderly Canadians ran counter to the paradigm of social citizenship entitlements. The provinces gradually became inclined towards entering into agreements with the federal government, and it took a decade for the Canadian old age pension to become national in scope.[14] Despite variations in the interpretation of the 1927 Old Age Pension Act among the provinces, the act gradually achieved a degree of stability and galvanized Canadians to view social security issues as national rather than purely local.[15] With the onset of the Great Depression, which led to a decline in both earned income and government revenues, the federal government assumed responsibility for 75 per cent of pension benefits provided by the provinces.[16] The emerging preoccupation with the financial calculation also led to the transfer of administrative responsibility for old age pensions from the Department of Labour to the Finance Department.

The 1927 Old Age Pension Act attached a number of stipulations to eligibility for old age pension benefits. Old age pension payments were subjected to means and income tests; besides this, the applicant had to provide proof that he or she had not transferred property to another person in order to qualify. The recipients were also required to be British subjects over seventy or widows of aliens who had been British subjects before marriage. A continuous twenty years of residency in Canada and five years in the province concerned was another strict requirement. The 1927 Old Age Pension Act also excluded Aboriginal people from old age benefits.[17] Under the act, the monthly amount of pension was set at $20 ($240 a year), and pensioners were allowed a total income of $365, including the pension. The pension benefit was to be reduced by any amount by which a pensioner's outside yearly income surpassed $125. Possession of property and assets was not in itself a basis for disqualification, but income value attached to assets and property was included in the calculation of income. Under the act's provisions, provincial authorities were authorized to recover from the estates of deceased pensioners the total amount of pension paid to them together with interest at 5 per cent compounded annually.[18] Due to variations in the interpretation of income and property by the provinces, many pensioners did not receive the maximum amount of pension payment that had been called for by the 1927 act. Consequently, a low average pension relative to the maximum established by the act became a central operational dimension of pension payments throughout Canada.[19] In his 1943 report on Canadian social security, which has been interpreted as the Canadian counterpart of the Beveridge social security blueprint for Britain, Leonard Marsh identified major regulatory and administrative factors that were limiting the opportunity for potential pensioners to receive an old age pension. These included:

1 Citizenship;
2 Residence restrictions, both Dominion and provincial;

3 Means testing in terms of the applicant's personal income, personal property qualification, and even the assumption of income from property where in fact such income does not exist;
4 The principle, zealously adhered to in certain provinces, of the responsibility of the children to the point of assuming that income is actually forthcoming from children for the support of the applicant, even in cases where it is not; and
5 Scaling-down of allowances below the amount permitted by the statute, on the finding that the pensioner does not require even that amount which is found to be the arithmetical maximum payable after the exhaustion of all statutory, regulatory and administrative means-test procedures.[20]

The retirement income system in Canada was reinforced by the Keynesian-inspired postwar socio-economic reconstruction. Indeed, it was after the Second World War that the basic components of retirement income were put in place and old age security came to constitute an institutionalized means of retirement.[21] Table 5.1 summarizes different tiers of the retirement income system in Canada during the postwar welfare state expansion.

First Tier

From the inception of the old age pension in 1927 until the late 1940s, the restrictive features of the Pension Act were subjected to only minor modifications. The provincial residency requirement (five years' residency immediately preceding the commencement of benefit) was gradually relaxed. In 1947, it was completely removed from the set of eligibility requirements governing the payment of pensions.[22] Under the 1947 amendment to the Pension Act, the residency requirement in Canada of twenty years immediately preceding the payment of pension was modified to allow the applicant to offset the non-residence restitution during those years by "an aggregate period at least equal to twice the aggregate periods of absence from Canada during those ten years."[23] The 1947 Act ended the exclusion of aliens from eligibility for old age pension payments. Besides raising the maximum amount of monthly pension, the 1947 Act raised the ceiling for permissible income.[24]

Despite the gradual relaxation of the eligibility requirements in the 1940s, the legacy of the 1927 Old Age Pension Act continued to be felt in the Canadian government's agenda, reflecting ongoing faith in the

Table 5.1 Retirement income system in Canada during the era of welfare state expansion

Pre–Second World War		
Old Age Pension (1927)		Voluntary private occupational pension plans and individual savings
Funding	Jointly funded by the federal and provincial governments	Employer/employee contribution. Individual savings
Eligibility	Citizenship/residency requirement and be age 70 and above	By contribution
Benefits	Income tested	Determined by accumulation of assets and returns on fund investment

Postwar welfare state expansion			
Tiers/features	First Tier	Second tier	Third tier
	Non-contributory	Publicly administered earnings-related contributory plan	Tax-assisted voluntary savings
Components	Old Age Security. Guaranteed Income Supplement Spouse's Allowance.	C/QPP	RPPs RRSPs
Year established	OAS (1951) GIS (1971) SPA (1975)	1966	RPPs (originated in 1800s, consolidated in 1900s) RRSPs (1957)
Coverage	OAS (all Canadians of retirement age) GIS (recipients of OAS with low income) SPA (spouses of OAS pensioners)	All employed and self-employed persons in Canada between 18 and 70 and who earn more than minimum level of earnings in a calendar year	RPPs (heavily concentrated in public sector and large firms in private sector) RRSPs (mostly confined to high-income earners)
Funding	Financed from federal government general tax revenue	Employee and employer contributions	RPPS (Employer/employee contribution). Investments. RRSPs (individual contribution).

Table 5.1 *continued*

	Postwar welfare state expansion		
Tiers/features	First Tier	Second tier	Third tier
Eligibility	OAS (age, residency requirement). Age of eligibility gradually lowered between 1966 and 1970, from 70 to 65. GIS (be recipient of OAS with low income) SPA (between 60 and 64 and has lived in Canada for at least 10 years)	By contribution.	By contribution
Benefits	OAS (flat rate, determined by how long s/he has lived in Canada)	Determined by level and number of years of contribution. Monthly payment equal to 25% of contributor's average monthly pensionable earnings during contributory period	Depends whether it is defined benefits (contributor is guaranteed a fixed percentage of earnings upon retirement) or defined contribution (determined by contribution plus the compounded returns on investment)
	GIS (determined by marital status and level of income). SPA (income tested benefits)	Provisions were put in place to provide pension disability benefits, survivor's benefits, death benefits, and dependent children benefits.	RRSPs (contribution plus compounded returns on investment)

market ethos of self-reliance. The restrictive dimensions of public pension provisions – the humiliation associated with the constant scrutiny of pensioners' personal affairs, the discrimination against aliens of long residence, the inclusion of property in the calculation of income, the residency requirements, and the assumption that children could support their parents when they could not even support themselves – continued to make it hard for aged people to receive pension benefits. Only during the economic expansion of the 1940s and 1950s did Canada begin taking steps to universalize the old age pension, marking a progressive departure from the residualism of the past.

In the early 1950s, the Canadian old age pension entered a new era marked by the progressive removal of restrictions on eligibility. The first steps towards universalism were the Old Age Assistance Act and Old Age Security Act in 1951. Both were promulgated in January 1952. Under the first of these, the federal government committed itself to providing 50 per cent of the costs of provincially administered means-tested pensions for people between sixty-five and sixty-nine. Also, Aboriginal Canadians were no longer barred from receiving a pension, and the income limitation was raised for both single and married pensioners. This act was solely concerned with the provisions of means-tested pensions, whereas its "partner act," the Old Age Security Act of 1952, universalized the pension for those over seventy, subject only to the residency requirement. It also authorized the federal government to assume full responsibility for financing and administering Old Age Security (OAS).

Monthly maximum pension payments were increased in 1957. Meanwhile, the residency restriction was significantly overhauled to the benefit of aged immigrants. In 1957 the residency requirement for pension eligibility was reduced to ten years immediately preceding the commencement of pension payment, with the same previous provision that allowed potential pensioners to offset the absences by prior residence equal to at least twice the total absences.[25] In a further attempt to remove barriers to pension eligibility, a 1960 amendment to the 1952 Old Age Security Act allowed long-term residents who were receiving the universal pension to continue to do so outside Canada if they had resided in Canada for twenty-five years after attaining the age of twenty-one. The increase in the maximum monthly pension in 1957 was accompanied by a higher allowable income for the recipients of the means-tested pension. In 1962, the permissible incomes for both single and married pensioners were raised.[26]

The progressive relaxation of eligibility requirements for the old age pension started in the 1950s and early 1960s and culminated in a significant change in the eligibility structure that completely universalized the old age pension. Until 1965, the qualifying age as the main requirement for receiving pension benefits had been seventy years. With the amendment to the Old Age Security Act in 1966, the qualifying age was reduced by one year per year until it became sixty-five in 1970.[27] The 1966 amendment to the act further liberalized the residency requirement. If a potential pensioner had not resided in Canada for ten years immediately preceding the submission of his or her application or was unable to offset the ten years by prior residence equal to twice the aggregate absence from Canada, the individual was still eligible if he or she had "resided in Canada after attaining eighteen years of age and prior to the day on which his application [was] approved for an aggregate period of at least forty years."[28]

After 1967, the basic universal pension payment was subjected to an upward adjustment in accordance with "multiplying the basic amount of such pension ... by the ratio that the pension index for that year bears to the pension index for the year 1967."[29] In 1971, the escalation of OAS benefits was removed and payment was frozen at $80 per month. In 1972, the upward adjustment of OAS payments was tied to the annual cost of living indexation (the increase in the consumer price index); this was subsequently replaced by a quarterly indexation in 1973. In accordance with the 1972 amendment, the payment of OAS was to be suspended for those who had resided outside Canada for six consecutive months, and would be resumed whenever the pensioner returned to Canada. However, if the pensioner had resided in Canada for twenty years after attaining the age of eighteen, his or her pension payment was exempt from such suspension.[30] In tandem with the progressive reduction of the age qualification and the corresponding progressive removal of means-tested pension benefits, the federal government gradually extended its authority over the financing and administration of the old age pension – a process that was complete by 1970.

The universalization of the old age pension in 1965 was accompanied by the introduction of the Guaranteed Income Supplement (GIS) in 1967. The GIS was designed to enhance the living conditions of the recipients of the universal pension who had been born on or before 1910 and who had little or no income except the old age security pension. In accordance with the provisions of the 1967 Act, the supplement amount was set at "forty per cent of the amount of the pension that may be paid to him for that month, minus one dollar for each full two dollars of his monthly base income."[31] In the calculation of income for a monthly supplementary benefit, other benefits under social assistance, and under worker's compensation legislation, war pension, disability, and gifts, were excluded.[32] With the removal of the date of birth as an eligibility criterion in 1970, the payment of the GIS to the recipients of the universal pension came to be solely determined by marital status and level of household income. Furthermore, no pensioner was to be completely disqualified unless his or her outside income exceeded double the maximum supplementary payment.[33] For the purpose of calculating income for GIS payments, income was defined as any money that "a pensioner receives in the form of an earnings-related retirement pension, interest, dividends, rents, wages, etc."[34] With respect to GIS payments, old age security pension, death benefits under the Canada/Quebec Pension Plan (C/QPP), home insulation grants, and provincial and territorial income supplements and welfare payments were exempt from the calculation of income.[35] The basic income above which the maximum monthly supplementary benefits would be reduced for both single and married pensioners was set at 1/12 and 1/24 of total income.[36] For single pensioners, the maximum monthly supplementary income was to be reduced by $1 for every $2 above the basic income. For married pensioners, the maximum monthly supplementary pension was to be reduced by $1 for every $4 above the basic income.[37]

During the 1970s, the Old Age Security Act was subjected to two significant amendments that were conducive to ameliorating the living conditions of elderly people. To improve the income of pensioners, the Spouse's Allowance (SPA) was introduced in 1975. In the 1975 amendment, the spouse of a pensioner was eligible for an allowance if he or she had not separated from the pensioner and had attained at least sixty years of age. The payment was to be halted when the spouse of the pensioner reached the age of sixty-five and, therefore, was eligible for Old Age Security. The monthly amount of spousal allowance was to be determined by the calculation of the couple's family income, which did not take into account the OAS pension and the GIS.[38] In 1972, the GIS maximum was increased in accordance with changes in the annual cost of living.[39]

In a further attempt to address the difficulties encountered by some elderly people who did not qualify for OAS due to residency requirements, the payment of a partial pension based on years of residency was introduced in 1977. According to the 1977 amendment, any person who was not eligible for a full monthly pension payment was permitted to receive a partial pension if he or she had attained sixty-five years of age and had resided in Canada after attaining eighteen years of age for an aggregate period of ten years but less than forty years.[40] In accordance with the 1977 changes in the residency requirement, full pension benefits would only be available upon the attainment of a maximum forty years of residency in Canada. In line with the 1977 amendment to the Old Age Security Act, partial benefits at the rate of 1/40 of the full pension for each year of residence after attaining eighteen years of age became payable to elderly people residing in Canada between ten and forty years.[41]

A progressive relaxation of eligibility criteria that culminated in the complete universalization of OAS in 1970 was correspondingly translated into a progressive increase in the percentage of elderly people who became eligible for the old age pension. As observed in table 5.2, after the universalization of OAS in 1970, almost all of those aged sixty-five and over became eligible for the benefits.

Second and Third Tiers

The postwar expansion of the non-contributory old age pension in Canada, which is regarded as the first tier of the retirement income system, was accompanied by other attempts to enhance the living conditions of elderly people. As in other liberal welfare systems, the purchasing of life insurance, government annuities, and tax-assisted employer-sponsored private occupational pension plans, known as Registered Pension Plans (RPPs), was encouraged as a means of supplementing state-provided flat rate benefits. In addition to this, tax-sheltered Registered Retirement Savings Plans (RRSPs) were introduced in 1957.[42] In the late nineteenth and mid-twentieth centuries, private occupational pension plans and individual life insurance had become a growing component of income retirement planning.[43] However, the growth of private occupational pension plans (reflected in private occupational expenditures as a percentage of the GDP and the percentage of workers covered by these employer-sponsored arrangements) was slower in Canada than in other countries such as Australia.[44] The growth of tax-subsidized private occupational pension plans and individual life insurance did not prevent Canada from establishing a publicly administered compulsory earnings–related pension plan. This established itself as the second pillar of the retirement

Table 5.2 Percentage of aged Canadians receiving non-contributory flat rate old age pension, 1930s–1970s

Year	%
1931	10
1941	24
1961	71
1971	95
1976	98

Sources: Calculated from F.H. Leacy, ed., *Historical Statistics of Canada* (2nd ed.) (Ottawa: Statistics Canada, 1983); and Canada, *The Income Security Programs of Health and Welfare Canada* (Ottawa: Ministry of Supply and Services Canada, 1983)

income system in Canada. Consequently, voluntary savings through RPPs and RRSPs became the main components of the third pillar of the Canadian retirement income system.

Despite the growth of private occupational pension schemes, private arrangements were not viewed as an effective mechanism for securing retirement income for Canadians. In the words of Judy LaMarsh, the Liberal health and welfare minister in the 1960s, the main purpose of a Canada-wide compulsory earnings-related pension plan was to overcome the shortcomings of private occupational pension plans and, thereby, to "provide elderly Canadian citizens with some measure to meet their retirement needs."[45] The implementation of a universal and comprehensive system of contributory retirement pensions was the outcome of prolonged deliberation and debate as well as intense federal–provincial negotiations. The second pillar of the Canadian retirement system, known as the Canada/Quebec Pension Plan, was enacted in 1965 and came into force in January 1966. The Canada and Quebec pension plans were set to be administered separately; even so, they have been brought into harmony through a series of agreements between the federal and Quebec governments. As a result of this coordination between the two plans, "benefits from either plan are based on pension credits accumulated under both, as if only one plan existed."[46]

As comprehensive social insurance for retirement income encompassing old age, survivor, death, and disability benefits, the C/QPP made it compulsory for both employees over eighteen and the self-employed to make contributions to the plan; they would then receive old age benefits in accordance with their past contributions. For participating employees, the rate of contribution was initially fixed at 1.8 per cent % of earnings between the basic exemption and the ceiling; this was to be matched by equal employer contributions.[47] The self-employed who participated were required to pay the full 3.6 per cent of their earnings. To ease the burden on low-income workers, a year's basic exemption (earnings below which contributions to the plan were not required) was introduced and was matched by the inclusion of a year's maximum pensionable earnings (the maximum earnings on which contributions to and benefits from the plan were determined). In 1965, the basic income exemption and earning ceilings were respectively set at $600 and $5,000; these in turn were subject to adjustment thereafter in accordance with the earning index.[48]

In line with the plan's provisions, the rate of retirement benefits was to be calculated at 25 per cent of an employee's adjusted average pensionable earnings over his or her contributory period. In accordance with the 1965 act's provisions governing retirement benefits, the payment of full retirement benefits was to commence in 1975. During the ten-year transition period, eligible retirees were to receive less than full benefits, which were set at 10 per cent of the potential maximum retirement benefits for each year between 1966 and the year of retirement.[49]

With respect to the impact of an increase in the cost of living on pension benefits, the 1965 act provided a provision for an annual increase in the level of retirement benefits. The 1965 C/QPP also specified a retirement test for pension eligibility. While the age of seventy was established as a requirement for receiving retirement benefits, the act nonetheless provided a basis for the progressive reduction of the qualifying age for pension benefits so that they could not be claimed at sixty-five until 1970.

The C/QPP also provided for disability and death benefits and the surviving spouse's pension benefits. In line with these provisions, the spouse of a deceased contributor would be entitled to receive monthly pension benefits equivalent to 60 per cent of the deceased contributor's retirement pension if the surviving spouse was over sixty-five.[50] If the surviving spouse was younger than sixty-five, the monthly benefit was composed of a flat rate component and an earnings-related component equivalent to 37.5 per cent of the actual retirement pension of the deceased contributor.[51] Under the CPP, if the survivor was younger than thirty-five years and she or he was not disabled and had no dependent children, he or she would not receive any benefits.

Unlike the CPP, the QPP retained its commitment to pay a survivor's pension to a non-disabled eligible spouse without dependents who was under thirty-five. In accordance with the 1965 act, the payment of surviving spouse pension benefits would be terminated if the spouse remarried.[52] Under the disability provisions of the 1965 act, any individual who lost his or her capacity to continue working due to mental or physical disability was entitled to receive monthly disability benefits. The disability benefits were set to be composed of a flat rate component unrelated to previous earnings contributions and an earnings-related component set at 75 per cent of his or her actual retirement benefits that he or she would have been entitled to receive during retirement. The disability benefits would be converted to retirement pension once the recipient reached the age of sixty-five. Under the 1965 act, the main qualification governing the disability and surviving spouse pension benefits was a requirement that the deceased contributor or the disabled individual had contributed to the plan during at least one-third of the numbers of calendar years in his or her contributory period. In line with the 1965 act, a lump sum of death benefits equal to six times the monthly retirement pension of the deceased contributor would be paid to his or her surviving spouse or next of kin, in that order. In addition to survivor, disability, and death benefits, the C/QPP provided for payments of benefits to the dependent children of deceased and disabled contributors as long as they were under eighteen or were full-time students aged eighteen to twenty-five. The first payments of retirement pension, survivors' benefits, and disability pensions began respectively in 1967, 1968, and 1970.[53]

In 1973, significant changes were made to the C/QPP, which came into force in 1974. The most crucial change to the structure of the original act was related to a simultaneous increase in the levels of the year's basic exemption and maximum pensionable earnings. While the 1965 Act called for an increase in the earnings ceiling by $100 a year, the 1973 legislation set the earnings ceiling for 1974 and 1975 at $6,600 and $7,400 respectively. Parallel to an increase in the earnings ceiling, the basic earnings exemption was increased from $600 to $700, and was set at 10 per cent of maximum pensionable earnings. Under the 1973 amendment, future increases in the earnings ceiling were set at 12.5 per cent a year until the ceiling reached the average earnings indicated by the Statistics Canada Industrial Composite of wages and salaries.[54] The 1973 amendment also repealed the 2 per cent limit on the annual adjustment of retirement benefits and replaced it with an annual adjustment in line with the increase in the full cost of living.

During the 1970s, the C/QPP underwent further progressive amendments. In line with the provisions of the 1965 act, the termination of regular employment was a compulsory requirement for receiving retirement benefits. In 1975, this retirement and employment earnings test was repealed and the CPP no longer required individuals between sixty-five and seventy to desist from regular employment in order to be eligible for retirement benefits. The same elimination of the retirement test was adopted by the QPP in 1977.[55] The 1975 amendment also stipulated the availability of retirement benefits for widowers and widows as well as their dependent children. In 1978, following the inclusion of credit splitting between ex-spouses in the QPP in 1977, the CPP introduced a provision that called for the division of pension credits between ex-spouses after a divorce or legal annulment of marriage.[56]

Greater state involvement in the provision of the old age pension, and less emphasis on private arrangements as a device for securing retirement income for elderly people, signified the prevalence of the principles of collectivity and universality in Canada's pension system. Private occupational pension schemes might signal freedom and individual responsibility, but they lack the crucial elements of community solidarity, caring, and progressive benefits redistribution embedded in a publicly administered compulsory social insurance program. While an earnings-related compulsory pension scheme nominally signifies a direct correlation between benefits and past contributions and, therefore, grants greater benefits to those who have earned more, it nevertheless contains built-in mechanisms of community solidarity and progressive benefit redistribution.[57] A publicly administered compulsory pension plan is also redistributive in the sense that it redistributes income to certain groups such as those with low wages and a larger number of dependants. Furthermore, a compulsory contributory earnings–related public pension plan is progressively redistributive since, under such a plan, "low income workers are granted a much higher return on their tax contribution than high income workers."[58] The solidarity dimension of a state-administered compulsory pension plan lies in the fact that all individuals stand together and contribute to a plan, which is designed as a device for pooling the risks and providing benefits to covered individuals upon the occurrence of certain predesignated losses such as old age, disability, and death.

By complementing the non-contributory universal flat rate Old Age Security pension with a compulsory earnings-related public pension plan, the Canadian retirement income system distinguished itself from its Australian counterpart, which remained based solely on selectivity principles and private occupational pension plans. The universalization of Old Age Security and the establishment of a universal compulsory earnings-related public pension plan in Canada were shaped largely by the political character of the postwar social class settlement.

The Postwar Social Settlement and the Canadian Pension System

As in Australia, postwar social reconstruction in Canada was launched by the Canadian state to ameliorate class antagonisms and thereby weaken the impact of radical socialism on the political order. Also, postwar reconstruction was designed to integrate the marginalized population by deploying national resources to provide social welfare programs. When Old Age Security was introduced in 1951, Paul Martin, Sr, the health and welfare minister in the Liberal cabinet of Louis St Laurent, viewed the enhancement of social income security for elderly people as part of a broader social welfare policy mechanism to combat the threat of radical socialism: "You cannot triumph over communism by force alone; that in the long run the victory over that ideology will be won by the determination of the free nations of the world to use their own capacities ... to provide within reasonable limits for social welfare of the masses of the people. That is what we are doing in this program."[59] A few days later in the House, Martin affirmed: "Canada's old age security program is a symbol of our determination to work for the well-being of all our citizens. This humanitarian action like every measure for social progress, help, to counter communism."[60]

The postwar political pressures leading to the adoption of social welfare policies provided a unique opportunity for the Canadian state to turn social policy into a mechanism for national unity, which has historically been threatened by the clash of nationalisms. To overcome the regional fragmentation compounded by the historical confrontation between Canada and Quebec, the Canadian state used the postwar reconstruction of the welfare state as a "cement" for the social union and harnessed social welfare programs to nurture national bonds. The employment of social welfare policy as a linchpin for national unity was intended to secure citizens' allegiance to the nation. This was, in turn, conducive to galvanizing the discourse of universalism. The emerging policy discourse around national unity was used to eclipse the language of class on the terrain of political struggle. The competition between nationalisms through the employment of social welfare policy helped cement the linkage between social citizenship and the principle of universalism. Paradoxically, the discourse of national unity and the competition for citizens' allegiance strengthened the position of the Co-operative Commonwealth Federation (CCF; later the New Democratic Party, NDP) as it amplified its calls for the universalization of retirement income. The CCF's strengthening call for universal social programs was compatible with the national discourse on social welfare policy. In other words, the fragmentation of the labour movement and the political weakness of the CCF/NDP were to some extent offset by the political imperative of employing universal and comprehensive social welfare policy as a tool for national integration. Such a discourse became an ally of working-class politics at a time of growing demands for a universal pension system.

Unlike in Australia, where the major debates over the postwar welfare state were taking place in the federal Parliament, the details of the expansion of existing social programs and the establishment of new programs in Canada were hammered out at intergovernmental forums, which were then brought to Parliament for ratification. The 1945 Dominion–Provincial Conference on Reconstruction – according to Mackenzie King, "the most important Canadian conference since Confederation" – served as a grand foundation on which the structures of social welfare programs were built. As pointed out, the Canadian state did not commit itself to accomplishing full employment through state intervention in business cycles; rather, Keynesianism in Canada continued to give a prominent role to the private sector as the engine of economic expansion. As Prime Minister Mackenzie King pointed out, "without excluding actions by the state, the reconstruction programs of the federal government are deliberately designed to encourage and foster employment-creating enterprise by individuals and corporations."[61] The Canadian state kept the focus of postwar social reconstruction on social welfare programs and found it politically imperative to provide goods and generous services as a way of building loyalty to the Canadian state. Due to Canada's politicized ethnic cleavages, a universal and generous pension system became much more tangible and effective than full employment in fostering citizens' allegiance to the national state.

As a blueprint for reconstruction in Canada, the 1945 Dominion–Provincial Conference focused on the details of social welfare programs and fiscal arrangements between the two levels of government with the aim of harnessing these programs to nurture national bonds. In his concluding remarks to the 1945 conference, King pointed to the intent of the Canadian state to employ social reconstruction as a tool for strengthening national unity:

> I wish in conclusion to emphasize anew that the fundamental purpose of this conference is to strengthen all the participating governments, provincial as well as the Dominion. Only in this way can we all work effectively towards the common goal of ensuring a strong, a united and a happy Canada. I am convinced that the future of our country depends upon its unity and strength as a nation ... We know that our country cannot make its full contribution to world peace and prosperity unless its government is strong and its people united.[62]

Almost two decades later, Lester Pearson, the Liberal prime minister, reiterated Mackenzie King's concern by emphasizing the maintenance of national unity as the first "among our national goals – prerequisite to all others, economic, social or cultural."[63] Even though the expansion of social security programs was often rationalized by the Canadian state as an essential tool of Keynesian demand management, social income security was simultaneously deemed indispensable to national unity. The postwar social settlement in Canada was thus given a "political character" in the sense that socio-economic restructuring was not based solely on labour market regulation. Rather, social welfare expenditures served as a device for enhancing a common sense of national unity across Canada. Echoing the statements by Prime Minister Mackenzie King and other premiers, J.B. McNair, the New Brunswick premier, identified the overriding objective of postwar social reconstruction as an attempt "to develop in the hearts of the people of Canada a feeling of oneness, a sense of nationhood."[64] During the 1945 conference, Brooke Claxton, the national health and welfare minister, highlighted social security programs as a mechanism of national integration:

> The Government believes that social security proposal which it is setting before this Conference would make a threefold contribution. They would provide a network of protection for the Canadian people that justifies itself on social and humanitarian grounds. They would provide an important degree of protection to buttress the nation's economy as a whole, in times of stress and strain. Less tangible perhaps, but in some ways most important of all, they would make a vital contribution to the development of our concept of Canadian citizenship and to the forging of lasting bonds of Canadian unity.[65]

A decade later, Claxton's statement on the linkage between social welfare policy and national unity was echoed by A.W. Matheson, the Prince

Edward Island premier during the 1957 Dominion–Provincial Conference. He reminded his colleagues that among all national policies, it was social welfare policy that "would contribute most to national unity and national spirit."[66] It is clear from the stated aims of the 1945 Dominion–Provincial Conference that the Canadian state associated the welfare state with social and national citizenship. The integration of Canadians was to be fostered by explicitly constructing citizenship rooted in social policy entitlements. A logical corollary of using social welfare policy as an instrument of national unity was "universalism" as a conceptual reflection of common national standards integral to citizenship. The need to adopt the principle of universalism had already been alluded to by the Rowell–Sirois Commission in 1930s, which called for the unification and equalization of services across Canada.[67] It was a direct ramification of converting social income security into a tool of national integration that the Dominion government identified the means test as "undesirable after a certain age" and regarded "the payment of pensions as [a] right."[68] After pointing to the shortcomings and residual character of the 1927 Old Age Pension Act, the federal government outlined its twofold proposal to overhaul and expand the existing old age pension program:

> (a) National Old Age Pensions at age 70
> It is proposed that the federal government would establish a system of National Old Age Pensions entirely financed and administered by the federal government, and paid at the uniform rate of $30 per month regardless of means to men and women of aged 70 and over in all parts of Canada.
>
> (b) Dominion–Provincial Old Age Assistance at age 65–69
> In addition, it is proposed to provide old age assistance for persons of ages 65–69, in cases of need and in accordance with local conditions and individual circumstances, under a Dominion–Provincial agreement broadly similar to those presently existing with respect to old age pensions for persons of age 70 and over. The proposal is that the provincial governments should administer the old age assistance and that the federal government should contribute 50 per cent of the cost.[69]

Building national identity and thereby securing citizens' allegiance to the nation through social welfare policy required the federal government to assume responsibility for providing the old age pension. Based on this political calculation, the Dominion government in 1945 proposed eliminating the means test. In the Dominion government's view, eliminating the means test "would make it possible for these pensions to be administered by the federal government alone on a uniform national basis."[70] It was because the federal government intended to use social welfare policy and public social expenditure to enhance its national image, particularly in Quebec, that Maurice Duplessis, the Quebec premier, fiercely criticized the centralizing tendency of the Dominion proposals as "the death [of] the confederated system."[71] From the beginning, Quebec nationalists resented the employment of social welfare policy by the Canadian state to enhance its own image across Canada, for it worked against the Quebec state's project of galvanizing French identity. Furthermore, for Quebec, the concept of "national standards" implied the presence of "one nation." This was construed by Quebec nationalists as leaving no room for the Quebec nation within Canada. The conversion of income security provisions into a nation-building mechanism by the federal government was seen by Quebec nationalists as a deliberate attempt to undermine the appeal of Quebec nationalism and thereby assimilate French Canadians. As Quebec's Tremblay Commission pointed out in 1957, "as far as the assimilation of French Canada is concerned, thirty years of social policy will thus have had more effect than a century and half of political history."[72]

The federal government's proposals for progressive improvements to the old age pension and the eventual elimination of the means test provided effective ammunition for the CCF and progressive labour organizations, especially the Canadian Congress of Labour, which had long called for the enhancement of the social wage, and for pensions in particular.[73] To bolster their struggle to eliminate the means test, labour centres and the CCF referred to the 1945 Dominion proposals as legitimate and as officially endorsing their case for universal principles. In its remarkable 1947 campaign to eliminate the means test on pensions, the CCF circulated a nationwide petition that received the signatures of 256,282 individuals. On 15 May 1947, M.J. Coldwell, the CCF's national leader, tabled the party's petition in the House of Commons. It called on MPs to:

(a) provide pensions no less than fifty dollars per month at the age of sixty five;
(b) eliminate the means test;
(c) provide in addition to the basic pension, a sort of living supplement, invalidity supplement, and free medical, dental, optical and hospital care;

(d) provide that all such pensions be paid in full from the dominion treasury.[74]

In 1950, referring to the 1945 proposal of the Dominion government to eradicate the means test, the CCL launched a massive postcard campaign to remind MPs of the promise that had been made in 1945.[75] In their fight to universalize the old age pension, CCF MPs also grounded their arguments in the Dominion government's 1945 proposals. In his attack on the Liberal government's procrastination in implementing those proposals, CCF MP Alistair Stewart asked: "If that [universalizing of old age pension] was the government proposal why has the government not implemented it? Why does the government not put that proposal into action?"[76] In his call for the abolition of the means test, Angus MacInnis, a CCF MP, reminded the Liberal government of Louis St Laurent that "the country came very close to having the means test abolished in 1945."[77] Stanley Knowles, a CCF MP and an ardent defender of the universal pension principle, urged the government to adhere to the pledge made in 1945: "One of those offers, one of those promises with which the people of Canada are familiar, is the offer made in August 1945 with respect to old age pension ... [I]t was to be payable at the age of seventy to all Canadians, without any means test, and it was to be financed and administered entirely by the federal government.[78]

Both the Liberals and the Progressive Conservatives occasionally raised the need to install a contributory pension plan as a precondition for eventually abolishing the means test. During the 1950 debate on the old age pension, Prime Minister St Laurent specified the position of the Liberal Party: "the only practical way in which an old [age] pension scheme without a means test could be provided is through a direct contributory system."[79] Similarly, Conservative MP Donald Fleming called for the elimination of the means test "in favour of a contributory scheme."[80] In contrast to the Liberal and Conservative parties, Stanley Knowles of the CCF stressed the 1945 Dominion proposals in which the call for the abolition of the means test was not tied to a nationwide contributory plan; he insisted on a two-tier system for old age income.[81] The Liberal government's delay in implementing its predecessor's pledge, and the position of the Progressive Conservative Party, to a great extent reflected the opposition of business organizations towards increasing pension payments, which were perceived as a threat to corporate profits.[82] The escalation of pension costs ensuing from the abolition of means test was perceived by business organizations as a burden on their community.

The delay in implementing the 1945 Dominion proposals for the old age pension was also questioned by some provincial premiers during the 1950 First Ministers' Conference.[83] Growing public desire for the elimination of the means test, galvanized by the CCF's constant references to the 1945 Dominion proposal as an official statement in favour of eradicating the means test, also generated strong support within other political parties. By the 1950s, despite differences in their political orientation towards the issue of the old age pension, there emerged a unanimous agreement among the three main political parties to tackle the means test. In conjunction with the CCF's insistence on eradicating it, the Conservatives pressured the Liberal government to expedite its policy action on the old age pension. Donald Fleming accused the Liberal government of resorting to a "Fabian tactic" in devising ways to evade the issue.[84]

The mounting pressures ultimately led to the announcement by the Liberal government that it would establish "a Joint Committee of both Houses to examine and study the operation of old age security in Canada."[85] After extensive public hearings, and evaluating various submissions and examining the related jurisdictional conflict between the two levels of government, the Joint Committee submitted its unanimous recommendations on 28 June 1950. The Joint Committee's recommendations were in line with the twofold plans that had been proposed by the Dominion–Provincial Conference of 1945. Regarding the debate over the introduction of the Old Age Assistance Act and the Universal Old Age Security Act, which were passed by the House of Commons in 1951, Paul Martin heralded these acts as "the greatest single advance made in this country in our [Canadian] provisions for senior Canadians."[86] The ensuing 1951 constitutional amendment allowed Parliament to make laws relating to the old age pension without affecting the operations of any law of a provincial legislature in relation to old age pension. Even though Martin commended his own government for choosing a midway position between the two extremes,[87] the passage of those two acts reflected the 1950 Dominion–Provincial agreement. In his opening statement to the 1955 Federal–Provincial Conference, Prime Minister St Laurent congratulated the provincial premiers: "In the field of social security, in regards to old age pensions we completed in 1951 what had been aimed at in 1945."[88]

The 1951 constitutional amendment provided jurisdictional grounds for joint and separate undertakings by the federal and provincial governments in the field of old age pensions. Following this constitutional amendment, the debate on old age security shifted to the establishment of a publicly administered contributory pension plan, which had already been contemplated in the 1940s and 1950s. The policy grounds for installing the social insurance plan were framed by Harry Cassidy's *Social Security and Reconstruction in Canada*[89] and Leonard Marsh's 1943 *Report on Social Security for Canada.*[90] Cassidy and Marsh, who had been influenced by British Fabian principles, were able to articulate the social and economic imperatives for comprehensive social insurance in Canada along lines similar to those of the Beveridge plan. Prime Minister Mackenzie King, for his part, felt he had already "anticipated" Beveridge's version of social income security in 1918.[91] By 1960, a universal earnings-related pension plan had generated interest among all the main political parties, labour groups, and even some business organizations.[92] The main opposition to a universal contributory pension scheme came from life insurance companies, who viewed it as adversely affecting their ability to sell private pension plans.[93] According to Stanley Knowles, life insurance companies were "enemies of the CPP" that had launched "disgraceful" campaigns against the CPP.[94] Life insurance companies contended that a publicly administered universal earnings-related pension plan would deprive companies of massive capital and trigger a corresponding increase in the costs of private pensions. J.G. Connor,[95] manager of insurance and pensions with the Steel Company of Canada, and a member of the Canadian Manufacturers' Association Committee on Portable Pensions, outlined the main reasons why insurance companies objected to a universal contributory public pension plan:

1 The cost of employer contributions to the Canada Pension Plan less any offsets which may result from adjustments to Private Pension plans.
2 Higher private plan costs if higher levels of Public Pensions makes earlier retirement particularly attractive.
3 That massive diversions of money from the private to the public sector of the economy may endanger the private capital formation required for necessary growth.
4 That the existence of such public pension funds may invite future extension of or increase in benefits without due attention to the costs.

Capitalizing on the general social consensus on the desirability of a publicly administered universal earnings-related pension plan, and on the 1951 constitutional amendment that empowered the national government to enact laws relating to the old age pension, Lester Pearson's Liberal government introduced a motion in the House of Commons on 18 July 1963. On introducing the motion on the Canada Pension Plan, Judy LaMarsh, the health and welfare minister, extolled the proposed universal public pension plan "as one of the most important and far reaching plans of action put forward by this or any other government."[96] She characterized the proposed plan as "comprehensive social insurance ... which provides help as a right rather than on a need or a means-test ... for those ... unable to carry on work." After highlighting the shortcomings of proposed provincial-based pension schemes, particularly that of Ontario, for failing to provide comprehensive coverage, she hailed the proposed nationwide public pension plan as an effective tool to guarantee universality and comprehensiveness. Since universal Old Age Security had acquired political acceptance across Canada, Pearson praised the proposed public pension as a second-tier old age income retirement plan designed to supplement, not replace, the universal OAS.[97] The introduction of the CPP as a supplementary scheme to the universal OAS was praised by Knowles as a crucial "step in moving into a new phase of social security in Canada."[98] The Liberals' move to endorse social security measures that had long been advocated by the CCF/NDP inspired Knowles to convey his party's satisfaction with the course of action: "I say quite frankly that we were delighted when the Liberals started talking in language similar to ours ... I call on her [Mrs LaMarsh] to launch various programs of education ... to sell the idea of the Canada Pension Plan."[99]

After minor modifications, the original draft of the CPP was tabled in the House Commons as Bill C-75 in 1964. In the House of Commons, there was a unanimously positive attitude towards the bill across the political spectrum; however, the plan's fate was not to be determined in Parliament. Setting aside the views of life insurance companies, the main challenge to a publicly administered universal pension plan arose from the clash of visions held by the federal, Quebec, and Ontario governments. Ontario was tepid about the federal proposal and promoted a private pension system. Quebec's vision was quite different from the federal one.[100] Pearson's diplomacy was able to overcome Ontario's opposition to the federal proposal.[101] However, the plan's ultimate shape reflected the exigencies of national unity. The competition between the Canadian state and Quebec, both of which set out to use a universal contributory pension scheme to shift citizens' allegiances towards their respective nation-building projects, culminated in a much more progressive and comprehensive public pension plan, one that was superior to what had first been proposed by the Liberal government.

The most formidable opposition to a nationwide universal contributory pension plan emanated from Quebec, which in the 1960s saw the socio-political transformation known as the Quiet Revolution, during which nationalists demanded that the province be harnessed as an instrument for nation-building. With the transformation of a passive and inward-looking nationalism into a more assertive, state-led nationalism in the 1960s, the Quebec government intensified its opposition to federal intrusion into its jurisdiction. The idea of establishing a publicly administered pension plan as an economic development tool was a typical product of the Quiet Revolution. Quebec's control over its own public pension plan was identified as vital to the process of nation-building launched by Jean Lesage's Liberal government in 1960. The Quebec government viewed the QPP reserve fund as a powerful weapon in its financial arsenal that would galvanize the growth of domestic industries – growth that was seen as a prerequisite for French Canadians' cultural development.[102] Lesage pointed out that the QPP's reserve fund "was very important for financing of government, hydro and municipalities."[103]

Quebec's administrative authority over its own pension fund was thus seen as essential to domestic economic development; it was also seen as "nationalist" glue for bonding Quebecers emotionally to their own province. In René Lévesque's words, it was the only "tool" that French Canadians "could really call their own."[104] According to the Quebec Pension Plan Committee Report, "the intention behind the Quebec Pension Plan is to place Quebecers in social conditions proportionally equivalent to those prevailing" in other countries.[105] The Lesage government was determined to use the public pension funds as an instrument of economic and social development. For the Quebec government, an autonomous public pension plan would symbolize the distinctiveness of Quebecers and serve the project of building Quebec identity.

Quebec's determination to control its own pension plan was bolstered by the 1951 constitutional amendment regarding old age pensions. The amendment vested constitutional authority in Ottawa to enact laws relating to the old age pension, but it also left room for provincial governments to exercise authority such pensions. During the Federal–Provincial Conference of 1963 held in Ottawa, Premier Lesage declared that the Quebec government was determined to establish its own public pension plan: "It has been known ... that Quebec refused that the Canadian

Pension Plan apply to its citizens. In this case we have elected to stick to the spirit of the contracting out formula and we shall institute in Quebec, a system which will be provincial, public universal."[106]

Quebec's quest for investment capital to finance its nation-building project brought it into direct confrontation with Ottawa. The competition between Canada and Quebec came to a head during the 1964 Federal–Provincial Conference, held in Quebec. The fate of the CPP as proposed by the federal government, and Quebec's threat to launch its own pension plan, dominated the conference's agenda. Sensing a threat to the Canadian federation, Prime Minister Pearson called for a re-examination of social welfare programs that would be "based on a look at the future and a full regard for the confederation which will truly maintain and strengthen the unity of our country in the years ahead."[107] At the same conference, Premier Lesage reiterated Quebec's strong preference for the opting-out formula and for the establishment of its own pension plan – a plan he deemed much more comprehensive than the one proposed by the federal government. Lesage presented his pension plan to the conference delegates in what LaMarsh later described as "a real bombshell."[108] Tom Kent, policy secretary to the prime minister, described the presentation of Quebec's pension plan by Lesage as a calculated move to eclipse the proposed CPP: "Jean Lesage came out with a much more attractive plan, wider in the scope of its benefits, on balance good, but funded, therefore capable of producing savings available to provincial governments for social capital. The response in the conference was electric. Lesage handled it very, very cleverly, there was no question that at that moment the Canadian Pension Plan was dead."[109]

Quebec's proposed public pension plan was so attractive because it could function as a reserve fund for economic development. Other provincial governments quickly noticed this.[110] To retain the Canada-wide character of the CPP and simultaneously accommodate Quebec's demands, Pearson launched a strategic operation that went far behind the mandate of federal–provincial conferences. The rescue team was composed of Tom Kent and Maurice Sauvé, the newly appointed forestry minister. As the political linchpin between Ottawa and Quebec, Sauvé was advised by the prime minister to carry out the mission "in great secrecy."[111] In Quebec City on 7 April 1964, the team engaged in secret negotiations with Quebec officials, including Premier Lesage. Their intense negotiations led to an agreement in principle, which was divulged to the public on 11 April 1964 when the Quebec delegation visited Ottawa to finalize the agreement. The revelation that an agreement had been negotiated in secrecy infuriated Judy LaMarsh: "I remember picking up a framed photograph ... of Mike [Prime Minister Pearson] and slamming it down on the desk and broke its face ... I really felt humiliated. Pearson never explained that to me and never did, in fact, discuss it with me."[112] Sauvé argued that the goal of the agreement was to deflect the threat of disruption to the Canadian federation:

> It was a reconciliation of the proposal that Quebec and the federal government had made on the Canadian Pension Plan, and we found ways of reconciling both which would give the province of Quebec and the rest of Canada a good pension plan with some possibilities for the provinces, if they so chose, to administer their own. It was in a way an opting-out formula applied to the Canadian Pension Plan. We came to full agreement on this.[113]

The national reconciliation over the CPP allowed the opting-out formula to become something of a provincial right and an accepted practice of federalism in Canada. The opting-out formula granted to Quebec became an option for all other provinces; in the end, though, no other provincial government sought administrative control over its own public pension plan. John Robarts, the premier of Ontario, the most financially powerful province, thought "it would be very divisive for the country as a whole" if Ontario used the opting-out option to install its own public pension plan.[114] Tom Kent has clarified how considerations of national unity propelled Robarts to accept a national pension plan:

> Mr. Robarts never received as much praise as he deserved for his willingness to put the Canadian national interest first. But large-minded as he was, his course would have been much more difficult ... if he had not been helped by Mr. Pearson's diplomatic persuasiveness, reflecting as it did the force of a concern for national unity that the two men shared. Without that quality ... a national pension plan for Canadians would have not been established.[115]

The opting-out formula for the pension plan came to be regarded as a logical mechanism of national accommodation since it sustained national standards of social services through coordination rather than centralization. National accommodation allowed Quebec to exercise jurisdiction over its own pension plan; at the same time, the harmonization of the two plans allowed the CPP to retain its universal and national character. Accommodating Quebec was key to the CPP's eventual success. As NDP MP Knowles pointed out, "the Canadian Pension Plan without that separate right for Quebec would not have succeeded."[116] The integration and harmonization of the two plans in terms of coverage, contributions, portability, and benefits became the basis for the final articulation of the CPP known as Bill C-136. The proposed bill was assailed by Social Credit MPs, who characterized the plan as "socialist and communist-inspired legislation of the worst kind" and as "a further step towards communism."[117] Setting aside these insignificant attacks, the unanimity among the main political parties allowed the Liberal government to pass the Bill on 29 March 1965.

Although the bill's contents were debated in the House of Commons, the features of the CPP were shaped mainly by Quebec's proposed pension scheme. Indeed, the federal government adjusted its own plan to Quebec's, which was more generous and comprehensive than the proposed federal counterpart. Walter Gordon, Pearson's finance minister, stated plainly that the "federal government agreed to change its Canadian Pension Plan to the Quebec style."[118] As table 5.3 shows, the competition over citizens' allegiance and the imperative of national unity led to the passage of a universal public pension plan that was much more progressive than what the federal government had previously proposed.

It can be seen that political competition over the nation-building project, and the ensuing national accommodation between the federal and Quebec governments, resulted in coverage, contributions, rates of replacement, and other related social benefits that went beyond the federal proposals. A universal contributory pension plan had positive ramifications for the flat rate non-contributory old age pension. As a natural corollary of the established qualifying age for public pension benefit eligibility, the age of eligibility for Old Age Security was to be progressively lowered to sixty-five by 1970. Reducing the age qualification to sixty-five had already been envisaged in the 1945 Dominion–Provincial Conference.[119] As a result of the progressive reduction of the age qualification for OAS, means-tested Old Age Assistance was bound to be discarded by 1970. During the 1965 Federal–Provincial Conference in Ottawa, Prime Minister Pearson heralded the gradual move towards complete elimination of the means test applied to OAS benefits: "[O]ld age assistance ... will be unnecessary after 1969, because of the progressive lowering of the age of eligibility for Old Age Security. Pensions at or above the old–age assistance level will then be available as of right, without a test of need for all Canadians over the age of sixty-five, provided only that they have the necessary length of residence in Canada."[120]

National reconciliation over the CPP entailed the consent of Quebec to a constitutional amendment that would allow the federal government to make laws on survivors' benefits that fell under provincial jurisdiction.

Table 5.3 Reconciliation between the proposed Canada and Quebec pension plans

Main features	Bill C-75 (initial federal proposal)	Quebec Committee Report (Quebec's proposal)	Bill C-136 (revised C/QPP)
Coverage	Compulsory for employees, voluntary for self-employed	Compulsory for employees and self-employed earning more than $1,000 a year	Compulsory for employees earning more than $600 per year and for self-employed earning at least $800 per year
Transition	10 years	20 years	10 years
Earning ceiling	$4,500 a year in first 5 years (adjustable thereafter)	$6,000 a year in first two years (adjustable thereafter)	$5,000 per year in 1966 (adjustable thereafter)
Basic exemption	Nil	$1,000 a year	$600 per year
Employee contribution rate	1% of earnings up to ceiling for first 15 years, upward revision thereafter	2% of earnings between basic exemption and ceiling	1.8% of earnings between basic exemption and ceiling, matched by same percentage by employers
Qualifying age	Unconditional at 70; retirement test at 65–9	Unconditional at 70; retirement test at 65–9	Progressively reduced from 70 in 1965 to 65 in 1970
Rate of benefits	20% of average adjusted earnings	25% of average adjusted earnings	25% of average adjusted earnings
Other benefits	Pension for surviving spouse at 65	Broad range of survivor, death, and disability benefits	Broad range of survivor, death, and disability benefits

Sources: Adapted from Kenneth Bryden, *Old Age Pensions and Policy-Making in Canada* (Montreal and Kingston: McGill-Queen's University Press, 1974); and Quebec Pension Legislation, 1965.

Also, it became a constitutional imperative that any change in the CPP would require the approval of two-thirds of the provinces with two-thirds of the population. This constitutional requirement for amending the CPP was instrumental in bringing Ontario in line with a national pension plan.[121] Parallel to the universalization of Old Age Security that brought the entire first tier of income security in retirement under federal control, the federal government retained the Guaranteed Income Supplement (which had been designed to operate for ten years, at which point the CPP would have reached its maturity to provide the full benefits) as another tool in its arsenal to maintain its direct relationship with Canadian citizens. The "national setting" and federal structure of the Canadian state also favoured the retention and expansion of the GIS, because unlike the reforms to the C/QPP over which provincial governments had veto power, it was completely under the control of the federal government. The concern of the federal government with the constitutional powers of provincial governments over elements of social income security was the main force behind the retention and subsequent extension of the GIS as an effective tool at its disposal for maintaining its relationship with Canadian citizens.

The federal government's concerns about the long-term implications of provincial powers over social welfare programs were echoed by Prime Minister Pierre Trudeau during the Constitutional Conference of 1971. Trudeau raised alarm by pointing out that provincial jurisdiction over social welfare programs "would over the years lead to an erosion of federal income security programs and their replacement by purely provincial plans" that would have adverse implications for national unity.[122] Trudeau's concern underlined the federal government's preoccupation with retaining the allegiance of Canadians towards the national state and countering the appeal of Quebec nationalism.[123] This necessitated the direct involvement of the national government in delivering social income security benefits to Canadians. In other words, maintaining ties between Ottawa and Canadian citizens through the provision of federal social services came to be identified as key to fostering national identity across Canada.

Conclusion

The postwar expansion of the retirement income system in Canada came to be characterized by universal flat rate Old Age Security as first tier, coupled with a publicly administered contributory social insurance program as the second tier and private arrangements as the third tier. The postwar trajectory of retirement income in Canada was structured by the postwar social settlement that manifested itself in a redistributive-oriented welfare state. In contrast to Australia, where social protection came to hinge on harnessing market forces to achieve full employment, which reinforced the principle of residualism, social income security in Canada was to be secured through a nationalist project of social welfare policy. While the political discourse of national unity eclipsed the language of class, the imperatives of national unity paradoxically galvanized the voices of federalist and pro-labour forces, which called for a generous and universal old age pension system. The social settlement in Canada reinforced the linkage between social citizenship, national identity, and the universality and collectivity dimensions of the retirement income system.

Moreover, in contrast to the vulnerability of the postwar social settlement of Australia to economic instabilities, the social settlement in Canada was less susceptible to the retrenchment pressures of neoliberalism that followed the economic crisis of the 1970s. Under the social settlement in Canada, the decline in the bargaining power of labour in the era of neoliberalism was in part offset by the discourse of national unity that partly shielded the welfare state from the neoliberal process of income security retrenchment. It is to this process of welfare state retrenchment, and the divergent patterns of pension adjustments between Canada and Australia, that this book now turns.

6 Welfare State Restructuring and Neoliberal Variations in Canada and Australia

It has become a common theme in the welfare state literature that the 1970s saw the beginning of a significant shift in the politics of the welfare state. The economic crisis of the 1970s provided an opportunity for the emergence of neoliberalism and the transformation of the postwar settlement. Since the 1980s, the welfare states of the advanced capitalist societies have faced ongoing restructuring and retrenchment. Changes in the balance of social forces in favour of the business classes, and the restructuring of the state's role, have meant a tough time for social welfare programs.

The transformation of the welfare state should not be construed as the *demise* of the welfare state or as a full-frontal assault on the postwar social settlement. But welfare state transformation is reflected in the alteration of the existing frameworks within which social welfare services are provided. No welfare state has been immune from neoliberalism, but the intensity of welfare state restructuring and retrenchment has been marked by variations across nations. These divergent patterns are reflected in differences in the levels of recommodification and privatization and in the degree of the shift from universality to selectivity.

Variations in welfare state restructuring reflect different national forms of neoliberalism as well as differences in the intensity of neoliberal inroads into social welfare policy. Both Canada and Australia experienced an embrace of the neoliberal paradigm in the 1980s and its consolidation by the mid-1990s. In both countries, right-wing think tanks and business organizations used the economic crisis of the 1970s to reshape social and economic policies so as to give more sway to market forces. However, the speed and the nature of neoliberal consolidation differed in these two countries. In Australia, the discourse of "economic rationalism" became a basis for implementing neoliberal principles; in Canada, pro-market forces capitalized on the imperatives of free trade with the United States and decentralization of governmental power as tools to facilitate the adoption of neoliberal policy. In Australia, the neoliberal push for recommodification, the privatization of retirement income, and the shift to selectivity gained significant momentum. In Canada, by contrast, neoliberal pressures to privatize retirement income and to eradicate the universality principle have failed.

This chapter has five sections. The first outlines the economic contraction in the 1970s that led to the rise of neoliberalism as a socio-political project. The second analyses the general impact of economic restructuring on the welfare state. The third discusses the emergence of neoliberalism and its impact on social welfare policy in Australia. The fourth focuses on neoliberalism's impact on social welfare policy in Canada. The final section prepares the ground for explaining the variations in retirement income restructuring in Australia and Canada in the two chapters that follow.

Economic Crisis and the Triumph of Neoliberalism

The Keynesian-based postwar social class compromise fell apart with the economic convulsions of the 1970s. Keynesian demand management had difficulty coping with the simultaneous rise in unemployment and inflation known as "stagflation."[1] The inability of Keynesian demand management to overcome stagflation dashed the golden age of three consecutive decades of capitalist growth and prosperity across Western states.[2] Economic instability provided an opening for the New Right to launch a theoretical attack on the foundations of Keynesianism.[3] The core of the New Right's ideology is "an economic doctrine which gives supremacy to free markets as a method of handling not only the economic affairs of nations, but also a political ideology which can be applied to all manner of government issues."[4] As an ideological project, the New Right sought to transform the political and economic foundations of the postwar social class settlement.[5] The breakdown of the postwar social settlement, and the ensuing demand by capital for social welfare retrenchment, also indicated "the limits of reform within capitalist democracies."[6]

The rise of the New Right in 1980s challenged the Keynesian framework across a variety of dimensions. Analysts have employed the terms neoconservatism and neoliberalism interchangeably to describe the ideology of the New Right. Although the term neoliberalism has become prevalent in political discourse, the tenets of the New Right were first put into a political formula by Conservative governments on both sides of the Atlantic.[7] Neoconservatism was intended to revive and embrace two elements of different traditions that had been eclipsed by the post-war success of Keynesianism.[8] As an ideological framework, neoconservatism attempts to combine the classical liberal theory of the free market economy with the social traditionalism of classical conservatism.[9] The classical liberal component of neoconservatism regards a free market economy as society's focal principle for economic activities. It is assumed that the maximization of self-interest emanates from a market that operates on the basis of free competition and the laws of supply and demand. While the economic liberalism of neoconservatism praises "rugged individualism," the classical conservative component of neoconservatism preaches moral values, order, stability, preservation of family, and community cohesion.[10]

Neoconservatism is full of contradictions. A striking contradiction of neoconservatism relates to the formidable task of creating an affinity between the classical liberal doctrines of the economy, which emphasize a "free market," and the social traditionalism of classical conservatism, which emphasizes family and community cohesion. A lasting affinity between classical liberal economic doctrines and the social traditionalism of classical conservatism is chimerical, for the centrifugal propensity of the former tends to corrode the basis for preserving the latter. It seems contradictory to call for the revival and maintenance of moral norms, family spirit, and community cohesiveness while simultaneously leaving members of the same community at the mercy of market forces. Greater latitude for market forces is bound to undermine the social structures upon which family and community cohesion can be maintained. While these two elements of neoconservatism are contradictory in theory, they complement each other in practice. Desmond King has commented on the internal unity between the two components: "Liberalism is the source of New Right economic and political theories and policy objectives; conservatism provides a set of residual claims to cover the consequences of pursing liberal policies. For example, the liberal objective of reducing public welfare provision implies a traditional role for women and family; conservatism provides an ideology justifying such outcomes from public policy."[11]

The rise of the New Right was a class-motivated response to a shift in the balance of class power towards the hitherto marginalized strata – a shift that had been encouraged by Keynesian policies.[12] The institutionalization of collective bargaining and the expansion of social programs during the 1950s and 1960s reflected a balance of power between labour and capital that weakened the absolute sovereignty of market forces.[13] As logical corollaries of Keynesianism, state intervention in economic activities and the expansion of social programs were regarded by the dominant classes as a threat to their hegemony.[14]

Within the discourse of economic and social welfare restructuring, most commentators use neoliberalism as an explanatory concept since the social traditionalism component of the New Right has lost its momentum. As Hartman has pointed out, neoliberalism should be understood "as an economic doctrine which gives supremacy to free markets as a method of handling not only the economic affairs of nations, but also a political ideology which can be applied to all manners of government issues."[15] The origins of neoliberal ideology can be traced back to the 1940s and 1950s, a time when Keynesian ideas dominated political discourse throughout the West. Intellectuals like Friedrich Hayek and Milton Friedman equipped early neoliberal commentators with ammunition to assault the Keynesian paradigm.[16] Hayek and Friedman linked market forces to the enhancement of individual freedoms as a general law of capitalism.[17] As classical liberal disciples of Adam Smith, Hayek and Friedman identified state intervention in the economic sphere as a direct infringement on individual freedoms. Through their intellectual arguments, Hayek and Friedman attempted to confine the state within the boundaries of the "night watchman" state that had been delineated by Smith in the eighteenth century. According to Hayek and Friedman, the state's role should be confined to defending the nation against external threats, maintaining social order, and providing certain goods and services that cannot be provided by the market.[18]

During the 1940s and 1950s, pro-market intellectuals, financed by the business community, established several think tanks whose goals were to expound the virtues of a free market economy in Europe and North America. Hayek was instrumental in mobilizing pro-market intellectuals to counter the growing momentum of Keynesianism.[19] In a letter sent to invitees to the first meeting of the Mont Pelerin Society in 1947, Hayek declared the need for an intellectual campaign to counter Keynesian ideas as a direct threat to individual liberty:

> Our goal ... must be the solution not of the practical task of gaining mass support for a given programme, but to enlist the support of the best minds in formulating a programme which has the chance of gaining general

> support. Our effort therefore differs from any political task in that it must be essentially a long run effort, concerned not so much with what would be immediately practical, but with the beliefs which must regain ascendancy if the dangers are to be averred which at the moment threaten individual freedom.[20]

The postwar intellectual crusade of neoliberal thinkers was, however, neutralized by the very success of Keynesianism during the postwar boom. The economic crisis of the 1970s challenged Keynesian macroeconomic management. The Keynesian response to stagflation proved to be not only ineffective but also counterproductive.[21] This provided an opportunity for neoliberal ideology to link the economic contraction to Keynesian policies.[22] Because of the susceptibility of Keynesian policies to right-wing attacks, the neoliberal doctrines of political economy triumphed as alternative public policy. In the capitalist welfare states, market-oriented neoliberal policies gradually rose to the top of the agenda of governments of all political and ideological stripes.[23]

With the rise of neoliberal doctrines of monetarism and supply-side economics, a wave of economic restructuring was encouraged; this included policies of deregulation and privatization as well as the removal of barriers to trade. These market-centred neoliberal policies shifted the balance of social forces towards capital. They also suggested that the state and capital accumulation were structurally interdependent.[24] The imperatives of competitiveness, the new emphasis on labour market flexibility, and the threat of capital flight became powerful weapons in the arsenal of businesses to discipline labour and to push for concessions in wages and working conditions.[25]

The replacement of Keynesian demand management by monetarism also heralded a shift in the locus of state authority from direct state intervention in the management of industrial conflict to the application of monetary policy to discipline labour through non-political agencies such as the central bank.[26] This shift in policy frameworks also meant a depoliticization of industrial confrontation management through "neutral" economic management. During the Keynesian era, managing relations between capital and labour had required direct state intervention. Under the Keynesian paradigm, the pursuit of tight anti-inflationary targets by the state was bound to exacerbate class conflict and, therefore, industrial confrontation, which took the form of a crisis of political authority.[27] By transferring authority for financial stability to formally independent agencies such as the central bank, the state externalized the imposition of disciplinary measures on labour and thereby depoliticized the industrial confrontation between capital and labour.[28]

The welfare state, which had been extolled as a measure of social development and as the missing link between capitalist production and social peace, now came to be identified as an impediment to economic growth. Social welfare programs that had been enacted as palliative measures to deflect the threat of radicalism were now interpreted as blocking capital accumulation.[29] Monetarism and supply-side economics became pivotal tools of neoliberalism to discourage progressive redistributive policies and encourage deregulation, labour market flexibility, upward redistribution of income, and privatization of publicly owned corporations. These neoliberal measures blocked the pursuit of further progressive social reforms.[30]

The shift from Keynesianism to neoliberalism should not be construed as a sign of decline in the power of the state over the market, but only as a change in its role. In other words, the ascendancy of neoliberalism should not be interpreted as an outright assault on the state in favour of the market, for "neoliberalism has operated through the institutions of the state."[31] Contrary to the discourse of the New Right, neoliberalism is less about smaller government than about shifting government's focus, techniques, and priorities.[32] State adaptation to the rhythms of market forces is not equivalent to a lessening of the state's power.[33] The state has remained central to facilitating and maintaining capital accumulation, both national and international.[34] The state's neoliberal restructuring role has accentuated the social power of the dominant classes and reduced the capacity of the subordinate classes to use the state as a tool to enhance their social positions.

By invoking the global imperatives of competitiveness, governments have justified subjugating redistributive policy to the demands of market forces.[35] The general adherence to fiscal restraint by governments reflects the contraction of the ideological landscape "into a singular view of what is to be considered as legitimate economic and social policy."[36] The shift in the balance of social forces and political terrain has even dragged labour and social democratic parties into "the magnetic field of their opponents."[37] As Albo has pointed out, "it is a cold hard fact of contemporary politics that regimes of different political stripes have all endorsed capitalist globalization ... We get neoliberalism even when we elect social democratic governments."[38] On the emerging ideological landscape, even social democratic and labour parties have internalized "the necessity of adapting to international market and the austerity policies that capital has demanded." They have, in turn, attempted to adulate their own technical capacity to "administer the neo-liberal policies that match[] market imperatives."[39]

The restructuring of the welfare state must be understood in the context of a socio-economic environment within which its role as a mechanism of social protection was bound to shift. As Gilbert has pointed out, "a fundamental change in the nature of capitalism whether to an advanced stage or a new form is likely to be accompanied by substantive changes in the character of social protection."[40] Under neoliberalism, the adaptability of government, labour, community, and social programs to the imperatives of market discipline has been seen as a historical necessity.[41]

Neoliberalism has not led to the demise of the welfare state.[42] The rhetoric of dismantling the welfare state is often used to "disguise a fundamental reliance upon forms of governance [neoliberal] which incorporates major elements of what has come to be known as the welfare state."[43] A reshaping of the welfare state, not its abolition, has been the neoliberal impact on social welfare policy. As Stein Kuhnle has observed, "cutbacks in social security and welfare programs ... have on average been modest during the 80s and 90s, and real social expenditure has ... in some places substantially increased."[44] There is also no evidence to corroborate the supposed convergence of a reduction in business taxes across the OECD countries, as has confidently been asserted by many welfare state analysts.[45] The ascendancy of the discourse of restraint in social welfare policy has come to reflect itself in the social policy practices of restriction (controlling budgetary growth), retrenchment (reorganizing the budgetary priorities of government and cutting some of resources of the base budgets of particular programs), privatization (ceding public involvement to the private sector), and vertical downloading (pushing social responsibility to lower levels of governments or the third sector).[46] Although these social policy practices of fiscal restraint have not signalled the end of the welfare state, welfare state restructuring has been accompanied by increases in both income inequality and poverty in most advanced industrialized countries.[47]

But the changes in the framework of social welfare provisions do reflect a fundamental change in normative views on the proper relationship between the state and the market economy. This has culminated in a new policy landscape on which the market is praised as the most effective allocator of resources and provider of social security benefits. This fundamental conversion in normative views about the interaction between the state and the market implies a shift in conception – from the state as provider of social goods to the state as guarantor of access to social goods, that is, the "enabling state."[48] As Dexter Whitfield has observed, the enabling state refers to "a model of government in which the state facilitates and supports but services are primarily provided by private and social economy."[49]

The normative view of the state's role as "enabling" has been accepted by the OECD since the 1990s. The OECD has called for a new orientation of social policy in which government serves not as the "provider of largesse" but as a partner with active, self-sustaining individuals.[50] A social democratic vision of the enabling state that has as its motto "the state should not row but steer" has also permeated the discourse of "Third Way" politics.[51] The emerging conceptualization of the enabling state implies a reorientation of the state's role in providing social protection. That reorientation is reflected in market-centred social policies in education, reskilling, and training that prepare the labour force for the demands of the new, knowledge-centred economy. The enabling state is also manifest in certain regulatory frameworks such as private arrangements for retirement benefits and welfare-to-work schemes through which access to social goods is secured.

The Three Dimensions of Welfare State Restructuring

The focus on cost containment and cost-cutting associated with the change in the conception of the state as enabling has translated into a shift from universality to selectivity, recommodification of labour, and privatization of social protection. The shift from universality to selectivity has been the most significant change in the framework of social welfare income security.[52] The use of selectivity in determining welfare benefits points to a retreat from universalism (generally seen as a defining characteristic of the ideal welfare state). During the postwar expansion of the welfare state, universalism came to be closely associated with the social rights of citizenship. The replacement of the universal provision of social services with means/income-tested social benefits signified a clear change in the character of the welfare state. During the period of welfare expansion, the link between universalism and social rights had been envisaged as a means to enhance inclusion and solidarity within a national community.[53] With the rise of neoliberalism, the fragility of the social rights component of citizenship has become evident.

The postwar emphasis on universality was a response to the selectivity of poor law relief. The discourse on welfare state restructuring has come to be dominated by the need to adopt selectivity as the most effective response to constrained fiscal circumstances.[54] Selectivity is predicated on the assumption that allocating national resources to those in need is still consistent with low levels of social expenditure and minimal disturbance of the market economy.[55] This entails directing social benefits towards those in greatest need, instead of towards all elderly people or children whatever their incomes. Targeting is justified on the basis that the redistributive impact of a given volume of social expenditure is greater when social benefits are targeted at low-income groups. But the shift from universalism to selectivity is also associated with the revival of social stigma for those on welfare or who are covered by state pensions.

The replacement of universalism by selectivity in old age pension policy has been achieved by restricting the criteria of eligibility, targeting benefits to low-income elderly people, flattening the benefits rate, and clawing back benefits through taxation.[56] Based on the data provided by Gilbert, between 1980 and the mid-1990s, income- and means-tested expenditures as a percentage of total social security increased sharply in most OECD countries.[57] This shift towards selectivity in the social policies of the advanced industrialized countries continued to gain momentum in the 2000s.

Recommodification is another prominent trend in neoliberal welfare state restructuring. Under neoliberalism, recasting social welfare policy along employment-centred lines has become a guiding principle for the social protection of the poor, the unemployed, and even the aged. The recommodification of labour results from subordinating public income supports to a series of rules and coercive measures to steer people back to work through tightening eligibility and reducing the duration of social benefits. These regressive practices have become widespread in advanced industrialized countries.[58] This reshaping of the links between economic and social policy is interpreted as an employment-friendly social policy and is advanced by neoliberals as indispensable to social protection. Compelling able-bodied recipients of social benefits to take jobs has become a pervasive social welfare policy development.[59]

In the guise of reducing demographic pressures on public pensions, retaining elderly people in the labour market through work incentives has become a growing dimension of retirement income restructuring.[60] First, removing incentives that encourage early retirement is emphasized as essential for maintaining the financial sustainability of the pension system.[61] The extension of working time is further justified by increasing life expectancy. It is also viewed as an effective strategy to compensate for a "shortage" of workers due to the aging of the population.[62] Finally, labour recommodification has manifested itself in the push for the abolition of early retirement and for raising the retirement age. This includes making the retirement age flexible and penalizing early receipt of pensions.[63]

As a political and institutional strategy for reshaping labour market policy, workfare schemes have become a prominent component of social welfare policy in advanced industrialized countries.[64] Tightening the eligibility criteria for social security benefits, including adopting workfare schemes to compel the poor to undertake work-related activities in order to receive social benefits, constitutes a decisive departure from the postwar development of the social right to state benefits.[65] In capitalist countries, engaging in work-related activities has become a requirement for accessing social benefits. Labour force participation has become the route to social citizenship.[66] As Dahrendorf has pointed out, under neoliberal welfare restructuring, "rights are dissolved into marketable commodities."[67] This qualitative break with the past has also marked the social protection mechanisms in Scandinavian countries, once known for their decommodifying social welfare measures.[68] Reform of the pension system and the privatization and market orientation of social care (reflected in a decline in the supply of home care and a sharp decrease in the number of institutional beds despite the rise in number of elderly people) have undermined the Swedish model.[69]

The recommodification of labour in welfare-to-work initiatives and the prolonging of employment are both intended to restore the authority of market forces. These welfare-to-work policy measures intensify the competition between the reserve army of labour and the employed workforce. Compelling the poor and the unemployed to re-enter the labour force reflects the neoliberal ideology that welfare benefits foster dependency on the state. By this line of neoliberal reasoning, welfare benefits sow dependency and indolence, which weaken self-reliance and individual initiative.[70] Compelling the poor and unemployed to take jobs by tightening eligibility criteria for social benefits is thus seen as an appropriate response to the overgenerosity of the postwar social welfare state.

The growing acceptance of the neoliberal definition of self-reliance is an attempt to repersonalize social responsibility for economic outcomes. The push to repersonalize social responsibility has been internalized even by many protagonists of the Third Way politics of social democracy. The slogan "no rights without responsibilities" we hear in Third Way politics has been adopted by social democracy as a means to recommodify labour. Third Way politics has accepted the imperatives of withdrawing and restricting welfare benefits as disciplinary mechanisms to coerce the poor and unemployed into re-entering the labour force.[71] The prevailing social democratic discourse on combating poverty and inequality by shifting emphasis from redistribution of income to the redistribution of possibilities (education and training-centred policies) as a means to enhance "social inclusion" is a form of the neoliberal compulsion to repersonalize social responsibility.

As part of the recommodification process, another trend in welfare state restructuring has been the privatization of the old age pension. The growing momentum to privatize social security is evident in the spread and growth of private arrangements for old age income. Although tax-assisted private occupational and personal arrangements for retirement income have historically constituted a component of general provisions for old age income, expanding the scope for privatizing retirement incomes has become a hallmark of welfare state restructuring. As Gilbert has observed, "without much fanfare, old age pensions in a number of countries are marching on steady course of incremental privatization."[72] The privatization of retirement income is reflected in the levels of tax expenditures on private occupational and personal arrangements for old age pensions. These trends have been on the rise in most of the advanced capitalist countries.[73] The privatization of old age pension is in line with the World Bank's exhortation for governments to place greater emphasis on privately managed government-mandated pension schemes as an effective strategy to reduce future pressure on public finances.[74]

The move towards privatizing income security is presented as an attempt to lessen the growing cost of retirement incomes on the public purse. This justification is in line with the enabling state paradigm and with expanding the scope of private sector activity so that individuals take responsibility for their own retirement income. The privatization of income security, which emphasizes the liberal ethos of choice and individual responsibility over collectivity, is reminiscent of the nineteenth-century classical liberal value of individualism. The transformation of the welfare state should thus be understood as a fundamental alteration in the framework within which social welfare income protection and services are provided. Differences in the pace and level of recommodification, selectivity, and privatization provide a basis for comparing the degree to which welfare states have been subjected to neoliberal transformation.

The 1970s economic contraction was acute in both Canada and Australia, yet each country pursued a different road to neoliberalism. As

Table 6.1 Unemployment in Canada and Australia, 1980–2010 (%)

Country	1980	1985	1990	1995	2000	2005	2010
Australia	6.1	8.2	6.9	8.4	6.7	5	5.2
Canada	7.5	10.1	8.1	9.4	6.8	6.7	7.9

Source: OECD, *World Economic Outlook* (September 2011) (Paris: 2011).

noted in chapter 4, in contrast to Australia, where achieving full employment was an official policy during the era of welfare state expansion, Canada tolerated higher levels of unemployment. As shown in table 6.1, the levels of unemployment in both countries began to rise in the second half of 1970s. In the 1980s, a general pattern of neoliberal social and economic policies became prevalent in both countries. By the mid-1990s, however, the pace and nature of neoliberal inroads were different between the two countries.

The Rise of Neoliberalism in Australia

After the 1970s, pro-business organizations engaged in popularizing neoclassical tenets of the free-market economy against Keynesian demand management. In Australia, the revived neoclassical ideas that prevailed in the debate about economic recovery came to be known as "economic rationalism," and these ideas shifted the political and economic agenda to the right.[75] Within the discourse of economic rationalism, social welfare programs and the postwar expansion of the public sector were identified as the main culprits behind mounting public debt that was contributing to economic decline.[76] The discourse of economic rationalism, which moved from think tanks to the upper echelons of the bureaucracy, emphasized the self-regulating tendencies of the market and its inherent capability of achieving equilibrium.[77] Underlying the discourse of economic rationalism was a strong policy framework to replace Australia's traditional interventionist policy "by an aggressive market-worshipping economic rationalism" that promoted "a laissez faire minimalist state."[78] The economic crisis manifested itself by raising the levels of unemployment and social public expenditures; this in turn reinforced the "fight back" crusade among the right-wing movement, which called for privatization, the decentralization of industrial relations, a retrenchment of social welfare programs, and the removal of barriers to trade.[79]

Right-wing think tanks and business organizations in Australia were instrumental in advancing the cause of free market economy and rationalizing the need to curtail the welfare state. Before the 1970s, there had been only a few right-wing think tanks, such as the Institute of Public Affairs (IPA), involved in articulating the right-wing agenda.[80] The effectiveness of these think tanks had been overshadowed by postwar economic prosperity. Even the IPA at the time endorsed state intervention in the economy and emphasized the imperatives of social welfare programs.[81]

The economic crisis of the 1970s led to the proliferation of right-wing think tanks in Australia.[82] Besides the IPA (established in 1943), two new think tanks, the Centre for Independent Studies (founded in 1976) and the Tasman Institute (founded in 1990), became advocates for neoliberal policy.[83] Both contended that the welfare state was a source of dependency, cultural laziness, and family disintegration.[84] Both deployed cultural explanations for poverty and disadvantages in Australian society, arguing that as a result of the welfare state, the poor had lost their initiative and had abandoned their obligations to family and community.[85]

The solutions proposed included cutting social welfare expenditures, enhancing self-reliance, and transferring the paternalistic roles of the state to private and community organizations. The IPA, for example, vigorously advocated replacing the existing welfare state provisions with "private welfare," which in its view "returns to taxpayers control over their own incomes and widens their freedom of choice."[86] The IPA's endorsement of "private welfare" echoed the calls already made by the Centre for Independent Studies.[87] In advocating private welfare, James outlined the virtues of the IPA's proposal for Australia:

> Private welfare is not just more efficient than state welfare; it embodies a different ethos. It encourages individuals to take primary responsibility for their own and their families' welfare, and to exercise some direct responsibility for the welfare of others. It recognizes that whatever residual role the state retains in distributing welfare, the sole source of welfare lies in the spontaneous and diverse activities of private individuals and their free-formed associations.[88]

In tandem with the intensification of right-wing think tank activities, the economic turmoil of the 1970s moved Australia's fragmented business organizations towards relative unity. Until the late 1970s, the national and sectoral organizations representing the interests of the business community in Australia had been marked by fragmentation.[89] Despite many attempts, Australian employers failed to form a nationally based umbrella organization.[90] However, fragmentation of the business community did not mean that business organizations did not coordinate their struggle against the labour movement whenever their long-term interests were threatened.[91]

Until the early 1980s, there were three main national associations representing the interests of business community: the Australian Council of Employers' Federations, the Associated Chambers of Manufactures of Australia, and the Associated Chambers of Commerce of Australia.[92] The rivalries among these three national business groups in the field of industrial relations reduced their capacity to form an overarching organization that could counterbalance the ACTU. As Matthews has pointed out, until the 1980s "no single association enjoyed a dominant and unchallenged position as the voice of business or as the voice of employers."[93]

The economic events of the 1970s and deliberations within the ranks of corporate executives led to the emergence of the Business Council of Australia (BCA) in 1983 as the most prominent business group representing the executives of leading Australian corporations.[94] During the successive Labor administrations from 1983 to 1996, the BCA established its authority as "the generator of broad business strategy on public policy questions."[95] After 1983, the BCA attempted to reshape industrial relations by shifting them towards a decentralized and enterprise-based bargaining system.[96] The BCA's rise was also a response to the growing influence of the ACTU. Through the merger with previously competing confederations of white-collar unions and ideological reconciliation within the labour movement, the ACTU had achieved growing authority and control over organized workers.[97] The BCA's advocacy of major reforms to industrial relations was a response to structural changes in the international economy; it was also "an attempt to wrest the initiative in the debate about the structural adjustment policy and industrial relations policy from the ACTU."[98] However, unlike the right-wing think tanks that had adopted a radical stance on restructuring the welfare state, the BCA took a pragmatic and incremental stance towards reshaping social and economic policy in terms of market forces.[99]

The push was from the right, yet the implementation of neoliberal principles in Australia was in fact carried out under Labor governments between 1983 and 1996. Even though the economic crisis had emerged during the Liberal coalition led by Malcolm Fraser between 1975 and 1983, Fraser's government made few unpopular decisions despite declaring itself the champion of economic rationalism.[100] As Kelly has pointed out, Fraser "was never a monetarist, never a Margaret Thatcher."[101] In spite of the anti-Keynesian monetarist rhetoric prevalent during the Fraser administration, "the Fraser Government still resorted to Keynesian economics in an attempt to break a particularly deep recession."[102] Under the Liberal coalition government, deficit reduction was accomplished by raising levels of taxation rather than cutting social welfare expenditure.[103] Social welfare reform revolved mainly around changing the Medibank system, linking the indexation for people over seventy to their income level, and restraining wages in the hope of curtailing inflation and creating jobs.[104]

Changes to the Australian welfare state that reflected a shift towards selectivity and expanding the scope of privatization of the retirement income system were implemented by the Labor administration. Before its election in 1983, the Labor Party had reached an agreement with the ACTU regarding incomes and prices. The pre-1983 election Income and Prices Agreement between the ALP and the ACTU provided the basis for a series of accords that were concluded over the Labor administration from 1983 to 1996. The accords were designed to secure wage restraint in an exchange for "a general commitment by government to consultation with unions and specific support for an agreed package of economic and social policies."[105] The accords shaped the basic framework for implementing neoliberal social and economic policies that had been vigorously advocated by right-wing think tanks.

After its electoral triumph, the Labor government undertook several measures that were in line with neoliberal ideas. Floating the dollar, reducing tariff protection for manufacturers, deregulating the financial system, and removing restrictions on the movement of capital were all market-friendly economic policies implemented by Bob Hawke's Labor government.[106] Some of these market-oriented economic measures, such as the deregulation of the financial system, undercut the policies of the Liberal Party, which had long called for such measures but had eschewed their implementation.[107]

The accords between the Labor government and the ACTU paved the way for a gradual shift from a centralized wage determination system to "enterprise bargaining," which had long been espoused by right-wing think tanks and business organizations, particularly the BCA.[108] With the Industrial Relations Reform Act of 1993, the Labor government for the first time removed the monopoly of unions over collective bargaining by allowing employers to negotiate collective agreements directly with their employees and then having those agreements certified without unions being involved.[109]

To reduce social welfare spending, as was being advocated by right-wing think tanks and business organizations, the Labor governments (1983–96) implemented several drastic measures intended to reshape the entire edifice of the Australian welfare state. The Labor administration also made several crucial changes to the rules and regulations governing the provision of social welfare programs. In 1995 the Labor government introduced the New Start Scheme designed to link unemployment benefits to compulsory training, revoked the traditional notion of the unemployment benefit as an entitlement, and introduced "mutual obligation" measures to tighten eligibility and make beneficiaries more accountable.[110] Also under the Labor administration, a fierce campaign was waged against welfare fraud, surveillance intensified, and eligibility was increasingly linked to commitment to labour force participation through the government's labour market strategy.[111]

The implementation of neoliberal policies by the Labor government provided strong legitimacy to the subsequent right-wing Howard government's aggressive pursuit of market-oriented social and economic policy throughout the second half of the 1990s and early 2000s.[112] Under Howard's Liberal coalition, which came to power in 1996, neoliberal principles acquired general political hegemony. The recommodification and more stringent targeting of social welfare benefits that had been launched by the Labor government were accelerated by the Howard government. Cutting spending on social services, attacking "incentives" to welfare dependency, introducing a "work for dole" scheme for the young unemployed, and contracting out employment training programs to the private sector were all measures implemented by the Liberal coalition government.[113] The Howard government intensified the process of welfare state restructuring.[114] The extension of "contractual welfare obligation" involved the compulsory social and economic participation of social welfare recipients, as well as extending the boundary of the "mutual obligation." There were also further reforms to industrial relations, which reduced the role of Industrial Relations Commission and gave greater power to employers in bargaining relations.[115] Castles, who had once defended the Australian welfare state as the leader of the "Fourth world" of welfare state capitalism, has depicted the progressive inroads of neoliberalism into Australian social welfare policy:

> From the time of the Hawke Labor government onwards, the situation of the welfare beneficiary has been changing and changing for the worse. There has been increasingly more policing of benefit eligibility, with the strongest element of forced compliance on unemployment work test which

has become increasingly onerous to fulfill. Under the Howard government, the conditions of this test have become extremely strict, with an increasingly explicit moral justification that recipients must return something to society in return for their benefits.[116]

Thus, while pro-business think tanks and organizations seized the opportunity provided by the economic crisis in the 1970s to push for austerity measures, it was the Labor government that most ardently pursued neoliberal policies. The inclination of the Labor government to implement neoliberal measures provided greater legitimacy for the even harsher austerity measures adopted later by the Howard government.

The Rise of Neoliberalism in Canada

As in Australia, the economic turmoil of the 1970s provided ground for right-wing think tanks and business organizations in Canada to attack the welfare state. These pro-market organizations popularized neoliberal policies as the only alternative to Keynesian macroeconomic management. Historically, a strong belief in a dynamic private sector as the engine of economic growth has been a cornerstone of successive federal governments' economic policies. However, the economic crisis in the 1970s prepared the ground for right-wing policy advocacy groups and business organizations to intensify their struggles to restrict the state's redistributive role. As Carroll and Shaw have pointed out, the economic crisis of the 1970s even reshaped the policy orientation of institutionalized business think tanks such as the C.D. Howe and the Conference Board of Canada, which had previously endorsed more than minimalist social welfare programs.[117] With the shift in the balance of class power, leading corporate executives began to revive the doctrines of the nineteenth-century free market economy.[118]

The economic crisis of the 1970s also paved the way for greater integration and class cohesion and for a sense of unity among diverse business interests that had been fragmented during the Keynesian era. Until the 1970s, the Canadian business class was relatively disorganized and had no coherent plan of action in place. The Canadian Chamber of Commerce and the Canadian Manufacturers' Association "tended to be spokespeople for narrow sectoral interests [and] … appeared capable only of reacting negatively and after the fact to government politics and programs."[119] National associations of businesses such as the Chamber of Commerce, the Canadian Manufacturers' Association, and the Canadian Federation of Independent Businesses had not built a unified national business interest.[120] The rise of the Business Council on National Issues (BCNI) in 1976, as an organization of the chief executives of the leading corporations in Canada, heralded the emergence of a unified business front determined to remove social and economic impediments to market forces.[121] The council functioned as a "cross sectoral peak organization for business activism, explicitly seeking to construct policy consensus not simply for bankers or manufacturers, but for the entire bourgeoisie."[122]

Neoliberal think-tanks and business organizations such as the Conference Board of Canada, the C.D. Howe, the Business Council on National Issues, and the Fraser Institute waged their struggle through publications, research reports, and submissions to governmental forums to shift political debate.[123] Through interlocking directorships between different elements of capital and strong ties between Canada's corporate elites and right-wing think tanks, the neoliberal project steadily gained policy ascendancy in Canada.[124]

Policy measures such as wage restraints and tight monetary policy had already been adopted by the Liberal government of Pierre Trudeau in the second half of the 1970s.[125] But it was in the findings of the 1985 Royal Commission on Economic Union and Development Prospects for Canada (the Macdonald Commission) that Canadian business and government elites found justification for implementing neoliberal policy programs.[126] Established by the Liberal government in 1982, the Macdonald Commission's recommendations contributed to a major shift in Canadian political discourse with regard to social and economic policy measures at the national level.[127] The commission "succeeded in integrating policy reforms in numerous fields into a coherent discourse of market liberalization."[128] In his evaluation of the impacts of the Macdonald Commission on social and economic policy, Bradford asserts that its report remains "the essential conceptual reference point for the host of era defining policy innovations, ranging from continental free trade to restrictions on unemployment insurance and retrenchment of the federal role in social assistance, legislated between 1985 and 1997 by successive Conservative and Liberal governments."[129]

The Macdonald Commission's Final Report, released in September 1985, made many recommendations that would reshape Canada's political and economic landscape. Its key recommendations included a reduction of social welfare expenditures, an end to universality, a shift to targeted social benefits, and free trade with the United States.[130] Its conclusions and recommendations, which would guide successive federal governments, had been influenced by business interests. The interaction between business associations and the commission contributed to the development of a consensus on implementing free trade with the United States.[131]

The Macdonald Commission's recommendations for reforming income security programs and undertaking major retrenchments encountered some difficulties in implementation. Brian Mulroney's Progressive Conservative government partly succeeded in cutting social transfers and altering the tax structure so as to favour business interests, but it failed to consolidate the neoliberal revolution in Canada.[132] It did not set about reintegrating major income security programs such as the Guaranteed Income Supplement, the Family Allowance, federal housing programs, federal transfers to the provinces for social assistance, and the income support functions of Unemployment Insurance into a single income-tested social security program called the Guaranteed Annual Income, which the commission had recommended.[133] However, it did succeed in introducing certain changes to universal programs such as Family Allowance and Old Age Security, and it triggered a surge in the privatization of Crown corporations.[134]

The Macdonald Commission's recommendations for free trade with the United States provided an opportunity for proponents of neoliberalism to convert neoliberal tenets into acceptable political mandates in Canada. In Anglo-Saxon countries such as the United States and Great Britain, conservative administrations in 1980s employed nationalism as an ideological imaginary of a unified interest between capital and workers in order to secure a "strong state and free economy." Canadian neoliberals were, however, unable to raise the flag of nationalism to advance their agenda.[135] Canada's dual nature has complicated appeals to Canadian nationalism as a tool for attacking unions and welfare recipients. According to Whitaker, Canadian neoliberals had no room for invoking any "tribal demons of national chauvinism ... to build support for neo-liberalism."[136] Furthermore, neoliberal forces encountered difficulties delinking the Canadian state from universal and national services, which had established themselves as sources of Canadian national identity.[137] Limiting the national government's capacity to perform its traditional role of nation-building through redistributive policy would have been equivalent to undermining the basis for the national identity, which was indispensable to the realization of a "strong state and free economy."[138]

Neoliberal forces viewed free trade with the United States in 1989 as an indirect strategy to delink the national state from its redistributive role, which had been crucial to maintaining national unity. By constraining the national state's capacity to pursue collectivistic policies, the Free Trade Agreement (FTA) functioned as a "conditioning framework" for harmonizing social and economic policy across North America.[139] Furthermore, the Free Trade Agreement came to function as an effective means to force provincial governments to embark on market-oriented reforms, since they would have more control over policy initiatives.[140]

In conjunction with the free trade agreement with the United States and its extension to Mexico through the North American Free Trade Agreement (NAFTA) in 1993, decentralization of political power through the transfer of responsibilities for social programs to sub-national states was found to be another approach to translating neoliberal tenets into a successful political formula. Pursued as a strategy for reconciling historically ingrained national tensions, decentralization of political authority was compatible with the implementation of neoliberal policies. Indeed, the triumph of neoliberalism in Canada has manifested itself in the devolution and offloading of political responsibility for social programs to provincial governments.[141]

The Mulroney government failed to constitutionalize the principle of "provincialization." Nevertheless, the Liberal administration in 1990s pursued decentralization of political responsibility for certain social programs. The Chrétien Liberal government also found decentralization to be the most effective means to implement neoliberal-oriented social welfare policy. On their return to power in 1993, the Liberals began a crusade of deficit reduction through retrenchment, program cutbacks, downsizing of the public sector employees, and offloading of political responsibility for social welfare programs to provinces.[142] The major part of social welfare reform undertaken by the Liberal administration in 1990s involved integrating federal transfers for the Canada Assistance Plan (CAP), health services, and post-secondary education (PSE) into a single transfer scheme called the Canada Health and Social Transfer (CHST) in 1996.[143] The CHST was accompanied by the devolution of legislative authority to sub-national governments, with the federal government also reducing its transfers to provincial governments.[144] The cuts to federal transfers to the provinces were accompanied by further cuts as well as more stringent eligibility criteria for receiving social welfare assistance on the part of sub-national governments.[145] Political decentralization as a means to accommodate national tensions indirectly served the interests of the neoliberal forces, for it translated their goals into concrete policies. However, the neoliberal push to privatize social protection and intensify targeting did not succeed completely.

Conclusion

In both Canada and Australia, neoliberal think tanks and business groups used the economic crisis of the 1970s to justify restructuring social and economic policies to meet the imperatives of market forces. The inability of Keynesian demand management to reverse the economic contraction of the 1970s strengthened the position of the New Right in Canada and Australia as it set out to bring the neoliberal policy framework to the centre of welfare state politics.

In Australia, the imperatives of economic competitiveness as found in the discourse of economic rationalism injected neoliberal principles into government policy. In Canada, the free trade agreement with the United States and the decentralization of political authority to address the alleged fiscal imbalance became the main avenues along which neoliberal tenets entered the domain of social welfare policy. In both Canada and Australia, the neoliberal inroads into social welfare policy of the late 1970s were consolidated in the second half of the 1990s. But despite the neoliberal pressures for welfare state retrenchment in Canada and Australia, there were variations in the levels of recommodification and privatization of social protection as well as in the shift from universality to selectivity.

As will be demonstrated in the following chapters, the restructuring of pension provisions in Canada and Australia has followed these more general patterns of welfare state restructuring and retrenchment. In Australia, neoliberal welfare state restructuring manifested itself in a decisive shift towards selectivity and the consolidation of a state-mandated privately arranged retirement income program. In contrast to the Australian experience, the Canadian retirement income system largely succeeded in retaining its universal and collectivistic characteristics. As well, compared to the success of neoliberalism in Australia, neoliberal attempts to fundamentally alter the structure of the retirement income system in Canada were not translated into the political gains that pro-market forces had contemplated. Variations in responses to the neoliberal pressures for restructuring and retrenchment were to a significant degree shaped by the differences in the nature of the postwar social settlement in Canada and Australia.

7 Restructuring of the Pension System in Australia

With the political ascendancy of neoliberalism, restraining social welfare expenditures became a cornerstone of the Australian government's fiscal strategy. Although the pressures for welfare state restructuring began to emerge in the 1970s, it was after the 1980s that the public pension system became the object of restructuring and retrenchment. Neoliberal pressures for welfare state restructuring steered Australian social policy on retirement income towards consolidating state-mandated, privately managed provision of retirement income and reviving an intrusive, means-tested retirement pension system.

The retrenchment of Australia's retirement income system was greatly conditioned by the market-centred nature of the postwar social class settlement. The Australian social compromise rested on market measures to attain full employment as a surrogate for universal social welfare protection. To boost economic growth and employment – which had historically been the guiding vision of the Australian labour movement – the industrial and political wings of the labour movement in Australia readjusted their strategies to the new imperatives of market forces after the 1970s. Intensifying residualism by reactivating means testing and by consolidating the privatization of retirement income provisions was an outcome not inconsistent with the Australian labour movement's historical vision of the welfare state.

This chapter has three parts. In the first, the significant changes to the Australian retirement income system are highlighted. The drift towards means-tested principles and the privatization of retirement income will be examined. In the second, the influence of the postwar social class compromise in shaping the patterns of retirement income restructuring and retrenchment are analysed. The final section prepares the ground for comparing the restructuring of the Australian retirement income system to that of Canada in the following chapter.

Changes to the Australian Retirement Income System

Welfare state restructuring triggered by the economic crisis of the 1970s set in motion a major transformation in the provision of retirement income in Australia. As a result of changes to its provisions, the Australian retirement income system came to be characterized by three tiers. This was a marked departure from the postwar era, during which the Australian system had two pillars. Table 7.1 illustrates the major changes to the Australian retirement income system.

The First Tier

Under the pressure to cut costs that became central to Australia's approach to tackling the economic crisis, the Age Pension – the first tier of retirement income – was fundamentally altered. As part of welfare state retrenchment, the Age Pension was gradually stripped of all universal features and returned to its pre-1960s residualism, characterized by a simultaneous application of income and asset tests to Age Pension payments.[1] Although the regressive changes to the non-contributory flat rate component of the retirement income system were initiated by Malcolm Fraser's Liberal coalition government in 1978, it was under Bob Hawke's Labor administration that residualism was fully revived.

As noted in chapter 5, under Gough Whitlam's Labor government the non-contributory flat rate Age Pension had acquired at least a partly universal character. It was also during the Whitlam administration that Age Pension payments to people seventy years of age and over were exempted from the income test. Fraser's Liberal coalition (1976–1982) halted this limited trend towards the abolition of the means test.[3] Starting in 1978, people aged seventy and over were assured of a fixed base rate Age Pension, but their receipt of further indexation increases was subject to their income level.[4] However, blind pensioners remained immune from the application of income test.[5] In 1982 the maximum rate of Supplementary Assistance was set at either $8 per week or one-half the amount by which rent paid or payable exceeded $19 per week. Under the changes to Supplementary Assistance, tenants in government housing lost their eligibility for Supplementary Assistance.[6] Supplementary Assistance, which

Table 7.1 Changes to the Australian retirement income system during era of neoliberal restructuring, 1980s–2000s

Tiers/features	First tier	Second tier	Third tier
	Non-contributory	State-mandated privately arranged compulsory superannuation plan established in 1992	Tax-assisted voluntary occupational superannuation plans and voluntary individual savings
Components	Age Pension Supplementary Assistance Wife's Pension	Superannuation guarantee charge	Voluntary occupational superannuation plans. Private savings (through property, homeownership, managed funds, and shares)
Funding	No changes Financed from federal government general tax revenue	Fully funded individual accounts. Compulsory contribution made by employers on behalf of their employees	By contribution
Eligibility	Age and residency. 2 In 1994, qualifying age for accessing Age Pension for women was raised from 60 to 65 (to be phased in over 20 years). In 1987, residency requirements were changed to exclude non-citizens and temporary residents from receiving age pension.	By contribution	By contribution
Benefits	Since 1984, benefits have been subject to income and asset tests. In 1983, Supplementary Assistance was renamed Rent Assistance. Since 1991, women younger than 21 without children in their care are no longer eligible for Wife's Pension. In 1998, to encourage pensioners to delay receiving Age Pension and continue working, the Pension Bonus was introduced.	Defined contribution. Fully vested, portable, and preserved to age 55 (will gradually be raised to 60 by 2025). Choice of lump sum or income streams. Benefits are determined by rate of contribution plus the compounded returns on investment.	Depends whether it is defined benefits (contributor is guaranteed a fixed percentage of his or her earnings on retirement) or defined contribution (determined by contribution plus compounded returns on investment). Individual savings: contribution plus compounded returns on investment.

had been introduced in 1958 to assist pensioners who paid rent, was renamed Rent Assistance in 1985.

The rollback of the universal component of the Age Pension was started by the Fraser government in 1978 and was continued by the Labor government in the 1980s. Through several significant changes initiated by Labor, the Age Pension ultimately regained its residual character. Under new measures adopted in 1983, the exemption under the income test for pension incomes from friendly societies and trade unions was removed.[7] After November 1983, the income test–free component of the Age Pension for people over seventy became subject to a special income test. This special income test was more generous than the one applied to people aged sixty-five to sixty-nine. Under this special income test, where income exceeded $200 per week for a single pensioner or $333 per week for a couple, there was to be a reduction of fifty cents for each dollar above those levels.[8] Under this income test, if the weekly income of a person aged seventy and over exceeded $302.90, he or she would not be eligible for any pension.[9]

Subsequent to these changes to the Social Security Act of 1984 (coming into effect in March 1985), the Labor government fully restored the means test by complementing the income test with an asset test. By tightening welfare expenditures and directing welfare funds to those most in the need of income support, the Labor administration extended the principle of targeting as a permanent aspect of the non-contributory flat rate component of the Australian income retirement system. With the reintroduction of an asset test, which was to be applied to all income-tested pensions except for blind or invalid pensioners (their supplementary benefits remained subject to both income and asset tests), the Labor government returned the Age Pension to its pre-1976 position.[10] With the Social Security Act of 1984, both tests became applicable, and the one that led to a lower pension level set the Age Pension payment. In line with changes to the Social Security Act in 1984, the Department of Social Services defined income as "[p]ersonal earning, moneys, valuable consideration or property earned or derived or received by that person for the person's own use or benefits by any means from any source whatsoever within or outside Australia, and includes a periodical payment or benefits by way of gift or allowance."[11]

Under the 1984 Social Security Act, the maximum rate of pension for an unmarried pensioner was to be reduced by one dollar for every two dollars that the pensioner's weekly income exceeded the permissible income level of $30 per week. The same adjustment was to be applied to a married pensioner. For a married pensioner, there was to be a reduction of one dollar for every two dollars above his or her permissible weekly income level of $50. The disqualifying incomes for a single and a married pensioner were established at $236.60 and $364.60 respectively. If their weekly income reached this level, they would lose their eligibility for the Age Pension. However, the disqualifying income level was raised for pensioners with dependent children.[12]

With the reintroduction of the asset test in 1984, only a pensioner's home, special aids for disabled people, prepaid funeral expenses, unrecovered inheritance, and the capital value of life insurance and annuities were disregarded when calculating assessable assets.[13] The Department of Social Services identified the following items as assessable assets: cars, caravans, and boats that are not the principal residence of the person, holiday homes, farms (excluding home and cottage) and businesses, household contents and personal effects for personal use including furniture, paintings and other works of art, soft furnishings (e.g., curtains), electrical appliances other than fixtures such as stoves and built-in heaters, clothing, jewellery, collections (e.g., stamps, coins), collections for trading or investment purposes, bullion, uncounted diamonds, bank accounts (including chequing or non-interest-bearing accounts), building societies, credit unions, interest-bearing deposits, investments such as property trusts, investments in friendly societies, the surrender of life assurance policies, cash on hand other than that held for day-to-day expenses or to pay outstanding bills, value of real estate apart from the home the claimant lives in, large amounts disposed without adequate financial return, and investment in family trusts.[14]

Under the 1984 Act, the value of permissible assets for single and married pensioners who owned their own home was set at $70,000 and $100,000 respectively.[15] In the case of a single person, the pension was to be reduced at the rate of $2 per week for each $1,000 of assets above allowable assets. In the case of a married couple, the pension was to be reduced at the rate of $1 per week for every $1,000 of assets in excess of the exemption level. Under the asset test, pensions of a single person and a married couple were to cease if their asset values exceeded $117,250 and $179,000 respectively. The disqualifying asset values beyond which a non-homeowning single and a married couple could not receive any pension payment were set at $167,250 and $229,000 respectively.[16]

To mitigate the disqualifying impact of the asset test on pensioners who were bound to encounter difficulty in sustaining their living, "hardship" provisions were introduced. Under these provisions, assets that could be disregarded were those that produced no income or that could not be sold or used as security for a loan. In line with the hardship provisions, the "Pensioner Loan Scheme" was introduced to assist those pensioners who were entitled to little or no pension due to the asset test. Under the scheme, pensioners for whom 70 per cent of their assets could not readily be converted into cash were permitted to receive their pensions if only the income test applied. The excess over the entitlement under the asset test was regarded as debt, with interest charged at 10 per cent per annum.[17]

In 1987, several major changes were again made to the provisions governing the payment of the Age Pension. After adjustments to the residency requirement in 1985 that required residency in Australia for five of the past ten years, the requirement was again altered to prohibit temporary residents and non-residents from receiving the Age Pension.[18]

Further changes were made to the income and asset tests in 1988 that entailed pension clawbacks. After February 1988, 50 per cent of the lump sum settlement of compensation for personal injury that had been deemed to be for economic loss became recoverable where a pension had been paid during the period of that economic loss. Money received from a home equity conversion loan was exempted from consideration under the income test, but only until it reached $40,000. In the calculation of the income test, "value free" or subsidized board and lodgings was to be disregarded.

At the beginning of the 1990s, the Labor government set out to mitigate the harshness of the income and asset tests on pensioners through several changes to the Social Security Act. After February 1990, income from compulsory preserved superannuation benefits was disregarded under the means test. In 1991, the amount a pensioner could give away without triggering the deprivation provisions was elevated to $10,000 per annum. The same year, that portion of annuity or funded superannuation payment made on the return on capital was excluded from consideration under the income test. Furthermore, to simplify the calculation of income and asset tests, a minimum interest rate was deemed on cash and deposits in financial institutions. The first $2,000 was exempt from this provision, and a 10 per cent interest rate or the actual rate of return was to be applied to income and assets beyond the threshold of $2,000. The income test "free area" was to be indexed annually.[19]

In 1993, the evaluation of income from managed investments was simplified and the categorization into market-linked investments and accruing return was removed. With this change in the means tests, all managed investments were assessed on their actual rate of return over the previous twelve months, and the losses assessed could be used to offset the gains during the same period on other managed investments. The same rules of income and asset assessment were extended to shares and other securities listed on the stock exchange. Under the measures introduced for assessing assets and income, non-cash credits from exchange trading systems were removed from consideration. The asset test was modified so that for every $1,000 of assets above the thresholds, the pension payment was to be reduced by $1.50 per week.[20]

During the final year of its administration, the Labor government made significant changes to the residency requirement affecting refugees and women applying for the Age Pension. After January 1995, refugees applying for the Age Pension were exempt from the length-of-residency requirement, which had previously prevented many refugees from receiving the Age Pension. From July 1995, the age of eligibility for women applying for the Age Pension was set to be raised gradually from sixty to sixty-five years. By increasing the age of eligibility for women by six months every two years, the process was to be completed by July 2013.[21]

With the shift in administration from Labor to the Liberal coalition government of John Howard in 1996, the provisions governing the payments of the Age Pension became subject to a significant transformation. At the outset, the Liberals subjected the treatment of financial assets to a major reform, termed "extended deeming." For the income test provisions, the total value of all financial assets was to be added together. Under extended deeming, a rate of return of 5 per cent was deemed to have been received on the first $30,000 (for a couple $50,000) worth of assets and rate of 7 per cent was imputed to assets held above these levels. It was assumed that these attributed rates of return were achievable as along as pensioners adhered to principles of safe and cautious investing. In introducing extended deeming, the Liberals exempted the first $2,000 ($4,000 for a couple) of asset values; however, it abolished this exemption in March 1997.[22] Even though the Liberal government removed items such cars, boats, caravans, antiques, and stamp and coin collections from the list of assessable assets introduced by the Labor government in 1985, it nonetheless maintained the assessment of all market-linked assets. In accordance with the 1995 reform of the assetstest, the following items were deemed assessable for when calculating Age Pension payments: bank, building society, and credit union accounts, cash, term deposits, friendly society bonds, managed investments,

investments in superannuation funds, approved deposit funds and deferred annuities after pension age, listed shares and securities, loans, debentures and bonds, shares in unlisted public companies, gifted assets above the allowable limits, and gold and other bullion.[23]

In 1997 the Liberal government abolished the earnings credit scheme that had been introduced by the Labor government in 1987. Beginning in 1997, elderly people who were receiving compensation and who were eligible to receive the Age Pension were affected by the compensation, which had previously been ignored with regard to the evaluation of their eligibility. The calculation of preclusion periods due to the receipt of compensation was altered, and the amount was divided by the amount above which no pension was payable to a single pensioner under the income test. Previously, the compensation had been divided by the pensioner's average weekly earnings. The preclusion compensation was only applied to the recipient, not to his or her spouse, as had previously been the case. After September 1997, where a person had been a recipient of pension for thirty-nine weeks after reaching the age of fifty-five, his or her superannuation assets were to be assessed under the income test.[24]

Through the 1997 changes made to the eligibility of farmers for the Age Pension, the Liberals facilitated the transfer of assets within farming families. Farmers who were eligible for the Age Pension were permitted to transfer farms and farming assets up to a value of $500,000 to the next generation without losing their eligibility for Age Pension entitlement. The only qualifications that farmers had to meet was the presence of their long-term involvement in farming activities and proof that they had low incomes. This exemption was to be effective only until 14September 2000.[25]

In 1998, the treatment of income streams such as superannuation pensions, allocated pensions, annuities, and roll-over and ordinary annuities also became subject to major alterations. The treatment of income streams was separated into three categories: income streams for life, life expectancy, or at least fifteen years with no access to capital and purchased after reaching the eligibility age were all exempted from the asset test. However, under the income test, a deduction based on the purchase price was applied. Other income streams with a term greater than five years but less than lifetime or life expectancy were included in the calculation of the asset test. Under the means test, income streams were subject to a deduction. While short-term income streams of five years or less were asset tested, under the income test they were treated as other financial investments.[26]

In 1998, the Liberal government introduced a measure, the Pension Bonus Scheme, that was geared to retain aged people within the labour market.[27] Under the Pension Bonus Scheme, aged people who were willing to postpone their retirement and continue working for at least twenty hours a week were given a tax-free bonus payment equal to 9.4 per cent of the basic pension entitlement for each year of deferral up to a maximum of five years, to be paid when the pension was received. Elderly people who lived in public housing but were not the primary tenants were to be excluded from eligibility for Rent Assistance. An exemption was applied where the primary tenant was unsubsidized or where the State Housing Authority had been notified of the tenant's presence and their income had been taken into account in setting the rent for the household.[28]

In 2000, the Liberal government increased the rate of pensions as part of a package of measures to compensate for the impact of the introduction of the goods and sales tax (GST). From July 2000, an Aged Persons Savings Bonus was to be paid to people aged sixty and over who had savings and investment income. This was a one-off untaxed lump sum of up to $1,000. The exact payment was calculated by providing one dollar for each dollar of savings and investment income received by the claimant up to the maximum of $1,000. Those with annual income above $20,000 received a smaller payment, and no payment was available for those whose income exceeded $30,000. An additional Self-Funded Retirees Supplementary Bonus also became available for people who did not receive a pension or benefits. It was worth up to $2,000 and was subject to an income test mechanism. From July 2004, the allowable period of temporary absence overseas for portable payments was reduced from twenty-six to thirteen weeks.[29]

The Age Pension's value was to increase in line with inflation as measured by the Consumer Price Index (CPI), and "where necessary a further increase is made in order to ensure that it does not fall below 25% of pre-tax Male Total Average Weekly Earnings."[30] Overall, the application of the means test tends to adversely affect pensioners in Australia. In 2006, "almost 40% of pensioners had their benefits reduced by the means test."[31]

Second Tier

In parallel to the dramatic retrenchment of the non-contributory flat rate Age Pension, the private occupational pension schemes that were complementary to the first tier of old age income security were also subject to a major modification. As pointed out in chapter 5, as an alternative to a publicly administered compulsory public pension plan, employer-sponsored private occupational plans had entrenched themselves as the second tier of the retirement income system in Australia by the 1960s. In spite of several government attempts to improve the coverage of the private superannuation schemes, they remained confined to white-collar workers in the public sector and managerial employees of large enterprises in the private sector. These tax-assisted private occupational plans were supposed to function as the main source of retirement income. However, these superannuation plans were characterized by low coverage, lack of portability, poor inclusion of female and part-time workers, poor vesting (vesting refers to an employee's entitlement to full pension benefits at the retirement age or partial benefits upon early retirement whether or not he or she works for the same employer), and the need for preservation requirements.[32]

To overcome the shortcomings of non-compulsory employer-sponsored private occupational pension plans, the Labor government and the ACTU launched an intense negotiation to establish a comprehensive national superannuation system. While various proposals and suggestions discussed in chapter 5 for a national superannuation plan provided policy background for privately arranged compulsory superannuation schemes in 1992, the main impetus for this system stemmed from the industrial relations arena. The negotiation between the Labor government and the ACTU, along with Australia's centralized wage determination system, contained the idea of building superannuation contributions into a nationally centralized wage-setting mechanism.[33] The union movement saw occupational superannuation as a mechanism through which it could obtain deferred wage increase in the form of retirement savings.[34] The newly elected Labor government in 1983 expressed its support for employee superannuation and initiated discussion on this issue with ACTU to broaden access to superannuation throughout the workforce.[35] The process of institutionalizing employee superannuation began in 1985. With the support of the Labor government, the ACTU, as part of its National Wage Case claim with the Conciliation and Arbitration Commission, sought 3 per cent superannuation contribution by employers to be paid into an industry fund.[36] To advance the cause of national superannuation, Accord II was concluded between the Labor government and the ACTU in 1985. A crucial element in that agreement was that while the increase in compensation to employees should be 6 per cent to keep pace with inflation, half the increase would accrue in the form of a 3 per cent employer superannuation contribution, to be paid into an individual account in an industry fund.[37] Following intense negotiations between the unions and the Labor government that culminated in an agreement to improve the social wage as a substitute for wage improvements, employers were expected to contribute 3 per cent of an employee's base earnings to a superannuation fund on behalf of each employee. The agreement between the ACTU and Labor government became known as the Productivity Award Superannuation and was ratified by the Conciliation and Arbitration Commission in 1986.[38] The 1985 government proposal also made it necessary that these industry funds be controlled by either representatives of both employees and employers or appointed independent trustees.[39]

Some employer organizations such as the Confederation of Australian Industry challenged the commission's decision in the High Court on the grounds that it was not within the jurisdiction of the Conciliation and Arbitration Commission to rule on payment of superannuation as part of industrial award since superannuation was not an industrial matter. The High Court rejected this line of interpretation and ruled that worker superannuation was indeed an industrial matter that fell under the jurisdiction of the Commission.[40]

However, despite the rapid growth in superannuation coverage for employees as a result of the Productivity Award superannuation negotiated between the Labor government and the ACTU, coverage in the private sector remained poor, and by 1991 only one-third of private sector employees were covered.[41] Furthermore, the 3 per cent award was seen to be too small to secure any significant improvement in retirement incomes for low-paid workers.[42] The failure of the award system to expand the levels of coverage emanated from two factors.[43] First, many employees who were entitled to superannuation under the provisions of an award had not received their entitlement. In some cases, employees were not aware of their entitlement, and in other cases, the unions had failed to establish industry funds into which employer contributions could be made. Second, compliance with the provisions of the National Wage Case could only be enforced through a case referred to the Conciliation and Arbitration Commission, which was a tedious process given the number of awards that fell under the commission's jurisdiction.

In 1991, the gap in superannuation coverage and compliance problems with award superannuation led the Reconciliation and Arbitration Commission, now renamed the Industrial Relations Commission, to reject an application supported by both the Labor government and the

ACTU for a further 3 per cent superannuation increase. The commission rejected the application on the grounds that there were shortcomings in implementation and administration of award superannuation that in the Commission's view, unless addressed, would frustrate any further development of the system and the achievement of an adequate national retirement income system.[44]

The problems with increasing the contribution rates under Productivity Award Superannuation led to the establishment of a compulsory National Superannuation Scheme, which had been the subject of political debates for more than a century.[45] In 1992 the National Superannuation Scheme came into effect as an addition to existing employer-sponsored private occupational plans. The introduction of compulsory national superannuation was the outcome of a series of agreements between the ACTU and the Labor government as part of overall social contract negotiations.[46] To convert its agreement with the ACTU into a compulsory National Superannuation Scheme, the Labor government legislated a Superannuation Guarantee Charge in 1992. The proposed legislation did not face opposition from the business community since a National Superannuation Scheme was viewed by major actors in the financial sector as an essential step to increase Australia's level of national savings.[47]

To encourage consensus among stakeholders, the Labor government convened a Select Senate Committee on superannuation to hear objections to the planned reform and to interpret and explain the national benefits of a privately managed compulsory national superannuation plan.[48] By emphasizing the significant contribution of the proposed national superannuation plan to national savings and economic growth, the Labor government succeeded in garnering support from the main players in the financial sector.[49] Major stakeholders and vested interests like life insurance companies welcomed the superannuation reform package and were well positioned to implement the Labor government's retirement proposals.[50] [51] In fact, the compulsory supernannuation "pleased the financial sectors, particularly the life offices and pension funds which gained access to the management of the compulsory store of savings."[52]

In line with the legislated Superannuation Guarantee Charge, the employer contribution to a fund on behalf of each employee became compulsory; also, benefits would be not only portable but also fully invested in individual workers. Employers were also required to provide a minimum level of superannuation support for their employees to a complying fund or a retirement savings account of the employee's choice. Although the minimum superannuation contribution by employers was to be calculated on a quarterly basis, employers were permitted to make the contribution annually. Employers who failed to make the superannuation contribution would be liable for the shortfall plus an interest component and administrative costs. The employer's initial contribution rate was set at 3 per cent of the employee's earnings and was to increase to 9 per cent by 2002. The provisions for the superannuation guaranteed contribution came about through union–employer negotiations and were provided by employers in place of pay rises. The Compulsory Superannuation Guarantee Charge was, therefore, regarded as "deferred pay."[53] Each of these steps to increase employer superannuation contributions to 9 per cent of an employees' salary was presented as an alternative to future wage increases. As John Daley has pointed out, "forgoing a future wage increase was less politically painful than any reduction to current wages."[54] Furthermore, the labour movement realized that comprehensive wage increases were becoming increasingly difficult to negotiate successfully. Therefore, the employer superannuation contribution on the behalf of employees as "deferred savings benefits seemed to be an alternative to simply striving for an increase in workers' net pay."[55]

In fact, the Superannuation Guarantee Charge could be regarded as a special purpose tax on employees, although the Labor government chose not to call it a tax. It was politically more palatable to unions and government to call it a charge on employers rather than a tax on employees, since income tax cannot discriminate, so imposing a tax on employees without imposing a tax on the self-employed would have been declared unconstitutional. Furthermore, although the Labor government avoided calling the Superannuation Guarantee Charge an impost on employees, then-treasurer John Dawkins explicitly asserted that future increases in employees' wages could take into account employers' contributions to employee superannuation accounts.[56]

The Superannuation Guarantee Charge shifted the risk to employees since future retirement benefits would depend on the cumulation of assets and return on investment.[57] Prior to the superannuation, most members were in defined benefit funds whereby benefits were predetermined based on the members' final salary and length of service.[58] With the shift to accumulation funds (defined contributions), members were required to bear the investment risk. The shift of investment risk to members and away from employers is a central feature of the decline in defined benefit funds as well as a defining feature of the compulsory Superannuation Guarantee Charge introduced in 1992.

The Superannuation Guarantee Charge is largely absorbed through slower wage growth. Thus, the working poor may suffer more from reduced access to consumption today than they might gain from increased retirement resources in the future. Also, the superannuation tax concession provides more of a tax break to the wealthy and to high-income individuals than to the poor, to part-time workers, and to low-wage workers and non-standard workers – such as women – who have long periods out of the workforce.[59]

Under the Superannuation Guarantee Charge, any superannuation contribution employers paid to a superannuating fund for employees under an award arrangement would count towards the employers' superannuation guarantee contributions. In other words, if the awarded superannuation happened to be below the required levels of the superannuation guarantee, employers would have to make further contribution up to the required levels.[60] The maximum superannuation above which employers were not required to make a contribution was set at $20,000 for 1992–3 and was to increase to $29,000 for 2002–3.[61] The maximum superannuation base was to be used as a benchmark for determining the maximum limit on any individual employee's earning base for each quarter of any financial year. There is no particular protection in the National Superannuation Plan for periods out of work (there are no credits in the superannuation scheme for periods of unemployment). However, voluntary contributions are allowed for periods out of paid work. Table 7.2 illustrates the changes in the contribution rates and the maximum and minimum contribution base.

Under the 1992 Act, employers were not required to provide minimum superannuation support for that part of earnings that exceeded the maximum superannuation base. Furthermore, employers were not required to make superannuation contributions for their employees under the following conditions:

1 Salary and wages paid to an employee who is 70 or over (from July 2002, working people aged 70 and over but less than 75 are still able to continue to make contributions to superannuation, if they are working at least 10 hours per week. However, employers will still beexempt from having to provide superannuation support for employees aged 70 years and over.
2 Salary and wages paid to an employee who is not resident of Australia for work done outside Australia. Salary and wages paid by an employer who is not resident of Australia to an employee who is resident of Australia for work done outside Australia.

Table 7.2 Employer contribution rates, 1992–2005

Year	Employer contribution rate (%)	Maximum contribution base per quarter ($)	Minimum contribution base ($)
1992–3	3	20.00	450
1993–4	3	20.16	450
1994–5	4	20.78	450
1995–6	5	21.72	450
1996–7	6	22.39	450
1997–8	6	23.63	450
1998–9	7	24.48	450
1999–2000	7	25.24	450
2000–1	8	26.30	450
2001–2	8	27.51	450
2002–5	9	39.22	450

Source: Australian Taxation Office, *The Superannuation Guarantee: A Guide for Employers* (Canberra: Australian Government Publishing Service, 2005). http://www.ato.gov.au/super/content.asp?doc=/content/19818.htm.

3 If an employer pays an employee less than $450 by way of salary and wages in a month; the salary and wages paid are not to be taken into account for the purpose of calculation.
4 Salary and wages paid to a part-time employee who is under 18.
5 If an employee receives an income that is exempt from income tax.
6 Employees paid to do work of a domestic or private nature for not more than 30 hours per week (e.g. part time nanny or housekeepers).
7 Employees electing not to receive superannuation guarantee support because their accumulated superannuation benefits exceed the pension reasonable benefit limit.[62]

In the original legislation, the Labor government also proposed that employees be encouraged to contribute 3 per cent of their earnings to the superannuation fund. The purpose was to increase the rate of contribution so that the adequacy of retirement income from compulsory national superannuation would be secured. In its 1995–6 budgetary proposal, the Labor government announced it would match the 3 per cent contribution by employees with an equivalent government contribution so that the total contribution rate would be raised to 15 per cent by 2002.[63] But the Labor government inserted a means test into its proposal. To promote equity and coverage, the government contribution would be capped at 3 per cent of average weekly "ordinary" earnings, and a means test would be applied.[64]

With the change in government in 1996, another crack opened in the universality of the National Superannuation Plan. The Liberal coalition of John Howard allowed employees earning between $450 and $900 monthly to opt out of the superannuation contribution and receive superannuation contributions as cash instead. Its proposal to increase the rate of contribution to 15 per cent faced an obstacle. The matching of the 3 per cent employee contribution by an equivalent government contribution, proposed by the Labor government in 1995, was ignored by the Liberal coalition.

As pointed out, the 1992 Superannuation Guarantee Charge Act permitted employers to make required superannuation contributions on an annual basis. This provided more latitude for employers to delay or evade the superannuation contribution due to insolvency and bankruptcy; it also imposed the loss of investment earnings on employees. The potential loss of investment earnings for employees, the potential loss of entitlements in the event of insolvency, the increased number of lost members, and the impact on disability and income protection insurance as shortcomings associated with the payment of a superannuation contribution on annual basis were highlighted by a 2001 report of the Senate Committee on Superannuation and Financial Services.[65]

The conversion of the compulsory National Superannuation Scheme into an effective vehicle of retirement income provision was to be reinforced by a change in the tax treatment of superannuation contributions, investment income from superannuation funds, and superannuation benefits. Employer contributions are tax deductible as long as they are made to a complying superannuation fund and are within age-based contribution limits. Subject to annual indexation for 1994–5, the tax deductibility of employer contributions was limited to $9,000 for employees younger than thirty-five, $25,000 for those aged thirty-five to forty-nine, and $62,000 for those over fifty.[66] Contributions by employees are typically made out of after-tax income, and employees earning less than $31,000 can claim a tax rebate up to $1,000. In conjunction with taxation on contribution to superannuation funds, investment incomes from superannuation funds are subject to a single statutory rate of 15 per cent.[67]

Superannuation benefits are also subject to varying tax treatment depending on factors such as the type of benefits, the size of benefits, whether benefits are above the Reasonable Benefits Limit (the limit on the amount of superannuation benefits a person is permitted to receive on an occasionally taxed basis, which restricts the availability of tax-preferred superannuation benefits for high-income earners), and the age at which the benefits are withdrawn.[68] The main rationale behind changes in the tax treatment of the superannuation benefits that were initiated during the 1980s was to turn superannuation benefits into regular pension benefits. Until 1983, lump sum was the main form of superannuation benefits since only 5 per cent of the amount of the lump sum was included in the recipients' assessable income that was subject to taxation. To address this trend, the Labor government changed the tax treatment of income from the superannuation fund by providing more favourable taxation consideration for retirees if they purchased a traditional annuity or allocated pension products (such as the drawdown policy that allows retirees to take income from their retirement fund within government specified limits without being locked into an annuity contract).[69 70]

Further changes to the tax treatment of superannuation benefits in 1988 raised the threshold of $55,000 to $60,000, and pre-retirement lump sum rates were lowered to 20 per cent. Under these changes, the first $60,000 of genuine retirement payout was exempt from taxes and the balance was to be taxed at 15 per cent. Further changes were made to the tax treatment of superannuation benefits in 1992. For a lump sum payment taken after the age of fifty-five, the first $112,405 (indexed annually) was to be tax free if it was paid from a taxed fund. The lump sum payment was to be taxed at a maximum of 15 per cent if it was paid from an untaxed fund. Any remaining component up to the individual's lump sum Reasonable Benefits Limit (RBL) was to be taxed at a maximum rate of 15 per cent if it was paid from a taxed fund (investment funds that are taxed) and 30 per cent if paid from an untaxed fund (investment funds that are not taxed).[71]

The restructuring and retrenchment of the first and the second tiers of the Australian retirement income system that began in the 1980s was all but complete by 1997. Howard's Liberal coalition made several more changes to the Superannuation Guarantee Charge Act in the early 2000s. In 2001, the Liberal coalition introduced the Government Co-contribution for low-income earners. This scheme was designed to replace the existing maximum $100 tax rebate for undeducted superannuation contributions made by eligible low-income earners. A maximum co-contribution of $1,000 was to be payable with respect to individuals whose assessable income and reportable fringe benefits did not exceed $20,000 per annum. The maximum government co-contribution was to be reduced by 8 cents for each dollar of assessable income and reportable fringe benefits over $20,000 (up to $32,500).[72] The Government Co-contribution was to be payable to a person if:

1 The person makes an eligible personal superannuation contribution during an income year, and
2 The person has employer-sponsored superannuation contribution for the income year, and
3 The person's total income for the income year is less than $32,500, and an income tax return for the person has been lodged, and
4 The person is less than 71 year[s] old at the end of the income year, and
5 The person does not hold an eligible temporary resident visa at any time during that year of income.[73]

In 2002, to encourage retirees to remain in the labour force, the maximum age for superannuation contribution increased from 70 to 75 as long as these retirees worked at least ten hours a week.[74] In 2004, the Liberal coalition passed the Choice Funds legislation, which has allowed employees to direct their employers' superannuation contributions to a fund of their choice. In 2005, as part of the transition to retirement, the Liberal coalition put regulations in place that allowed members of superannuation funds to access their superannuation in the form of an income stream before they had left the workforce.[75] The coalition's objective was to reduce the incentives for early lump sum withdrawals by allowing workers reaching the preservation age to access the balances in their superannuation accounts. These new regulations were meant to encourage workers to remain in the workforce while gradually withdrawing their superannuation savings.

By the end of its transition period, the Superannuation Guarantee Charge had advanced two of its main significant objectives: securing savings for investment, and improving coverage of the workforce. In 2007, superannuation assets were recorded at $1,153.3 billion, or 119 per cent of GDP.[76] The Superannuation Guarantee Charge also significantly improved the coverage of the workforce. Poor coverage had previously been the main shortcoming of non-compulsory private occupational

Table 7.3 Coverage of employees under the superannuation guarantee charge, 1986–2005

Year	Full-time (%)	Part-time (%)	Total (%)
1986	46.5	7	39.4
1989	55.1	17.8	48.1
1992	88	54.1	80.3
1995	94.4	71.6	89.4
1999	96.9	76.3	91
2000–5	N/A	N/A	92

Source: Australian Bureau of Statistics, *Australian Social Trends.* 2009. http://www.abs.gov.au/AUSSTATS/abs@.nsf/Lookup/4102.0Main+Features20Sep+2009.

pension plans. Table 7.3 illustrates the progressive increase in the percentage of workers covered by the National Superannuation Scheme.

Third Tier

Even though the National Superannuation Plan was state mandated, it never became universal. Besides the specified limitations mentioned earlier, the National Superannuation Scheme did not cover self-employed individuals. Under the 1992 Superannuation Guarantee Charge, self-employed individuals were excluded from the requirement to make mandatory superannuation contributions. Instead, self-employed individuals were encouraged to provide for their own retirement through tax deductions for personal superannuation contributions such as property investment, owning a house, shares, and financial securities.[77] This is part of the third tier of Australia's retirement income (voluntary savings) system, which includes voluntary member superannuation contributions, contributions made usually by a member of superannuation funds over and above the compulsory superannuation contribution, and contributions made on behalf of a person who is not eligible for superannuation guarantee contributions.[78] Furthermore, preferential treatment for some forms of savings exists for the family home, which is tax free in terms of capital gains acquired from the sale. There are also some tax concessions in the form of negative gearing (borrowing money for a residential investment that is rented out) for investment properties that are allowed as the third tier of pensions.[79]

The Postwar Social Class Settlement and Retirement Income Restructuring

The flag of fiscal austerity was raised during the Liberal coalition of Malcolm Fraser in the late the 1970s, but it was under the Labor administrations of Bob Hawke and Paul Keating that fundamental changes to the old age income system came to be implemented. The regressive measures taken by the Fraser government were characterized by William Hayden, then Labor leader of the Opposition, as an "ice age social concern" that "turns the clock back – a long way back on social welfare reform."[80] Fraser's Liberal coalition also refrained from implementing the recommendations of the Committee of Inquiry for a National Superannuation Scheme. In contrast to its previous rhetoric on the need for a national scheme to overcome the stigma of the means test, once in power the Liberal government emphasized individual choice and self-help. These values would, of course, be hampered by a compulsory contributory social security plan. John Howard, the treasurer in the Fraser government, explained why the government had decided to forgo a National Superannuation Scheme:

> This type of scheme would involve the compulsory payment of a national superannuation contribution. In effect, this would be an additional tax on personal income. Such a supercharge would impose a very heavy burden on middle and lower income workers ... This scheme involves a major compulsory transfer of resources away from those in the workforce to the aged ... This government believes that it is essential that social welfare planning be undertaken on a co-coordinated basis and those available resources should be directed primarily to those people who are most in need of assistance ... In addition, the government believes that the freedom of choice individuals currently enjoy in arranging their own affairs in respect of income in retirement should be retained.[81]

In 1982, the Labor Party commenced its electoral campaign with a firm commitment to social justice and social democratic reforms. But once in power in 1983, it promptly began to embrace neoliberal principles of economic rationalism. The implementation of these social policy changes by the Labor government did not constitute a historical departure for the Labor Party. The revival of a stringent means test and the privatization of the pension system under the Labor government could be seen as a legacy of the postwar social settlement in Australia. With the economic crisis, the Australian labour movement adjusted itself to the limits it had played a crucial role in establishing. In the words of Gough Whitlam, the ALP was "a prisoner of its own past."[82] The Australian labour movement and the ALP had been the main architects of the postwar social compromise, which rested on the maintenance of full employment and which directed social assistance to those who had fallen outside the realm of market exchanges. It was because of this narrower sense of solidarity and the implicit identification of citizenship with labour/capital relations that residualism had been built into the Australian welfare state. The Labor government's embrace of neoliberal policies was not, in fact, a radical departure from the Australian labour tradition. The seeds for market-oriented principles had been contained within the structure of the postwar social class compromise. Keating highlighted the continuity of labour's philosophy: "Both Curtin and Chifley fully appreciated that growth and jobs were central to any attempt to make Australia a fairer and more effective society ... In continuing to pursue this growth objective, the Hawke Labor Government is operating completely within the tradition of the Labor movement. In adopting practical, pragmatic measures to create growth and jobs, the Labor Party is doing nothing out of the ordinary."[83]

Reflecting on the Whitlam era, during which the governing Labor Party achieved partial universality in the Age Pension, Keating, the treasurer in the Hawke government who became Labor prime minister in 1993, clarified the historical necessity that required the Labor government to adjust itself to new market pressures:

> The problem of the Whitlam Government was that the gap between ideas and outcomes grew to a chasm over that three year period. The party, at last hungry for government and in government, had failed to mature as a government. The ideals and objectives were constant but the economic growth upon which the program was based, was disappearing. The task became, not the distribution of wealth but its creation, but neither Whitlam nor his successor as prime minister seemed to recognize it ... Although Labor had to remain true to its basic faith, the means of achieving its objectives must adapt in a changing world. The mismatch of ends and means was the fatal flaw in the makeup of the Whitlam Government. It is a flaw well understood by this Government.[84]

Keating's rationalization for adjusting to market forces partly reflected his vision of the relationship between the economy and social welfare:

the welfare state depended on a vibrant market economy. Since the social vision of Labor rested on economic growth for full employment, the need to boost economic growth and employment had support from the industrial *and* political wings of the labour movement. This left political space for a Labor-led neoliberal project. A less regulated market economy to promote high levels of employment with minimum inflation became a guiding principle of the Labor government's macroeconomic policy from the 1980s on.[85]

Prior to its electoral victory in March 1983, the ALP, through consultation with the ACTU, prepared the political ground for more market-oriented policies. In a speech to the Australian Institute of Political Science on 30 January 1983, Labor Party leader Bob Hawke questioned the merits and effectiveness of industrial confrontation as a means to advance the labour movement.[86] Hawke pledged that once in government the Labor Party "will undertake the task of national reconciliation rather than the intensification of divisiveness." The inclination of the ALP and the ACTU to adjust to the constraints of market forces was facilitated by a series of accords. The accords concluded between the ALP and the ACTU between 1983 to 1996 became integral to the Labor government's social and economic policies during its time in government.[87] Those accords were the conduit through which neoliberal social and economic policies would be institutionalized. The ACTU became incorporated into policy development and implementation, and this locked in continuing support of the unions for the social and economic restructuring undertaken by the Hawke government.

In their statement endorsing the accord concluded in February 1983, which became part of the ALP's election platform, unions accepted wage restraint in exchange for improvement in the social wage. The first accord came to be known as the Prices and Incomes Policy. Both parties came to an agreement that "wage increases should not generate impetuses for inflation and unemployment and that the government will aim to ... raising social security expenditures and making other improvements to social wage."[88] The first accord triggered a transformation in industrial relations so that they became more responsive to the demands of market forces. During a speech about Australian Labor Party policy on 16 February 1983, Hawke pointed to the economic imperatives that required the Australian labour movement to make concessions: "The whole thrust of our policy is to attack the twin evils of unemployment and inflation together. The Accord equally recognizes that these great goals cannot be achieved overnight, or without real equality of sacrifice."[89]

The Labor Party's call for concessions did not generate opposition within the ACTU leadership. Bill Kelly, the secretary of the ACTU and the person who supervised the implementing of successive accords between the ACTU and the ALP, also emphasized the need for the labour movement to sacrifice. According to Kelly, the Australian labour movement needed to "recognize that, in the current environment, wage and salary earners should be prepared to accept lower standards than they are otherwise entitled to."[90] Within a month of being elected, the governing Labor Party arranged a national summit that brought state officials together with workers and business people. In a speech to the National Economic Summit in Canberra on 11 April 1983, Hawke reiterated that the Australian labour movement must accept constraints: "If a genuine consensus is to emerge, it must mean an understanding on the part of all sections of Australian community of the constraints that they will be called upon to make to the process of national reconciliation, national recovery and national reconstruction."[91]

In establishing a consensus between itself and the business community, the Labor government pre-empted its political opponents in accomplishing what could hardly have been achieved by the Liberal coalition. Treasurer Keating boasted about inviting the representatives of major companies to the National Economic Summit and disparaged the opposition for never having "been able to assemble a group like that."[92] To secure the confidence of the business community, Keating pledged the Labor Party to "smaller government," which was to be achieved through fiscal restraint.[93] The Labor government placed great emphasis on limiting government expenditures, reducing taxes, and restricting public borrowing to the rate of economic growth as essential steps to creating wealth. The Labor Party's conception of "small government" implicitly incorporated the state's neoliberal view. Echoing Keating's view on the role of government, John Howard, the leader of Liberal Party who would become prime minister in 1997, stated that "government should always be strategic and limited."[94] This was the new cross-party neoliberal consensus with respect to the welfare state in Australia.

Although the Labor Party had historically regarded the welfare state as a corrective adjunct to capitalism, its view of the welfare state now echoed the neoliberal conviction that an excessive redistributive state damaged wealth creation and employment. The restructuring of retirement income programs was tied to the Labor government's adherence to fiscal constraint and tightening of the public purse as the basis for promoting economic growth and employment. The views of the Labor government regarding the adverse impact of the welfare state on economic growth became clear when Keating, the treasurer, criticized Fraser's Liberal coalition for failing to curtail income security programs. According to Keating, if the previous Liberal coalition had reintroduced the asset test and reimposed the income test on people aged seventy and over, those measures would "have led to a diminution in the structural deficit ... and to the strengthening of [the] private sector."[95] In an address to the Australian Social Service Council Conference in Canberra on 8 September 1983, Hawke explicitly linked the need to reform welfare programs to the imperatives of economic restructuring: "We have not sought to use the economic crisis as an alibi against reform. On the contrary, we believe that the very seriousness of the general economic problems lend an added urgency to the need to tackle the reform of the social welfare system. Indeed, the inadequacies of the system are themselves part and parcel of the wider economic problem."[96]

The primary goals of the Labor movement were to boost economic growth and raise employment. These things provided a justification for the Labor government to subject retirement income payments to restraint. In its 1983 estimates in the House of Representatives on 1 November 1983, the Labor government declared its determination to reintroduce asset and income tests in order to contain public expenditures. In the Labor government's calculation, the reimposition of income testing on people over seventy was "expected to reduce age pension outlays by $160m in 1983–1984."[97] The revival of means testing for people over seventy who had previously been exempted was compatible with the Labor government's philosophy of a needs-based redistribution of resources. On 1 June 1984, Prime Minister Hawke questioned the desirability of the principle of universality in an era of restructuring and emphasized the imperatives of applying stringent means tests to the Age Pension: "The Government is firmly committed to the principle that pensions be directed to those reliant upon those expenditures and not dissipate upon those who by any standard do not require such assistance ... In a world of unlimited resources, a Government might prefer to avoid such tests, but we do not live in such a world, and do not expect to do so for the foreseeable future."[98]

Although the Labor government was clearly shifting its social welfare policy to neoliberal principles, it attempted to argue that the pursuit of a rigorous means test was a sincere attempt to accomplish the goals of social justice and equity. As in the postwar period, social justice and equity became appendages to market-led economic growth. Keating pointed out that the main agenda of the Labor government was "to restore and sustain economic growth and to more equitably distribute its rewards."[99] The Labor Party's subordination of social welfare to economic growth had the support of the opposition parties. In its 1988 statement, the Liberal coalition declared that "in the long term, the best way to help the needy people is to improve economic growth and defeat inflation through the creation of a more productive, competitive economy."[100]

For the Hawke government, universality became synonymous with inequity and means testing became the means to realize social justice. Raising taxes on lump sum pension benefits and applying asset and income tests were, for the Labor government, indispensable to turn Australia into "a more just society."[101] For Dr Neal Hewlett, Hawke's health minister, "Labour's concern for social justice demands that we honor those undertakings."[102] Keating interpreted the reintroduction of the asset test as "a test that no reasonable Australian can take exception."[103]

Within the emerging discourse on social welfare policy embracing economic rationalism, the principle of universality as the basis for social democratic solidarity was construed, paradoxically, as an assault on social justice. In Hawke's words, the restoration of an asset test would "stop wealthy people exploiting or even cheating the ... pension system."[104] In his address to the Australian Council of Social Services on 8 September 1983, Hawke justified reintroducing an asset test as a prelude to the achieving of the goal of social justice: "It is simply unfair that people with substantial assets are able to receive a full pension ... clearly this situation is completely out of line with the Government's objective of a just distribution of social welfare payments."[105]

The reimposition of the asset and income tests on people over seventy put an end to partial universality in the Australian pension system. But this neoliberal direction taken by the Labor government can be seen as congruent with the historical philosophy of the Australian labour movement. That movement's philosophy had long relegated notions of citizenship to relations between labour and capital.[106] The reversion to the mechanism of targeting social benefits reflected a historically entrenched assumption by the Australian labour movement that the market and collective bargaining should be internalized as the most effective means for income distribution. The ACTU's preoccupation with employment was prominent in the accords that formed the social and economic policies during the Labor administration from 1983 to 1996. The ACTU made it clear that the "Accord has always been concerned with employment."[107] In its 1989 congress, the ACTU explicitly endorsed tightening the means test and reiterated its long-held aspiration for the "right to work." According to the ACTU, "every Australian resident who is available for and willing to work must be able to do so. Priority must be accorded to assisting those groups in greatest needs."[108]

Although the opposition parties were able to argue against the reintroduced asset test, tightening the means tests had always been a central component of their social welfare policy as well. According to Howard, the Leader of Opposition in 1995, "the Australian ethos is one of caring for the less fortunate. It is an extension of our greatest tradition of mateship."[109] The opposition parties attacked the reintroduction of the asset test as a "callous attack on the very aged" and "a backward step."[110]

However, the Labor government's cuts to the Age Pension enjoyed widespread popularity within the business community, which had historically been averse to the principle of universality. In a speech in the House of Representatives, Hawke boasted about having implemented what had long been demanded by the business community. Two prominent right-wing think tanks, the Institute for Public Affairs and the Centre for Independent Studies, praised the Labor government's bold undertakings in the field of social welfare programs, which included better targeting of welfare, consolidation of the means test mechanism, a campaign against welfare fraud, and the withdrawal of unemployment benefits for teenagers.[111] In his reflections on the legacy of the Labor government from 1983 to 1996, Michael Warby, a former IPA researcher, declared that "there is a very good argument that the ALP government engaged in a more thorough economic reform than a Liberal Government would have."[112] In his response to the opposition's attack on the reintroduction of the asset test, Hawke proudly recited the endorsement by the Business Council of Australia of his government's bold action on the Age Pension – action that the other parties had failed to undertake: "Over recent years business leaders have urged that welfare payments be means tested and we have said that the Government deserves support for attempting to tackle this politically difficult problem now."[113]

By implementing neoliberal economic policies and the residual social policy on the Age Pension, the Labor government was trying to gain the confidence of the Australian business community. That community had long called for fiscal constraint as a guiding principle of socio-economic policy. Prime Minister Hawke reminded the business community and the labour unions that his government had succeeded in creating "one million new jobs" within five years and that the rate of employment growth under the Labor government "has been twice the rate of the rest of western industrialized world."[114] In his 1988 budget speech, Keating proclaimed the success of the Labor government in accomplishing what had never been achieved by previous governments in the postwar era:

> I can report to the people of Australia that the nation is successfully emerging from the most serious economic crisis in a generation ... Tonight I announce a budget surplus of historical proportion – a surplus made possible because this Government has been the first in the post-war years with the courage to make real inroads into public spending ... No major OECD country has reduced the size of its government sector on such a vast scale.[115]

In tightening the eligibility requirements for the Age Pension in order to target benefits, the Labor government also consolidated the compulsory privatization of retirement provisions, which was designed to reduce the future demographic burden on state coffers. In his address to the House of Representatives, the Labor Party's John Charles Kerin clarified the intention of the Labor government to implement National Superannuation as a substitute for the state-provided non-contributory Age Pension. According to Kerin, superannuation "is a measure which would help people provide for their old age rather than rely on the social security system."[116] Even though the introduction of mandatory National Superannuation under the Labor administration had been hailed as a major innovation in Australian social welfare policy, it was in fact judged as an alternative to market-based wage increases. At its 1995 congress, the ACTU clarified that "superannuation improvements may form part of a broader wage settlement in an industry or in a workplace as part of an enterprise/workplace agreement."[117] The Labor government viewed state-mandated employer superannuation contributions as compensation for the loss of industrial power by the labour movement. Addressing the ACTU in 1991, Keating attempted to convince organized labour that the acceptance of wage restraint for employer superannuation contributions would allow Labor and the ACTU to substitute control over the funds for its loss of industrial leverage: "Listen boys, you are losing industrial muscle; you had better start and grasp management control of the funds. You will have to exert some financial muscle."[118]

As pointed out earlier, in the first accord between the ALP and the ACTU in 1983, the union leadership agreed to relax claims for higher wages and lower unemployment in return for the maintenance of social wages through tax cuts, indexation, more jobs, and increased government spending on welfare programs. In the second accord between the

Labor government and the ACTU, concluded in 1986, both parties accepted the conversion of productivity gains into employer contributions to a superannuation fund on behalf of each employee rather than payments in the form of a wage increase: "This agreement is designed to reduce the level of inflation by overcoming problems associated with depreciation whilst maintaining the high level of growth necessary to ensure further increase in employment and capacity to improve living standards through superannuation ... [The ALP] will establish a national safety net superannuation scheme to which employers will be required to contribute where they have failed to [provide] coverage for their employees under an appropriate scheme."[119]

In the sixth accord, concluded in 1990, the Labor government and the ACTU agreed that "additional superannuation equivalent to 3 percent of ordinary time earning be available from May 1991 and the superannuation increase shall be phased in aggregate three year period in a manner negotiated by the award parties."[120] In the ensuing wave of concessions, which were rationalized as necessary to promote economic growth and employment, the ACTU and the Labor government initiated a trend towards a flexible wages system that was bound to reduce the power of unions to stand in the way of economic development.[121]

The seventh accord was designed to systematically reduce the wage-fixing power of the federal industrial tribunal. A main objective of this accord was "to continue the devolution of wage fixation by encouraging bargaining at the industry and workplace levels involving employees and their unions."[122] The ACTU justified the trends towards decentralizing industrial bargaining as an essential prelude to "provide consultative solution and improve efficiency and productivity of compan[ies]."[123] In the words of Tim Pallas, the ACTU's assistant secretary, enterprise bargaining was "to ensure that our [Australian] enterprises are more flexible and resilient to the forces of international competition."[124] In the seventh accord, the ACTU accepted that "it will not embark on any general campaign for improvement in superannuation beyond the legislated minimum,"[125] which was designed to reach 9 per cent by 2000.[126]

The ACTU's concession – wage restraint in an exchange for improved superannuation contributions by employers – was compatible with its overriding goal, which was to restore economic growth and employment in order to secure the welfare of workers. The pool of savings generated by compulsory superannuation was compatible with the ACTU's historical aspiration to maintain full employment as the main mechanism of social welfare protection.[127] In the final accord, agreed upon in 1995, the

Labor government and the ACTU returned to emphasizing contributions to savings for investment as an indispensable means for promoting economic growth and employment: "It is understood that to maintain a healthy growth in production and employment, Australia's businesses need additional investment in up to date plants and equipment for their enterprises ... The capacity of the Australian economy to support investment generally is enhanced through the existence of an increased flow of domestic savings generated by superannuation and from a decreased reliance on the international financial community and foreign debt."[128]

This intensifying of the privatization of retirement income provisions reflected the Labor government's inclination to internalize the concept of the state as an enabling entity consistent with the neoliberal view. The resort to increased use of state-mandated privately managed retirement income provisions did not run counter to the political platform of the non-labour political parties. In their joint 1991 statements of principles and objectives, *Fight Back! It Is Your Australia*, the Liberal and National parties called for a reduction in government intervention in order to give individual Australians the chance to pursue their own goals in life.[129] The main difference between the Labor government and the other parties over the National Superannuation Plan related to the latter's endeavour to reduce the influence of unions over the superannuation funds. During the debate on the proposed compulsory National Superannuation Plan, the Liberal Party's Ray Braithwaite outlined the position of the non-labour parties: "The Coalition supports the extension of occupational superannuation so that everybody in the whole workforce will be covered by adequate and genuine superannuation but ... [A]ll employees should have the freedom of choice to join whatever superannuation scheme they wish and not to be directed by the unions."[130]

Consolidation of private arrangements for retirement income was also compatible with the Australian labour movement's traditional calls for self-development and self-reliance. This particular inclination ran counter to social democratic tenets such as solidarity, universality, and collectivity. During the debate on the proposed legislation for a mandatory National Superannuation Plan, James Scott, a Labor MP, clarified how the proposed legislation would encourage self-reliance and independence, themes long held by the Australian labour movement: "Through award-based superannuation, average Australians are being given the foundation for greater independence when they enter their retirement ... The superannuation is the best way to save for retirement. Far too long generations of Australian workers slaved through their working lives not being able to look towards ... independence once they retired."[131]

Historical aspirations for self-reliance and self-development have been entrenched in the social vision of the Australian Labor Party. Thus, the ALP's political platform for the welfare state countenanced a market-based, individualistic, enterprise approach to retirement income that was compatible with the non-labour parties' support for extending occupational superannuation.[132] The Labor government's stance on pension provisions unequivocally highlighted its vision of the state as an enabling entity whose role is to promote self-reliance and self-provision. During the debate on the legislation for compulsory National Superannuation in 1991, Robert Elliott, another Labor MP, reiterated his colleague's statement that the primary objective of the legislation was to encourage self-reliance in Australia: "Besides savings for retirement, another aspect of this legislation is the concept of social wage in terms of superannuation. We [the Labor Government] on this side of the House make no apology for seeing the provision of that social wage, of a real retirement incomes policy ... [W]e have now made retirement incomes policy which encourages people to provide for their retirement."[133]

Compulsory National Superannuation was largely endorsed by the non-labour parties since it was in line with their ideological orientation. The compulsory National Superannuation plan was geared to promote a vision that emphasized self-financing individuals. Its main thrust was to enhance capital markets that "actually serve to create wealth and hence provide the foundation of self-funded retirement."[134]

As Bryan has asserted, pension policy under both Labor and Liberal coalition governments has intended to "systematically affirm[] incentives for self-funded retirement rather than reliance on a state pension."[135] The shift to private provision of superannuation was justified on the grounds that the new policy would make "the ageing baby boomers more self-reliant ... and retirement would be self-funding individually."[136] Regarding the promotion of self-provision and self-reliance as the overriding objective of the Superannuation Guarantee Charge, no one was more clear than John Dawkins, treasurer in the Keating government. During the parliamentary debate on 2 April 1992, he asserted that the introduced Superannuation Guarantee Charge "will ensure that, by the beginning of the next century, virtually all employees will be accumulating substantial superannuation savings to help fund their retirement income. The increased self provision for retirement will permit a higher standard of living in retirement than if we continue to rely on the age pension alone."[137]

The objective of superannuation pension plans was thus to reduce the number of aged people on the non-contributory flat rate Age Pension.[138] Indeed, the employer superannuation contribution operates somewhat like a clawback. As Sara Rix has pointed out, "as workers' superannuation guarantee accounts grew, workers would have greater assets and thus no longer qualify for some of or even any of the age pension."[139] Underpinning the Labor government's quest to promote compulsory superannuation was and still is a strong faith in the capacity of the capital market "to conjure future wealth and solve the generational funding dilemma."[140]

The Labor government's course of action facilitated later efforts by John Howard's Liberal coalition to extend and deepen neoliberal-oriented social welfare policy. Greg Combet, who succeeded Bill Kelty as ACTU secretary in 1999, admitted that the changes in industrial relations launched by the Labor government provided an opportunity for "conservative governments to wind the clock back on employee rights."[141] Adhering to the principles of fiscal austerity, tax cuts, reduced social welfare expenditures, tightened means testing, extended scope for occupational pension plans, and decentralization of industrial relations was consistent with the social welfare policy adopted by the Liberal coalition that came to power in 1997.

Even in opposition, the Labor Party engaged in a fierce dispute with the Liberal coalition over the authorship of "mutual obligation" or "reciprocal obligation," which had been designed to consolidate workfare schemes as a mechanism for disciplining unemployed people.[142] Prime Minister Howard reminded the members of the Labor Party in the House of Representatives that his government had inherited the work-for-dole scheme "from the Labor government and he [welcomed] the conversion by the Australian Labor Party towards that approach."[143] Senator Jocelyn Newman, the coalition's family and community services minister, maintained that reducing welfare dependency and fostering greater self-reliance were the objectives of her government and called for the extension of mutual obligation to all welfare recipients, including jobless people aged up to sixty-four.[144] Tony Abbott, the Howard government's employment services minister, praised work-for-dole as a means to replace a "passive culture" with a more "self-reliant" one.[145] For Abbott, the point of work-for-dole was "to strengthen individuals in community rather than extend the reach of central government."[146]

The Labor government's enhancement of the principles of self-reliance and self-development also facilitated the Howard government's justification for changing the retirement income provisions. It was under the rubric of expanding the scope of individual choice that the Liberal coalition allowed low-income earners to opt out of employer superannuation contributions and replaced the Labor government's proposed 3 per cent employee superannuation contribution matched by an equivalent government contribution with a government co-contribution. According to the Liberal coalition, "individuals should be able to choose whether to make additional voluntary contribution over and above the Superannuation Guarantee." The coalition would also enact choice-of-fund legislation on the grounds that "Australians take a more active interest in the management of their superannuation."[147]

The ALP's support of the principle of mutual obligation brought greater legitimacy to the Liberal coalition's efforts at social welfare retrenchment. As Mendes has pointed out, "some of the Howard government's agenda arguably also built on earlier ALP government policies and programs."[148] In opposition, Mark Latham, who became the ALP leader in 2003, endorsed the enabling state and even the use of intrusive sanctions if necessary to coerce the poor to adhere to their obligations to society.[149] Latham asserted that the traditional model based on full employment had been sapped by socio-economic changes brought about by globalization. In line with the ascendancy of neoliberalism in Australia, Latham stated that "the era of tax and spend politics has ended."[150] In his keynote presentation in Brisbane on 14 June 2001, he claimed that "at the next federal election ... labor is committed to spend less and tax less than the Howard government ... At the bottom line, Labor stands for a smaller public sector."[151] In his budget reply speech in 2004 as the Labor leader, he revealed the ALP's "belief in limiting the size of government" and stated that "too much spending, too much bureaucracy is bad for the Australian economy."[152] Even in opposition, the ALP continued to endorse small government and express a fascination with enabling. In his address to the 2004 ALP National Conference, Latham urged party members not to expect government to invest in the public sector in the "old way" because government no longer had "a monopoly on solutions in our society."[153]

Conclusion

The official discourse of restraint and fiscal austerity in the 1980s and 1990s generated momentum for the restructuring and retrenchment of the retirement income system in Australia. The emerging discourse of economic rationalism justified retrenchment and the privatization of retirement income provisions. The reconfiguration of the retirement income system in Australia was marked by intensifying privatization and the revival of intrusive means testing. The partial universalism of the Age Pension that had been accomplished in the 1970s was halted by welfare state retrenchment under neoliberalism. As a result of restructuring and retrenchment, the Australian retirement income system came to be characterized by three-tiers: a non-contributory Age Pension, a state-mandated privately arranged National Superannuation Plan, and a voluntary private occupational plan.

The pattern of old age income retrenchment in Australia was structured largely by the nature of the postwar social class compromise. The postwar social class settlement shaped the social policy responses to the economic crisis in the 1970s. As noted in the introductory chapter, the postwar social class settlement in Australia acquired a market-centred character. That is, it hinged on market-led growth for full employment and national wage setting as surrogates for social income security. This led to a particular fusion of social justice with individual self-reliance. Under the Australian social class settlement, social citizenship was tacitly replaced by industrial citizenship in the sense of access to employment in the market. This is neither industrial democracy nor a democratized universal welfare state.

The survival and effectiveness of the Australian social class compromise was intimately linked to the health of the Australian market economy. Economic instability was bound to trigger major changes in Australia's postwar social class settlement and shape the adjustments to neoliberal policies. The market-centred postwar social class settlement in Australia was, therefore, vulnerable to drastic measures that were deemed imperative to tackle the economic crisis of the 1970s. Re-establishing economic growth and accomplishing full employment in the neoliberal period required the industrial *and* political wings of the Australian labour movement to accommodate market forces and make social concessions. In other words, the return to residualism and the deepening privatization of the old age pension system in Australia were rooted in the structure of its postwar social class settlement, the Australian labour movement's vision of the welfare state, and the political choices made under the accords.

The vulnerability of the market-centred postwar social class settlement in Australia to neoliberal retrenchment was in a sharp contrast to the situation in Canada, where the postwar settlement acted as a brake on neoliberal inroads into the retirement income system. This will be discussed in the following chapter.

8 Restructuring of the Pension System in Canada

With the economic crisis in the 1970s, the Canadian state's discourse on the welfare state came to be permeated with the imperative of fiscal restraint. Parallel to the Australian experience, in the 1980s and late 1990s the retirement income system in Canada was reshaped by several significant changes. However, the restructuring of the retirement income system in Canada did not entail embracing the neoliberal objectives of residualism and privatization that prevailed in Australia. Canadian retirement income policy has revolved around consolidation of existing programs. Despite the neoliberal push for reviving residualism and providing greater latitude for the privatization of old age pensions, the Canadian retirement income system has largely retained its universal and collectivistic features.

The explanation for the resistance of the Canadian retirement income system to the forces of retrenchment, and the failure of neoliberal forces to advance the cause of privatization and residualism, reflect the nature of the postwar social settlement in Canada, where the redistributive-oriented nature of the postwar settlement strongly linked universality with citizenship and national unity. Consequently, the postwar settlement functioned as a brake on neoliberal inroads into the retirement income policy.

This chapter has three sections. In the first, major changes to the three pillars of the Canadian retirement income system are highlighted. In the second, the role of the postwar social settlement in shaping the patterns of retirement income restructuring is analysed. The link between the postwar social settlement in Canada and the restructuring of the Canadian retirement income system is established. The third section draws together a series of points about the Canadian pension system under neoliberalism.

Changes to the Retirement Income System

The economic crisis of the 1970s was accompanied by the ascendancy of the discourse of fiscal austerity. It also triggered government attempts to re-evaluate social income security programs. As solutions to fiscal crisis, the imperative of cost-cutting and the rearrangement of income security programs marched to the top of the government's agenda in Canada. As a result of neoliberal pressures, several changes were made to the Canadian retirement income system. These changes were in line with the consolidation of existing retirement income programs. Table 8.1 highlights changes to the Canadian retirement income system.

The First Tier

The pressures for changes to the first pillar of the retirement income system in Canada gained momentum in the 1980s. Under the perceived imperatives of fiscal restraint, the governing Liberal Party imposed limits on the escalation of Old Age Security (OAS) payments. To control the rise in OAS expenditures, OAS indexation for 1983 and 1984 was set at 6 per cent and 5 per cent respectively.[2] However, the same restriction was not applied to the Guaranteed Income Supplement (GIS), which had become a favoured social security instrument of the federal government. The federal government's preoccupation with saving costs and diverting resources to the most needy people to tackle poverty among elderly Canadians was conducive to upgrading the GIS component of the first tier of the retirement income system in the 1980s.[3] The resulting reduction in the value of OAS payments due to the limitation on indexation was to be compensated for by a special increase in GIS payments. In its 1985 budget speech, the Progressive Conservative government of Brian Mulroney declared its intention to place limits on the scope of OAS indexation. The indexation of OAS payments was to be applied only to inflation in excess of 3 per cent a year. However, due to political pressure from seniors organizations and considerations of national unity (discussed in the second part of this chapter), the Conservative government retreated from implementing its proposal. After an amendment to the 1985 Social Security Act that came into force in 12 December 1988, the quarterly adjustment of OAS payment was restored to reflect increases in the CPI.[4]

In 1985, the Conservative government extended the Spouse's Allowance to low-income widows and widowers. Under the legislation, a widow

Table 8.1 Changes to the Canadian retirement income system during the era of neoliberal restructuring, 1980s–2000s

Tiers/features	First tier	Second tier	Third tier
	Non-contributory	Publicly administered earnings-related contributory plan	Tax-assisted voluntary savings
Components	Old Age Security Guaranteed Income Supplement Spouse's Allowance	C/QPP	RPPs RRSPs
Funding	No changes Financed from federal government general tax revenue	Increasing contribution rates by employers/ employees and return on pension fund investments. Gradual move from pay-as-you-go to partly funded	RPPS (employer/ employee contribution). RRSPs (individual contribution)
Eligibility	OAS benefits (age and residency).1 SPA benefits are extended to low-income widows and widowers	By contribution. Has made at least a valid contribution to the C/QPP. Since 1987, flexible retirement is in place (access to retirement benefits at 60 with reduced benefits or access to retirement benefits at 70 with increased benefits)	By contribution
Benefits	Since 1989, OAS benefits are subject to clawback	Modifying formula for retirement, disability, and survivor benefits	Depends whether it is defined benefits (contributor is guaranteed a fixed percentage of his or her earnings on retirement) or defined contribution (determined by contribution plus compounded returns on investment). RRSPs (contribution plus compounded returns on investment)

or widower who had reached the age of sixty and had resided in Canada for an aggregate of at least ten years prior to the approval of his or her application became eligible for benefits. The payment of income-tested Spouse's Allowance to a widow or widower was to be terminated when she or he died, reached the age of sixty-five, or ceased to be a widow or widower.[5]

Having escaped the threat of deindexation, universal OAS became subject to restructuring again in 1989. This took the form of a clawback, which was incorporated into Bill C-28 as an amendment to the Income Tax Act implemented as part of the 1989 budget provisions. The Conservative administration's preoccupation with cost-saving and the political attractiveness of income targeting pushed the Conservative government to introduce a recovery provision or clawback. The new provision required pensioners whose net income exceeded a specific threshold to repay some part of their OAS benefits at the rate of 15 per cent of the net income above the specified threshold. The introduced clawback provision was phased in over three years, and by 1991 it had been fully implemented. With the clawback, single pensioners were required to pay back fifteen cents of their OAS benefits for each dollar of their net income over $53,216. OAS benefits for a single pensioner were to be fully clawed back when his or her annual net income reached the threshold of $85,000.[6] For the 1995 tax year, OAS payments were to be fully recovered when the combined income of married pensioners reached the threshold of $187,000.[7]

Further changes to the OAS were pursued by the Chrétien Liberal government in the 1990s. In its 1996 budget proposal, it brought two significant changes to the residency requirement intended to tighten the rules for immigrants' eligibility for OAS and GIS. Until 1995, recipients of a partial OAS pension who had come from countries with which Canada had no social security agreement were required to have lived in Canada for a minimum of ten years before being considered eligible for OAS benefits. Under the new provisions, elderly people with less than ten years' residence in Canada who qualified for benefits only through a social security agreement with Canada were able to qualify for benefits at the rate of one-tenth of the GIS and Spouse's Allowance for each year of residence in Canada. However, newcomers from countries without a social security agreement with Canada were still required to complete ten years' residence before qualifying for benefits.[8] Under the new provisions, sponsored immigrants from countries that had social security agreements with Canada would not be eligible for the GIS or Spouse's

Allowance for the period of sponsorship up to ten years except in cases where sponsors could not meet their commitment (e.g., in the case of the sponsor's death or elder abuse). Sponsored immigrants were nonetheless eligible for the OAS benefits.[9] The same year, the Liberal government introduced a non-resident tax for OAS and CPP beneficiaries living outside Canada. This new provision imposed a 25 per cent withholding tax on pensions paid abroad unless the recipients were living in a country that had concluded a tax agreement with Canada.[10] In accordance with the new provisions, OAS benefits paid to non-residents became subject to a clawback calculated on their worldwide income rather than only their taxable income in Canada. Beginning in July 1996, the clawback was to be imposed before the payment of OAS benefits. In line with these changes, payment of OAS benefits in any year was to be based on the incomes that seniors had declared on their income tax returns the previous year.[11]

The most serious threat to the universality of the OAS in Canada emanated from the Liberal government's 1996 budget proposals. In its 1995–6 budget, the Chrétien government declared its intention to integrate the OAS, the GIS, and related pension income and age credits into a single program called the Seniors Benefit, which was to be determined by the individual's marital status and family income. The Seniors Benefit was to be tax free and would have incorporated the existing age and pension income tax credits. To moderate the scope of reform and deflect opposition to the new initiative, the Liberal government presented its proposed plan as voluntary: "seniors will have a choice between moving to the new system or maintain their currently OAS/GIS payments, as currently structured – whichever is more advantageous to them."[12] The Liberal government justified its proposal on the grounds that it would reduce the soaring cost of OAS payments and direct limited resources to needy seniors: "The new Seniors Benefit will slow the long-term growth in the cost of public pension that are paid out of the government's general revenues ... It will do this by better targeting assistance to those most in need."[13]

The proposed Seniors Benefit was an attempt by the Liberal government to end the universality of the OAS and convert it into a purely income-tested social assistance program geared to operate on the principles of targeting. Under the new proposal, benefits for single pensioners and married pensioners would be eliminated if their income surpassed the threshold of $52,000 and $78,000 respectively.[14] The proposal, which would have come into effect in 2001, was ultimately abandoned by the

Liberals in 1998 as a result of pressure from seniors' organizations and Quebec, as discussed below.[15]

The Second Tier

The second pillar of old age income security in Canada was also subject to modification. From the 1980s to the 1990s, major changes were undertaken to consolidate the Canada and Quebec Pension Plans. In 1984, Quebec introduced a degree of flexibility into retirement age; Canada followed suit in 1987. Until 1987, individuals were not allowed to receive retirement pension before the age of sixty-five. In accordance with the newly introduced flexible retirement provisions, individuals were given the option of early or even late retirement (at age sixty and seventy respectively). In the case of early retirement, the benefits were to be decreased by 0.5 per cent per month before the age of sixty-five. Similarly, for postponed retirement, retirement pensions were to be increased by 0.5 per cent per month of postponed retirement up to and including age seventy.[16] The same year, the QPP removed the provision that halted survivors' benefits upon remarriage; this was subsequently adopted by the CPP in 1987.[17]

In the late 1980s, two significant changes were made to the provisions governing the C/QPP. In 1988, for the first time, Aboriginal people earning income on reserves were allowed to contribute to the CPP and receive benefits.[18] Before 1988, the Income Tax Act had treated C/QPP contributions as tax deductions; after that year, those contributions would be treated as a non-refundable federal tax credit of 17 per cent of the employee's or a self-employed individual's contributions.[19] In 1989, significant amendments were made to the provisions governing spouses' claims to pension benefits. New provisions were put in place to allow the sharing of a retirement pension between spouses. Also, credit splitting was extended to cover the separation of married or common law spouses.[20] In 1991, legislation was passed to assist those who had been denied a credit split as a result of provisions contained in a spousal agreement entered into prior to June 1986. The amendment provided that applicants who were divorced, or whose marriage had been annulled on or after January 1987, would be credited with the same amount of credits he or she would have received otherwise.[21]

In 1992, three major changes significantly reshaped the C/QPP. After negotiation between the federal and provincial governments, a new twenty-five-year schedule for employee and self-employed contribution rates was established. In accordance with already introduced changes to the contribution rate, the C/QPP contribution rates were set to increase annually by 0.1 per cent of covered earnings for both employees and employers over the next five years.[22] Children's benefits were also increased, and provision was made for individuals who had been denied disability benefits due to late application.[23]

The most significant alteration to the C/QPP took place in the late 1990s. This fundamental reconfiguration was the outcome of a long negotiation between the federal and provincial governments. The agreed changes to the C/QPP were embodied in Bill C-2, introduced in the House of Commons on 25 September 1997 and coming into effect in 1998. To put the CPP on firmer financial footing and secure its long-term viability, three significant changes were made: there was an accelerated increase in contribution rates, the benefit formula was modified, and the plan's investment practices were improved.

In line with the goal of securing the long-term sustainability of the C/QPP, a new schedule of contribution rates was introduced.[24] The contribution rate increase was based on a six-year schedule; the rate was structured to increase from 6 per cent in 1997 to 9.9 per cent in 2003 and would remain constant thereafter. In tandem with progressive increases in contribution rates, changes were also made to income exemption and maximum pensionable earnings.[25] The Year's Basic Exemption (YBE) was to be frozen at $3,500 and was no longer to be indexed. But the Year's Maximum Pensionable Earnings (YMPE) was set to increase in accordance with the indexation. Table 8.2 illustrates the changes made to the C/QPP.

To ensure the long-term sustainability of the second tier of the retirement income system in Canada, the 1997 changes assigned the management of public pension reserve assets to an independent investment board accountable to the federal government but operating independently of the CPP.[26] This was meant to move the second tier of the retirement income system from pay-as-you go to a partly funded plan. The CPP Investment Board was given two objectives: to manage the public pension reserve assets entrusted to the board; and to maximize investment returns without incurring undue risk. Previously, the public pension reserves had been invested solely in risk-free federal and provincial securities. The 1997 modification to the management of public pension assets authorized the CPP Investment Board to diversify the investment opportunity from exclusively government bonds to a blend of bonds, equities, and stocks.[27]

Table 8.2 C/QPP contribution rates, YBE and YMPE history, 1967–2005

Year	YBE ($)	YMPE ($)	Contribution rate (%)
1967	600	5,000	3.6
1987	2,500	25,900	3.8
1997	3,500	35,800	6.0
1998	3,500	36,900	6.4
1999	3,500	37,400	7.0
2000	3,500	37,600	7.8
2001	3,500	38,300	8.6
2002	3,500	39,100	9.4
2003	3,500	39,190	9.9
2005	3,500	41,100	9.9

Sources: Canada, Social Development Canada, *The CPP and OAS Stats Book: Social Development Canada.* 2004, http://www.esdc.gc.ca/en/isp/statistics/pdf/statsbook.pdf; and Canada, *Service Canada: Income Security Program Information Card* (2005), http://www.servicecanada.gc.ca/eng/isp/statistics/rates/julsep05.shtml).

YBE = Year's Basic Exemption
YMPE = Year's Maximum Pensionable Earnings

Changes were also made to the calculation of public pension benefits. Under the 1997 changes, the retirement pension payable to a contributor over sixty-five remained as the basic monthly amount equal to 25 per cent of the contributor's average monthly pensionable earnings adjusted to reflect the average of the YMPE over the last five years. Before the 1997 changes, it had been only the last three years.[28] Significant changes were made to the criteria governing eligibility for disability benefits. Before 1997, for a contributor to receive disability benefits from the CPP, he or she must have contributed to the plan in five of the last ten or two of the last three calendar years (for the QPP, for half the contributory period). Beginning on 31 December 1997, to be entitled to disability benefits, pensioners had to have contributed to the plan for four of the last six years on earnings that were at least 10 per cent of the YMPE (for the QPP, two of the last three or five of the last ten years).[29] The 1997 changes also restructured the calculation of retirement benefits for disabled people. Retirement pensions for people with disabilities were to be based on maximum pensionable earnings at the time of disability and then price-indexed to age sixty-five (under the previous calculation, retirement pension for people with disabilities was based on maximum personable earnings at the time the recipient reached sixty-five). Under the 1997 changes, lump sum death benefits were reduced from a maximum $3,500 to $2,500 and were frozen at that level for those who die after 31 December 1997.[30]

Under the 1997 benefits calculation that came into effect in 1998, the beneficiaries of spouse-survivor's benefits would receive reduced payments.[31] The 1997 changes to the calculation of pension benefits mostly affected payments of the Survivors' Benefit, particularly the combined payment of retirement pension and survivor benefits. Under the 1997 amendments, the combined retirement pension and survivor benefits for a survivor over sixty-five was set at the sum of retirement pension plus the lesser of (1) 60 per cent of deceased's retirement pension minus the lesser of 40 per cent of that amount and 40 per cent of the survivor's retirement pension before an actuarial adjustment; or (2) the ceiling of the maximum retirement pension in the year of entitlement to the second benefit. For a survivor between sixty and sixty-five, the amount of the combined pension was set as the adjusted retirement pension plus the survivor's flat rate benefits plus the lesser of (1) 37.5 per cent of the deceased's retirement pension minus the lesser of 40 per cent of that amount, or (2) the maximum survivor's retirement pension in the year of entitlement to the second benefits plus the survivor's flat rate.[32] Table 8.3 shows the maximum monthly payments for the beneficiaries of C/QPP.[33] In July 2000, with the Modernization of Benefits and Obligations Act, benefits and coverage were extended to same-sex partners. Under the new provisions, the same-sex partners were to be provided with the same benefits and coverage as those provided to common law partners of the opposite sex. It was due to this modernization initiative, intended to bring about equality of treatment, that the term "Common-Law partner" came to substitute for the term "spouse" in both the C/QPP and the OAS. As a result of this modification, Spouse's Allowance was replaced with Allowance, and Widowed Spouse's Allowance was renamed Allowance for the Survivor. Similarly, eligibility for C/QPP survivors' benefits and credit splitting was extended to same-sex couples.[34]

The Third Tier

At the same time as the changes to the first and second pillars of the retirement income system, voluntary private occupational plans known as

Table 8.3 Maximum monthly amount paid out by the C/QPP, 1972–2005, in 2011 dollars (CPI: 2002 = 100)

Year	Retirement pension	Disability pension	Spouse pension	Dependent children pension	Lump sum death payment
1972	369.55	613.08	382.09	151.11	3,011.19
1982	671.90	658.29	406.33	154.36	3,603.55
1992	907.97	1,118.91	513.40	227.95	4,596.17
2000	926.17	1,153.04	528.87	213.75	3,142.03
2002	945.71	1,146.30	525.15	220.34	2,997.50
2005	928.66	1,132.02	557.20	224.64	2,801.40

Sources: Adopted from the CPP and OAS Statistic Tables in Canada, Social Development Canada, *The CPP and OAS Stats Book: Social Development Canada.* 2004, http://www.esdc.gc.ca/en/isp/statistics/pdf/statsbook.pdf; and Canada, *Service Canada: Income Security Program Information Card* (2005), http://www.esdc.gc.ca/en/isp/statistics/pdf/statsbook.pdf, For deflating prices, StatsCan's consumer price index (CPI) has been used (http://www.statcan.gc.ca/tables-tableaux/sum-som/l01/cst01/econ46a-eng.htm).

Registered Pension Plans (RPPs) and personal savings plans or Registered Retirement Savings Plans (RRSPs), as the main components of the third tier of the retirement income system, were also subject to major modifications. These changes were intended to encourage individuals to make provision for their own retirement income. The most significant change to the rules governing private occupational pension plans was the enactment of the Pension Benefits Standards Act of 1985 (taking effect on 1 January 1987). That act was intended to enhance coverage, vesting, indexation, and portability of benefits so as to address what had long been shortcomings of employer-sponsored private pension plans.[35] To equalize tax concessions for retirement savings through both RPPs and RRSPs, Bill C-52 amended the Income Tax Act and related acts in 1990.[36] The 1990 act changed the rules for granting tax assistance and equalized the limit on the tax-deductible contribution, which was scheduled to increase over the years. The annual dollar limit was initially set at 18 per cent of earned income in the previous year for RRSPs and 18 per cent of remuneration for RPPs (defined contribution) up to a specified threshold. Contribution limits to RPPs were set at $11,500 in 1991 and reached $13,500 in 2001.[37] Even though 86 per cent of private occupation plan members belonged to defined benefit plans in 1998, the share of defined contribution plans has been growing in recent years.[38]

To further advance the privatization of old age income security, greater incentives were provided to encourage individuals to use RRSPs as a private provision for their retirement income. Since 1991, tax filers who did not use their annual RRSP contribution limit had been allowed to use the unused room in the following years.[39] Also since 1991, tax filers were permitted to use an additional $8,000 lifetime over the contribution limit. This amount had to be used as part of future eligibility deduction before the end of the year during which the tax filer reached the age of retirement.[40] In its 1995 budget, the federal government reduced this additional amount to $2,000. Tax filers with contributions exceeding this margin were subject to a penalty at the rate of 1 per cent of the excess amount per month.[41]

Despite the progressive upgrading of concessional tax treatment of private provisions for retirement income, private arrangements for retirement income have not eclipsed or diminished the centrality of the first and second pillars of the retirement income system as the main sources of income for over two-thirds of seniors.[42] In sharp contrast to the intended purpose of encouraging private occupational and personal pension plans, the proportion of the workforce participating in private occupational pension plans began to decline by 1999. In 1991, 37 per cent of workers were covered by employer-sponsored occupational plans; by 1999, only 33 per cent. However, due to sustained growth and employment, the percentage of the workforce covered by employer-sponsored programs had risen to 39 per cent by 2000.[43]

Even though there has been an increase in the percentage of tax filers who use RRSPs as a retirement savings vehicle, RRSPs are used mainly by people with high incomes. In 1983, 15 per cent of tax filers made contributions to RRSPs.[44] In 2006, only 20 per cent of Canadians made contributions to RRSPs.[45] The vast majority of those who contributed to both RPPs and RRSPs were in higher income brackets.[46] Due to the correlation between income and contributions to private pension plans, in 2001, 25 per cent of families in Canada owned 84 per cent of pension assets held by RPPs and RRSPs and three out of ten families had no private pension assets at all.[47] Indeed, plans such as RRSPs reinforce economic inequality, since it is mainly high-income earners with extra disposable income or assets who benefit from RRSPs, which do not serve as an alternative to the CPP or RPPs for lower-income citizens.

The Postwar Social Settlement and Retirement Income Restructuring in Canada

The push for welfare state retrenchment came mainly from organizations representing the interests of the business community. With the economic crisis of the 1970s, the business community saw an opportunity to call for fiscal austerity and for the replacement of universality by a need-based redistribution of social welfare benefits. In its 1979 statements on the status of social security in Canada, the Canadian Council on Social Development (CCSD) reflected the business community's view on social welfare policy when it urged the federal government to end the principle of universality and adopt selectivity as an appropriate means to address poverty. According to the CCSD, the emerging reality meant that social welfare policy had to be confined to "ensuring that the major objective of income redistribution is the reduction of poverty. Completely recovering family allowances and old age security payments from recipients with income above average family income."[48]

Despite the pressures for the retrenchment and overhauling of social welfare programs, the Liberal government of Pierre Trudeau was reluctant to embark on a major transformation of existing social programs in the late 1970s. The Liberal government had already adopted market-oriented regulatory and monetary measures and also more interventionist policies such as wage and price controls to tackle the economic crisis. However, considerations of national unity limited its capacity to subject retirement income programs to the forces of retrenchment emanating from the business community. Under the Liberal government of the late 1970s and early 1980s, the discourse of national unity mitigated the pressures for social welfare retrenchment. The political nature of income security retirement as an instrument of nation-building was reiterated by Prime Minister Trudeau, who reminded the provincial premiers that income security programs were indispensable to the unity and national identity of Canadians: "We must take greater care not to damage the social fabric of our society by a loss of compassion for aged ... and less favoured."[49]

During the Conference of the First Ministers on the Constitution in 1981, Trudeau called the participants "nation builders" and warned them that social welfare retrenchment might jeopardize Canada's cohesion.[50] In his opening statement to the First Ministers Conference on the Economy in 1982, he emphasized the significance of social welfare programs to the preservation of Canadian unity: "The course we are on is a course made in Canada, it is not here that you will find massive cutbacks in the great social programs which serve the people. These programs for Canadians – health insurance, assistance for our senior citizens, family allowance, unemployment insurance and many others – were and are an expression of our national will, of our desire to work together, to share together. Their importance is greater than ever in these difficult times, and we are dedicated to making them better still."[51]

With the changes in the international and national political climate in the mid-1980s, neoliberal ideas in Canada led to the ascendancy of the Progressive Conservative government of Brian Mulroney in 1984. Under that government, the neoliberal discourse of restraint found an amicable atmosphere. The Mulroney government prepared the ground for neoliberalism to permeate the economic and social policy agenda in Ottawa.[52] In the emerging neoconservative climate, even state intervention in the economy in support of social policy came to be construed as a restriction on individual freedom, and momentum grew to "liberate market forces" from the state. In his 1985 budget speech outlining the Conservative agenda for social transfer cuts, changes to the tax structure, and privatization of publicly owned corporations, finance minister Michael Wilson contended: "The actions I am proposing are realistic, effective and fair. They represent a fundamental break with the past. For too long government decided what is best for Canadians. My budget calls for Canadians, not government, to choose what is best for Canada. Government is not only too big, it also reaches too far into almost every aspect of the economy ... Too often government frustrates entrepreneurship and discourages initiative."[53]

By the beginning of the second term as prime minister, Mulroney was praising his own government for launching "a process of deregulation and privatization aimed at ensuring that the market was allowed to work efficiently and effectively."[54] But although it partly succeeded in cutting social transfers and altering the tax structure to favour the business community, the Mulroney government failed to fully launch a neoliberal revolution in Canada.[55]

The Mulroney government encountered obstacles to reconstructing the state along neoliberal policy lines. Active involvement by the Canadian state has historically been indispensable to national unity. Despite the neoconservative pledge to trim the Canadian bureaucracy, the public service in fact grew by 13,000 during the Progressive Conservative administration from 1984 to 1993.[56] At the annual conference of first ministers held in Ottawa on 9–10 November 1989, Mulroney reiterated the significance of national unity for Canadian politics: "You and I and our fellow Canadians from coast to coast who share our commitment to this idea could not unite in a more compelling or historical cause or a more urgent one. The cause is Canada. One Canada. And that, above everything else is unity. Unity is the linchpin of our growth, it is the linchpin of our prosperity; and it is the cornerstone of our future, without unity, that future is not what it could be or what it should be."[57]

With the entrenchment of the Canadian welfare state as a significant pillar of national unity, even a Conservative government found it difficult to embark on a fundamental retrenchment of the welfare state, particularly in the areas of pensions and health care.[58] The historical links between the principle of universality in old age security, Canadian identity, and national unity became prominent during the passionate debate over the restructuring of the OAS in 1989. The emphasis on the principle of universality in OAS benefits as the basis for Canadian identity was reiterated by both the government and the opposition parties. John Turner, the Liberal leader of the opposition, identified the universal OAS as "part of the social contract in Canada."[59] In her defence of the principle of universality governing the OAS, Albina Guarnieri of the Liberal Party argued that "universal right is not a gift, it is an integral part of the Canadian identity."[60] At the beginning of his administration, Mulroney had emphasized the sacrosanct nature of universality in Canada. In his speeches on 7 March 1984 and 15 October 1988 that were quoted in the House of Commons debates in 1989, Mulroney underscored his government's determination to preserve the principle of universality: "Our position is simple and straightforward, we are in favor of universality in social programs, and it shall not be touched ... Let me [say] a special word to the senior citizens. In the future Canada will be doing more, not less, for all of you. As long as I am Prime Minister of Canada, social benefits and especially those for the elderly will be improved, not diminished by our government[,] which is committed to justice and fairness for Canadians."[61]

During the Mulroney government, pensions were subject to several improvements. The equalization of tax shelters obtainable from private and occupational pension plans, the flexibility of the retirement age under the contributory public pension plan, the extension of credit splitting to common law spouses, and, finally, the extension of the Spouse's Allowance to low-income widows and widowers, all were major progressive improvements to the existing retirement income system. But after its retreat from partial deindexation of OAS payments due to pressure from the opposition parties and senior citizens' groups,[62] the Conservative government found an alternative strategy for pursuing its cost containment policy. This was the introduction of the clawback on OAS payments in 1989. Even though the clawback has been interpreted as the end of universality, the Conservative government did not regard it as a violation of the principle of universality. During the debates on the introduction of the clawback in the House of Commons, Alan Redway, the parliamentary secretary to the government house leader, clarified this point: "This particular proposal [surtax on high income earners] that is before the House clearly observes the principle of universality. There is no question about it ... [W]ho applies for old age pension has in the past received an old age pension cheque and will continue to receive an old age pension cheque. The tax is at higher level for people with higher income."[63 64]

In fact, the generosity of the clawback meant that it only affected the small proportion of OAS recipients who had high incomes, and all eligible recipients received their OAS cheques. Consequently, the less intrusive nature of the clawback reinforced the Conservative government's claim to have preserved the principle of universality. The clawback provision modified the OAS but did not eclipse its universal character for the vast majority of pensioners. The form of the clawback was such that it could be construed as a surcharge tax on high-income recipients of a universal OAS. It cannot be seen as the reintroduction of the pre-1952 residual principles into the first tier of the Canadian retirement income system, as all individuals over sixty-five still received their OAS cheques regardless of their income. In the national accounts, repayments were treated as income tax revenue, not as a reduction in the cost of OAS expenditures or as a surtax of 15 per cent on income above the threshold of $57,000 in 2002.[65]

From its inception in 1989 to 2005, the clawback provision affected only a small percentage of OAS recipients. In 2000–1, only 5 per cent of pensioners received reduced OAS benefits and only 2 per cent of high-income pensioners lost their entire OAS benefits.[66] In a comparative study of retirement income systems in OECD countries, Whitehouse concluded that the "OAS is near universal because entitlement is based on residency" and covers almost all retired Canadians.[67] Furthermore, the surtax on high-income OAS recipients enhanced the political marketability of a universal state pension, given that the clawback was quite different from the stigmatizing means test of a residual welfare state – a test that Canada had in the past and that Australia was adopting.

The real threat to the Canadian welfare state – one that had not transpired during the neoconservative retrenchment under the Mulroney government – began to loom when the Liberals returned to power in 1993. The Liberals' proposed sweeping reforms of social welfare programs were outlined in a 1994 discussion paper called *Improving Social Security in Canada*, produced by the Department of Human Resources. In its discussion paper on the proposed social welfare reforms, Chrétien's Liberal government characterized those programs as a drain on the economy.[68] Furthermore, the governing Liberals emphasized limits on welfare programs as necessary in order to diminish disincentives to work and boost labour market participation. According to *Improving Social Security in Canada*, the main objectives were cost containment, the targeting of social benefits, a shift from passive social security to active and employment-centred social welfare programs, an enhanced role for the voluntary sector in the delivery of social services, and a shift in the locus of responsibility and decision-making over social programs to provincial governments.[69] Under the proposed reforms to social security made in the 1994 and 1995 budgets, the principle of universality in the OAS was to be breached. The Liberals proposed integrating the three components of the first tier of the retirement income system into an income-tested single plan called the Seniors Benefit, which was to come into effect in 2001.

During the run-up to the Quebec referendum on sovereignty-association in October 1995, the Liberal government was accused of hiding its sweeping reform of social welfare programs, for the reforms would have a decisive impact on the referendum's outcome. The Liberal government's drastic reforms to social programs had been leaked to and revealed by Gerald Larose, the head of la Confederation des Syndicats Nationaux (CSN).[70] The Liberals' reluctance to elaborate on their proposed reforms to the retirement income system had already been brought to light by the opposition parties in Parliament.[71] The CSN's revelation that the Liberals proposed a retrenchment and restructuring of social welfare programs was interpreted by Sheila Copps, the deputy prime minister, as "pure separatist propaganda" intended to tarnish the Canada's image and galvanize support for Quebec separation.[72] To counter the political attacks and to reassure Quebecers of the generosity of the Canadian welfare state, Copps re-emphasized the principles of universality, generosity, and progressivity of social programs as "a part of the Canadian dream."[73]

As the Quebec referendum loomed, the political competition between Canada and Quebec nationalists with regard to generous and universal social welfare programs underscored that social welfare programs, and especially pensions, had long been the political glue of national unity. Consequently, the Canadian welfare state set out to mitigate the neoliberal push for a sweeping social welfare retrenchment that had been contemplated by the Liberal government. During the Quebec referendum campaign, Lucien Bouchard, the leader of the Bloc Québécois, argued that Canada had abandoned its tradition of promoting social justice and generosity towards those in need. According to him, there was "a cold wind from English Canada" that was bound to lead to a crueller and harsher Canada, and only in an independent Quebec would generous social programs be maintained.[74] To heighten the appeal of sovereignty-association in Quebec and to weaken the federal government's capacity to employ the welfare state as a bargaining chip to maintain Quebecers' allegiance to Canada, Bouchard urged Chrétien to disclose his government's social welfare reforms, which he contended were being delayed until after the referendum. During the debate, Bouchard asked the prime minister to "[t]able his social program reform now, so that Quebecers can make an informed decision on the kind of society they want on October 31 ... The Prime Minister wants to postpone the tabling of this reform, because he has every reason to fear the devastating scope of cuts he is about to make. Does he not realize that by taking his clue from simplistic and heartless solutions proposed by Mike Harris [the Ontario premier], he is preparing the ground for a fractured and divided society in Canada and Quebec."[75]

Underpinning Bouchard's statement was an explicit admission that Canada had historically employed the welfare state as a means to secure French Canadians' loyalty. He was suggesting to Quebecers that since Canadian social welfare programs would inevitably decline in generosity after the referendum, there was no justification to oppose sovereignty-association for Quebec. To counter the appeal of Quebec nationalism, Chrétien labelled the BQ's statements as "blackmail" and "scaremongering." He was forced to assure Quebecers that generous retirement income programs would be preserved:

> If really we want to reassure retired people in Quebec the best way to do so is to tell them that they will continue to receive their old age pensions from the government of Canada after October 30, while the Parti Quebecois [PQ] is creating extreme uncertainty with its separatist plans. The best way to reassure seniors is to tell them. The government of Canada still is there after October 30 to pay your old age pensions. There will be no doubt about

that. We will never compromise the security of seniors who depend on government pensions. To those who are afraid today because PQ members are trying to scare them I say do not be afraid.[76]

The historical role of the Canadian welfare state as a fount of national unity paradoxically increased the political weight of the NDP, which had long campaigned for generous, progressive, and universal social programs. Capitalizing on the need to preserve generous social programs in order to dissuade French Canadians from endorsing sovereignty-association, the NDP MPs emphasized the political ramifications of social welfare retrenchment for the survival of a united Canada. On the eve of the Quebec referendum of 30 October 1995, Chris Axworthy of the NDP reminded the Liberal government that a generous and progressive welfare state was indispensable to national unity: "[Is] tearing down the very institutions which define us as Canadians and which we hold dear [...] the way to build a strong, united country[?]"[77]

In line with Axworthy's statement, which highlighted the link between national unity and the welfare state, Bill Blaikie, another NDP MP, seized the opportunity provided by the desire to preserve national unity as grounds to promote social and economic justice in Canada. During the debate on the Quebec referendum in the House of Commons, Blaikie emphasized the importance of a progressive and generous welfare state to Canada's survival: "A house divided against itself cannot stand, but even an apparently united house – without a foundation of social and economic justice, is a house built on sand."[78]

The political manoeuvring of the BQ MPs forced the Liberal government to revisit its plan to reform retirement income programs, indirectly bolstering the NDP's political project. The BQ's strong opposition to any trimming of social welfare programs had been highlighted by Ed Broadbent, a prominent NDP MP, in the *Globe and Mail*. The BQ now harnessed his words to its own political agenda. In a passionate parliamentary statement meant to enhance the BQ's progressive image, Claude Bachand boastfully repeated Broadbent's remarks so as to depict the BQ as a progressive political force: "Ed Broadbent wrote in the *Globe and Mail* that, the strongest voice in Ottawa in defence of Canadians' social and economic rights was that of the Bloc Quebecois."[79]

Even after a narrow victory of the "No" side in the referendum, the question of national unity continued to shape debates on the future of retirement income programs. The day after the Quebec referendum, the BQ MPs continued to pressure the Liberal government to adhere to its pre-referendum pledges. During the parliamentary debate of 31 October 1995, Gilles Duceppe of the BQ called on Prime Minister Chrétien to "reiterate the commitment made on numerous occasions during the referendum campaign that his government will not cut the old age pensions."[80] The same day, Pauline Ricard, also of the BQ, reminded the prime minister of the inconsistency of his government's hidden agenda for cutting social welfare programs with the quest to maintain national unity: "The federal government has deliberately been cruising in neutral since the end of September while waiting for the Quebec referendum results. Major changes to ... old age pension will be introduced, and they will hit harder than ever before since the inception of these programs ... We know that this choice is totally inconsistent with Quebec's aspiration in terms of society. The wind of change coming from Ottawa is really a flurry of drastic cuts that has Quebec shivering."[81]

Under political pressure over national unity, Chrétien was forced to reiterate that his government would adhere to its pre-referendum promises. In response to a question from Duceppe, Chrétien stated that his government had no intention of "cutting the federal pension benefits being received by those who are already retired."[82] Chrétien's statement left room for his government's long-contemplated plan to fold OAS and GIS into a single income-tested program called the Seniors Benefit. However, considerations of national unity and the Liberals' pre-referendum promises to retain the integrity of the OAS became obstacles to the replacement of these programs with the Seniors Benefit.

During the debate over the proposed 1996 budget, which included major cuts to social welfare programs, the Liberals were reminded of the political implications of social welfare retrenchment for national unity. In a passionate statement on the 1996 budget, Duceppe reminded the Liberal government of its stance on the link between social welfare programs and national unity. He did not think that social welfare cuts were "helping national unity on the Canadian point of view" and declared that his party "will be ready to fight that budget and have an election on that budget at any time."[83]

The links between the welfare state, national identity, and national unity had become so strong that it was now difficult to fully implement the neoliberal objectives of welfare state retrenchment. The Liberal government deployed a number of senior officials to make a link between a core welfare state and national unity. During the Senate debate on the 1996 budget, Joyce Fairbairn, the leader of the government in the Senate, again emphasized that generous social programs such as health care, OAS, and CPP were indispensable to the "unity of this country" and that they had helped define "the very nature of the society in which we [Canadians] wish to live ... and that have become a basic right of Canadian citizenship."[84] The imperative to maintain national unity through a universal and generous welfare state was strong and could not easily be subordinated to the exigencies of social welfare retrenchment. In his address to the Canadian Club on 18 November 1996, Stéphane Dion, then president of the Queen's Privy Council and the intergovernmental affairs minister, relegated the economic argument for securing national unity to a secondary position and instead identified "solidarity" as the main mechanism for fostering national unity. Invoking the trade union movement's famous slogan that "an injury to one is an injury to all," he pointed out that Canadians "have been able to achieve a strong sense of solidarity through our national social programs and collective action ... The social programs Canada enjoys ... will be preserved for future generations."[85]

The Canadian Labour Congress opposed the proposed Seniors Benefit;[86] in addition to this, the plan was unpopular in Quebec. The Quebec government warned its citizens that the Seniors Benefit, if implemented, "will have a far greater impact than the recovery measure [clawback] currently applied to the Old Age Security pensions."[87] Quebecers were told that the proposed Seniors Benefit would not only jeopardize "the long term financial security of retirees" but also "reduce the financial independence of the spouse with lower income," since the calculation of benefits would be based on family income.[88] It was under these pressures that on 28 July 1998, Paul Martin, the Liberal finance minister, announced that the government intended to set aside the Seniors Benefit. But he attributed the government's retreat to the strengthening of the Canadian economy: "In light of the structural enhancements to the public pension system, the turnaround in the country's economic prospects, and because of our commitment to sound fiscal management, the government is today announcing that the proposed Seniors Benefit will not proceed, the existing OAS/GIS will be fully maintained."[89]

National unity also played a decisive role in the restructuring of the earnings-related public pension plan when its affordability and long-term sustainability became a subject of intense debate in the mid-1990s. It was for reasons of national unity that neoliberal efforts to dismantle the universal public pension and replace it with voluntary or mandatory individual saving accounts were halted.

The future of the earnings-related component of the retirement income system had been debated since the late 1970s, but it was only in the mid-1990s that reforms to the universal public pension plan gained momentum. By tabling a dire projection made in the Fifteenth Actuarial Report on the CPP in the House of Commons in February 1995, the federal government prepared the ground for reforming the earnings-related component of the retirement income system. That report, released on 31 December 1993, projected that "if changes were not made, the fund would be exhausted by 2015 and the contribution rate would have to jump to over 14.2%."[90] The Liberal government raised the alarm by reminding Canadians of the rising costs of the public pension plan and the need to place it on sustainable foundations.[91] In February 1996, after consulting with provincial governments, the federal finance department released a join assessment of the CPP's long-term sustainability. The 1996 information paper raised the questions of "fairness," "equity," and "intergenerational conflict." It also warned Canadians that the "sustainability of the CPP was in question because young people will be asked to pay more into the CPP than their parents did ... yet receive no more in the way of benefits ... This is why Canadians are concerned about the future sustainability of the CPP."[92] By questioning the long-term viability of the CPP and proposing alternative measures, the 1996 information paper set the tone for public consultation. The main options proposed were as follows: increasing the contribution rate so as to reduce the replacement rate from 25 to 22.5 per cent; raising the age of entitlement from sixty-five to sixty-seven; partly indexing benefits; increasing the years required for full benefits; tightening eligibility requirements for disability pension; establishing a partial pension; eliminating death benefits; changing survivors' and disability benefits; and launching a new investment policy for CPP funds.[93] In their subsequent joint statement on guiding principles released in November 1996, the federal and provincial governments emphasized that the CPP was a "key pillar of Canada's retirement income system." They also emphasized that it was imperative to invest pension funds in the interests of plan members and to "maintain a proper balance between returns and investment risk."[94]

The fears generated by the statements of the federal and provincial governments, compounded by the shift towards various forms of privatized pension schemes in several countries, provided an opportunity for neoliberal-oriented research institutes and right-wing political parties to intensify their efforts to undermine the CPP's collectivist character. In the media, Andrew Coyne, a neoliberal-oriented writer, called for the privatization of retirement income; in his view, this would allow Canada to become "a Nation of Savers."[95] In his study for the C.D. Howe Institute published in September 1994, Tom Courchene called for the abolition of the earnings-related component of the retirement income system. He argued that Canadians "do not need two nearly comprehensive public programs for elderly people," and he suggested that OAS, GIS, and CPP be combined into a single plan based on "negative income or tax credit funded out of general revenue."[96] In another study for the C.D. Howe Institute published in January 1996, William Robson called for the CPP to be replaced with "mandatory RRSP contributions" that would re-establish individual responsibility and control over old age retirement income.[97] Reflecting the political sentiment of the C.D. Howe Institute, Robson called for the expansion of the third tier of the retirement income system. According to him, "particular attention must be given to providing choices to employees and employers that will allow them to adopt compensation packages and investment ... tailored to individual needs."[98] The business community's most elaborate view of reforms to Canada's retirement income system was articulated by the British North American Committee, which coordinates and represents the interests of the business sector in Britain, the United States, and Canada. In its 1997 statement on pension reform, the BNAC recommended that "governments should educate the population on the need to save by providing fiscal incentives and regulations to encourage individuals to make provision for their futures. This would involve modifying caps and other obstacles to private pensions. Employers should emphasize the promotion of cost-effective provision of retirement savings [as] a key element of their employees['] compensation ... Individuals who are in a position to do so should take responsibility for their own future – that is saving and investing with a view to maintaining their living standards through a lengthy retirement."[99]

On the political front, the Reform Party (which would later transform itself into the Canadian Alliance and then the Conservative Party) became the voice of corporate interests. In a pamphlet, *Renewing CPP*, released on 11 October 1995, the Reform Party proposed eliminating the CPP and replacing it with "Super-RRSPs."[100] On 9 November 1995, the Reform Party tabled its proposal in the House of Commons. A neoliberal party in economic matters, it called loudly for restrictions on state involvement in social welfare programs. Chuck Strahl, a Reform MP, argued that "[i]n order for Canada to prosper, the socialist tendency of this overwhelmingly intrusive central government must be permanently laid to rest."[101]

Reform's calls to curtail the federal government's power by decoupling it from social income security were rebutted by Prime Minister Chrétien during the debate on Quebec sovereignty. Chrétien depicted the Reform vision of Canada as a threat to Canadian unity. He again emphasized the historical link between social welfare programs and national unity. In his attack on Reform's divisive political program, Chrétien highlighted the importance of national social policies to Canada's image in Quebec: "If the leader of the Third Party had been in Quebec, he would have realized that nobody in Quebec voted to dismantle Medicare ... Nobody voted for the agenda of the Reform Party to destroy the social safety net that exists in Canada. What the leader of the Third Party is trying to do at this moment is sell its very right wing agenda, to the right of Gingrich [the Speaker of the US House of Representatives in the 1990s]. He is using this occasion to pass his own political agenda rather than arguing for the survival of the country."[102]

The concerted attempts by neoliberal forces to advance the privatization of Canada's retirement income system and undermine the integrity of the universal public pension did not enjoy wide public support. Cross-Canada public hearings led to a report on the Canadian Pension Plan Consultation in June 1996. That report confirmed that "most Canadians want the CPP preserved and protected now as a key pillar of retirement income system."[103] Representatives of business groups opposed higher contribution rates and endorsed a reduction in benefits and opting out of the CPP; but other groups, such as labour and women organizations, opposed benefit reductions and supported higher contribution rates.[104] Some representatives of business, such as taxpayers' associations, also proposed that the CPP be replaced by a privately managed mandatory defined contributory plan. All groups that had been consulted endorsed the investment of CPP funds in financial markets. Labour representatives argued that "the broader interests of Canadians should be taken into account in developing an investment policy and that maximizing returns should not be the only objective."[105]

The suggestion that the earnings-related component of the retirement income system (CPP) be privatized did not elicit a positive response from the federal and provincial governments. In sharp contrast to the privatization crusade launched by the defenders of corporate interests, "all governments in Canada have rejected the idea of replacing the CPP with mandatory 'RRSPs,'" and they were "committed to maintain fair and sustainable Canada and Quebec pension plans for seniors."[106] After releasing a public consultation paper, the federal government and eight of the ten provincial governments reached an agreement on a three-part approach to restoring the financial sustainability of the CPP.[107] It was proposed that the fairness, affordability, and sustainability of the CPP be secured for future generations by:

1 Moving to fuller funding by accelerating the legislated contribution rate increases;
2 Improving the rate of return on the CPP fund by adopting new investment policy; and
3 Slowing the growth in costs by tightening the administration of benefits, and changing the way benefits are calculated.[108]

The February 1997 agreement between the federal and provincial governments on proposed changes to the CPP was clearly influenced by the exigencies of national unity. Some of the radical changes to the CPP that had been proposed by the federal and the other English-speaking provincial governments in the February 1996 information paper had been modified by the stance of the Quebec government. In its own 1996 information paper released for public consultation, the Quebec government declared that some of the options proposed by the federal and other provincial governments "cannot be applied in Quebec because they would call into question the foundation of the plan."[109] The Quebec government declared that it would never endorse an agreement that threatened the integrity and progressivity of the QPP. It vowed to retain the plan's four main features: an income replacement rate of 25 per cent; retirement at sixty-five; indexation of benefits; and the exclusion of years when earnings are low or nil.[110]

Owing to its weight within the Canadian federation, the Quebec government was in a strong position to block the changes proposed by the federal and other provincial governments. With the help of the NDP provincial governments in BC and Saskatchewan, Quebec was in a position to veto the proposed changes. Given the need to harmonize the Canada and Quebec Pension Plans, which has been a key policy arrangement between Canada and Quebec since the inception of both plans in 1966, the February 1997 final agreement on the proposed changes had to address Quebec's proposals released in its own 1996 information paper. As can be observed in Table 8.4, the proposed changes in the February 1996 information paper were watered down in order to accommodate Quebec's demands.

The proposed changes that were agreed upon by the federal government and eight of the ten provincial governments in February 1997 were incorporated into Bill C-2, which was tabled in the House of Commons in December 1997. During the debate on that bill, the Reform Party continued trying to undermine the integrity of the universal public pension. Diane Ablonczy, a Reform MP, argued that "younger Canadians should be allowed to opt out of a bad plan into mandatory pension

Table 8.4 Interaction between proposed changes and final agreement on changes to C/QPP

Features of C/QPP	February 1996 information paper	The 1996 Quebec information paper	February 1997 final agreement
Income replacement rate	Reduce from 25% to 22.5%, which would reduce CPP pension benefits by 10%	Maintain it at 25%	No change
Retirement age	Increase it from 65 to 67	Maintain it at 65	No change
Indexation of benefits	Partly index benefits (CPI minus 1%)	Maintain full indexation	Retain full indexation
Calculation of drop-out years	Reduce number of years excluded from calculation of pension benefits from 15% to 10%	No change in existing calculation	No change
Contribution rate	Large increase and then remain steady state	Large increase and then remain steady state	Raise to 9.9% by 200[illegible] and then hold steady
Year's basic exemption	Cut to 5% of YMPE rather than 10%, or freeze it at 1997 level	Freeze it at 1997 level. Allow more low-income workers to be covered by the plan	Frozen at $3,500
Year's maximum pensionable earnings (YMPE)	No option proposed	No option proposed	No change
Investment policy	Diversify the investment of CPP	Already diversified	New funds invested in a diversified portfolio
Eligibility for disability pensions	Must have worked and contributed in 4 of last 6 years	This option was not considered for QPP because of its strict and fair administration (since 1993, 2 of the last 3 years for temporary disability benefits and half of the contributory period for chronically disabled people)	Must work and contribute in 4 of last 6 years
Death benefits	Eliminate death benefits	Priority should be given to person who paid the funeral expenses	6 months' retirement benefits to maximum $2,500, and frozen

Sources: Canada, *An Information Paper for Consultations on the Canada Pension Plan Released by the Federal, Provincial, and Territorial Governments of Canada* (February, Department of Finance) (Ottawa: Canadian Government Publishing, 1996); Québec, Direction des Communications Regie Des Rentes du Quebec, *For You and Your Children: Guaranteeing the Future of the Quebec Pension Plan* (1996), http://www.rrq.gouv.qc.ca/SiteCollectionDocuments/www.rrq.gouv.qc/Anglais/publications/regime_rentes/rrq_livvert_en.pdf; Canada, *Proceedings: First Ministers Meeting December 11–12: Final Agenda, Framework for Social Union* (Ottawa: Canadian Government Publishing, 1997)

investment accounts that would deliver a fully funded individually owned pension."[111] She revealed the plan the Reform Party had for the CPP: "The fact is the CPP is not a pension plan, it is a political promise backed up by a government's ability to tax citizens the fund needed to pay for the promises. Political promises change with change in power. They change with changing reality. They change with circumstances and with shift in voter support."[112]

Reform's attempts to advance the cause of privatization were frustrated by the unanimity of agreement among the other political parties to retain the CPP's integrity. Indeed, the other political parties emphasized the significance of the CPP to national unity. Tony Valeri, the parliamentary secretary to the finance minister, identified the CPP as "the most important social policy initiative ever taken in this country," and one that should not be replaced by RRSPs.[113] Gilles Bernier, a Progressive Conservative MP, argued that "it is a fundamental part of the Canadian social safety net; an obligation that the government must honour ... [T]he CPP is worth saving."[114] In conjunction with the NDP's attacks on the Reform Party's radical proposals, Paul Crete of the BQ argued that the Chilean road as suggested by the Reform Party "would create a major imbalance in society and would not respect the entire tradition we have built upon."[115] In his statement on the bill, Robert D. Nault, the parliamentary secretary to the human resources development minister, emphasized that the CPP was a symbol of solidarity that signalled the collectivity and progressiveness of the Canadian welfare state. According to Nault, "[t]he CPP is also a symbol of the kind of society we as Canadians have built, a society where we encourage individual effort but strive to use our national wealth to enable a basic standard of living for all."[116] Paul Martin, the finance minister, hailed the restructured CPP as one of the most progressive retirement insurance plans: "As a result of fuller funding, as a result of the changes to the benefits, in fact, we have now preserved the Canadian pension plan for future generations of Canadians ... In fact we have now put in place along with provinces one of the most modern and one of the most progressive retirement systems in the world.[117]

Paul Martin's description of the C/QPP is, of course, an overstatement with regard to the progressiveness of the retirement system in Canada. But faced with neoliberal forces, the Canadian pension system has sustained a universal social insurance program that pools risks and addresses the loss of income faced by workers who retire or become disabled. The OAS is nearly universal; the income-tested GIS is generous; the C/QPP includes a redistributive mechanism: "The earnings-related pension

[C/QPP] offers a flat, 25 percent replacement rates at first, but the replacement rate declines once the earnings threshold is reached. Adding the components together, the Canadian public pension system is highly progressive, paying much higher replacement rates to low income than to higher income workers."[118]

In Canada, national cohesion is expected to emerge from the interregional, intergroup, and interpersonal redistribution of resources.[119] The strong links between national unity, Canadian identity, and the welfare state have acted as a counterweight to neoliberal welfare state retrenchment. Some neoliberal writers view national unity as a fundamental force behind Canada's universal national programs. In *De-confederation,* Bercuson and Cooper assert that only with the departure of Quebec from Canada could Canadian society truly embrace the neoliberal spirit: "The departure of Quebec would provide a magnificent opportunity for Canadians to undertake a genuine restructuring of the political order in which they live. So long as Quebec is part of Canada we will have to deal with Quebec's political problems first. Since those problems are insoluble so long as Quebec is part of Canada, the real problems of the rest of the country will never come to the top of the agenda and will never get dealt with. The expenditure crisis, the deficit crisis, the debt crisis, however you identify it, symbolize this fact."[120]

Canadian neoliberals understand that national unity has had a crucial impact on the development and maintenance of universal social welfare programs. In the competition between Quebec and Canada for citizens' allegiance to their respective states, social welfare programs such as old age pensions have played a central role. This became evident in the 1980s and the 1990s during the debates over reforming the retirement income system. Maurice Lamontagne, the president of the Privy Council and the secretary of state in the Pearson Liberal government pointed out in the 1960s: "I think it [the opting out formula] was a very useful formula at that time because we applied it systematically; and if we had not applied that systematically, Quebec would not have gone for these strong social welfare programs; if Quebec had not gone for these programs it would have been very difficult to advance them for the rest of the country."[121]

The reform of the CPP in 1997 was the culmination of a series of attempts to restructure and retrench the Canadian retirement income system that started with the OAS clawback in 1989.[122] Indeed, in the decade following the reform of the CPP in 1997, no major changes or amendments were made to either the OAS Act or the CPP Act.[123] Since the 1997 reform, attention has shifted to enhancing the CPP Investment Board's investment strategies, increasing the range of retirement income through the introduction of Pooled Registered Pension Plans (PRPPs), providing monetary incentives for late retirement, and increasing the pension eligibility age (see the following chapter).

Conclusion

In the face of neoliberal pressures for welfare state restructuring in Canada and Australia, retirement income reconfiguration in those two countries took different directions. The reform and restructuring of the Canadian retirement income system entailed consolidating existing old age income programs. Even the introduction of the clawback to the first tier of retirement income system has not completely ended the universalism of the OAS. Nor have neoliberal pressures succeeded in subjecting the second tier of the retirement system to the forces of privatization. Despite ongoing neoliberal-inspired efforts to advance the privatization of retirement income and revive intrusive means-tested mechanisms, the Canadian retirement income system has largely retained its universal and collectivistic features.

This particularity of the social policy response to the imperatives of welfare state restructuring in Canada can be explained by the nature of its postwar social settlement. The politically constructed redistributive-oriented nature of that settlement made it very difficult for neoliberal forces to invade the field of social welfare policy. The key to understanding the neoliberals' failure to make decisive inroads into retirement income policy lies in the centrality of the Canadian political discourse on national unity – a discourse that is conducive to maintaining the principles of collectivity and universalism.

The postwar discourse on national unity cemented itself as the governing principle of the postwar social settlement. The prevailing discourse of national unity strongly links social welfare programs to Canadian identity, social citizenship, and national unity. The postwar social settlement has impeded social welfare retrenchment and retirement income privatization, however vehemently corporate interests have lobbied for these things. As long as national unity retains its significance in the national political discourse, the redistributive-oriented postwar social settlement will act as a bulwark against neoliberal inroads into retirement income policy in Canada.

Conclusion

This final chapter brings together my main findings and draws out their implications. It also evaluates the Australian and Canadian pension reforms in the context of the global financial crisis. It has five sections. The first recapitulates this book's main findings. The second presents the theoretical implications of this study. The third highlights this book's main contributions to scholarship as well as its limitations. The fourth briefly explains the impact of the global financial crisis on pension funds and pension policy. The fifth reflects on current and future trends in retirement income policy in Canada and Australia.

The Main Findings

Within the comparative welfare state literature, it has become common to characterize Canada and Australia as liberal regimes distinguished by their reliance on means-tested social assistance as the primary mechanism of social protection. Yet the Canadian and Australian retirement income systems were marked by divergent patterns of development during the postwar welfare state expansion; they also varied in their responses to neoliberal welfare state restructuring and retrenchment. While Australia complemented the means-tested non-contributory flat rate Age Pension with tax-subsidized private occupational pension plans, Canada supplemented private occupational pension schemes with a universal non-contributory old age security pension and a publicly administered earnings-related universal public pension plan. Similarly, despite neoliberal pressure to restructure and retrench the public pension systems in both Canada and Australia, social policy responses to the neoliberal push in these two countries took different directions. In Canada, the forces of welfare state restructuring have not completely eclipsed the universality and collectivity features of the retirement income system; in Australia, the restructuring of the retirement income system has been marked by the intensification of selectivity and the expansion and consolidation of privatization. These divergent patterns of retirement income expansion, and subsequent variations in retirement income restructuring and retrenchment, reveal the explanatory weaknesses of mainstream theoretical paradigms. The shortcomings of the existing theoretical literature in terms of explaining variation in retirement income systems in Canada and Australia provided the impetus for writing this book.

Comparative welfare state studies have focused mainly on factors such as demographic composition, institutional structures, levels of economic development, and levels of the power resources of labour as variables for explaining variation in retirement income expansion and restructuring. Less attention has been paid to the role of national settings as a crucial variable shaping postwar welfare expansion. The shortcomings of the mainstream theoretical perspectives in explaining variations between welfare states emanate from their failure to account for the differences in postwar political strategies built around class, nation, and social alternatives. The inability of mainstream theoretical approaches to explain variations in postwar expansion and subsequent processes of restructuring of retirement income systems does not imply that power resources, institutional settings, demographic composition, or levels of economic development are irrelevant to analyses of welfare states. The significance of these variables to analyses of pension systems should be taken into account within the wider political and national settings that shaped the postwar social settlement. Yet prevailing theoretical perspectives fail to integrate the interplay of national settings, social classes, and the state's role in shaping the postwar social class settlement. Postwar national settlements structured welfare state expansion and have shaped responses to welfare state restructuring and retrenchment.

No single theoretical framework can completely explain differences in welfare state expansion and subsequent retrenchment, so it would be helpful to synthesize the various theoretical explanations. A theoretical framework that can adequately explain the interplay of national settings, the role of the state, and the specific form of postwar social class settlement requires us to combine elements of Marxian class analysis and the power resources model. Such a synthesis can provide a theoretical template to explain variations in welfare state expansion as well as differences in the degree of resistance to welfare state retrenchment. The approach

I propose highlights the differences in the character of the postwar social settlement as the main explanatory variable behind welfare state variation. It can also explain why the retirement income systems in Canada and Australia diverged. Having grounded the analysis of variations in welfare state expansion and restructuring within this integrated approach, I restate this book's main arguments as follows: As the political manifestation of the postwar social class compromise, the welfare state came to be harnessed to counter the threat of radicalism to the existing socio-political order. Contrary to prevailing assumptions held by mainstream theoretical perspectives on the welfare state, the presence of a single nationalism within a given social formation was not sufficient to ensure the emergence of a comprehensive and generous welfare state. Nor did the clash of competing nationalisms within a social formation necessarily pave the way for the adoption of a residual social welfare policy. National configurations in Canada and Australia played a crucial role in shaping the labour movements in these countries. National settings in Canada deepened the fragmentation of the labour movement, whereas the national configuration in Australia fostered a united labour movement. Differences in national settings decisively structured the interplay of class, party, and nation in Canada and Australia, and this in turn paved the way for variations in Keynesianism between these two countries. Relative ethnic homogeneity in Australia (notwithstanding the presence of the Aboriginals) was conducive to the emergence of a united labour movement, which became a crucial to a centralized industrial relations system. However, the social vision of the labour movement in Australia was restricted to capital/labour relations. This political strategy emphasized securing the social wage through market-based regulatory measures such full employment, a centralized wage-setting system, and protecting the home market from external competitors.

In Canada, rivalries between fragmented labour union centres led to a weak and decentralized industrial relations system. The fragmentation of Canada's labour movement contributed to the pursuit of a form of Keynesianism that placed less emphasis on market regulation and full employment as means to provide income security. But in Canada, Keynesianism was found to be an effective device for promoting national unity, which in turn was conducive to establishing progressive and universal social welfare programs. Variations in the Keynesian-inspired postwar social settlements in Canada and Australia decisively shaped the retirement income systems in these countries.

All postwar social class settlements were politically constructed; nonetheless, they acquired different characteristics. A politically constructed market-oriented social class compromise formed in Australia, where relative ethnic homogeneity and the presence of one nationalism cemented the labour movement. However, the Australian labour movement's aspirations did not extend beyond capital/labour relations. The postwar expansion and consolidation of Australia's retirement income system was heavily structured by the nature of the market-centred social class compromise. This market-centred social class settlement emphasized full employment and centralized wage-setting as a surrogate for social welfare protection. By emphasizing "industrial citizenship" over "social citizenship," the market-centred social settlement in Australia reinforced the continuity of selectivity, encouraged private arrangements for old age income, and stymied the collectivization of retirement income through a publicly administered earnings-related pension plan. The postwar reliance on private occupational plans for securing old age income in Australia signified the weakness of the principles of collectivity and solidarity, which are essential to universalism and direct state involvement in retirement income.

Conversely, a politically constructed redistributive-oriented social settlement emerged in Canada, where politicized national heterogeneity had reinforced the fragmentation of the working class. But within this particular social environment, the management of national unity required a progressive and comprehensive social welfare policy, which in turn was conducive to strengthening the links between the welfare state, social citizenship, universalism, and national identity. Despite the fragmentation of labour and the historical absence of a social democratic government at the national level, a universal pension system became a reality in Canada. The trajectory of Canada's retirement income system was shaped by the character of the postwar social settlement. In contrast to Australia, where social protection was secured by harnessing market forces to achieve full employment, social income security in Canada came to be maintained through a nationalist project of state-building through social welfare policy. The political discourse of national unity shifted the language of class away from the centre of Canadian politics, but paradoxically, the imperative of maintaining national unity amplified the voices of federalist and pro-labour forces calling for a generous and universal old age pension system. Consequently, the need to promote national unity through social welfare programs in Canada reinforced the links between social citizenship, national identity, and the universality and collectivity dimensions of the retirement income system.

In line with the role of the postwar social settlement in shaping postwar pension policy, the responses to neoliberal pressures for retirement income restructuring were also largely shaped by the legacy of the postwar social settlement. In both Canada and Australia, pro-business organizations and think tanks used the economic crisis of the 1970s as an opportunity to subordinate social and economic policies to the imperatives of market forces. But despite the neoliberal pressures to retrench and restructure the retirement income systems in both countries, there were striking variations in governmental responses. In Australia, the exigencies of economic competitiveness couched in the discourse of "economic rationalism" paved the way for neoliberal principles to permeate the governmental agenda. In Canada, pro-market forces used the free trade agreement with the United States and the push for greater decentralization of political authority to inject neoliberal tenets into social welfare policy. Pursued as a strategy to reconcile historically ingrained national tensions, the decentralization of political power was conducive to the implementation of the neoliberal paradigm.

The market-centred postwar social settlement in Australia was highly susceptible to drastic market measures, which were deemed imperative to tackle the economic crisis of the 1970s. With the economic contraction of that decade, the imperatives of welfare state retrenchment set in motion a profound restructuring of Australia's retirement income system. The forces of welfare state reconfiguration propelled Australian social policy on retirement income towards the consolidation of state-mandated privately managed retirement income and the revival of intrusive and stringent means testing. The restructuring of the Australian retirement income system was shaped by the nature of the postwar social class settlement, which had rested on full employment and a centralized wage-setting system as substitutes for social income security. To restart the engine of economic growth and employment, which had historically been envisaged as the guiding principles of the Australian labour movement, the industrial and political wings of the labour movement had to adjust to the exigencies of market forces. The intensification of residualism through iniquitous means testing and the consolidation of privatized retirement income led to compulsory employer superannuation contributions on behalf of employees as "deferred pay" or a substitute for wage increases. This was a logical corollary of Australian labour's historically ingrained vision of the welfare state.

The redistributive-oriented social settlement in Canada was less susceptible to alteration in the balance of class forces leading to a wave of economic restructuring. The postwar social settlement in Canada did much to block neoliberal inroads into old age pension policy. Owing to the discourse of national unity, Canadian retirement income policy came to revolve around consolidating existing retirement income programs. Despite neoliberal pressures from businesses to revive means testing for old age pension and to provide greater scope for private retirement income, the Canadian retirement income system has largely retained its universal and collectivist features.

Theoretical Implications

Differences in the historical trajectory of postwar welfare state expansion in Canada and Australia generate a puzzle for mainstream theoretical paradigms. This is particularly so for institutional approaches and the power resources model, both of which have acquired analytical hegemony within welfare state studies. The central theoretical claim of the power resources model is brought into question by the methodological and empirical evidence that is used to substantiate its explanatory strength. The power resources model attributes decommodification and universality to class mobilization and patterns of class coalition, which serve as criteria for stratifying welfare states along a hierarchical line of comprehensiveness. Yet empirical findings presented by proponents of the power resources model demonstrate that the degree of decommodification and universality in societies such as Canada, where class is fragmented and social democracy has never exercised governmental power at the national level, is in fact greater than in societies such as Australia, where the labour movement has retained its unity and social democracy has held governmental power. The trends towards stringent means-tested Age Pension and the privatization of retirement income in Australia were guided by the ALP, a party that is supposed to advance the social democratic principles of collectivity and universalism. Yet it was the Canadian retirement income system that acquired the principles of collectivity and universalism, and it did so under the aegis of the Liberal Party, which has historically been identified as a pro-market political force. What seems to have escaped the attention of adherents to the power resources model is that the effectiveness of the power resources of labour is conditioned by national political settings and the ideological underpinnings of the labour movement. Within a given social formation, these factors do much to shape social welfare policy.

With respect to welfare state expansion, it is the central assumption of institutionalism that the fragmentation of political authority systematically limited the scope for progressively implementing social welfare programs. As well, institutionalists contend that a centralized political authority is essential to universal and comprehensive social income security programs. According to this principal line of institutional explanation, which identifies the national configuration of decision making within the polity as an overarching independent variable, a relatively centralized federation in Australia should have fostered a comprehensive and universal income retirement program. But it was under a relatively *de*centralized political authority in Canada that universalism, collectivity, and comprehensiveness came to define the retirement income system. This book demonstrates that institutions and organizational structures are not the debris from an eruption that can be analysed in abstract and independently of societal forces that shape social, political, and economic institutions. Rather, institutional structures are the "congealed" outcomes of past struggles. Those structures play a crucial role in channelling socio-political pressures. However, they cannot be diagnosed independent of the historical and national settings of each specific social formation.

This book also challenges the place of nationalism within the class mobilization thesis. The Canadian case shows that the clash of nationalisms can reinforce working-class disunity, as leftist intellectuals have astutely pointed out. Yet the exigencies of national reconciliation, which may require adoption of the principles of universality and collectivity in social policy, have had spillover benefits for the working class. In other words, the clash of nationalisms in Canada has been an ally of the working class and has, paradoxically, advanced its interests. This brings into question leftist intellectuals' perennial assumptions about the interplay of nationalism and working-class interests. Leftist intellectuals in Canada have contended that the chronic clash of nationalisms and considerations of national unity have allowed the status quo political parties to obfuscate their positions on class and thereby remove class issues from the national political discourse. But as this book has shown, the clash of nationalisms and the imperatives of national unity have in fact advanced the interests of Canada's working class.

Conversely, the Australian case contradicts the widely held assumption that homogeneity and the presence of one nationalism within a social formation are crucial to the adoption of progressive and comprehensive social welfare policy. Homogeneity and one nationalism in Australia boosted working-class unity but did not guarantee the entrenchment of universality and collectivity in social welfare policy, as leftist intellectuals have long assumed to be the case.

This book's findings also call for the reformulation of the Marxian concept of the relative autonomy of the state. They have demonstrated that the challenge of maintaining national unity so as to increase the state's relative autonomy must be added to other variables (political organization of the working class, intensity of social struggle) that structural Marxists have identified as determinants of the relative autonomy of the state.

Finally, this book's findings have significant implications for policymakers. Reliance on the privatization of retirement income system might appear to be a sound policy to reduce the fiscal burden on the public purse. But privatization of retirement income might in the long term generate more problems for governments if pension fund performance is negatively affected by the volatility of market forces.[1]

Contributions and Limitations

This book enriches the existing welfare state literature and advances the scholarship on several grounds. Its primary contribution is to bring the explanatory significance of the structure and character of the national basis of the postwar social class compromise into the literature on the welfare state. Most comparative welfare studies refer to the postwar class compromise as a uniform phenomenon across the advanced industrial countries. None of these studies have elaborated on the variations in the postwar social settlement and how these variations shaped the postwar development of public pension systems. This book has introduced new conceptual tools such as "politically constructed market-based" social class settlement and "politically constructed redistributive-oriented" social class settlement into the welfare state literature. These analytical tools can be useful for future studies on the welfare state in general and on retirement income systems in particular. The second contribution of this book is that it focuses on the impact of national settings (homogeneity/heterogeneity) on social welfare policy, thereby filling a gap in the pensions literature. The existing comparative welfare studies on pension systems have rarely reflected on ethnicity as a variable that shapes social income security. A third contribution this book makes to the scholarship relates to its detailed empirical analysis of the historical trajectory of pension provisions in Canada and Australia. This will be helpful for future comparative welfare state studies.

This book has, however, two primary limitations. The first is its restricted number of case studies, which makes it difficult to generalize findings and to uncover patterns and tendencies in social welfare policy. However, given the time frame of this project, which covers eras of welfare state expansion *and* restructuring, this limitation is unavoidable. It can be overcome by including more countries and by confining the scope of the study to a specific period of retirement income policy. The second limitation of this book is that it focuses on a single social welfare program. The public pension system has been identified as "the paradigm setter for welfare politics," but there are other social welfare programs (such as unemployment insurance, social assistance, and health care) that have decommodifying effects that express the character of welfare states. This limitation is also unavoidable, since these social welfare programs cannot all be integrated into a single research project covering a long period of old age pension policy across two countries. This limitation could be surmounted by applying the themes of this book to the development, consolidation, and restructuring of each of these social welfare programs. Therefore, this book will broaden the scope for welfare state studies.

Pension Policy and the Global Financial Crisis

Pension fund performance and, consequently, pension policy have been adversely affected by the ongoing global financial crisis since 2007. The financial turmoil that erupted in the United States has become a worldwide phenomenon and has impacted all segments of the financial industry, including pension funds. Allowing for variation in the degree of impact due to the nature of pension plans, pension funds have been affected by the global financial crisis.[2] The shock to pension assets resulting from the fall in equity markets and the shock to pension contributions as a result of economic slowdown have severe fiscal implications for pension plans.[3] In just the first ten months of 2008, "private pensions in OECD countries reported US$4 trillion losses in asset value."[4] In 2008, the global financial turmoil reduced "the values of assets accumulated to finance retirement by around 20–25% on average according to the latest OECD figures."[5] The key factor in variation in the degree of impact across countries has to do with the degree of exposure to collapsing equity markets. The impact on investment returns has been more severe in countries where "equities represent over a third of total assets invested."[6]

The financial crisis has affected pension plans in different ways. Due to the poor performance of pension funds and subsequent decline in rates of return, members of defined contribution plans will have less retirement income in the future. And for defined benefit plans, the financial crisis has increased the risk of a funding gap. As a direct consequence of the financial crisis, rising unemployment has reduced the amount of individual pension savings and will negatively affect the ratio of assets to expenses. This chain of impacts calls for either cutting pension benefits or increasing contribution rates.[7]

The current travails of pension funds and ensuing pressures on pension policy are the results of the neoliberal push to privatize pensions.[8] It was because of the spread of neoliberal ideas by national and international advocacy groups, the IMF, and the World Bank that "from 1981 to 2007, more than thirty countries worldwide fully or partially replaced their pre-existing social security pay-as-you-go (PAYG) pension systems with ones based on individual, private pension savings accounts in a process labelled 'pension privatization.'"[9] As neoliberalism spread in the 1980s and 1990s, pension privatization seemed to offer a comprehensive solution to the fiscal woes of public pension systems. The rationale for moving towards pension privatization was part and parcel of free market capitalist ideas: "it is based on the ideas that market can provide income-related pension benefits more effectively than governments and private companies are better managers of pension funds than governments."[10] Privatization of pensions was advanced on the grounds that it was an effective strategy to address the unsustainability of public pensions due to demographic change (an increase in the population of elderly citizens) and that funded pensions would increase savings, which would consequently increase the supply of capital investment for the real economy.[11]

The implications of the financial crisis have generated controversy about pension privatization. The desirability and effectiveness of pension privatization has even been questioned by some ardent defenders of the free market, and public opinion has turned against financial institutions.[12] According to Orenstein, "a wide variety of voices from all parts of the world have questioned the relevance of free market ideology in economic policy. This new ideological climate undoubtedly has made it harder to advocate or defend pension privatization in most countries."[13]

Pension privatization has lost credibility, yet banks and insurance companies continue to support it.

Because it has failed to deliver what it promised, "pension privatization fever" has lost its grip. Because of the adverse implications of the global financial crisis, many countries have scaled back their efforts to privatize pensions, and countries such as Argentina and Hungary have reversed the trend by eliminating their private pension systems.[14] In some Central and Eastern European countries, there are policy discussions and debates about reverting back towards PAYG public pension systems.[15] As a result of the negative impact of financial turmoil on pension funds and the global campaign by International Labour Organization for a minimum pension guarantee, leading international organizations such as the IMF and World Bank have once again begun to emphasize minimum pensions.[16]

The Future of the Pension Policy in Australia and Canada

Recent changes to retirement income systems in Canada and Australia are in line with this book's main arguments. Those changes to retirement income systems in both countries do not constitute major departures from the restructuring and retrenchment processes of the era of neoliberalism in the 1980s and 1990s.

In Australia, the defeat of the Liberal coalition and the electoral victory of the Labor Party in 2008 did not herald a radical departure from the market-oriented social and economic policies of the Howard Liberal government. Labor prime minister Kevin Rudd called for an end to "extreme capitalism," but he also reaffirmed the Labor government's commitment to a balanced budget, constrained spending, and lower business taxes. Having regained political power in 2008, the Labor government made several changes to the retirement income system that were in line with the restructuring and retrenchment under previous Labor and Liberal administrations.[17] As Ben Spies-Butcher has pointed out, after the Labor Party's electoral triumph under Rudd in 2008, "it seems the alternative to neoliberalism looks remarkably similar to neoliberalism itself."[18] The Labor government's adherence to fiscal discipline underscored its affinity with the Howard's government's policy platform with regard to social policy. Julia Gillard, the Labor prime minister from 2011 to 2013, declared that "we have moved beyond the days of big government and big welfare state."[19] In her criticism of the Liberal Party, Gillard stated that "the growing extremism of the Abbott Liberals, is such, the party of Howard is disappearing from view." As Quiggin has pointed out, Gillard's statement reflected her attempt to present "her own government as the legitimate heir of consensus embodied by Howard's."[20]

Australian pension funds have been hard hit by the financial crisis. The impact of this economic downturn on Australian pension funds has raised questions about the desirability and effectiveness of pension privatization in securing an adequate level of retirement income for Australians.[21] Despite the crushing impact of the financial crisis on pension fund performance, the ALP continues to trust market forces to deliver the social goods. In his address to the Institute of Actuaries Australia Biennial Convention 2009 in Sydney, Nick Sherry, the minister for superannuation and corporate law in the Rudd government and the minister for small businesses in the Gillard government, articulated the Labor government's faith in market forces: "While we cannot dismiss the effects of the financial turbulence, we must remember that the superannuation is a long-term investment ... There will be time for markets to recover. And history tells us that markets will recover over time."[22]

In Canada, the recent changes to the retirement income system are also consistent with the consolidation of existing retirement programs. After the 1997 reform of the CPP, it took almost a decade to make additional changes to the retirement income system.[23] In the most recent triennial review, announced by the federal, provincial, and territorial finance ministers on 25 May 2009, it was asserted that the CPP "remains on sound financial footing and is well positioned to weather the recent market downturn. Canadians can count on the CPP to be there for them when they retire."[24]

There are no misgivings that as socio-economic conditions change, there will be corresponding changes in social welfare programs. The trajectory of retirement income policy in Canada and Australia will undoubtedly be affected by the ongoing global economic crisis. Global financial turbulence has provided the grounds to impose further austerity measures, as well as to increasingly resist retrenchment and cutbacks. While pension privatization has been discredited by the global financial crisis, the underlying conditions (population aging, demographic pressure on state finances, and concerns about the financial sustainability of social programs) that were used to justify pension privatization have not been resolved. These unresolved conditions can still be harnessed by governments to impose austerity measures.

Income security systems are changing and will be subject to further reforms. It would be mere speculation to predict how the present global financial crisis will unfold and how it will affect social security programs such as the retirement income system. But based on the present conditions, it can be argued that Australia's retirement income system does not seem to be at a crossroads, since it has already moved towards residualism and privatization. There are no signs of either a further scaling back or a reversal of the tide of pension privatization in Australia. Australia's retirement income system already promotes self-reliance and self-financing. The compulsory Superannuation Guarantee Charge is geared towards bringing about a psychological shift whereby the Age Pension "is seen more as welfare than any entitlement."[25]

The Canadian retirement income system may experience some minor changes. But those changes are unlikely to constitute a sharp departure from current developments. As Keith Ambachtsheer has pointed out, as a result of the cooperative efforts of Ottawa and the provinces in the 1990s that placed retirement income programs "on a more fiscally sound footing ... experts agree that the universal OAS/GIS and CPP/QPP components of Canada's retirement income system are in better shape today than their counterparts in many other developed countries."[26] Furthermore, Canadian social programs such as pensions and health care are closely tied to notions of Canadian identity and national unity. As Brodie has aptly pointed out, despite the deep penetration of neoliberalism in Canada, "the historical mixture of pan-Canadian nationalism with social citizenship rights has presented a formidable barrier to a wholesale conversion to neoliberalism in Canada."[27] As long as Quebec remains within Confederation and as long as Quebec nationalism remains a force, the neoliberal project will continue to encounter formidable obstacles in Canada. And as long as the clash of nationalisms is perceived as a menace to Canadian unity, the Canadian state is bound to employ social policy as a mechanism to deflect this perceived threat. As Myles has asserted, "the welfare state has been the pot of glue to which the elites have turned to hold the country together even when party ideology has dictated otherwise."[28] Thus, the imperatives of maintaining national unity in Canada will continue to weaken neoliberal pressures for social needs to be subjugated to the demands and exigencies of market forces.

Notes

Note to reader: Throughout the notes, citations for parliamentary debates have been condensed as follows:

For Australia: Australia, *Commonwealth Parliamentary Debates,* First Session, 19th Parliament, Vol. 3, 18 May (Canberra: F. Johnston, Commonwealth Government Printer, 1950), 2879, is hereafter cited as CPD, First/19th/v3, 18 May, 1950, 2879.
For Canada: Canada, *House of Commons Debates,* Fourth Session, 21st Parliament, Vol. V, 21 June (Ottawa, ON: King's Printer for Canada, 1951), 4424, is hereafter cited as HCD, Fourth/21st/v5, 21 June, 1951, 4424.

Introduction

1 Wilensky, *Comparative Social Policy*, 1.
2 Briggs, "The Welfare State," 18.
3 Pierson, "Coping with Permanent Austerity."
4 OECD, "Key Employment Policy Challenges."
5 World Bank, *Averting the Old Age Crisis*; World Bank, *Social Protection Sector Strategy*; World Bank, *Pension Reform.*
6 UN Department of Economic and Social Affairs, *World Public Sector,* 33.
7 Gillion et al., *Social Security Pensions.*
8 Cutler and Johnson, *The Birth and Growth.*
9 Myles, *Old Age in the Welfare State,* 2. See also Cutler and Johnson, *The Birth and Growth.*
10 Esping-Andersen, *The Three Worlds,* 79–80.
11 Ozanne, "Ageing Citizens"; Timonen, *Ageing Societies.*
12 Shaver, "Consideration of Mere Logic," 105.
13 Wilensky, *Comparative Social Policy.*
14 Torfing, *Politics.*

15 Gilbert, *Transformation of the Welfare State*; Torfing, *Politics*.
16 Huo, "Comparing Welfare States."
17 Both countries have remained net importers of production technology, the bulk of which is imported from the United States. The primary sector dominates the structure of both countries' economies. For example, from 1980 to 2000, "55% of Australia's exports [were] in the forms of raw materials, compared with 46% for Canada." Canada, Statistics Canada, *Canada and Australia*, 1.
18 In Canada, senators are appointed and first-past-the-post is used to elect members to the House of Commons. In Australia, by contrast, a preferential voting system is used for electing members to the House of Representatives and proportional representation is employed for electing members of the Senate.
19 Esping-Andersen, *The Three Worlds*; O'Connor and Olsen, eds., *Power Resources Theory*; Goodin et al., *The Real Worlds of Welfare Capitalism*.
20 Williamson and Pampel, *Old Age Security*, 227.
21 Ragin, *The Comparative Method*, 4.
22 Bhatia and Coleman, "Ideas and Discourse."
23 Olsen, *The Politics of the Welfare State*.
24 Allan and Scruggs, "Political Partisanship"; Esping-Andersen, *The Three Worlds*.
25 Gilbert, *Transformation of the Welfare State*; Clayton and Pontusson, "Welfare State Retrenchment Revisited."
26 Olsen, *The Politics of the Welfare State*.
27 Bradley et al., "Distribution and Redistribution"; Moller et al., "Determinants of Relative Poverty."
28 Huber and Stephens, "The Social Democratic Welfare State"; Saunders, *The Ends and Means*.
29 Castles and Mitchell, "Worlds of Welfare"; Goodin et al., *The Real Worlds of Welfare*.
30 Castles and Mitchell, "Worlds of Welfare," 13–15.
31 Castles and Mitchell, "Worlds of Welfare."
32 Esping-Andersen, *The Three Worlds*; Korpi and Palme, "New Politics and Class Politics."
33 Esping-Andersen, *The Three Worlds*.
34 Castles and Mitchell, "Worlds of Welfare," 103.
35 Saunders, *The Ends and Means*.

1 Theoretical Perspectives on the Welfare State

1 Wallace and Wolf, *Contemporary Sociological Theory*; Ritzer, *Contemporary Sociological Theory*.

2 Parsons, *The Evolution of Societies.*
3 Wilensky, *The Welfare State and Equality*; Kerr et al., *Industrialism and Industrial Man*; Timonen, *Restructuring the Welfare State.*
4 Wilensky, *The Welfare State and Equality.*
5 Wilensky, *Comparative Social Policy.*
6 Wilensky, *The Welfare State and Equality*; Wilensky, *Rich Democracies.*
7 Kerr et al., *Industrialism and Industrial Man*; Wilensky, *The Welfare State and Equality.*
8 Esping-Andersen, *The Three Worlds*, 13.
9 Flora and Alber, "Modernization."
10 Alber, "Continuity and Changes."
11 Torfing, *Politics*, 170.
12 Wilensky, *Rich Democracies.*
13 Ibid.
14 Janowitz, *Social Control of the Welfare State*; Olson, *The Rise and Decline of Nations.*
15 Pratt, *Gray Agendas.*
16 Therborn, "Karl Marx Returning," 159.
17 Olsen, *The Politics of the Welfare State.*
18 Ibid., 95.
19 Castles, *Australian Public Policy*; Olsen, *The Politics of the Welfare State*; Pierson, "Coping with Permanent Austerity."
20 Confalonieri and Newton, "Taxing and Spending."
21 Olsen, *The Politics of the Welfare State;* Pierson, "Coping with Permanent Austerity."
22 Collier and Messick, "Prerequisites versus Diffusion"; Francis G. Castles, "The Impact of Parties"; Huo, "Comparing Welfare States."
23 Cutler and Johnson, *The Birth and Growth.*
24 Myles, *Old Age in the Welfare State.*
25 Olsen, *The Politics of the Welfare State.*
26 Ibid.; Gilbert, *Transformation of the Welfare State*; Therborn, *When, How, and Why*; Lynch, *Age in the Welfare State.*
27 Esping-Andersen, *The Three Worlds*; Clayton and Pontusson, "Welfare State Retrenchment"; Gilbert, *Transformation of the Welfare State.*
28 Therborn, "Karl Marx Returning."
29 Skocpol, "Bringing the State Back In"; Orloff and Skocpol, "Why Not Equal Protection?"
30 Skocpol, "Bringing the State Back In"; Orloff and Skocpol, "Why Not Equal Protection?"; de Swan, *In the Care of the State*; Ashford, *The Emergence of Welfare States.*
31 Weiss, *The Myth of Powerless State*, 38; Evens, *Embedded Autonomy*, 49–50.
32 Cammack, "Review Article," 263–4.

33 Therborn, "Karl Marx Returning," 147.
34 Gordon, "The New Feminist Scholarship."
35 Radice, "Taking Globalization Seriously."
36 Immergut, "Institutions"; Swank, "Political Institutions"; Swank, *Global Capital*; Bonoli, *The Politics of Pension Reform*; Rothstein and Steinmo, "Restructuring Politics"; Hicks, *Social Democracy and Welfare Capitalism.*
37 Swank, "Political Institutions"; Bonoli, "Political Institutions."
38 Immergut, "Institutions"; Bonoli, "Political Institutions"; Swank, "Political Institutions"; Swank, *Global Capital*; Pierson, "Coping with Permanent Austerity."
39 Castles, "The Impact of Parties."
40 Bonoli, "Political Institutions," 264.
41 Korpi, "Power, Politics, and State Autonomy"; Pampel and Williamson, *Age, Class, Politics.*
42 Hall, *Governing the Economy*; Kitschelt et al., "Convergence and Divergence"; Huber and Stephens, "The Social Democratic Welfare State"; Huber and Stephens, "Welfare States and Production Regimes."
43 Soskice, "Divergent Production Regimes"; Kitschelt et al., "Convergence and Divergence."
44 Schmitter, "Still the Century of Corporatism"; Streeck, "Neo-Corporatist Industrial Relations."
45 Hicks, *Social Democracy and Welfare Capitalism*, 128.
46 Ibid.
47 O'Connor and Olsen, *Power Resources Theory.*
48 Panitch, "The Role and Nature of the Canadian State."
49 Therborn, "Karl Marx Returning."
50 Ibid., 143.
51 Stephens, *The Transformation.*
52 Therborn, "Karl Marx Returning."
53 Therborn, "Social Democracy in One Country."
54 Ewer et al., *Politics and Accord*; Saunders, *The Ends and Means.*
55 Therborn, "Karl Marx Returning," 144-5
56 Rothstein and Steinmo, "Restructuring Politics," 17.
57 Pontusson, "From Comparative Public Policy."
58 Rothstein, "Labour Market Institutions," 306.
59 Pierson, "The New Politics"; Stephens, "The Scandinavian Welfare States."
60 Pierson, "The New Politics."
61 Ibid.
62 Pierson, *Dismantling the Welfare State?*, 29.
63 Scarbrough, "West European Welfare States," 59; Clayton and Pontusson,

"Welfare State Retrenchment"; Allan and Scruggs, "Political Partisanship."
64 Clayton and Pontusson, "Welfare State Retrenchment," 11.
65 Scarbrough, "West European Welfare States"; Korpi, and Palme "New Politics and Class Politics"; Castles and Mitchell, "Worlds of Welfare"; Anderson, "The Politics of Retrenchment."
66 Timonen, *Restructuring the Welfare State*, 28–9.
67 Poulantzas, *State, Power, Socialism*; Offe, *Contradictions of the Welfare State*; O'Connor, *The Fiscal Crisis*; Block, "The Ruling Class."
68 Offe, *Contradictions of the Welfare State.*
69 O'Connor, *The Fiscal Crisis*; Poulantzas, *State, Power, Socialism*; Offe, *Contradictions of the Welfare State.*
70 Poulantzas, *State, Power, Socialism.*
71 Poulantzas, *Political Power.*
72 Poulantzas, *Political Power*; Block, "The Ruling Class."
73 Poulantzas, *Political Power*, 289.
74 Poulantzas, *State, Power, Socialism*, 184.
75 Hirsch, *Social Limits to Growth.*
76 O'Connor, *The Fiscal Crisis*; Offe, *Contradictions of the Welfare State.*
77 Offe, *Contradictions of the Welfare State*, 153.
78 Poulantzas, *State, Power, Socialism*; Panitch, "Rethinking the Role of the State"; Panitch, "The Impoverishment of State Theory"; Burnham, "The Politics of Economic Management."
79 Ibid.
80 Poulantzas, *State, Power, Socialism*, 185.
81 Therborn, "Karl Marx Returning."
82 Skocpol and Amenta, "States and Social Policies"; Olsen, *The Politics of the Welfare State.*
83 Ibid.
84 Esping-Andersen, *The Three Worlds*; Torfing, *Politics*; Therborn, "Karl Marx Returning."
85 O'Connor, *The Fiscal Crisis.*
86 Huber and Stephens, "The Social Democratic Welfare State."
87 Poulantzas, *Political Power*, 287–9.
88 Bronner, *Socialism Unbound.*
89 Przeworski, *Capitalism and Social Democracy*; Gay, *The Dilemma.*
90 Bronner, *Socialism Unbound*, 204.
91 Crosland, *The Future of Socialism*, 63.
92 Ibid., 114–15.
93 Korpi, *The Democratic Class Struggle*; Esping-Andersen and Korpi, "Social Policy"; Korpi, "Power."

94 Korpi, *The Democratic Class Struggle.*
95 Miliband, *Marxism and Politics,* 72.
96 Przeworski, *Capitalism and Social Democracy,* 40.
97 Esping-Andersen, *The Three Worlds,* 30.
98 Ibid.
99 Ibid.
100 Ibid.
101 Myles, *Old Age in the Welfare State*; Castles, "The Impact of Parties"; Cameron, "The Growth of Governmental Spending."
102 Banting, "Images of the Modern State"; Saunders, *Welfare and Inequality*; Saunders, *The Ends and Means.*
103 Ibid.
104 Titmuss, *Essays on the Welfare State.*
105 Ragin, "A Qualitative Comparative Analysis."
106 Banting, "The Multicultural Welfare State"; Gould and Palmer, "Outcomes."
107 Kymlicka, *The Multicultural Welfare State,* 3.
108 McEwen, *Nationalism and the State*; Gagnon, Guibernau, and Rocher, eds., *The Conditions of Diversity*; Banting, "The Multicultural Welfare State"; Béland and Lecours, "Sub-State Nationalism."
109 Ragin, "A Qualitative Comparative Analysis."
110 McEwen, *Nationalism and the State*; Béland and Lecours, "Sub-State Nationalism"; Kymlicka, *The Multicultural Welfare State*; Banting et al., "Do Multiculturalism Policies Erode the Welfare State?"; Banting, "The Multicultural Welfare State."
111 Wright, "Class Analysis"; Przeworski, *Capitalism and Social Democracy*; Panitch, *Working Class Politics*; Glyn, *Capitalism Unleashed*; Wahl, *The Rise and Fall*; Rhodes, "The Political Economy."
112 Wahl, *The Rise and Fall.*
113 Boyer, "The Convergence Hypothesis"; Rhodes, "The Political Economy."
114 Williamson and Pampel, *Old Age Security.*
115 Johnson and Johnson, "Civil Political Discourse," 291.
116 Jenson, "Different but Not Exceptional."
117 Campbell, "Institutional Analysis."
118 Miller, *On Nationality*; Tamir, *Liberal Nationalism.*
119 Miller, *On Nationality.*
120 Putnam, *Who Bonds?*
121 Marx and Engels, *The Communist Manifesto,* 79–80.
122 Lewis, "Marxism and Nationalism," 3.
123 Davis, *Toward a Marxist Theory,* 4.

124 Ibid., 56.
125 Lipset and Marks, *It Didn't Happen Here.*
126 Lowy, *Fatherland or Mother Earth?*
127 Stephens, *The Transformation.*
128 Eger, "Even in Sweden."
129 Banting et al., "Do Multiculturalism Policies Erode."
130 Marshall, *Citizenship and Social Class,* 33–4.
131 Ibid., 40.
132 Bendix, *Nation-Building,* 73–4.
133 Papillon and Turgeon, "Nationalism's Third Way?"
134 Brodie, "Citizenship and Solidarity."
135 Poulantzas, *State, Power, Socialism.*
136 Burnham, "The Politics of Economic Management."
137 Poulantzas, *Political Power and Social Classes,* 289.
138 Stephens, *The Transformation*; Pierson, *Beyond the Welfare State?*
139 Cuperus, Duffek, and Kandel, eds., *The Challenges of Diversity.*
140 Rhodes, "The Political Economy."

2 Pension Systems: Canadian and Australian Cases

1 Blackburn, *Banking on the Death.*
2 Kennedy, "Introduction."
3 Higgins, "To Him That Hath," 222.
4 Blackburn, *Banking on the Death.*
5 Esping-Andersen, *The Three Worlds.*
6 Kennedy, "Introduction"; Myles, *Old Age in the Welfare State.*
7 Bruce, *The Coming of the Welfare State,* 30.
8 Heclo, "Towards a New Welfare State?"
9 Therborn, *When, How, and Why*; Pierson, *Beyond the Welfare State?*
10 Bruce, *The Coming of the Welfare State*; Therborn, *When, How, and Why*; Przeworski, *Capitalism and Social Democracy*; Pierson, *Beyond the Welfare State?*
11 Heclo, "Towards a New Welfare State?"
12 Bruce, *The Coming of the Welfare State,* 31.
13 Marshall, *Class, Citizenship, and Social Development.*
14 Albo and Jenson, "Remapping Canada."
15 It has been established that wars were instrumental in the formation of various types of pensions such as veterans' pensions and service pensions, which provided the precedent for the later development of civil servant and other types of pensions. See Skocpol, *Protecting Soldiers and Mothers*; Teipe, *America's First Veterans*; National Union, "A Brief History of

Pensions." However, this book does not deal with this area and retains its focus on the trajectory of public pension systems in Australia and Canada.

16 Myles and Pierson, "The Comparative Political Economy."
17 Turner and Rajnes, "Can Private Pension Systems"; Little, *Fixing the Future.*
18 Whitehouse, *Canada's Retirement Income Provision,* 2.
19 Ibid.
20 Ibid.
21 Harris, *Pension Reforms,* 5; Weaver, "Whose Money Is It?"; Rein and Turner, "How Societies Mix."
22 Myles, and Pierson, "The Comparative Political Economy," 310.
23 Little, *Fixing the Future.*
24 Turner and Rajnes, "Can Private Pension Systems?"; Myles and Quadagno, "The Politics of Income Security."
25 Stanford, *Paper Boom.*
26 Holzmann and Hinz, *Old Age Income Support*; Hyung Hur, "A Comparative Study."
27 Ibid.
28 Kerr et al., *Industrialism and Industrial Man.*
29 Wilensky, *The Welfare State and Equality.*
30 Ibid.; Kerr et al., *Industrialism and Industrial Man.*
31 Palme, *Pension Rights.*
32 Holzmann and Hinz, *Old Age Income Support.*
33 Olsen, *The Politics*; Gilbert, *Transformation*; Therborn, *When, How, and Why*; Lynch, *Age in the Welfare State.*
34 Janowitz, *Social Control of the Welfare State*; Olson, *The Rise and Decline*; Pampel and Williamson, *Age, Class, Politics.*
35 Williamson and Pampel, *Old Age Security,* 13.
36 Pratt, *Gray Agendas.*
37 Pampel and Williamson, *Age, Class, Politics, 176.*
38 Modigliani and Muralidhar, *Rethinking Pension Reform.*
39 Castles, "The Impact of Parties"; DeViney, "Characteristics of the State and the Expansion."
40 Castles, "The Impact of Parties."
41 Weaver and Pierson, "Imposing Losses," 143.
42 Korpi, "Power, Politics"; Pampel and Williamson, *Age, Class, Politics.*
43 Bonoli, *The Politics of Pension Reform.*
44 Ibid., 150.
45 Williamson and Pampel, *Old Age Security.*
46 Bõrsch-Supan and Meinhard, eds., *Pension Reform in Six Countries*; Weaver, "Cutting Old Age Pensions."

47 Orloff, "Gender and the Social Rights"; Kangas, Lundberg, and Ploug, *Three Routes.*
48 Béland and Shinkaw, "Public and Private Policy Change"; Myles and Pierson, "The Comparative Political Economy."
49 Weaver and Pierson, "Imposing Losses"; Pal and Weaver, "The Politics of Pain"; Béland and Shinkaw, "Public and Private Policy Change."
50 Korpi, *The Democratic Class Struggle*; Myles, *Old Age in the Welfare State*; Esping-Andersen, *Politics against Markets*; Esping-Andersen, *The Three Worlds*; Palme, *Pension Rights.*
51 Esping-Andersen, *The Three Worlds*; Palme, *Pension Rights.*
52 Ibid., 119–20.
53 Esping-Andersen, *The Three Worlds.*
54 Myles, *Old Age in the Welfare State*; Myles and Quadagno, "Recent Trends"; Esping-Andersen, *The Three Worlds*; Lynch, *Age in the Welfare State.*
55 Ibid., 9–10.
56 Myles and Quadagno, "Recent Trends"; Rein and Turner, "How Societies Mix."
57 Béland and Gran, "Introduction"; Preece, *Dismantling Social Europe*; Evans and Williams, *A Generation of Change*; Plant, *The Neo-Liberal State.*
58 Quadagno, *The Transformation.*
59 Dilnot, "Public and Private Roles," 52.
60 Wonik, "Social Insurance Expansion."
61 Langley, "In the Eye."
62 Blackburn, *The Great Pension Crisis.*
63 Blackburn, *Banking on the Death*; Langley, "In the Eye"; Clark, *Pension Fund Capitalism.*
64 Orenstein, "Pension Privatization in Crisis," 180.
65 Blackburn, *Banking on the Death.*
66 Ibid.; Langley, "Pension Fund Capitalism."
67 Barr and Diamond, "The Economics of Pensions."
68 Blackburn, *Banking on the Death*; Langley, "Pension Fund Capitalism"; Ferguson, *Reclaiming Social Work.*
69 Davis, Lukomnik, and Pitt-Watson, *The New Capitalists.*
70 Blackburn, *The Great Pension Crisis.*
71 Blackburn, "A Global Pension Plan."
72 Blackburn, "A Global Pension Plan."
73 Wilson, *Retreat from Governance*); McBride and Shields, *Dismantling a Nation*; Grinspun and Kerklewich, "Consolidating Neo-Liberal Reform"; Drache and Ranachan, "Ground Zero"; Bakker and Scott, "From the Post-War"; Salter and Salter, "Displacing the Welfare State"; Pulkingham

and Ternowetsky, "The Changing Landscape"; Guest, *The Emergence of Social Security*; Jackson, "The Impacts"; Richards, *Retooling the Welfare State*; Campbell, *False Promise*; Finkel, *Social Policy and Practice.*

74 Miliband, *Marxism and Politics*; Rice and Prince, *Changing Politics*; Daniel Drache, "The Eye of the Hurricane"; Frankman, "The Fight"; Workman, *If You're in My Way.*

75 Levitt, *The Silent Surrender*, 149.

76 Rice and Prince, *Changing Politics.*

77 Rimmer, *Australian Labour Market*; Bell and Head, "Australia's Political Economy"; Walter, *Tunnel Vision*; Schwartz, "Internationalization"; Shaver, "Australian Welfare Reform"; Ewer et al., *Politics and Accord*; Macintyre, "After Social Justice"; Hancock, "Labour Market Deregulation."

78 Saunders, *Welfare and Inequality*; Bell, "The Unemployment Crisis"; Quiggin, "Social Democracy"; Jones, *The Australian Welfare State: Evaluating Social Policy*; Ozanne, "Ageing Citizens"; Smyth, "Australian Social Policy."

79 Shaver, "Australian Welfare Reform"; Mendes, *Australia's Welfare Wars Revisited.*

80 Kelly, *A Life of One's Own*; Zijderveld, *The Waning of the Welfare State*; Albo and Christ, "European Industrial Relations."

81 Moschonas, *In the Name of Social Democracy*, 2.

82 Piven, *Labor Markets*, 18.

83 Shields and Evans, *Shrinking the State.*

84 Haddow and Klassen, *Partisanship*, 34–40.

85 Myles, *Old Age in the Welfare State.*

86 Myles and Pierson, "The Comparative Political Economy."

87 Gash, *Anticipatory Budgeting*, 266.

88 Lynch, *Age in the Welfare State*, 115.

89 Esping-Andersen, *The Three Worlds*; O'Connor and Olsen, *Power Resources Theory*; Riches, "Australian Responses to Unemployment."

90 Esping-Andersen, *The Three Worlds*; Huber and Stephen, "The Social Democratic Welfare State."

91 Castles and Mitchell, "Worlds of Welfare."

92 Olsen, *The Politics.*

93 Saunders, *The Ends and Means.*

94 Ozanne, "Ageing Citizens"; Saunders, *The Ends and Means.*

95 Rothstein, "Social Capital," 234.

96 Campbell, *The Full Employment Objectives*; Apple, "The Rise and the Fall."

97 Wolfe, "The Canadian State"; Campbell, *The Full Employment Objectives*; Haddow, "Canada's Experiment."

98 Brown, *Market Rules*; Courchene, "Subnational Budgetary and Stabilization Policies."

99 Jenson, "Different but Not Exceptional"; Jenson, "Representation in Crisis"; Banting, *The Welfare State*; Banting, "Neo-Conservatism"; Myles, "When Markets Fail"; Pierson, "Coping with Permanent Austerity."
100 Hiller, "Region as a Social Construction."
101 Richmond, "Immigration and Multiculturalism"; Jaensch, *The Australian Party System*; Sayers, "Regionalism."
102 Porter, *The Vertical Mosaic.*
103 Watts, "Federalism and Diversity."
104 Nemni, "Two Nationalisms"; Brown, *Market Rules.*
105 Hodgins, Wright, and Hieck, eds., *Federalism in Canada and Australia.*
106 Watts, "Federalism and Diversity."
107 Irving, "Citizenship and Subject-Hood"; Smith, "Indices of Citizenship."
108 Guest, *The Emergence of Social Security.*
109 Kewley, *Australia's Welfare State.*
110 Woodsworth, "Book Review," 125.
111 Finkel, *Social Policy and Practice.*
112 Bryden, *Old Age Pensions.*
113 Simeon, "Studying Public Policy," 551.
114 Banting and Boadway, "Reforming Retirement Income Policy"; Rice and Prince, *Changing Politics*; Myles, *Income Security.*
115 Ibid., 5.
116 Banting and Boadway, "Reforming Retirement Income Policy," 6.
117 Ascah, *The Great Pension Debate*; Battle, "A New Old Age Pension"; Townson, *Pensions under Attack*; Baldwin, *Pension Reform in Canada*; Carmichael, *Pension Power*; Drover, "Tilting toward Marketization."
118 Battle, *Thinking the Unthinkable*; Battle, "A New Old Age Pension"; Myles, *The Market's Revenge*; Baldwin, *Pension Reform in Canada*; Drover, "Tilting toward Marketization."
119 Ibid.
120 Battle, *Relentless Incrementalism.*
121 Baldwin, *Pension Reform in Canada,* 9.
122 Quarter et al., "Social Investment"; Carmichael and Quarter, *Money on the Line.*
123 Deaton, *The Political Economy of Pensions*; Carmichael, *Pension Power.*
124 Robson, *Putting Some Gold in the Golden Years*; Pesando, *From Tax Grab to Retirement Saving*; Lam and Walker, *The Next Step.*
125 Mintz and Wilson, "Private Provision."
126 Estelle, "Canada's Old Age Crisis," 37–8.
127 Myles and Quadagno, "Recent Trends"; Weaver, "Cutting old Age Pensions"; Drover, "Tilting toward Marketization"; Rein and Turner, "How Societies Mix."

128 Klassen and Forgione, "Forced Retirement."
129 Béland, "Review."
130 Pixley, "Economic Democracy."
131 Carney and Hanks, *Australian Social Security Law*, 13–14.
132 Castles, *The Working Class and Welfare State.*
133 Castles, "A Farewell"; Castles, *Comparative Public Policy.*
134 Kirkwood, *Social Security Law*; Jones, *The Australian Welfare State*; Pixley, "Economic Democracy"; Carney and Hanks, *Australian Social Security Law*; Whiteford, "Reforming Pensions."
135 Saunders, *Welfare and Inequality*; Pixley, "Economic Democracy"; Jones, *The Australian Welfare State*; Shaver, *Universality and Selectivity*; Ozanne, "Ageing Citizens"; Shaver, "Australian Welfare Reform"; Nursey-Bray and Bacchi, *Left Directions*; Smyth, "Australian Social Policy."
136 Creedy and Disney, "Pension Schemes."
137 Hartcher, "Sun, Surf."
138 Harris, *Pension Reforms.*
139 Scheiwe, *Was Comparability Overstated*; Scheiwe, *Why Australia's Pension System.*
140 Rosenman, "Restructuring Australian Retirement Income."
141 Rosenman and Warburton, "Retirement Policy."
142 Rein and Turner, "Public–Private Interactions."
143 Ibid.; Creedy and Disney, "Pension Schemes."
144 Bryan, "Superannuation," 113.

3 National Settings, Class Forces, and Keynesianism

1 Johnson, "Independent Commodity Production."
2 Panitch, "Dependency and Class"; Fox, "Women's Role in Development."
3 Avakumovic, *Socialism in Canada*; Palmer, *Working Class Experience.*
4 Johnson, "The Development of Class."
5 Avakumovic, *Socialism in Canada*, 24.
6 Innis, *The Fur Trade in Canada*; Lipton, *The Trade Movement*; Morton and Copp, *Working People*; Palmer, *Working Class Experience.*
7 Pentland, *Labour and Capital*; Kealey and Palmer, "The Working Class."
8 Kovacs, "The Philosophy."
9 Horowitz, *Canadian Labour in Politics*; Howard and Scott, "International Unions."
10 Isbester, "Quebec Labour in Perspective"; Bennett, *The History of the Labour Movement in Quebec.*
11 Ibid.

12 Miller, "Organized Labour and Politics."
13 Avakumovic, *Socialism in Canada.*
14 McKay, *Rebels, Reds, and Radicals.*
15 Avakumovic, *Socialism in Canada*; McKay, *Rebels, Reds, and Radicals.*
16 Young, *The Anatomy of a Party*; Penner, *The Canadian Left*; Horowitz, *Canadian Labour in Politics.*
17 Avakumovic, *Socialism in Canada.*
18 Young, *The Anatomy of a Party.*
19 Cross, ed., *The Decline and Fall*, 19.
20 Ibid.
21 Caplan, *The Dilemma of Canadian Socialism*, 110–11.
22 Campbell, *The Full Employment Objectives*, 4.
23 Pickersgill, *The Mackenzie King Record*, vol. 1, 643.
24 Ibid., vol. 2, 22.
25 Young, *The Anatomy of a Party*; Lipset, *Agrarian Socialism.*
26 McKay, *Rebels, Reds, and Radicals*, 111.
27 Cross, *The Decline and Fall.*
28 Wolfe, "The Canadian State."
29 Langille, "The Business Council on National Issues," 47–8.
30 Isbester, "Quebec Labour in Perspective"; Bercuson and Bright, eds., *Canadian Labour History.*
31 Swartz, "The Politics of Reform"; Williams, *The Story of Unions*; Miller and Isbester, eds., *Canadian Labour in Transition.*
32 Pammett, "Class Voting"; Nevitte et al., *Unsteady State.*
33 Robinson and Simeon, *State, Society.*
34 Alford, *Party and Society*; Jaensch, *The Australian Party System.*
35 Panitch, *Working Class Politics*, 16.
36 Kautsky, *The Class Struggle.*
37 Przeworski, "Class, Production, and Politics," 177.
38 Brodie and Jenson, *Crisis, Challenge and Change.*
39 Clarke et al., *Absent Mandate.*
40 Macpherson, *Democracy in Alberta.*
41 Lemoine, "The Growth."
42 Porter, *The Vertical Mosaic.*
43 Ibid., 369.
44 Ibid., *The Vertical Mosaic.*
45 Carty, "Three Canadian Party Systems."
46 Stevenson, "Political Decentralization."
47 Nemni, "Two Nationalisms," 67.
48 Whitaker, *A Sovereign Idea.*

49 Horn, *Frank R. Scott*, xxviii.
50 Hargrove, *Labour of Love*, 193.
51 Drache, "Formation and Fragmentation."
52 Palmer, *Working Class Experience*, 211–13.
53 Macleod, "Nationalism and Social Class."
54 McMullin, *The Light on the Hill.*
55 Ehrensaft and Armstrong, "The Formation of Dominion Capitalism"; Albinski, *Canadian and Australian Politics*; Schedvin, "Staples and Regions."
56 Mayer, "Social Stratification," 34.
57 Rawson, *Labor in Vain?*; Markey, "The ALP"; Albinski, *Canadian and Australian Politics*; McMullin, *The Light on the Hill.*
58 Ledger, *Australian Socialism*; Albinski, *Canadian and Australian Politics.*
59 Aitkin, "The Australian Country Party."
60 Ledger, *Australian Socialism*, 48.
61 McMullin, *The Light on the Hill*, 11.
62 Ibid., 56.
63 Jupp, "Their Labour and Ours"; Markey, *The Making of the Labor Party.*
64 McMullin, *The Light on the Hill.*
65 Hancock, *Australia.*
66 McMullin, *The Light on the Hill*; Jupp, "Their Labour and Ours"; Ehrensaft and Armstrong, "The Formation of Dominion Capitalism."
67 Hancock, *Australia*; Matthews, "Employers' Associations."
68 Connell, *Ruling Class.*
69 Ibid.; Matthews, "Employers' Associations."
70 Tsokhas, *A Class Apart?*, 122.
71 Ledger, *Australian Socialism*, 235.
72 Stevens and Weller, eds., *The Australian Labor Party*, 22.
73 Ledger, *Australian Socialism*; Brugger and Jaensch, *Australian Politics*; McMullin, *The Light on the Hill.*
74 Ledger, *Australian Socialism*; McMullin, *The Light on the Hill.*
75 Jupp, "Their Labour and Ours," 232.
76 McMullin, *The Light on the Hill*, 38.
77 Ibid., 90.
78 Ibid., 90.
79 Castles, *The Working Class*; Kelly, *The End of Certainty.*
80 Ibid.; Pixley, "Economic Democracy."
81 Rawson, *Labor in Vain?*
82 Stevens and Weller, eds., *The Australian Labor Party*, 48.
83 Hancock, *Australia*, 67.
84 Australia, Department of Immigration and Ethnic Affairs, *Australia and Immigration, 1788–1978.*

85 McCarty, "The Economic Foundation."
86 Ledger, *Australian Socialism.*
87 Markey, "The ALP."
88 Higgins, "A New Province."
89 Pixley, "Economic Democracy."
90 Saunders, *The Ends and Means*, 49.
91 Higgins, "A New Province," 14.
92 Tsokhas, *A Class Apart?*, 122.
93 Pixley, "Economic Democracy."
94 Castles, *The Working Class*; Hagan, *The History of the ACTU.*
95 Miliband, *The State in Capitalist Society.*
96 Crisp, *The Parliamentary Government*, 83.
97 Hancock, *Australia*; Ledger, *Australian Socialism*; Markey, "The ALP"; Brugger and Jaensch, *Australian Politics.*
98 Markey, "The ALP."
99 Ibid.; Beilharz, *Transforming Labor*; Nairn, *Civilizing Capitalism.*
100 Stevens and Weller, eds., *The Australian Labor Party.*
101 Ibid., 89.
102 Ibid., 90.
103 Jupp, "The Australian Labor Party," 33.
104 Apple, "The Rise and the Fall."
105 Caporaso and Levine, *The Theories of Political Economy.*
106 Nemni, "Two Nationalisms"; Brown, *Market Rules.*
107 Rhodes, "The Political Economy."
108 Teeple, *Globalization*; Yargin and Stanislaw, *The Commanding Heights.*
109 Iversen, *Capitalism.*
110 Yargin and Stanislaw, *The Commanding Heights*, 41.
111 Harris, "Beveridge's Social and Political Thought," 23; Cassidy, *Social Security.*
112 Baldwin, "Beveridge in the Longue Durée."
113 Australia, *Full Employment in Australia*, 26–7.
114 Ibid., 27.
115 Whitlam, *The Whitlam Government*, 184.
116 Campbell, *The Full Employment Objectives in Canada, 1945-85: Historical, Conceptual and Comparative Perspectives*; Apple, "The Rise and the Fall of Full Employment Capitalism."
117 Campbell, *The Full Employment Objectives*, 3.
118 Ibid.
119 Bradford, "The Policy Influence," Howlett, Netherton, and Ramesh, *The Political Economy of Canada.*
120 Canada, *Green Book*, 175.
121 English, "Canada."

122 Canada, *Green Book.*
123 Heron, *The Canadian Labour Movement.*
124 Apple, "The Rise and the Fall."

4 Postwar Expansion of the Pension System in Australia

1 Kennedy, "Introduction"; Dickey, *No Charity There.*
2 Australia, Department of Social Security, *Developments in Social Security*; Kirkwood, *Social Security Law.*
3 Ziguras, "Australian Social Security Policy."
4 Kirkwood, *Social Security Law*, 2.
5 Dixon, *Australia's Policy Towards the Aged*; Carney and Hanks, *Australian Social Security Law.*
6 Ibid., 27.
7 Ibid.
8 Kewley, *Australia's Welfare State*; Jones, *The Australian Welfare State.*
9 Kewley, *Australia's Welfare State.*
10 Deacon and Bradshaw, *Reserved for the Poor.*
11 Australia, Department of Social Security, *Developments in Social Security.*
12 Ibid., 1.
13 Ibid.
14 Shaver, "Consideration of Mere Logic."
15 Australia, Department of Social Security, *Developments in Social Security.*
16 Ibid., 4.
17 Jones, *The Australian Welfare State*, 19.
18 Smith and Wearing, "Do Australians Want the Welfare State?"
19 Australia, Department of Social Security, *Financing Social Security.*
20 Australia, Department of Social Security, *The Social Security Review.*
21 Australia, Department of Social Security, *Developments in Social Security*, 13–18.
22 Ibid.
23 Kirkwood, *Social Security Law*, 49.
24 Australia, Department of Social Security, *The Social Security Review.*
25 Australia, Department of Social Security, *Developments in Social Security.*
26 Ibid., 30.
27 Australia, Department of Social Security, *The Social Security Review*, 30.
28 Australia, Department of Social Security.
29 Kirkwood, *Social Security Law and Policy.*
30 Australia, Department of Social Security, *Developments in Social Security.*
31 Ibid.

32 Ibid.
33 Ibid., 36.
34 Ibid., 38.
35 Carney and Hanks, *Australian Social Security Law.*
36 Australia, Department of Social Security. *Developments in Social Security*, 41.
37 Australia, Department of Social Security, *The Social Security Review*; Australia, Department of Social Security, *Developments in Social Security.*
38 Ibid., 36.
39 Carney and Hanks, *Australian Social Security Law*, 20.
40 Australia, Department of Social Security, *Developments in Social Security*, 44.
41 Carney and Hanks, *Australian Social Security Law.*
42 Australia, Department of Social Security. *Developments in Social Security*, 47.
43 Kirkwood, *Social Security Law.*
44 Australia, Department of Social Security, *Developments in Social Security.*
45 Australia, Department of Social Security, *Developments in Social Security.*
46 Kirkwood, *Social Security Law and Policy.*
47 Australia, Department of Social Security, *Developments in Social Security*, 45.
48 Carney and Hanks, *Australian Social Security Law.*
49 Australia, Department of Social Security, *Developments in Social Security*; Kirkwood, *Social Security Law*, 14.
50 Australia, Department of Social Security, *Developments in Social Security.*
51 Podger, Raymond, and Jackson, "The Relationship."
52 Kirkwood, *Social Security Law*, 2–3.
53 Australia, Department of Social Security, *Financing Social Security*, 8.
54 Australia, Department of Social Security, *Financing Social Security*; Dixon, *Australia's Policy Towards the Aged.*
55 Jones, *The Australian Welfare State.*
56 Australia, Department of Social Security, *Financing Social Security.*
57 Australia, *Official Year Book*, 969–71.
58 Jones, *The Australian Welfare State*; Dixon, *Australia's Policy Towards the Aged.*
59 Australia, *Official Year Book*, 969.
60 Australia, Department of Social Security, 8.
61 Jones, *The Australian Welfare State*; Dixon, *Australia's Policy Towards the Aged.*
62 Australia, Department of Social Security, *Financing Social Security.*
63 Australia, *National Superannuation*, 183.
64 Ibid., 186–7.
65 Australia, Department of Social Security, *Financing Social Security.*
66 Australia, *National Superannuation*, 186.
67 Australia, Department of Social Security, *Financing Social Security.*
68 Esping-Andersen, *The Three Worlds.*

69 Jones, *The Australian Welfare State*, 120.
70 Bateman and Piggott, "Mandatory Retirement Saving."
71 Ibid.
72 Australia, Australian Bureau of Statistics, *Employment Benefits*.
73 Ibid.
74 Australia, Department of Social Security, *Financing Social Security*.
75 Sax, *Ageing and Public Policy*.
76 CPD, First/19th/v. 3, 18 May, CGP, 1950, 2879.
77 CPD, First/18th/v1, 7 April, CGP, 1948, 609.
78 Chifley, *Things Worth Fighting For*, 65.
79 Crisp, *Ben Chifley*, 319.
80 Menzies, *Speech of Time*, 203.
81 Chifley, *Things Worth Fighting For*, 85.
82 Kewley, *Social Security in Australia*.
83 Chifley, *Social Security and Reconstruction*, 1.
84 CPD, First/18th/v1, 26 February, CGP, 1948, 257.
85 CPD, Third/17th/v1, 21 February, CGP, 1945, 12.
86 Chifley, *Things Worth Fighting For*, 29.
87 Whitlam, *The Whitlam Government*.
88 Department of Social Security, *Developments in Social Security*.
89 CPD, Second/15th/v1, 24 May, CGP, 1938, 1329–30.
90 CPD, First/16th/v1, 3 March, CGP, 1943, 1132–3.
91 CPD, First/17th/v3, 7 September, CGP, 1944, 596.
92 Kewley, *Social Security in Australia*.
93 CPD, Third/17th/v3, 12 September, CGP, 1945, 5305.
94 CPD, Third/17th/v3, 12 September, CGP, 1945, 5303.
95 CPD, Third/17th/v3, 13 September, CGP, 1945, 5394–5.
96 CPD, Second/18th/v1, 26 February, CGP, 1948, 245.
97 CPD, Third/17th/v3, 19 September, CGP, 1945, 5564.
98 CPD, Third/17th/v3, 19 September, CGP, 1945, 5638–41.
99 Stevens and Weller, eds., *The Australian Labor Party*.
100 Whitlam, *The Whitlam Government*, 277.
101 Kewley, *Social Security in Australia*.
102 Whitlam, *The Whitlam Government*, 358.
103 CPD, Third/17th/v1, 26 February, CGP, 1948a, 239–45.
104 CPD, First/19th/v3, 25 May, CGP, 1950, 3246–7.
105 Watts, "The Origins."
106 Ibid.
107 Kewley, *Australia's Welfare State*, 102–3.
108 CPD, First/21st/v1, 28 September, CGP, 1954, 1663.

109 CPD, First/19th/v3, 18 May, CGP, 1950c, 2883.
110 CPD, Second/25th/v1, 13 May, CGP, 1964, 1862.
111 Kewley, *Social Security in Australia.*
112 CPD, Second/27th/v2, 11 May, CGP, 1972, 2397.
113 CPD, First/28th/v1, 15 March, CGP, 1973, 665.
114 CPD, First/28th/v1, 11 April, CGP, 1973, 1345.
115 CPD, First/28th/v1, 12 April, CGP 1973, 1388.
116 CPD, First/28th/v1, 12 April, CGP, 1973, 1380–1.
117 CPD, First/29th/v1, 13 February, CGP, 1975, 249; CPD, First/29th/v1, 26 February, CGP, 1975, 712.
118 CPD, First/28th/v1, 15 March, CGP, 1973, 665.
119 Whitlam, *The Whitlam Government,* 351.
120 Australia, Department of Social Security, *Financing Social Security.*

5 Postwar Expansion of the Pension System in Canada

1 Finkel, *Social Policy and Practice.*
2 Guest, *The Emergence.*
3 Ibid., 34–5.
4 Bryden, *Old Age Pensions,* 49.
5 Guest, *The Emergence,* 35.
6 Knight, Nassar, and Pettit, *Canada and Quebec,* 3–4.
7 Guest, *The Emergence,* 37.
8 Bryden, *Old Age Pensions.*
9 Guest, *The Emergence,* 75.
10 Ibid., 71–2.
11 Bryden, *Old Age Pensions.*
12 Finkel, *Social Policy and Practice.*
13 Ibid.; Guest, *The Emergence.*
14 Ibid.; Bryden, *Old Age Pensions.*
15 Laycock, *The Canadian System.*
16 Bryden, *Old Age Pensions.*
17 Ibid.
18 Ibid.
19 Marsh, *Report.*
20 Ibid., 161.
21 Perrin, "Reflections."
22 Laycock, *The Canadian System*; Bryden, *Old Age Pensions.*
23 Canada, *Old Age Security Act,* 5.
24 Bryden, *Old Age Pensions.*

25 Canada, *The Canada Pension Plan and Changes.*
26 Canada, *Proceedings: Constitutional Conference.*
27 Ibid.
28 Canada, *Old Age Security Act,* 4.
29 Ibid., 4.
30 Canada, *Canada Pension Plan and Old Age Security Legislation* (4th ed.).
31 Canada, *Old Age Security Act and Old Age Security Regulation,* 7.
32 Canada, *Proceedings: Constitutional Conference.*
33 Ibid.
34 Canada, *The Income Security Programs,* 6.
35 Canada, Minister of Public Works and Government Services, *A Pension Primer.*
36 Canada, *Canada Pension Plan and Old Age Security Legislation* (6th ed.), 8.
37 Ibid., 6–7.
38 Canada, *Canada Pension Plan: Bill C-75.*
39 Canada, Statistics Canada, *Canada's Retirement Income Programs.*
40 Canada, *Statutes of Canada,* 1 (C9).
41 Canada, Statistics Canada, *Canada's Retirement Income Programs.*
42 Pesando, *Public and Private Pensions*; Clark, *Canada's Income Security Programs.*
43 Tamagno, *Occupational Pension Plans in Canada*; Edwards, *Canadian Private Pension Plans*; Clark, *Canada's Income Security Programs.*
44 Esping-Andersen, *The Three Worlds,* 83–4; Deaton, *The Political Economy of Pensions,* 430; Clark, *Canada's Income Security Programs,* 96–101.
45 Canada, *Canada Pension Plan: Bill C-75,* 6.
46 Canada, Human Resources Development. *Income Security Programs: Overview,* 18.
47 Canada, *Proceedings: Federal–Provincial Conference July 19–22.*
48 Ibid.
49 Canada, Statistics Canada, *Canada's Retirement Income Programs.*
50 Canada, *The Canada Pension Plan and Old Age Security Legislation with Regulations.*
51 Canada, *The Canada Pension Plan and Changes.*
52 Canada, *Statutes of Canada,* 1 (C9).
53 Canada, Statistics Canada, *Canada's Retirement Income Programs.*
54 Bryden, *Old Age Pensions.*
55 Statistics Canada, *Canada's Retirement Income Programs.*
56 Ibid.
57 Barr, *Economics of the Welfare State.*
58 Munnell, *The Future of Social Security,* 93.
59 HCD, Fourth/21st/v5, 21 June, 1951, 4424.

60 HCD, Fourth/21st/v5, 23 June, 1951b, 4553.
61 Canada, *Green Book*, 5.
62 Ibid., 6–7.
63 Canada, *Proceedings: Federal–Provincial Conference August 31–September 2*, 8.
64 Canada, *Green Book*, 28.
65 Ibid., 85.
66 Canada, *Proceedings: Dominion–Provincial Conference November 25–6*, 126.
67 Canada, *Report of the Royal Commission on Dominion–Provincial Relations*, 1940.
68 Canada, *Green Book*, 96–8.
69 Ibid., 97.
70 Ibid., 98.
71 Ibid., 529.
72 Canada, *Proceedings: Dominion–Provincial Conference November 25–6*, 129–30.
73 Knowles, *The New Party*.
74 HCD, Third/20th/v4, 15 May, 1947, 3139.
75 Bryden, *Old Age Pensions*.
76 HCD, Third/20th/v1, 24 February, 1947, 110.
77 HCD, Second/21st/v1, 24 March, 1950, 1119.
78 HCD, Second/21st/v1, 6 March, 1950, 469.
79 HCD, Second/21st/v1, 20 February, 1950, 62.
80 HCD, Second/21st/v1, 10 March, 1950, 651.
81 HCD, Second/21st/v1, 6 March, 1950, 475.
82 Bryden, *Old Age Pensions*, 53–7.
83 Canada, *Proceedings: Federal–Provincial Conference January 10–12*, 34.
84 HCD, Second/21st/v1, 10 March, 1950, 648.
85 HCD, Second/21st/v1, 9 March, 1950, 634.
86 HCD, Fourth/21st/v5, 23 June, 1951, 4548.
87 HCD, Fourth/21st/v5, 21 June, 1951, 4422.
88 Canada, *Proceedings: Federal–Provincial Conference April 26*, 9.
89 Cassidy, *Social Security and Reconstruction*.
90 Marsh, *Report*.
91 Pickersgill, *The Mackenzie King Record*, 564.
92 HCD, First/26th/v3, 18 July, 1963, 2340–81.
93 LaMarsh, *Memoirs*.
94 HCD, First/26th/v5, 4 November, 1963, 4751.
95 Connor, "How Industry Views," 52–3.
96 HCD, First/26th/v3, 18 July, 1963, 2340.
97 Canada, *Proceedings: Federal–Provincial Conference November 28–9*, 16.
98 HCD, First/26th/v3, 18 July, 1963, 2375.
99 HCD, First/26th/v5, 14 November, 1963, 4751.

100 Kent, *A Public Purpose*, 272–84.
101 Kent, *A Public Purpose*.
102 Béland and Babich, “Policy Change,” 265.
103 Stursberg, *Lester Pearson*, 195.
104 Provencher, *René Lévesque*, 166.
105 Quebec, *Quebec Pension Legislation*, 91.
106 Canada, *Proceedings: Federal-Provincial Conference November 28–9*, 49.
107 Canada, *Proceedings: Federal–Provincial Conference August 31–September 2*, 10.
108 Stursberg, *Lester Pearson*, 187.
109 Ibid., 186.
110 Kent, *A Public Purpose*, 271–84.
111 Stursberg, *Lester Pearson*, 191.
112 Ibid., 194.
113 Ibid., 192.
114 Ibid., 196.
115 Kent, *A Public Purpose*, 290.
116 Stursberg, *Lester Pearson*, 197.
117 HCD, Second/26th/v12, 23 March, 1965, 12777.
118 Stursberg, *Lester Pearson*, 195.
119 Canada, *Green Book*, 97.
120 Canada, *Proceedings: Federal–Provincial Conference July 19–22*, 14.
121 Kent, *A Public Purpose*, 285–91.
122 Canada, *Proceedings: Constitutional Conference*.
123 The consideration of maintaining national unity also permeated regional economic policy. In his opening statement on the review of social security in 1973, Marc Lalonde, the Minister of National Health and Welfare, declared that regional economic policy would “remain as cornerstone not only of job creation in parts of Canada but also of national unity” (Canada, *Working Papers*, 7). It was also mainly due to the rivalry between Quebec and Canada that the Unemployment Insurance (UI) was transformed “from insurance coverage into an instrument for wider social support through income transfer” (Drache, “The Eye of the Hurricane,” 35).

6 Welfare State Restructuring and Neoliberal Variations in Canada and Australia

1 In this chapter, the main attention is paid to how economic restructuring has triggered the transformation of the welfare state. The analysis of economic crisis in the 1970s is beyond the scope of this book. There are various explanations for the emerging crisis in the 1970s. For Marxist

explanations that relate the crisis to the inherent contradictions of capitalism, see Offe, *Contradictions*; and O'Connor, *The Fiscal Crisis*. For liberal theoretical explanations of the crisis, see Crozier, Huntington, and Watanuuki, *The Crisis*. For a Weberian explanation that emphasizes changes in the levels of technology and the imperatives of organizational adaptation to those changes, see Castells, *The Rise of Network Society*.

2 Harvey, *The Condition of Postmodernity*.
3 Alber, "Continuity and Changes"; Anderson, "The Politics of Retrenchment."
4 Hartman, "In Bed with the Enemy," 58–9.
5 Campbell and Pedersen, "Introduction."
6 Panitch, *Working Class Politics*, 6–7.
7 McBride and Shields, *Dismantling a Nation*; Hoover and Plant, *Conservative Capitalism*; Gamble, *The Free Economy*.
8 Ibid.
9 Harrison, *Of Passionate Intensity*.
10 Segal, *Beyond Greed*; Harrison, *Of Passionate Intensity*.
11 McBride and Shields, *Dismantling a Nation*, 37.
12 Harrison, *Of Passionate Intensity*; Broadbent, "Social Democracy."
13 Esping-Andersen, *Politics against Markets*; Broadbent, "Social Democracy."
14 Gamble, *The Free Economy*; Harvey, *The Condition of Postmodernity*.
15 Hartman, "In Bed with the Enemy," 58–9.
16 Giddens, *The Third Way*; Gamble, *The Free Economy*.
17 Hayek, *The Road to Serfdom*, 204–5; Friedman, *Capitalism and Freedom*, 10–21.
18 Hayek, *The Road to Serfdom*, 54–65; Friedman, *Capitalism and Freedom*, 27–36.
19 Cockett, *Thinking the Unthinkable*, 100–21.
20 Ibid., 104.
21 Harvey, *The Condition of Postmodernity*, 141–2.
22 Hoover and Plant, *Conservative Capitalism*.
23 Anderson, "The Politics of Retrenchment"; Albo, "Neoliberalism."
24 Offe, *Contradictions*; Panitch, "Rethinking."
25 Tilly, "Globalization"; Ross and Trachte, *Global Capitalism*.
26 Hall, *Governing the Economy*; Stanford, *Paper Boom*.
27 Burnham, "The Politics."
28 Ibid.
29 Pierson, *Beyond the Welfare State?*
30 McBride and Shields, *Dismantling a Nation*; Anderson, "The Politics of Retrenchment."
31 Albo, "Neoliberalism," 51.
32 Isin, "Governing Toronto," 173.
33 Panitch, "Rethinking"; Kagarlitsky, "The Challenges."

34 For Castells, the national state has become powerless because globalization has exerted enormous pressure on the national political power to diffuse in both upward (towards supranational organizations) and downward (towards local and regional political entities) directions (*The Rise*, 242–307). This diffusion of state power is in line with the neoliberal recasting of social responsibility.

35 Within the political economy literature, the welfare state reconfiguration accompanied by neoliberal restructuring has often been attributed to globalization, which has supposedly restricted the political manoeuvrability of the state to implement national policy (Kennedy, *Preparing*; Castells, *The Rise*; Strange, *The Retreat*; Held et al., *Global Transformations*; Mishra, *Globalization*). This interpretation insinuates that capital was subservient to the power of the state in the postwar period and that globalization has diminished the state's power over the operation of capital. In contrast, other analysts have questioned the validity of the supposed impact of globalization on the welfare state (Hirst and Thompson, *Globalization*; Boyer and Drache, *States against Markets*; Gilpin, *Global Political Economy*). Sceptics have argued that domestic variables are much more significant than globalization in explaining welfare state restructuring.

36 Bazowski, "Contrasting Ideologies," 103.

37 Moschonas, *In the Name of Social Democracy*, 3.

38 Albo, "Neoliberalism," 47.

39 Piven, *Labor Markets*, 18.

40 Gilbert, *Transformation*, 37.

41 Anthony Giddens, *The Third Way and Its Critics.*

42 Clarke, *Changing Welfare.*

43 Hartman, "In Bed with the Enemy," 57.

44 Kuhnle, "The Nordic Welfare States," 116.

45 Kiser and Laing, "Have We Overestimated."

46 Shields and Evans, *Shrinking the State*, 36–41.

47 Glyn, *Capitalism Unleashed*; OECD, *Society at a Glance.*

48 Gilbert, *Transformation.*

49 Whitfield, *Public Services or Corporate Welfare*, 84.

50 OECD, "New Orientations."

51 Giddens, *The Third Way and Its Critics.*

52 Gilbert, *Transformation*; Shaver, *Universality and Selectivity.*

53 Marshall, *Class, Citizenship.*

54 Shaver, *Universality and Selectivity.*

55 Friedman, *Capitalism and Freedom*; Hayek, *The Road to Serfdom.*

56 Shaver, *Universality and Selectivity.*

57 Gilbert, *Transformation*, 38.
58 Ibid.
59 Finn, "Welfare to Work"; Quaid, *Workfare*; Shragge, "Workfare."
60 OECD, *Ageing and Employment Policies.*
61 Hinrichs and Aleksandrowicz, "Reforming European Pension Systems."
62 OECD, *Ageing and Employment Policies.*
63 Vidlund, *Old Age Pension Reforms.*
64 Peck, *Workfare States.*
65 Shragge, "Workfare."
66 Pixley, *Citizenship and Employment.*
67 Dahrendorf, "The Changing Quality of Citizenship," 13.
68 Nordlund, "Social Security."
69 Blomqvist, "The Choice Revolution."
70 Carlson, "The Family"; Mead, *Beyond Entitlement.*
71 Giddens, *Where Now for New Labour?*; Blair, *The Third Way.*
72 Gilbert, *Transformation*, 41.
73 Gruber and Wise, eds., *Social Security Programs.*
74 World Bank, *Averting the Old Age Crisis.* http://ieg.worldbank.org/Data/reports/pensions_evaluation.pdf
75 Pusey, *Economic Rationalism.*
76 Kelsey, *Economic Fundamentalism.*
77 Pusey, *Economic Rationalism.*
78 Ibid., 106–7.
79 Broomhill and Spoehr, "Altered State Governments."
80 Mendes, "Australian Neoliberal Think Tanks."
81 Hay, "The Institute."
82 Mendes, "Australian Neoliberal Think Tanks."
83 Ibid.
84 Beder, *Global Spin.*
85 Mendes, "Australian Neoliberal Think Tanks."
86 Michael James, "How to Reform," 33.
87 James, "Welfare Coercion."
88 James, "How to Reform," 35.
89 Matthews, "Employers' Associations."
90 Bray and Walsh, "Different Paths."
91 McLaughlin, "How Business Relates."
92 Matthews, "Employers' Associations," 198.
93 Ibid.," 197–8.
94 Bray and Walsh, "Different Paths."
95 Matthews, "Employers' Associations," 204.

96 McLaughlin, "How Business Relates."
97 Bray and Walsh, "Different Paths."
98 Matthews, "Employers' Associations," 214.
99 McLaughlin, "How Business Relates."
100 Kelly, *The Hawke Ascendancy*, 426.
101 Ibid.
102 Wanna, "Can the State Manage," 228.
103 Kelly, *The Hawke Ascendancy*.
104 Ibid.; Wanna, "Can the State Manage."
105 Bray and Walsh, "Different Paths," 367.
106 Bell and Head, "Australia's Political Economy."
107 Bray and Walsh, "Different Paths."
108 Matthews, "Employers' Associations."
109 Bray and Walsh, "Different Paths."
110 Matthews, "Employers' Associations"; Castles, "A Farewell."
111 Bryson, "The Welfare State," 292.
112 Castles, "A Farewell."
113 Argy, *Australia at the Crossroads*; Mendes, "Australian Neoliberal Think Tanks."
114 In 1986, the Labor government attempted to introduce a "work for dole" scheme for young unemployed people to do community work in return for unemployment benefits (Bryson, "The Welfare State").
115 Bray and Walsh, "Different Paths."
116 Castles, "A Farewell," 21.
117 Carroll and Shaw, "Consolidating the Neoliberal Policy Bloc," 204.
118 Howse and Chandler, "Industrial Policy," 246.
119 Langille, "The Business Council," 47–8.
120 Wolfe, "The Canadian State."
121 Langille, "The Business Council," 70.
122 Carroll and Shaw, "Consolidating the Neoliberal Policy Bloc," 197.
123 Ibid.
124 Brownlee, *Ruling Canada*.
125 McBride, *Paradigm Shift*.
126 There were other social policy review committees and task forces whose recommendations for restructuring social welfare programs were adopted by federal governments. The impacts of these social policy reform recommendations will be examined in chapter 8.
127 Bradford, "The Policy Influence."
128 Clark, "Neoliberalism and Public Service Reform," 775.
129 Bradford, "Writing Public Philosophy," 158–9.

130 Inwood, *Continentalizing Canada*, 34–5.
131 Wolfe, "The Canadian State"; Inwood, *Continentalizing Canada.*
132 Mishra, *The Welfare State*; Smardon, "The Federal Welfare State."
133 Inwood, *Continentalizing Canada.*
134 Baker, "The Restructuring of the Canadian Welfare State."
135 Whitaker, *A Sovereign Idea*, 223.
136 Ibid.
137 Taylor, *Reconciling the Solitudes*, 158–60.
138 McBride and Shields, *Dismantling a Nation*, 38–9.
139 Grinspun and Kerklewich, "Consolidating Neo-Liberal Reform"; Panitch, "Capitalist Restructuring"; Wolfe, "The Canadian State"; McDougall, *Drifting Together*; Johnson and Mahon, "NAFTA, the Redesign."
140 Chant, "Macro Stability and Economic Growth."
141 Shields and Evans, *Shrinking the State.*
142 Prince, "Federal Budgeting."
143 Banting, "The Social Policy Divide"; Baker, "The Restructuring."
144 Banting, "The Social Policy Divide"; Baker, "The Restructuring."
145 Banting, "The Social Policy Divide."

7 Restructuring of the Pension System in Australia

1 Jones, *The Australian Welfare State.*
2 The Labor government made an amendment to the Social Security Act in 2009 in order to raise the qualifying age for the Age Pension by six months for every two years until it reached sixty-seven years in July 2024. Australia, *Social Security Payments*, 2010.
3 Carney and Hanks, *Australian Social Security Law.*
4 Australia, Department of Social Security *Government Support of Retirement Incomes.*
5 Australia, "The History of Pensions."
6 Australia, Department of Social Security, *Developments in Social Security.*
7 Australia, "The History of Pensions."
8 Australia, *Social Security Payments for the Aged*, 2004.
9 Ibid.
10 Jones, *The Australian Welfare State*; Carney and Hanks, *Australian Social Security Law.*
11 Kirkwood, *Social Security Law*, 150.
12 Australia, *Social Security Payments for the Aged*, 2004.
13 Australia, Department of Social Security, *The Social Security Review.*
14 Kirkwood, *Social Security Law*, 162–3.

15 Australia, *Social Security Payments for the Aged*, 2004.
16 Kirkwood, *Social Security Law*, 163–4.
17 Australia, *Social Security Payments for the Aged*, 2004.
18 CPD, First/35th/v36N9, 16 February, 1988, 7–8.
19 Australia, *Social Security Payments for the Aged*, 2010.
20 Australia, *Social Security Payments for the Aged*, 2004.
21 Australia, *Social Security Payments for the Aged*, 2010.
22 Australia, *Social Security Payments for the Aged*, 2004.
23 Ibid.
24 Australia, *Social Security Payments for the Aged*, 2010.
25 Australia, *Social Security Payments for the Aged*, 2004.
26 Ibid.
27 Australia, *Social Security Payments for the Aged*, 2010.
28 Ibid.
29 Ibid.
30 OECD, *Pensions at a Glance 2009*, 166.
31 Ibid., 166.
32 Australia, Department of Social Security, *The Social Security Review*.
33 Bateman and Piggott, "Australia's Mandatory Retirement Policy."
34 Australia, Senate Select Committee, *Enforced Superannuation Guarantee Charge*.
35 Australia, "Towards Higher Retirement Incomes."
36 Ibid., 78.
37 Bateman and Piggott, "Australia's Mandatory Retirement Policy," 4.
38 Australia, Department of Social Security, *The Social Security Review*.
39 Ibid., 8.
40 Australia, "Towards Higher Retirement Incomes," 79.
41 Australia, Department of Social Security, *The Social Security Review*, 15–20.
42 Borowski, "The Economics and Politics," 35.
43 Australia, "Towards Higher Retirement Incomes," 81.
44 Ibid., 82.
45 CPD, First/35th/v3N10, 23 August, 1988, 183–5.
46 Bateman and Piggott, "Australia's Mandatory Retirement Policy."
47 Harris, *Pension Reforms*, 5.
48 Ibid.
49 Ibid.
50 Ibid., 5–6.
51 The tacit support of the Australian business community for the Labor government's superannuation reform was in part coordinated by major financial players such as the Life Insurance Federation of Australia (IIFA), which

is now known as Investment and Financial Services Association (IFSA), and the Association of Superannuation Funds of Australia (ASFA), which eagerly welcomed the superannaution reform. Harris, *Pension Reforms,* 5.

52 Bryan, "Superannuation," 101.

53 Australia, ACTU, *History of Super.*

54 Daley, "Self-Reliance in Retirement," 1.

55 Harris, *Pension Reforms,* 3.

56 Scheiwe, *Why Australia's Pension System,* 3–5.

57 Bryan et al., "Agents with Too Many Principals?"

58 Bateman, Kingston, and Piggott, *Forced Saving.*

59 Ibid., 203–5.

60 Australia, Australian Taxation Office, *The Superannuation Guarantee.*

61 Ibid.

62 Australia, Department of the Attorney General, *Superannuation Guarantee Administration Act 1992,* 54–5.

63 Australia, Parliamentary Library, *Budgetary Review.*

64 Australia, Parliamentary Library. *Budgetary Review,* 2001b.

65 Australia, Senate Select Committee, *Enforced Superannuation Guarantee Charge.*

66 Australia, Australian Taxation Office. *Superannuation.*

67 OECD, *Directorate for Education.*

68 Reasonable benefit limits were abolished from 1 July 2007. Superannuation concessions are now limited by caps on contributions to superannuation. Concessional contributions (which encompass all contributions made by an employer on an individual's behalf) that exceed an annual threshold ($50,000 in 2007–8) are subject to an additional tax levied on the individual (at 31.5 percent on the excess contributions). The individual may choose to pay this tax by withdrawing amounts from the fund. OECD, *Pensions at a Glance 2011.*

69 Harris, *Policy Approach,* 7.

70 A flat rate of 31.25 per cent (including the medical levy of 1.25 per cent) on lump sum benefits taken prior to age fifty-five, and a lower rate of 16.25 per cent (including the medical levy of 1.25 per cent) in respect of the first $55,000 taken after the age of fifty-five (access to superannuation benefits is possible for retirement on or after age fifty-five, which will be increased to 60 by 2025), with the remainder taxed at 31.25 per cent (including the medical levy). Australia, *The Social Security Review,* 40.

71 OECD, *Directorate for Education*; Harris, *Policy Approach.*

72 Australia, Parliament of Australia, *Superannuation.*

73 Ibid., 1–2.

74 Australia, Senate Select Committee, *Retirement Income Modelling.*

75 Australia, *Budget Speech 2005–06.* http://www.budget.gov.au/2005-06/speech/download/speech.pdf

76 Australia, *APRA Quarterly Superannuation Performance June 2007.*

77 Australia, Department of the Attorney General, *Superannuation Guarantee Administration Act 1992.*

78 Burner, "Private Pensions Supervisory Methods," 183.

79 Harris, *Policy Approach*, 7.

80 CPD, First/31st/v6N17, 11 October, 1978, 1749–50.

81 Australia, Department of Social Security, *Financing Social Security*, 11–12.

82 Whitlam, *The Whitlam Government*, 351.

83 Keating, *Address to the Victorian Fabian Society*, 72–3.

84 Ibid., 13.

85 Mendes, *Australia's Welfare Wars Revisited*, 155–78.

86 Hawke, *National Reconciliation*, 57.

87 Saunders, *The Ends and Means.*

88 Australia, ACTU, *Prices and Incomes Accord*, 1983, 2.

89 Hawke, *National Reconciliation:* 84.

90 Australia, ACTU. *Prices and Incomes Accord.*

91 Hawke, *National Reconciliation*, 42.

92 CPD, First/33rd/v33N1, 3 May, 1983, 99.

93 Keating, *Address to the Victorian Fabian Society*, 19–22.

94 Howard, *The Role of Government*, 5.

95 CPD, First/33rd/v33N5, 4 May, 1983, 160.

96 Hawke, *National Reconciliation*, 88.

97 CPD, First/33rd/v33N5, 3 May, 1983, 115–16.

98 CPD, First/33rd/v33N7, 1 June, 1984, 2718.

99 Keating, *Address to the Victorian Fabian Society*, 186.

100 Liberal and National Parties of Australia, *Future Directions*, 71.

101 Hawke, *National Reconciliation*, 92.

102 CPD, First/33rd/v33N6, 6 September, 1983, 379.

103 CPD, First/33rd/v3N5, 24 August, 1983, 119.

104 CPD, First/33rd/v33N5, 24 August, 1983, 159.

105 Hawke, *National Reconciliation*, 92.

106 The subordination of citizenship to relations between capital and labour was also evident in the labour movement's endorsement of tax cuts that directly benefited the employed but limited the scope for social welfare initiatives that would have had a direct impact on those outside the labour market. See the ALP platforms in Stevens and Weller, *The Australian Labor Party*. See also Shaver, "Australian Welfare Reform."

107 Australia, ACTU, *All You Want to Know,* 10.
108 Australia, ACTU, *Accord V,* 2.
109 Howard, *The Role of Government,* 14.
110 CPD, First/33rd/v33N1, 1 November, 1983, 2099; CPD, First/33rd/v33N5, 6 September, 1983, 378.
111 Mendes, "Australian Neoliberal Think Tanks," 37.
112 Ibid., 38.
113 CPD, First/33rd/v33N7, 1 June, 1984, 2719.
114 CPD, First/35th/v36N9, 16 February, 1988, 7–8.
115 CPD, First/35th/v3N10, 23 August, 1988, 183–5.
116 CPD, First/37th/v36N19, 8 October, 1991, 364.
117 Australia, ACTU, *Accord VII.*
118 CPD, First/37th/v36N6, 10 April, 1991, 2315.
119 Australia, ACTU, *Prices and Incomes,* 1986, 2.
120 Australia, ACTU, *Accord VI,* 3.
121 The ACTU hailed the accords as major accomplishments; nonetheless, it deplored the decline in real wages and the soaring of profits. "Under the Accord, wages have been restrained with nominal growth of 6.0% compared to 11% in the pre-Accord … at the same time, real unit labour costs have fallen by 8% since … 1983 consistent with supporting both employment and investment. Australia, ACTU, *The Accord and Enterprise Bargaining,* 3.
122 Australia, ACTU, *Accord VII,* 2.
123 Australia, ACTU, *All You Want to Know,* 10.
124 Australia, ACTU, *The IR Reform Act of 1993,* 2.
125 Australia, ACTU, *Accord VII,* 2.
126 By 2004, the ACTU admitted that the 9 per cent contribution rate was not sufficient to secure retirement income for workers. In his speech on 15 October 2004, Greg Combet, the ACTU secretary, asserted that "all evidence therefore points to the fact that 9% will not provide sufficient retirement savings for workers currently in the workplace, or entering the workplace today. Australia, ACTU, *A New Vision for Super,* 4.
127 Bryan, "Superannuation," 101.
128 Australia, ACTU, *Accord VII.*
129 Hewson and Fischer, *Fightback,* 28–32.
130 CPD, First/36th/v171N2, 16 May, 1990, 593.
131 CPD, First/37th/v36N6, 10 April, 1991, 2317–19.
132 CPD, First/36th/v171N2, 16 May, 990, 593.
133 CPD, First/37th/v36N6, 8 October, 1991, 2310.
134 Bryan, "Superannuation," 102–3.

135 Bryan, "Minimum Living Standards," 213.
136 Bryan, "Superannuation," 102.
137 CPD, First/36th/v38N4, 2 April, 1992, 1763.
138 Sax, *Ageing and Public Policy.*
139 Rix, "Old Age Income Security," 1.
140 Bryan, "Superannuation," 102.
141 Australia, ACTU, *Greg Combet's Address*, 4.
142 CPD, First/38th/v138N18, 17 November, 1997, 10460–1.
143 CPD, First/38th/v138N18, 17 November, 1997, 10461.
144 Newman, *The Challenge of Welfare Dependency*, 12–23.
145 As leader of the Liberal Party of Australia, Tony Abbott has been the prime minister since September 2013.
146 Abbott, "Renewing the Social Fabric," 42.
147 *The Howard Government Election 2004 Policy*, 18.
148 Mendes, *Australia's Welfare Wars Revisited*, 139.
149 Latham, *Civilising Global Capital*, xix, xxx; Latham, "The New Economy."
150 Latham, "The Myths of the Welfare State," 2
151 Ibid., 2.
152 Latham, *Budget Reply Speech.*
153 Latham, *Opportunity for All.*

8 Restructuring of the Pension System in Canada

1 In its 2012 budget, the Conservative government raised the age eligibility for OAS benefits to sixty-seven, which is scheduled to be phased in by 2023 (Canada, *Canada Pension Plan and Old Age Security Benefit Rate Effective January 1, 2012.*
2 Canada, *Canada Pension Plan and Old Age Security Legislation* (6th ed.).
3 Canada, *The Income Security Programs.*
4 Canada, *Canada Pension Plan, Old Security Act, and Pension Benefits Standards Act with Regulations* (8th ed.).
5 Canada, *Canada Pension Plan, Old Age Security Act and Pension Benefits Standards Act* (1987).
6 Canada, Statistics Canada, *Canada's Retirement Income Programs*, 109.
7 Ibid., 21.
8 Ibid.
9 Ibid., 67.
10 Ibid.
11 Canada, Human Resources Development, *Income Security Programs.*
12 Canada, Department of Finance, *Seniors Benefits*, 28.
13 Ibid., 33.

14 Ibid., 9.
15 Canada, Human Resources Development, *Income Security Programs.*
16 Canada, *Canada Pension Plan, Old Age Security Act and Pension Benefits Standards Act* (1987).
17 Ibid.
18 Canada, *Canada Pension Plan, Old Security Act and Pension Benefits Standards Act with Regulations* (8th ed.).
19 Canada, Statistics Canada, *Canada's Retirement Income Programs.*
20 Canada, Human Resources Development, *Income Security Programs.*
21 Ibid.
22 Ibid.
23 Ibid.
24 Ibid.
25 Canada, Statistics Canada, *The CPP and OAS Stats Book.*
26 Canada, Statistics Canada, *The CPP and OAS Stats Book.*
27 Ibid.
28 Little, *Fixing the Future.*
29 Ibid.
30 Ibid.
31 Killeen and James, *Annotated Canada Pension Plan.*
32 Greenan, *The Handbook*, 70.
33 The spouse benefits paid by the QPP are slightly higher than the amount paid by the CPP. On the other hand, the dependent children benefits paid out by the CPP are much higher than the same benefits paid out by the QPP.
34 Little, *Fixing the Future.*
35 Canada, *Canada Pension Plan, Old Security Act and Pension Benefits Standards Act with Regulations* (8th ed.). Note that the regulation of employer-sponsored private occupational plans falls within the jurisdiction of provincial governments. With respect to legislation governing minimum standards and the funding and investment of pension funds, there are variations across Canada.
36 Canada, Statistics Canada, *Canada's Retirement Income Programs.*
37 Ibid.
38 Greenan, *The Handbook.*
39 Canada, Statistics Canada, *Canada's Retirement Income Programs.*
40 Ibid.
41 Ibid.
42 Canada, Statistics Canada, *Canada's Retirement Programs.*
43 Canada, *Canada's Retirement Income Programs: A Statistical Overview.* Statistics Canada, Catalogue No. 75–507-XIE (Ottawa: Statistics Canada, 1999–2000), 7–8.
44 Canada, Statistics Canada, *Retirement Savings.*

45 Clark, *Retirement and Estate Planning*, 119.
46 Canada, Statistics Canada, *Retirement Savings.*
47 Canada, Statistics Canada, *Survey of Financial Security.*
48 Canadian Council on Social Development, *The Future of Social Security*, 10.
49 Canada, *Federal–Provincial Conference of First Ministers* (1978), 9.
50 Canada, *The Federal and Provincial Conference of the First Ministers* (1981), 3.
51 Canada, *Federal–Provincial Conference of First Ministers* (1982), 5.
52 Drache and Ranachan, "Ground Zero."
53 HCD, First/33rd./v4, 23 May, 1985, 5012, 5016.
54 Canada, Canadian Intergovernmental Conference Secretariat., *The Federal–Provincial Annual Conference*, 2.
55 According to Sylvia Bashevkin (*Welfare Hot Buttons*, 21), "Brain Mulroney was less ideological and more pragmatic than his US and UK counterparts." However, through "his pursuit of a decentrist domestic agenda, he opened the door for the adoption of US-style welfare rhetoric by Canadian provincial leaders."
56 Inwood, *Understanding Public Administration*, 262. During the Mulroney era, there was an insignificant decline in the number of full-time public service employees. However, there was also a significant increase in the number of term and part-time public employees as the Mulroney government launched new initiatives such as the goods and services tax (Lindquist and Paquet, *Government Restructuring*, 13–14).
57 Canada, Canadian Intergovernmental Conference Secretariat, *The Federal–Provincial Annual Conference*, 19.
58 According to Bercuson and Cooper, it was due to considerations of national unity and the Quebec question that the Mulroney government refrained from implementing the 1986 Forget Commission on unemployment insurance, which had recommended deep cuts to unemployment insurance benefits. See their *De-Confederation*, 53–4.
59 HCD, Second/34th/v4, 18 October, 1989, 4839.
60 HCD, Second/34th/v1, 1 May, 1989, 1395.
61 HCD, Second/34th/v1, 5 May, 1989, 1380.
62 HCD, Second/34th/v4, 17 May, 1989, 1850, 4840.
63 HCD, Second/34th/v1, 5 May, 1989, 1396.
64 Even the Liberal Party in government did not regard the clawback as a violation of the universality principle. The federal finance department's statement on the OAS confirms this assertion. According to that department's 1997 description, "Old Age Security provides benefits to Canadians age 65 and over based on years of residence in Canada. Benefits are taxable and paid to all seniors." Canada, Department of Finance, *Securing Canada's*

Retirement Income System, 3.

65 Dickinson, "Six Common Misperceptions," 178; Baldwin, *Pension Reform*, 3.

66 Canada, Statistics Canada, *Retirement Savings*. In 2010–11, 4.9 million seniors received an OAS cheque. Canada, Human Resources and Skills Development Canada, *Annual Report*. In other words, almost 98 per cent of the elderly Canadians received OAS benefits during this period.

67 Whitehouse, *Canada's Retirement Income Provision*, 5.

68 Canada, *Improving Income Security in Canada*.

69 Ibid. A massive reduction in the federal social transfer that was tied to the integration of federal grants into a single block called the Canada Health and Social Transfer (CHST), which provided the provinces with greater power over social welfare programs. This was projected as a means to maintain national unity. The trends towards further devolution of authority over social welfare programs were hailed as a collaborative approach to the use of the federal spending power. It became the main principle of the Social Union Framework Agreement between the federal and provincial governments Canada, *Proceedings: First Ministers Meeting December 11–12*.

70 HCD, First/35th/v133N238, 30 October, 1995, 15968.

71 HCD, First/35th/v133N165, 13 March, 1995, 10385.

72 HCD, First/35th/v133N238, 30 October, 1995, 15968.

73 HCD, First/35th/v133N238, 30 October, 1995, 15971.

74 HCD, First/35th/v133N225, 28 September, 1995, 14993.

75 HCD, First/35th/v133N225, 28 September, 1995, 14993.

76 HCD, First/35th/v133N225, 28 September, 1995, 14996–7.

77 HCD, First/35th/v133N248, 30 October, 1995, 16023.

78 HCD, First/35th/v133N248, 30 October, 1995, 16020.

79 HCD, Second/35th/v133N002, 28 February, 1996, 33. Ironically, the Bloc Québécois was the only political party that called for the universalization of the RRSP by "replacing the RRSP deductions with a tax credit of $268 for everyone." HCD, Second/35th/v135N44, 4 December, 1997, 2707.

80 HCD, First/35th/v133N238, 31 October, 1995, 16024.

81 HCD, First/35th/v133N248, 31 October, 1995, 16021.

82 HCD, First/35th/v133N238, 31 October, 1995, 16024.

83 HCD, Second/35th/v133N8, 7 March, 1996, 430.

84 Canada, *Senate Debates*, vol. 135N2, 18 March, 1996, 52.

85 Dion, *Straight Talk*, 68–72.

86 Canadian Labour Congress, *The Upcoming Debate*.

87 Quebec, Direction des Communications, *For You and Your Children*, 51.

88 Ibid., 57.

89 Canada, Department of Finance, *Finance Minister's Statement*, 8.

90 Canada, Department of Finance, *Budget Plan*, 4.
91 Ibid.
92 Canada, *An Information Paper*, 21.
93 Ibid., 33–42.
94 Ibid.
95 Coyne, "Let's Create a Nation of Savers."
96 Courchene, *Social Canada in the Millennium*, 10–13.
97 Robson, *Putting Some Gold in the Golden Years.*
98 Ibid., 6.
99 BNAC, *The Future of Pension Policy*, vii.
100 Reform Party of Canada, *Responsible Social Reform.*
101 HCD, First/35th/v133N251, 31 October, 1995, 16023.
102 HCD, First/35th/v133N251, 31 October, 1995, 16025.
103 Canada, *Principles to Guide Federal-Provincial Decisions*, 13.
104 Ibid., 22–3. Some business representatives, such as the Canadian Chamber of Commerce and many local chambers, the Metro Toronto Board of Trade, and the Retail Council of Canada, argued that increased contribution rates amounted to higher payroll taxes, which would be "job killers." Canada Federal, Provincial, Territorial CPP Consultation Secretariat, *Report*, 21.
105 Canada, *Principles to Guide Federal-Provincial Decisions*, 23.
106 Canada, Department of Finance, *Securing Canada's Retirement Income System*, 21. According to Daniel Béland, whose insight had been shaped by information acquired from anonymous federal public servants, "because the pressure not to alienate Quebec voters became stronger than ever after the 1995 referendum when separation almost triumphed, privatization became implicitly related to 'national unity' issues." See his *Pension Reform*, 31.
107 Canada, *Proceedings: First Ministers Meeting December 11-12*, 10. Despite the disapproval of the proposed changes by the NDP governments in BC and Saskatchewan, the agreement between the federal and other eight provincial governments satisfied the statutory requirement that changes to the CPP must receive the concurrence of at least two-thirds of the provinces with two-thirds of Canada's population.
108 Canada, *Proceedings: First Ministers Meeting December 11-12*, 10.
109 Quebec. Direction des Communications, *For You and Your Children*, 38.
110 Ibid., 38.
111 HCD, Second/36th/v135N44, 4 December, 1997, 2706.
112 HCD, Second/36th/v136N44, 4 December, 1997, 2704.
113 HCD, Second/36th/v135N44, 4 December, 1997, 2698–2701.
114 HCD, Second/36th/v136N41, 1 December, 1997, 2490.

115 HCD, Second/36th/v135N04, 1 December, 1997, 2709. Bloc Québécois MPs boasted about their province's influence on the CPP's restructuring, especially on its new investment policy. In her statement on Bill C-2, Christine Gagnon of the Bloc declared that the bill "is an indirect tribute to the initiative taken by the Quebec government in the mid-sixties when Jean Lesage's team decided to create the Caisse de depot et placement du Quebec." HCD, v135N 44, 1 December 1997, 2481. The Bloc's claim is corroborated by Daniel Béland, who asserts that the existence of the Caisse de depot et placement in Quebec facilitated the establishment of an investment board in the rest of Canada (ROC) to invest CPP funds in equities in order to generate high returns to help pay benefits. See Béland, *Pension Reform.*
116 HCD, Second/36th/v135N04, 4 December, 1997, 2722.
117 HCD, Second/36th/v135N04, 4 December, 1997, 100.
118 OECD, "The Value of Pensions Entitlement," 29.
119 Paquet, "Governance," 252.
120 Bercuson and Cooper. *De-Confederation,* 159.
121 Stursberg, *Lester Pearson,* 201.
122 Béland and Myles, "Policy Change."
123 Knight, Nassar, and Pettit, *Canada and Quebec,* 4–7.

Conclusion

1 Since two of the main objectives of the welfare state are poverty alleviation and income inequality reduction, the findings in this book would be of great interest for policy-makers. In its recent report card on elderly poverty reduction in OECD countries, the Conference Board of Canada has given Canada an "A" grade. Australia has received a "D" grade on the poverty reduction indicator. According to this report, 6.7 per cent of elderly Canadians live in poverty but close to 40 per cent of the elderly do in Australia.
2 Detje, "Systemic Danger?"
3 Impavido and Tower, "How the Financial Crisis Affects Pensions," 19.
4 Impavido, and Tower, "How the Financial Crisis Affects Pensions," 19.
5 Antolín and Stewart, "Private Pensions," 4; Blackburn, "Crisis 2.0."
6 Detje, "Systemic Danger?," 24.
7 Ibid.
8 Blackburn, "Crisis 2.0," 35.
9 Orenstein, "Pension Privatization in Crisis," 65–6; Blackburn, "Crisis 2.0," 41.
10 Orenstein, "Pension Privatization in Crisis," 70.

11 Detje, "Systemic Danger? The Effects of the Financial Crisis on Private Pensions," 7.
12 Blackburn, "Crisis 2.0," 33–4.
13 Orenstein, "Pension Privatization in Crisis," 70.
14 Orenstein, "Pension Privatization in Crisis," 73.
15 Antolín and Stewart, "Private Pensions."
16 Orenstein, "Pension Privatization in Crisis," 75.
17 Raising the qualifying age for the Old Age Pension by six months for every two years until it reaches sixty-seven in July 2024. Also, the superannuation guarantee rate is scheduled to be raised to 12 per cent between 2013–14 and 2019–20 (Australia, *Social Security Payments for the Aged* [2010].
18 Spies-Butcher, "Labor," 26.
19 Quiggin, "Labor Vision against Tradition," 1.
20 Ibid., 1.
21 Bateman, "Retirement Incomes in Australia."
22 Sherry, "Australia's Policy Response," 1.
23 The raising of the age eligibility for the OAS benefits to sixty-seven, scheduled to be phased in by 2023, and the introduction of the pooled registered pension plans (PRPPs) by the federal government, are the main changes since 1997. The PRPPs are defined contribution plans; they are voluntary and are intended to enhance workplace coverage in small and medium-sized companies where employees have no workplace savings plan. Canada, *Ensuring a Strong Retirement System.*
24 Canada, Human Resources and Skills Development Canada, *Annual Report of the Canada Pension Plan 2010–2011.*
25 Daley, "Self-Reliance in Retirement," 1.
26 Ambachtsheer, "Pension Reform," 46.
27 Brodie, "Citizenship and Solidarity," 392.
28 Myles, "When Markets Fail," 130.

Bibliography

Australia

ACTU (Australian Council of Trade Unions). *Accord V.* 1989. http://www.actu.asn.au/public/papers/89socialwelfare

– *Accord VI: Agreement between the Federal Government and the ACTU.* 1990. http://www.actu.org.au/our-work/publications

– *Accord VII: Putting Jobs First.* 1993. http://www.actu.org.au/public/papers/accord7/index.html

– *The Accord and Enterprise Bargaining.* 1992. http://www.actu.org.au/public/news/1063077679_30362.htm

– *ACTU Congress: Social Justice Policy.* 1995. http://www.actu.org.au/public/papers/95superannaution

– *All You Want to Know About ACTU but Were Afraid to Ask.* 1994. http://www.actu.org.au/public/news/1058420227_29131.html

– *Greg Combet's Address to the SDP National Council.* 1999. http://www.actu.org.au/public/papers/95superannaution

– *History of Super.* 2005. http://www.actu.org.au/super/about/super_history.html

– *The IR Reform Act of 1993, a Union Perspective: Labouring towards Workplace Reform.* 1994. http://www.actu.org.au/public/news/1060305701_401.html

– A New Vision for Super. 2004. http://www.actu.org.au/super/news/1102472562_4354.html

– *Prices and Incomes.* 1986. http://www.actu.org.au/public/papers/accord2/index.html

– *Prices and Incomes Accord.* 1983. http://parlinfo.aph.gov.au/parlInfo/search/display/display.w3p;query=Id%3A%22library%2Fpartypol%2F992745%22

– *Wages Policy.* 1991. http://www.actu.org.au/public/papers/accord6/index.html

APRA Quarterly Superannuation Performance June 2007. Australian Bureau of Statistics, Cat. no. 5206.0. 2007.

Australian Bureau of Statistics. *Employment Benefits*. Catalogue no. 6332 (May). Canberra: Australian Government Publishing Service, 1979.

– *Australian Social Trends*. 2009. http://www.abs.gov.au/AUSSTATS/abs@.nsf/Lookup/4102.0Main+Features20Sep+2009

– "The History of Pensions and Other Benefits in Australia." *Year Book Australia*. Publication no. 1301.0. Canberra: Department of Social Security, 1988.

– "History of Pensions and Other Benefits in Australia." *Year Book Australia*. Cat. no. 1301.0, No. 82. Canberra: Department of Social Security, 2001.

– "Paid Work: Labour Force Characteristics of People with Disability." *Australian Social Trends*. Cat. no. 4102.0, Australian Bureau of Statistics, Canberra. 2005. https://www.ato.gov.au/super/content.asp?doc=content%2F60489.htm&pag=1&H=

Australian Taxation Office. *Superannuation: Key Superannuation Rates and Thresholds*. 2005. https://www.ato.gov.au/super/content.aspx?doc=%2Fcontent%2F60489.htm

– *The Superannuation Guarantee: A Guide for Employers*. Canberra: Australian Government Publishing Service, 2005. https://www.ato.gov.au/super/content.asp?doc=%2Fcontent%2F19818.htm

Budget Speech 2005–06. 2005. http://www.budget.gov.au/2005-06/speech/download/speech.pdf

Budget Speech 2006–07. 2006. http://www.budget.gov.au/2006-07/speech/html/Speech.htm

Department of the Attorney General. *Superannuation Guarantee Administration Act 1992*. Canberra: Office of the Legislative and Publishing, Attorney-General's Department, 2005.

Department of Immigration and Ethnic Affairs. *Australia and Immigration, 1788–1978*. Canberra: Australian Government Publishing Service, 1978.

Department of Social Security. *Developments in Social Security: A Compendium of Legislative Changes Since 1908*. Canberra: Australian Government Publishing Service, 1983.

– *Financing Social Security: An Analysis of the Contributory Social Insurance Approach*. Canberra: Australian Government Publishing Service, 1982.

– *Government Support of Retirement Incomes in Australia*. Canberra: Australian Government Publishing Service, 1984.

– *Income Support for the Retired and the Aged: An Agenda for Reform, Report of the Senate Standing Committee on Community Affairs*. Canberra: Australian Government Publishing Service, 1988.

– *A Guide to Payments and Services.* Canberra: Government Publication Services, 1996.

– *The Social Security Review: Occupational Superannuation Arrangements in Australia.* Canberra: Australian Government Publishing Service, 1987.

– *Social Welfare Policy Secretariat: Alternative to Meet the Income Needs of the Aged.* Canberra: Australian Government Publishing Service, 1982.

Full Employment in Australia. Canberra: Australian Government Printer, 1945.

National Superannuation in Australia: Interim Report of the National Superannuation Committee of Inquiry. Canberra: Australian Government Publishing Service, 1974.

Official Year Book of the Commonwealth of Australia. No. 33. Canberra: Australian Government Publishing Service, 1940.

Parliamentary Library. *Budgetary Review,* 2001. http://www.aph.gov.au/About_Parliament/Parliamentary_Departments/Parliamentary_Library/pubs/rp/rp1314/CommOfAudit

Parliament of Australia. *Superannuation: Government Co-contribution for Low Income Earners, Bill 2003.* (Bills Digest no. 178 2002–03). Canberra: Australian Government Publishing Service, 2003. http://www.aph.gov.au/Help/404?item=%2flibrary%2fpubs%2fbd%2f2002-03%2f03bd178&user=extranet%5cAnonymous&site=website

Select Committee of Inquiry into Superannuation and Living Standards in Retirement. Canberra: Australian Government Publishing Service, 2002.

Senate Select Committee on Superannuation and Financial Services. The Commonwealth Treasury. *Enforced Superannuation Guarantee Charge.* Australian Government Publishing Service, 2001. http://www.aph.gov.au/Help/404?item=%2fsenate%2fcommittee.superfinan_ctte%2fsqc%2fsgc+report&user=extranet%5cAnonymous&site=website

– *Retirement Income Modelling: Inquiry into the Superannuation and Standards of Living in Retirement.* Canberra: Australian Government Publishing Service, 2002. http://rim.treasury.gov.au/content/submission/index.asp

Social Security Payments for the Aged, People with Disabilities and Carers 1909 to 2010. Parliament of Australia. Canberra, Australian Government Publishing Service. 2010. http://www.aph.gov.au/About_Parliament/Parliamentary_Departments/Parliamentary_Library/pubs/BN/1011/SSPayments1

Social Security Payments for the Aged, People with Disabilities and Carers 1909 to 2004. Parliament of Australia. Canberra, Australian Government Publishing Service, 2004. http://www.aph.gov.au/Help/404?item=%2flibrary%2fpubs%2fonline%2faged3&user=extranet%5cAnonymous&site=website

"Towards Higher Retirement Incomes for Australians: A History of the Australian Retirement Income System since Federation." *Economic Round-Up*

Centenary, 2001, 65–92. http://search.informit.com.au/documentSummary;dn=537834436390974;res=IELBUS

Canada

Canada Pension Plan: Bill C-75. Ottawa: CCH Canadian, 1964a.

The Canada Pension Plan and Changes in Old Age Security Act. Ottawa: Department of National Health and Welfare, 1965.

Canada Pension Plan, Old Age Security Act, and Pension Benefits Standards Act. Ottawa: CCH Canadian, 1987.

Canada Pension Plan, Old Security Act, and Pension Benefits Standards Act with Regulations (8th ed.). Ottawa: CCH Canadian, 1991.

Canada Pension Plan and Old Age Security Legislation (4th ed.). Ottawa: CCH Canadian, 1975.

Canada Pension Plan and Old Age Security Legislation (5th ed.). Ottawa: CCH Canadian, 1978a.

The Canada Pension Plan and Old Age Security Legislation with Regulations. Don Mills: CCH Canadian, 1968.

Canada's Retirement Income Programs: A Statistical Overview. Statistics Canada, Cat. no. 75–507- XIE. Ottawa: Statistics Canada, 1999–2000.

Canadian Intergovernmental Conference Secretariat. *The Federal-Provincial Annual Conference*. Ottawa: Canadian Government Publishing, 1989.

Department of Finance. *Budget Plan*. Ottawa: Canadian Government Publishing, 1995.

– *Ensuring a Strong Retirement System, Support for Provinces and Territories While Moving Towards Budget Balance*. Canada News Centre, 2010. http://news.gc.ca/web/article-en.do?nid=581189

– *Finance Minister's Statement on the Seniors Benefit*. News Release. Ottawa: Canadian Government Publishing, 1998.

– *Securing Canada's Retirement Income System*. Ottawa: Canadian Government Publishing, 1997.

– *Seniors Benefits: Securing the Future*. Ottawa: Canadian Government Publishing, 1996.

Federal and Provincial Conference of the First Ministers on the Constitution (November 2–3). Ottawa, ON: Canadian Government Publishing, 1981.

Federal–Provincial Conference of First Ministers on the Economy. Ottawa: Canadian Government Publishing, 1978.

Federal–Provincial Conference of First Ministers on the Economy. Ottawa: Canadian Government Publishing, 1982.

Federal, Provincial, Territorial CPP Consultation Secretariat. *Report on the Canada Pension Plan Consultations* (June). Ottawa: Canadian Government Publishing, 1996.

Green Book: Dominion–Provincial Conference. Ottawa: Edmound Coultier, 1945.

Human Resources Development. *Income Security Programs: Overview.* Ottawa: Canadian Government Publishing, 1998.

– *Income Security Programs.* Ottawa: Canadian Government Publishing, 1998.

Human Resources and Skills Development Canada. *Annual Report of the Canada Pension Plan 2010–2011: Ensuring Financial Sustainability.* 2012. http://www.esdc.gc.ca/eng/oas-cpp/reports/2011/page08.shtml

– *Canada Pension Plan and Old Age Security Benefit Rate Effective January 1, 2012.* Canada News Centre, 2012. http://news.gc.ca/web/article-eng.do?nid=641249

Improving Income Security in Canada: A Discussion Paper. Ottawa: Human Resources Development Canada, 1994.

The Income Security Programs of Health and Welfare Canada. Ottawa: Ministry of Supply and Services Canada, 1983.

An Information Paper for Consultations on the Canada Pension Plan Released by the Federal, Provincial, and Territorial Governments of Canada (February, Department of Finance). Ottawa: Canadian Government Publishing, 1996.

Minister of Public Works and Government Services. *A Pension Primer: A Report by the National Council of Welfare.* Ottawa: Canadian Government Publishing, 1999.

Old Age Security Act and Old Age Security Regulation. Ottawa: Queen's Printer for Canada, 1970.

Parliament of Canada. *Bill C-36: An Act to Amend Canada Pension Plan and the Old Age Security Act.* 2007. http://www.parl.gc.ca/ErrorPage/Default.aspx?Url=http%3A%2F%2Fwww%2Eparl%2Egc%2Eca%3A80%2FAbout%2FParliament%2FLegislativeSummaries%2Fbills&UrlReferrer=&StatusCode=404&Encoding=ISO-8859-1

Principles to Guide Federal–Provincial Decisions on the Canada Pension Plan (October). Ottawa: Canadian Government Publishing, 1996. http://www.cpp.rpc.gc.ca/principles/principle.htm

Proceedings: Constitutional Conference. June 14. Victoria, BC. Ottawa: Canadian Government Publishing, 1971.

Proceedings: Dominion–Provincial Conference: Submissions and Preliminary Conference Discussions. Ottawa: King's Printer, 1945.

Proceedings: Dominion–Provincial Conference November 25–26. Ottawa. Ottawa: Queen's Printer, 1957.

Proceedings: Federal–Provincial Conference January 10–12. Constitutional Conference of Federal and Provincial Governments. Ottawa: King's Printer, 1950.

Proceedings: Federal–Provincial Conference April 26. Preliminary Meeting. Ottawa: Queen's Printer, 1955.

Proceedings: Federal–Provincial Conference November 28–29. Ottawa: Queen's Printer, 1963.

Proceedings: Federal–Provincial Conference August 31–September 2. Ottawa: Queen's Printer, 1964.

Proceedings: Federal–Provincial Conference July 19–22. Ottawa: Queen's Printer, 1965.

Proceedings: First Ministers Meeting December 11–12: Final Agenda, Framework for Social Union. Ottawa: Canadian Government Publishing, 1997.

Report of the Royal Commission on Dominion–Provincial Relations. Ottawa: King's Printer, 1940.

Report of Royal Commission of Inquiry on Constitutional Problems vol. 3, bk 1. Ottawa: Queen's Printer, 1957.

Royal Commission on Dominion–Provincial Relations, Report, bk. 2: *Recommendations.* Ottawa: King's Printer, 1945.

Service Canada: Income Security Program Information Card. 2005. http://www.servicecanada.gc.ca/eng/isp/statistics/rates/julsep05.shtml

Statistics Canada. *Canada and Australia: A Comparison of Economic Performance, 1980–2000,* 2003. http://www.statcan.gc.ca/maintenance/maintenance.html

– *Canada's Retirement Income Programs.* Cat. no. 74–507. Ottawa: 1996.

– *Canada's Retirement Programs.* Cat. no. 74–507. Ottawa: 2003.

– *The CPP and OAS Stats Book: Social Development Canada.* 2004. http://www.esdc.gc.ca/en/isp/statistics/pdf/statsbook.pdf

– *Retirement Savings through Employer-Sponsored Plans and Registered Retirement Savings Plans.* Ottawa: 2001.

– *Survey of Financial Security.* Ottawa: 2001. http://www.statcan.gc.ca/daily-quotidien/011214/dq011214a-eng.htm

Statutes of Canada, 1 (C9). Ottawa: Queen's Printer, 1977.

Statutes of Canada, 1 (C58). Ottawa: Queen's Printer, 1978b.

Working Papers on Social Security in Canada. Ottawa: King's Printer, 1973.

Other Sources

Abbott, Tony. "Renewing the Social Fabric: Mutual Obligation and Work for the Dole." *Policy Magazine* 17, no. 3 (2000): 38–42.

Aitkin, Don. "The Australian Country Party." In *Australian Politics: A Reader,* edited by Henry Mayer, 294–300. Canberra: F.W. Cheshire, 1966.

Alber, Jens. "Continuity and Changes in the Idea of Welfare State." *Politics and Society* 16, no. 4 (1988): 451–68.

Albinski, Henry S. *Canadian and Australian Politics in Comparative Perspective.* Toronto: Oxford University Press, 1973.

Albo, Gregory. "Competitive Austerity and the Impasse of Capitalist Employment Policy." In *Socialist Register: Between Globalism and Nationalism,* edited by Ralph Miliband and Leo Panitch, 144–70. London: Merlin Press, 1994.

– "Neoliberalism, the State, and the Left: A Canadian Perspective." *Monthly Review* 54, no. 1 (2002): 46–55.

– "The New Realism and Canadian Workers." In *Canadian Politics: An Introduction to the Discipline,* edited by James Bickerton and Alain G. Gagnon, 471–501. Peterborough: Broadview, 1990.

Albo, Gregory, and Robert Christ. "European Industrial Relations or Model Forward?" In *Rising from the Ashes? Labor in the Age of Global Capitalism,* edited by Peter F. Meiksins, Michael D. Yates, and Ellen Meiksins Wood, 164–78. New York: Monthly Review Press, 1998.

Albo, Gregory, and Jane Jenson. "Remapping Canada: The State in the Era of Globalization." In *Understanding Canada,* edited by Wallace Clement, 215–34. Montreal: McGill–Queen's University Press, 1997.

Alford, Robert R. *Party and Society: The Anglo-American Democracies.* Chicago: Rand McNally, 1963.

Allan, James P., and Lyle Scruggs. "Political Partisanship and Welfare State Reform in Advanced Industrial Societies." *American Journal of Political Science* 48, no. 3 (2004): 496–512.

Ambachtsheer, Keith. "Pension Reform: How Canada Can Lead the World." *Policy Options,* March 2010, 46–52.

Anderson, Karen M. "The Politics of Retrenchment in a Social Democratic Welfare State: Reform of Sweden Pensions and Unemployment." *Comparative Political Studies* 34, no. 9 (2001): 1063–91.

Antolín, Pablo, and Fiona Stewart. "Private Pensions and Policy Responses to the Financial and Economic Crisis." OECD Working Papers on Insurance and Private Pension, No. 36 (2009). http://www.oecd.org/redirect/dataoecd/37/54/42601323.pdf

Apple, Nixon. "The Rise and the Fall of Full Employment Capitalism." *Studies in Political Economy* 4 4(August 1980): 5–36.

Argy, Fred. *Australia at the Crossroads.* Sydney: Allen and Unwin, 1998.

Arrowsmith, David. J. *Canada's Trade Unions: An Information Manual.* Kingston: Industrial Relations Centre, Queen's University, 1992.

Ascah, Louis. *The Great Pension Debate: Federal and Provincial Pension Reform, Missing, Misleading, and Shrinking Proposals.* Ottawa: Canadian Centre for Policy Alternatives, 1991.

Ashford, Douglas E. *The Emergence of Welfare States.* Oxford: Blackwell, 1986.

Avakumovic, Ivan. *Socialism in Canada.* Toronto: McClelland and Stewart, 1978.

Baker, Maureen. "The Restructuring of the Canadian Welfare State: Ideology and Policy." *Social Policy Research Centre* 77 (June 1997). https://www.sprc.unsw.edu.au/dp/dp077.pdf

Bakker, Isabella, and Katherine Scott. "From the Post-War to the Post-Liberal Keynesian Welfare State." In *Understanding Canada: Building on the New Canadian Political Economy*, edited by Wallace Clement, 286–306. Montreal, and Kingston: McGill–Queen's University Press, 1997.

Baldwin, Bob. *Pension Reform in Canada in the 1990s: What Was Accomplished? What Lies Ahead?* Ottawa: Canadian Labour Congress, 2004.

Baldwin, Peter. "Beveridge in the Longue Durée." In *Beveridge and Social Security: An International Perspective*, edited by John Hills, John Ditch, and Howard Glennerster, 37–55. Oxford: Clarendon Press, 1994.

Banting, Keith G. "Images of the Modern State: An Introduction." In *State and Society: Canada in Comparative Perspective*, edited by Keith G. Banting, 1–20. Toronto: University of Toronto Press, 1986.

– "The Multicultural Welfare State: International Experiences and North American Narratives." *Social Policy and Administration*, 39, no. 2 (2005): 98–115.

– "Neo-Conservatism in an Open Economy: The Social Role of the Canadian State." *International Political Science Review* 13 (1992): 149–70.

– "The Social Policy Divide: The Welfare State in Canada and the United States." In *Degrees of Freedom: Canada and the United States in a Changing World*, edited by Keith G. Banting, George Hoberg, and Richard Simeon, 267–309. Montreal and Kingston: McGill–Queen's University Press, 1997.

– *The Welfare State and Canadian Federalism.* Montreal and Kingston: McGill–Queen's University Press, 1982.

Banting, Keith G., and Robin W. Boadway. "Reforming Retirement Income Policy: The Issues." In *Reform of Retirement Income Policy: International and Canadian Perspectives*, edited by Keith G. Banting and Robin W. Boadway, 1–26. Montreal and Kingston: McGill–Queen's University Press, 1997.

Banting, Keith G., Richard Johnston, Will Kymlicka, and Stuart Soroka. "Do Multiculturalism Policies Erode the Welfare State? An Empirical Analysis." In *Multiculturalism and the Welfare State: Recognition and Redistribution in Contemporary Democracies*, edited by Keith G. Banting and Will Kymlicka, 49–91. Oxford: Oxford University Press, 2006.

Barr, Nicholas. *Economics of the Welfare State* (4th ed.). New York: Oxford University Press, 2004.

Barr, Nicholas, and Peter Diamond. "The Economics of Pensions." *Oxford Review of Economic Policy* 22, no. 1 (2006): 15–30.

Bashevkin, Sylvia. *Welfare Hot Buttons: Women, Work, and Social Welfare Policy.* Toronto: University of Toronto Press, 2002.

Bateman, Hazel. "Retirement Incomes in Australia in the Wake of the Global financial Crisis." Discussion Paper 03/10. Centre for Pension and Superannuation. (2010). https://www.business.unsw.edu.au/research-site/cps-site/Documents/H.%20Bateman%20-%20Retirement%20incomes%20in%20Australia%20in%20the%20wake%20of%20the%20global%20financial%20crisis%20.pdf

Bateman, Hazel, and John Piggott. "Australia's Mandatory Retirement Policy: A View from the Millennium." Social Protection Discussion Paper Series, No. 0108. Human Development Network, The World Bank, 2001.

– "Mandatory Retirement Saving in Australia." *Annals of Public and Cooperative Economics* 69, no. 4 (1998): 547–69.

Bateman, Hazel, Geoffrey Kingston, and John Piggott. *Forced Saving: Mandating Private Retirement Incomes.* Cambridge: Press Syndicate of the University of Cambridge, 2001.

Battle, Ken. "A New Old Age Pension." In *Reform of Retirement Income Policy: International and Canadian Perspectives,* edited by Keith G. Banting and Robin W. Boadway, 135–89. Montreal and Kingston: McGill–Queen's University Press, 1997.

– *Relentless Incrementalism: Deconstructing and Reconstructing Canadian Income Security Policy.* Ottawa, ON: Caledon Institute of Social Policy, 2001 (September).

– *Thinking the Unthinkable: A Targeted, Not Universal, Old Age Pension.* Ottawa: Caledon Institute of Social Policy, 1993.

Bazowski, Raymond. "Contrasting Ideologies in Canada: What's Left? What's Right?" In *Canadian Politics* (3rd ed.), edited by James Bickerton and Alain G. Gagnon, 79–103. Peterborough: Broadview, 1999.

Beder, Sharon. *Global Spin.* Melbourne: Scribe Publications, 1997.

Beilharz, Peter. *Transforming Labor: Labor Tradition and the Labor Decade in Australia.* Melbourne: Cambridge University Press, 1994.

Béland, Daniel. "Pension Reform and Financial Investment in the United States and Canada." SEDAP Research Paper, No. 120, September 2004. http://www.socserve2.mcmaster.ca/sedap

– "Review of C.T. Gillin, David MacGregor, and Thomas R. Klassen, eds., *Time's Up! Mandatory Retirement in Canada.*" *Canadian Journal on Aging* 25, no. 3 (2006): 331–2.

Béland, Daniel, and Kristina Babich. "Policy Change and the Politics of Ideas: The Emergence of the Canada/Quebec Pension Plans." *Canadian Review of Sociology* 46, no. 3 (2009): 253–71.

Béland, Daniel, and Brian Gran. "Introduction: Public and Private?" In *Public and Private Social Policy: Health and Pension Policies in a New Era,* edited by Daniel Béland and Brian Gran, 1–27. New York: Palgrave Macmillan, 2009.

Béland, Daniel, and André Lecours. "Sub-State Nationalism and the Welfare State: Quebec and Canadian Federalism." *Nations and Nationalism* 12, no. 1 (2006): 77–96.

Béland, Daniel, and John Myles. "Policy Change in the Canadian Welfare State: Comparing the Canada Pension Plan and Unemployment Insurance." Social and Economic Dimensions of an Aging Population (SEDAP), Research Paper No. 235 (2008). http://socserv.mcmaster.ca/sedap/p/sedap235.pdf

Béland, Daniel, and Toshimitsu Shinkaw. "Public and Private Policy Change: Pension Reform in Four Countries (United States, Canada, Britain, and Japan)." *Policy Studies Journal* 1 (August 2007): 349–71.

Bell, Daniel. *The Coming of Post-industrial Society: A Venture in Social Forecasting.* New York: Basic Books, 1976.

Bell, Stephen. "The Unemployment Crisis and Economic Policy." In *The Unemployment Crisis in Australia*, edited by Stephen Bell, 1–20. Cambridge: Cambridge University Press, 2000.

Bell, Stephen, and Brian Head. "Australia's Political Economy: Critical Themes and Issues." In *State, Economy, and Public Policy in Australia*, edited by Stephen Bell and Brian Head, 1–21. Melbourne: Oxford University Press, 1994.

Bendix, Reinhard. *Nation-Building and Citizenship: Studies of Our Changing Social Order.* New York: John Wiley and Sons, 1964.

Bennett, Arnold. *The History of the Labour Movement in Quebec.* Montreal: Black Rose Books, 1989.

Bercuson, David J., and David Bright, eds. *Canadian Labour History.* Toronto: Copp Clark Longman, 1994.

Bercuson, David J., and Barry Cooper. *De-Confederation: Canada without Quebec.* Toronto: Key Porter Books, 1991.

Bernstein, Eduard. *Evolutionary Socialism: Criticism and Affirmation.* New York: Schocken Books, 1961.

Bhatia, Vandna, and William Coleman. "Ideas and Discourse: Reforms and Resistance in the Canadian and German Health Systems." *Canadian Journal of Political Science* 36, no. 4 (2003): 791–817.

Blackburn, Robin. *Banking on the Death: The History and Future of Pensions.* London: Verso, 2002.

– "Crisis 2.0." *New Left Review* 72 (November–December 2011): 33–62.

– "A Global Pension Plan." *New Left Review* 47 (September–October 2007): 71–92.

– *The Great Pension Crisis: From Grey Capitalism to Responsible Accumulation*, 2003. https://www.ssc.wisc.edu/~wright/Published%20writing/Pensions-Blackburn.pdf

Blair, Tony. *The Third Way: New Politics for the New Country.* London: Fabian Pamphlet, 1998.

Blair, Tony, and Gerhard Schroeder. *Third Way/Die Neue Mitte Manifesto.* 2000. http://webcache.googleusercontent.com/search?q=cache:f6Ov5tXFbisJ:library.fes.de/pdf-files/bueros/suedafrika/02828.pdf+&cd=2&hl=en&ct=clnk&gl=ca

Block, Fred. "The Ruling Class Does Not Rule." *Socialist Review* 7 (May–June 1977): 6–28.

Blomqvist, Paula. "The Choice Revolution: Privatization of Swedish Welfare Services in the 1990s." *Social Policy and Administration* 38, no. 2 (2004): 139–55.

BNAC (British North American Committee). *The Future of Pension Policy: Individual Responsibility and State Support.* Washington, DC: 1997.

Bonoli, Giuliano. "Political Institutions, Veto Points, and the Process of Welfare State Adaptations." In *The New Politics of the Welfare State*, edited by Paul Pierson, 238–64. London: Oxford University Press, 2001.

– *The Politics of Pension Reform: Institutions and Policy Change in Western Europe.* Cambridge: Cambridge University Press, 2000.

Borowski, Allan. "The Economics and Politics of Retirement Incomes Policy in Australia." *International Social Security Review* 44, nos. 1–2 (1991): 27–40.

Börsch-Supan, Axel H., and Miegel Meinhard, eds. *Pension Reform in Six Countries: What Can We Learn from Each Other?* New York: Springer Verlag, 2001.

Boyer, J. Patrick. *Direct Democracy in Canada: The History and Future of Referendums.* Toronto: Dundurn Press, 1992.

Boyer, Robert. "The Convergence Hypothesis Revisited: Globalization But Still the Century of Nations?" In *National Diversity and Global Capitalism*, edited by Suzanne Berger and Ronald Dore, 29–59. Ithaca: Cornell University Press, 1996.

Boyer, Pierre, Linda Cardinal, and David John Headon, eds. *From Subjects to Citizens: A Hundred Years of Citizenship in Australia and Canada.* Ottawa: University of Ottawa Press, 2004.

Boyer, Robert, and Daniel Drache, eds. *States against Markets.* New York: Routledge, 1996.

Bradford, Neil. "The Policy Influence of Economic Ideas: Interests, Institutions, and Innovation in Canada." *Studies in Political Economy* 59 (1999): 17–54.

– "Writing Public Philosophy: Canada's Royal Commissions on Everything." *Journal of Canadian Studies* 34, no. 4 (1999–2000): 136–67.

Bradley, David, Evelyne Huber, Stephanie Moller, François Nielsen, and John Stephens. "Distribution and Redistribution in Postindustrial Democracies." *World Politics* 55 (2003): 193–228.

Bray, Mark, and Pat Walsh. "Different Paths to Neo-Liberalism: Comparing Australia and New Zealand." *Industrial Relations* 37, no. 3 (1998): 356–82.

Briggs, Asa. "The Welfare State in Historical Perspective." In *The Welfare State Reader*, edited by Christopher Pierson and Francis G. Castles, 18–31. London: Polity Press, 2000.

Broadbent, Edward. "Social Democracy or Liberalism in the New Millennium." In *The Future of Social Democracy*, edited by Peter Russell, 73–93. Toronto: University of Toronto Press, 1999.

Brodie, Janine. "Citizenship and Solidarity: Reflection on the Canadian Way." *Citizenship Studies* 6, no. 4 (2002): 337–94.

Brodie, Janine, and Jane Jenson. *Crisis, Challenge, and Change: Party and Class in Canada.* Toronto: Methuen, 1991.

Broomhill, Ray, and John Spoehr. "Altered State Governments and Vampire Economics." In *Altered States,* edited by John Spoehr and Ray Broomhill, 13–25. Adelaide: Centre for Labour Studies, University of Adelaide, 1995.

Bronner, Stephen Eric. *Socialism Unbound* (2nd ed.). Boulder: Westview Press, 2001.

Brown, Douglas M. *Market Rules: Economic Union Reform and Intergovernmental Policy Making in Australia and Canada.* Montreal and Kingston: McGill–Queen's University Press, 2002.

Browne, Paul Leduc. *Love in a Cold World? The Voluntary Sector in the Age of Cuts.* Ottawa: Canadian Centre for Policy Alternatives, 1996.

Brownlee, Jamie. *Ruling Canada: Corporate Cohesion and Democracy.* Halifax: Fernwood, 2005.

Bruce, Maurice. *The Coming of the Welfare State.* London: B.T. Batsford, 1968.

Brugger, Bill, and Dean Jaensch. *Australian Politics: Theory and Practice.* Sydney: Allen and Unwin, 1985.

Bryan, Dick. "Minimum Living Standards and the Working Class Surplus: Higgins, Henderson, and Housing." *Labour History* 95 (2008): 213–22.

– "Superannuation: The Ricardian Crisis." *Journal of Australian Political Economy* 53 (2004): 100–15.

Bryan, Dick, Gillian Considine, Roger Ham, and Mike Rafferty. *Agents with Too Many Principals? An Analysis of Occupational Superannuation Fund Governance in Australia.* Workplace Research Centre, University of Sydney, 2009.

Bryden, Kenneth. *Old Age Pensions and Policy-Making in Canada.* Montreal and Kingston: McGill–Queen's University Press, 1974.

Bryson, Lois. "The Welfare State and Economic Adjustment." In *State, Economy, and Public Policy in Australia,* edited by Stephen Bell and Brian Head, 291–314. Melbourne: Oxford University Press, 1994.

Burner, Greg. "Private Pensions Supervisory Methods in Australia." In *Private Pensions Series: Supervising Private Pensions,* edited by OECD, 183–224. Paris: OECD Publications, 2004.

Burnham, Peter. "The Politics of Economic Management in the 1990s." *New Political Economy* 4, no. 1 (1999): 37–54.

Cahill, Damien. "Contesting Hegemony: The Radical Neo-Liberal Movement and the Ruling Class in Australia." In *Ruling Australia*, edited by Nathan Hollier, 87–105. Melbourne: Australian Scholarly Publishing, 2004.

Calwell, Arthur Augustus. *Labor's Role in Modern Society*. Melbourne: Landsdowne Press, 1963.

Cameron, David. "The Growth of Governmental Spending: The Canadian Experience in Comparative Perspective." In *State and Society: Canada in Comparative Perspective*, edited by Keith G. Banting, 21–47. Toronto: University of Toronto Press, 1986.

Cammack, Paul. "Review Article: Bringing the State Back In?" *British Journal of Political Science* 19, no. 2 (1989): 261–90.

Campbell, Bruce. *False Promise: Canada in the Free Trade Era* (EPI Briefing Paper, April). Ottawa: Canadian Centre for Policy Alternatives, 2001.

Campbell, John L. "Institutional Analysis and the Role of Ideas in Political Economy." *Theory and Society* 27 (1998): 377–409.

Campbell, John L., and Ove K. Pedersen. "Introduction: The Rise of Neoliberalism: An Institutional Analysis." In *The Rise of Neoliberalism: An Institutional Analysis*, edited by John L. Campbell and Ove K. Pedersen, 249–81. Princeton: Princeton University Press, 2001.

Campbell, Robert Malcolm. *The Full Employment Objectives in Canada, 1945–85: Historical, Conceptual, and Comparative Perspectives*. Ottawa: Economic Council of Canada, 1991.

Canadian Council on Social Development. *The Future of Social Security in Canada*. Ottawa: 1979.

Canadian Labour Congress. *The Seniors' Benefits Must Be Opposed*. Ottawa: 1997.

– "Submission to the House of Commons on Finance Regarding the Pooled Registered Pension Plans (PRPPs). March 12." 2012. http://canadianlabour.ca/sites/default/files/prpp-submission-2012-02-24-en.pdf

– *The Upcoming Debate on Public Pensions: Issues as Seen by the Federal Government, the Reform Party, and the CLC*. Ottawa: 1995.

Caplan, Gerald L. *The Dilemma of Canadian Socialism: The CCF in Ontario*. Toronto: McClelland and Stewart, 1973.

Caporaso, James A., and David P. Levine. *The Theories of Political Economy*. Cambridge: Cambridge University Press, 1992.

Carlson, Alan. "The Family and the Welfare State." In *After Liberalism: Essays in Search of Freedom, Virtue, and Choice*, edited by William D. Gairdner, 93–106. Toronto: Stoddart, 1998.

Carmichael, Isla. *Pension Power: Unions, Pension Funds, and Social Investment in Canada*. Toronto: University of Toronto Press, 2005.

Carmichael, Isla, and Jack Quarter. *Money on the Line: Workers' Capital in Canada.* Ottawa: Canadian Centre for Policy Alternatives, 2003.

Carney, Terry, and Peter Hanks. *Australian Social Security Law, Policy and Administration.* Melbourne: Oxford University Press, 1986.

Carroll, William K., and Murray Shaw. "Consolidating the Neoliberal Policy Bloc in Canada, 1976 to 1996." *Canadian Public Policy* 27, no. 2 (2001): 195–217.

Carty, R. Kenneth. "Three Canadian Party Systems: An Interpretation of the Development of National Politics." In *Party Politics in Canada* (6th ed.), edited by Hugh G. Therborn, 124–43. Scarborough: Prentice-Hall, 1991.

Cassidy, Harry M. *Social Security and Reconstruction in Canada.* Toronto: Ryerson Press, 1943.

Castells, Manuel. *The Rise of Network Society.* Oxford, UK: Blackwell, 1996. 2nd ed., 2000.

Castles, Francis G. *Australian Public Policy and Economic Vulnerability.* Sydney: Allen and Unwin, 1988.

– *Comparative Public Policy: Patterns of Postwar Transformation.* Northampton: Edward Elgar, 1998.

– "A Farewell to Australia's Welfare State." *Eureka Street* 11, no. 1 (January–February 2001): 1–17.

– *The Future of the Welfare State: Crisis Myth and Crisis Reality.* New York: Oxford University Press, 2004.

– "The Impact of Parties on Public Expenditures." In *The Impact of Parties,* edited by Francis G. Castles, 21–96. Beverly Hills: Sage, 1982.

– "Social Protection by Other Means: Australia's Strategy for Coping with External Vulnerability." In *The Comparative History of Public Policy,* edited by Francis G. Castles, 16–55. Cambridge: Polity Press, 1989.

– *The Working Class and Welfare State: Reflections on the Political Development of the Welfare State in Australia and New Zealand 1890–1980.* Sydney: Allan and Unwin, 1985.

Castles, Francis G., and Deborah Mitchell. "Worlds of Welfare and Families of Nations." In *Families of Nations: Patterns of Public Policy in Western Democracies,* edited by Francis G. Castles, 93–126. Sydney: Dartmouth, 1993.

Chant, John. "Macro Stability and Economic Growth: What the Macdonald Commission Said." In *Prospects for Canada: Progress and Challenges 20 Years after the Macdonald Commission,* edited by David Laidler and William Robson, 13–24. Toronto: C.D. Howe Institute, 2005.

Chifley, Joseph Benedict. *Social Security and Reconstruction.* Canberra: Department of Post War Reconstruction, 1945.

– *Things Worth Fighting For.* Speeches by Joseph Benedict Chifley, edited by A. Stargardt. Melbourne: Melbourne University Press, 1952.

Clark, Christopher. *Canada's Income Security Programs.* Ottawa: Canadian Council on Social Development, 1998.

Clark, Coleen. *Retirement and Estate Planning in Canada* (2nd ed.). Toronto: Captus Press, 2009.

Clark, David. "Neoliberalism and Public Service Reform: Canada in Comparative Perspective." *Canadian Journal of Political Science* 33, no. 4 (2002): 771–93.

Clark, Gordon L. *Pension Fund Capitalism.* New York: Oxford University Press, 2000.

Clarke, Harold D., Jane Jenson, Lawrence LeDuc, and Jon H. Pammett. *Absent Mandate: Canadian Electoral Politics in an Era of Restructuring* (3rd ed.). Toronto: Gage, 1996.

Clarke, John. *Changing Welfare, Changing States: New Directions in Social Policy.* London: Sage, 2004.

Clayton, Richard, and Jonas Pontusson. "Welfare State Retrenchment Revisited: Entitlement Cuts, Public Sector Restructuring, and Inegalitarian Trends in Advanced Capitalist Societies." *World Politics* 51, no. 1 (1998): 67–98.

Cockett, Richard. *Thinking the Unthinkable: Think-Tanks and the Economic Counter-Revolution, 1931–1983.* London: Fontana Press, 1995.

Collier, David, and Richard E. Messick. "Prerequisites versus Diffusion: Testing Alternative Explanations of Social Security Adoption." *American Political Science Review* 69 (1975): 1299–315.

Confalonieri, Maria A., and Kenneth Newton. "Taxing and Spending: Tax Revolt or Tax Protest?" In *The Scope of Government,* edited by Elinor N. Scarbrough and Ole Borre, 121–48. Oxford: Oxford University Press, 1995.

Conference Board of Canada. "How Canada Performs: Elderly Poverty" (2013). http://www.conferenceboard.ca/hcp/details/society/elderly-poverty.aspx

Connell, Raewyn W. *Ruling Class, Ruling Culture.* Melbourne: Cambridge University Press, 1977.

Connor, J.C. "How Industry Views the Canadian Pension Plan." In *Symposium of Views on the Canada Pension Plan,* edited by Laurence E. Coward, 47–53. Don Mills: Commerce Clearing House Canadian, 1964.

Coughlin, Richard M. *Ideology, Public Opinion, and Welfare Policy: Attitudes Towards Taxing and Spending in Industrialized Societies.* (Monograph Series No. 42). Berkeley: Institute of International Studies, University of California, 1980.

Courchene, Thomas. "The Comparative Nature of Australian and Canadian Economic Space." In *Reforming Fiscal Federalism of Global Competition:*

A Canada–Australia Comparison, edited by Paul Boothe, 7–12. Edmonton: University of Alberta Press, 1996.

– *Social Canada in the Millennium: Reforming Imperatives and Restructuring Principles.* Toronto: C.D. Howe Institute, 1994.

– "Subnational Budgetary and Stabilization Policies in Canada and Australia." In *Fiscal Institutions and Fiscal Performance: A National Bureau and Economic Conference Report*, edited by James Poterba, and Jurgan Hagen, 301–348. Chicago: University of Chicago Press, 1999.

Coward, Laurence E. *Mercer Handbook of Canadian Pension and Welfare Plans.* Ottawa, ON: CCH Canada, 1977.

Coyne, Andrew. "Let's Create a Nation of Savers." *Globe and Mail*, 17 August 1994.

Creedy, John, and Richard Disney. "Pension Schemes and Incentives: Case Studies from Australia and the United Kingdom." *Australian Economic Review* 25, no. 1 (2008): 23–32.

Crisp, Leslie Finlay. *Ben Chifley.* Melbourne: Longmans, Green, 1961.

– *The Parliamentary Government of the Commonwealth of Australia.* London: Longmans, 1961.

Crosland, Anthony. *The Future of Socialism.* New York: Schocken Books, 1963.

Cross, Michael S., ed. *The Decline and Fall of a Good Idea: CCF–NDP Manifesto 1932–1969.* Toronto: New Hogtown, 1974.

Crozier, Michel J., Samuel P. Huntington, and Joji Watanuki. *The Crisis of Democracy. Report on the Governability of Democracies to the Trilateral Commission.* New York: NYU Press, 1975.

Cuperus, René, Karl Duffek, and Johannes Kandel, eds. *The Challenges of Diversity: European Social Democracy Facing Migration, Integration, and Multiculturalism.* Innsbruck: StudienVerlag, 2003.

Cutler, David M., and Richard Johnson. *The Birth and Growth of the Social Insurance State: Explaining Old Age and Medieval Insurance across Countries.* Federal Reserve Bank of Kansas City Research Working Paper, RWP 01–13, 2001.

Dahrendorf, Ralf. "The Changing Quality of Citizenship." In *The Condition of Citizenship*, edited by Bart van Steenbergen, 10–19. London: Sage, 1994.

Daley, John. "Self-Reliance in Retirement: Australian Lessons for U.S. Pension Schemes" (2011). http://www.gailfosler.com/self-reliance-in-retirement-australian-lessons-for-u-s-pension-schemes

Davis, Horace, B. *Toward a Marxist Theory of Nationalism.* New York: Monthly Review Press, 1978.

Davis, Stephen M., Jon Lukomnik, and David Pitt-Watson. *The New Capitalists: How Citizen Investments Are Reshaping the Corporate Agenda.* Cambridge, MA: Harvard Business School Press, 2006.

de Swan, Abram. *In the Care of the State: Health Care, Education, and Welfare in Europe and the USA in the Modern Era.* Cambridge: Polity Press, 1988.

Deacon, Alan, and Jonathan Bradshaw. *Reserved for the Poor: The Means Test in British Social Policy.* London: Basil Blackwell and Martin Robertson, 1983.

Deaton, Richard Lee. *The Political Economy of Pensions: Power, Politics, and Social Changes in Canada, Britain, and the United States.* Vancouver: UBC Press, 1989.

Detje, Richard. "Systemic Danger? The Effects of the Financial Crisis on Private Pensions." *Transform.* (2010). http://www.transform-network.net/de/publikationen/publikationen-2010/news/detail/Publications/systemic-danger-the-effects-of-the-financial-crisis-on-private-pensions.html

DeViney, Stanley. "Characteristics of the State and the Expansion of Public Social Insurance Expenditures." *Comparative Social Research* 6 (1983): 151–74.

Dickey, Brian. *No Charity There: A Short History of Social Welfare in Australia.* Melbourne: Nelson, 1980.

Dickinson, Paul. "Six Common Misperceptions about the Canada Pension Plan." In *When We're 65: Reforming Canada's Retirement Income System,* edited by John Richards and William G. Watson, 171–220. Toronto: C.D. Howe Institute, 1996.

Dilnot, Andrew. "Public and Private Roles in the Provision of Retirement Income." In *Reform of Retirement Income Policy: International and Canadian Perspectives,* edited by Keith G. Banting and Robin W. Boadway, 49–60. Montreal and Kingston: McGill–Queen's University Press, 1996.

Dion, Stéphane. *Straight Talk: On Canadian Unity.* Montreal and Kingston: McGill–Queen's University Press, 1999.

Dixon, John E. *Australia's Policy Towards the Aged, 1890–1972.* Canberra: Canberra College of Advanced Education, 1977.

Drache, Daniel. "The Eye of the Hurricane: Globalization and Social Policy Reform." In *Warm Heart, Cold Country: Fiscal and Social Policy Reform in Canada,* edited by Daniel Drache and Andrew Ranachan, 23–50. Toronto: Robarts Centre for Canadian Studies, 1995.

– "Formation and Fragmentation of the Canadian Working Class 1820–1920." *Studies in Political Economy* 15 (Fall 1984): 43–89.

Drache, Daniel, and Andrew Ranachan. "Ground Zero: Rebuilding the Future: Fiscal and Social Policy Reform in Canada." In *Warm Heart, Cold Country: Fiscal and Social Policy Reform in Canada,* edited by Daniel Drache and Andrew Ranachan, 1–18. Toronto: Robarts Centre for Canadian Studies, 1995.

Drover, Glenn. "Tilting toward Marketization: Reform to Canada Pension Plan." *Review of Policy Research* 19, no. 3 (2002): 88–104.

Economy Watch. *Unemployment Rates (% of Labour Force) Data for all Countries.* 2011. http://www.economywatch.com/economic-statistics/economic-indicators/Unemployment_Rate_Percentage_of_Labour_Force

Edwards, Adrian Charles. *Canadian Private Pension Plans: A Study of Their History, Trends, Taxation, and Investment.* PhD diss., Ohio University, 1967.

Eger, Maureen A. "Even in Sweden: The Effects of Immigration on Support for Welfare Social Expenditure." *European Sociological Review* 26, no. 2 (2010): 203–17.

Ehrensaft, Philip, and Warwick Armstrong. "The Formation of Dominion Capitalism: Economic Truncation and Class Structures." In *Inequalities: Essays on Political Economy of Social Welfare,* edited by Allan Moscovitch and Glenn Drover, 121–49. Toronto: University of Toronto Press, 1981.

English, M.D. "Canada." In *Macro-Economic Policy: A Comparative Study: Australia, Canada, New Zealand, South Africa,* edited by James Oliver Newton Perkins, 57–92. Toronto: University of Toronto Press, 1973.

Esping-Andersen, Gøsta. *Politics against Markets.* Princeton: Princeton University Press, 1985.

– *The Three Worlds of Welfare Capitalism.* Princeton: Princeton University Press, 1990.

– *Welfare States in Transition: National Adaptation in Global Economies.* London: Sage, 1996.

Esping-Andersen, Gøsta, and Walter Korpi. "Social Policy and Class Politics in Post-War Capitalism: Scandinavian, Austria, and Germany." In *Order and Conflict in Contemporary Capitalism,* edited by John H. Goldthrope, 179–208. Oxford: Clarendon Press, 1984.

Estelle, James. "Canada's Old Age Crisis in International Perspective." In *Reform of Retirement Income: International and Canadian Perspectives,* edited by Keith G. Banting, and Robin W. Boadway, 29–47. Montreal and Kingston: McGill–Queen's University Press, 1997.

Evans, Martin, and Lewis Williams. *A Generation of Change, a Lifestyle of Difference: Social Policy in Britain Since 1979.* Bristol: Policy Press, 2009.

Evens, Peter. *Embedded Autonomy: State and Industrial Transformation.* Princeton: Princeton University Press, 1995.

Ewer, Peter, Ian Hampson, Chris Lloyd, John Rainford, Stephen Rix, and Meg Smith. *Politics and Accord.* Leichhbordt: Pluto Press, 1991.

Ferguson, Iain. *Reclaiming Social Work: Challenging Neo-Liberalism and Promoting Social Justice.* Los Angeles: Sage, 2008.

Ferreira, Maurizio, Anton Hemerijck, and Martin Rhodes. "The Future of Social Europe: Recasting Work and Welfare in the New Economy." In *The*

Global Third Way Debate, edited by Anthony Giddens, 114–33. Cambridge: Polity Press, 2001.

Fine, Ben, and Laurence Harris. *Reading Capital*. London: Macmillan, 1979.

Finkel, Alvin. *Social Policy and Practice in Canada: A History*. Waterloo: Wilfred Laurier University Press, 2006.

Finn, Dan. "Welfare to Work: The Local Dimension." *Journal of European Social Policy* 10, no. 1 (2000): 43–57.

Flora, Peter, and Jens Alber. "Modernization, Democratization, and the Development of the Welfare State in Western Europe." In *The Development of Welfare States in Europe and America*, edited by Peter Flora and Arnold Joseph Heidenhemier, 37–80. London: Transaction Books, 1982.

Forcese, Dennis. *The Canadian Class Structure*. Toronto: McGraw-Hill Ryerson, 1997.

Fox, Bonnie. "Women's Role in Development." In *Perspectives on Canadian Economic Development*, edited by Gordon Laxer, 333–51. Toronto: Oxford University Press, 1991.

Frankman, Myron J. "The Fight to Preserve Universal Social Programs: A Canadian Perspective on the Great Capitalist Restoration." *Journal of Economic Issues* 32 (June 1998): 489–96.

Friedman, Milton. *Capitalism and Freedom*. Chicago: University of Chicago Press, 1962.

Gagnon, Alain G., Montserrat Guibernau, and François Rocher, eds. *The Conditions of Diversity in Multinational Democracies*. Montreal: Institute for Research on Public Policy, 2003.

Gamble, Andrew. *The Free Economy and the Strong State: The Politics of Thatcherism*. Durham: Duke University Press, 1994.

Gash, Alexander. *Anticipatory Budgeting: A Long-Term Analysis of Old Age Pension in Australia, Canada, and Sweden*. PhD diss., Griffith University, 2005.

Gay, Peter. *The Dilemma of Democratic Socialism*. New York and London: Collier Books and Collier-Macmillan, 1962.

Gibbens, Roger. *Regionalism: Territorial Politics in Canada and the United States*. Toronto: Butterworths, 1980.

Giddens, Anthony. *The Third Way: The Renewal of Social Democracy*. London: Polity Press, 1998.

– *The Third Way and Its Critics*. Cambridge: Polity Press, 2000.

– *Where Now for New Labour?* Malden: Blackwell, 2002.

Gilbert, Neil. *Transformation of the Welfare State: The Silent Surrender of Public Responsibility*. New York: Oxford University Press, 2002.

Gillion, Colin, John Turner, Clive Bailey, and Denis Latulippe. *Social Security Pensions: Development and Reform.* Geneva: International Labour Office, 2000.

Gilpin, Robert. *Global Political Economy.* Princeton: Princeton University Press, 2001.

Glyn, Andrew. *Capitalism Unleashed: Finance Capitalization and Welfare.* Toronto: Oxford University Press, 2006.

Goodin, Robert E., Bruce Headey, Ruud Muffels, and Henk-Jan Dirven. *The Real Worlds of Welfare Capitalism.* New York: Cambridge University Press, 1999.

Gordon, Linda. "The New Feminist Scholarship on the Welfare State." In *Women, State, and Welfare,* edited by Linda Gordon, 9–35. Madison: University of Wisconsin Press, 1999.

Gough, Ian. *The Political Economy of the Welfare State.* London: Macmillan, 1979.

Gould, Stephanie, and John Palmer. "Outcomes, Interpretation, and Policy." In *The Vulnerable,* edited by John Palmer, 31–51. Washington: Institute of Urban Studies Press, 1988.

Greenan, Jennifer. *The Handbook of Canadian Pension and Benefit Plans* (12th ed.). Toronto: CCH Canadian, 2002.

Grinspun, Ricardo, and Robert Kerklewich. "Consolidating Neo-Liberal Reform: Free Trade as a Conditioning Framework." *Studies in Political Economy* 43 (Spring 1994): 33–61.

Gruber, Jonathan, and David A. Wise, eds. *Social Security Programs and Retirement Income around the World.* Chicago: University of Chicago Press, 2004.

Guest, Dennis. *The Emergence of Social Security in Canada.* Vancouver: UBC Press, 1980.

Guest, Dennis. *The Emergence of Social Security in Canada* (3rd ed.). Vancouver: UBC Press, 1997.

Haddow, Rodney. "Canada's Experiment with Labour Market Neocorporatism." In *Labour Market Polarization and Social Policy Reform,* edited by Keith G. Banting and Charles M. Beach, 205–29. Montreal and Kingston: McGill-Queen's University Press, 1995.

Haddow, Rodney, and Thomas Klassen. *Partisanship, Globalization and Canadian Labour Market Policy: Four Provinces in Comparative Perspective.* Toronto: University of Toronto Press, 2006.

Hagan, Jim. *The History of the ACTU.* Melbourne: Longman, 1981.

Hall, Peter A. *Governing the Economy. The Politics of State Intervention in Britain and France.* Cambridge: Polity Press, 1989.

– "The Political Economy of Europe in an Era of Interdependence." In *Continuity and Change in Contemporary Capitalism,* edited by Herbert Kitschelt, Peter Lange, Gary Marks, and John Stephens, 135–63. New York: Cambridge University Press, 1999.

Hancock, William Keith. *Australia.* London: Ernest Benn, 1930.

– "Labour Market Deregulation in Australia." In *Reshaping the Labour Market: Regulations, Efficiency, and Inequality in Australia,* edited by Sue Richardson, 38–83. Cambridge: Cambridge University Press, 1999.

Hargrove, Buzz. *Labour of Love.* Toronto: Macfarlane Walter and Ross, 1998.

Harris, David O. *Pension Reforms and Aging Populations: Lessons from Australia,* 2004. http://www.aging.senate.gov/imo/media/doc/hr123dh.pdf

– *Policy Approach to Promote Private and Occupational Old Age Pensions in Australia* (2002). http://www.bertelsmann-stiftung.de/fileadmin/files/BSt/Publikationen/GrauePublikationen/GP_Policy_approaches_to_promote_private_and_occupational_old-age_provision_in_Australia.pdf

Harris, Jose. "Beveridge's Social and Political Thought." In *Beveridge and Social Security: An International Retrospective,* edited by John Hills, John Ditch, and Howard Glennerster, 23–36. New York: Oxford University Press, 1994.

Harrison, Trevor. *Of Passionate Intensity.* Toronto: University of Toronto Press, 1995.

Hartcher, Peter. "Sun, Surf, and the Birth of New Economic Model." *Financial Times,* 10 May 2006.

Hartman, Yvonne. "In Bed with the Enemy: Some Ideas on the Connections between Neoliberalism and the Welfare State." *Current Sociology* 53, no. 1 (2005): 57–73.

Harvey, David. *The Condition of Postmodernity.* London: Basil Blackwell, 1990.

Hawke, Bob. *National Reconciliation: The Speeches of Bob Hawke.* Selected by John Cook. Sydney: Fontana/Collin, 1984.

Hay, James. "The Institute of Public Affairs and Social Policy in World War II." *Historical Studies* (October 1982): 198–216.

Hayek, Friedrich von. *The Road to Serfdom.* London: Routledge, 1944.

Heclo, Hugh. "Towards a New Welfare State?" In *The Development of Welfare States in Europe and America,* edited by Peter Flora and Arnold Joseph Heidenheimer, 384–406. London: Transaction Books, 1981.

Held, David, Anthony G. McGrew, David Goldblatt, and Johnathan Perraton. *Global Transformations: Politics, Economics, and Culture.* Stanford: Stanford University Press, 1999.

Heron, Craig. *The Canadian Labour Movement: A Short History.* Toronto: James Lorimer, 1989.

Hewson, John, and Tim Fischer. *Fightback: It's Australia.* Sydney: Liberal Party, 1991.

Hicks, Alexander. *Social Democracy and Welfare Capitalism: A Century of Income Security Politics.* Ithaca: Cornell University Press, 1999.

Higgins, Henry Bournes. "A New Province for Law and Order: Industrial Peace through Minimum Wage Arbitration." *Harvard Law Review* 29 (November 1915): 13–39.

Higgins, Winton. "To Him that Hath ...: The Welfare State." In *Australian Welfare History: Critical Essays*, edited by Richard Kennedy, 199–222. Melbourne: Macmillan of Australia, 1982.

Hiller, Harry H. "Region as a Social Construction." In *Regionalism and Party Politics in Canada*, edited by Lisa Young and Keith Archer, 24–36. Toronto: Oxford University Press, 2002.

Hinrichs, Karl, and Paula Aleksandrowicz. "Reforming European Pension Systems for Active Ageing." *International Social Science Journal* 58, no. 190 (2008): 585–99.

Hirsch, Fred. *Social Limits to Growth.* Cambridge, MA: Harvard University Press, 1978.

Hirst, Paul, and Grahame Thompson. *Globalization in Question.* Cambridge: Polity Press, 1996.

Hodgins, Bruce, Don Wright, and Welf Hieck, eds. *Federalism in Canada and Australia: The Early Years.* Waterloo: Wilfrid Laurier University Press, 1978.

Holzmann, Robert, and Richard Hinz. *Old Age Income Support in the Twenty-First Century.* Washington: World Bank, 2005.

Hoover, Kenneth, and Raymond Plant. *Conservative Capitalism in Britain and the United States.* London: Routledge, 1989.

Horn, Michiel. *Frank R. Scott: A New Endeavour.* Toronto: University of Toronto Press, 1986.

Horowitz, Gad. *Canadian Labour in Politics.* Toronto: University of Toronto Press, 1968.

Howard, John. *The Role of Government: A Modern Liberal Approach.* Menzies Research Centre (6 June 1995). http://australianpolitics.com/1995/06/06/john-howard-headland-speech-role-of-govt.html

Howard, Roger, and Jack Scott. "International Unions and the Ideology of Class Collaboration." In *Capitalism and the National Question in Canada*, edited by Gary Teeple, 68–87. Toronto: University of Toronto Press, 1972.

Howard Government Election 2004 Policy: A Stronger Economy, A Stronger Australia, 2004. http://www.scribd.com/doc/27771186/John-Howard-s-election-platform

Howlett, Michael, Alex Netherton, and Mishra Ramesh. *The Political Economy of Canada: An Introduction* (2nd ed.). Toronto: Oxford University Press, 1999.

Howse, Robert, and Marsha Chandler. "Industrial Policy in Canada and the United States." In *Degrees of Freedom: Canada and the United States in a Changing World*, edited by Keith G. Banting, George Hoberg, and Richard Simeon, 231–67. Montreal and Kingston: McGill–Queen's University Press, 1997.

Huber, Evelyne, and John Stephens. "The Social Democratic Welfare State." In *Social Democracy in Neo-Liberal Times: The Left and Economic Policy Since 1980*, edited by Andrew Glyn, 276–93. New York: Oxford University Press, 2001.

– "Welfare States and Production Regimes in the Era of Retrenchment." In *The New Politics of the Welfare State*, edited by Paul Pierson, 107–45. New York: Oxford University Press, 2001.

Huo, Jingjing. "Comparing Welfare States in Australia and Canada: A Party Competition Theory of Welfare State Development." *Commonwealth and Comparative Politics* 44, no. 2 (2004): 167–89.

Hyung Hur, Mann. "A Comparative Study of the Relationship between Pension Plan and Individual Savings in Asian Countries from an Institutional Point of View." *International Journal of Social Welfare* 19, no. 4 (2010): 379–89. http://www.ilo.org/pub;ic/english/protection/socfas/research/intros.htm Immergut, Ellen M. "Institutions, Veto Points, and Policy Results: A Comparative Analysis of Health Care." *Journal of Public Policy* 10 (1990): 391–416.

Impavido, Gregorio, and Ian Tower. "How the Financial Crisis Affects Pensions and Insurance and Why the Impacts Matter." International Monetary Fund Working Paper. WP/09/151 (2009). http://www.imf.org/external/pubs/ft/wp/2009/wp09151.pdf

Innis, Harold Adams. *The Fur Trade in Canada*. New Haven: Yale University Press, 1930.

International Labour Organization. *Cost of Social Security*. Social Protection – Financial, Actuarial Statistical Services Branch, 1997.

Inwood, Gregory J. *Continentalizing Canada: The Politics and Legacy of the Macdonald Royal Commission*. Toronto: University of Toronto Press, 2005.

– *Understanding Public Administration: An Introduction to Theory and Practice*. Toronto: Pearson Prentice Hill, 2004.

Irving, Helen. "Citizenship and Subject-Hood in Twentieth-Century Australia." In *From Subjects to Citizens: A Hundred Years of Citizenship in Australia and Canada*, edited by Pierre Boyer, Linda Cardinal, and David John Headon, 9–18. Ottawa: University of Ottawa Press, 2004.

Isbester, Fraser. "Quebec Labour in Perspective: 1949–1969." In *Canadian Labour in Transition*, edited by Richard Ulric Miller and Fraser Isbester, 240–66. Scarborough: Prentice-Hall, 1971.

Isin, Engin F. "Governing Toronto without Government: Liberalism and Neo-Liberalism." *Studies in Political Economy* 56 (1998): 169–91.

Iversen, Torben. *Capitalism, Democracy, and Welfare*. Cambridge: Cambridge University Press, 2005.

Jackson, Andrew. "The Impacts of the Canada–US Free Trade Agreement (CUFTA) and the North American Free Trade Agreement (NAFTA) on

Canadian Labour Markets." In *Pulling Apart: The Deterioration of Employment and Income in North America under Free Trade*, edited by Bruce Campbell, 85–122. Toronto: Canadian Centre for Policy Alternatives, 1999.

Jaensch, Dean. *The Australian Party System.* Sydney: George Allen and Unwin, 1983.

James, Estelle. "Canada's Old Age Crisis in International Perspective." In *Reform of Retirement Income Policy: International and Canadian Perspectives*, edited by Keith G. Banting and Robin W. Boadway, 29–45. Montreal and Kingston: McGill–Queen's University Press, 1997.

James, Michael. "How to Reform Australia's Social Security System." *Institute of Public Affairs Review* 46, no. 4 (1994).

– "Welfare Coercion and Reciprocity." In *The Welfare State*, edited by Michael James, 3–23. Sydney: Centre for Independent Studies, 1989.

Janowitz, Morris. *Social Control of the Welfare State.* New York: Elsevier, 1976.

Jenson, Jane. "Different but Not Exceptional: Canada's Permeable Fordism." *Review of Sociology and Anthropology* 26, no. 1 (1989): 69–84.

– "Representation in Crisis: The Roots of Canada's Permeable Fordism." *Canadian Journal of Political Science* 4 (1990): 663–83.

Johnson, David W., and Roger T. Johnson. "Civil Political Discourse in a Democracy: The Contribution of Psychology, Peace, and Conflict." *Journal of Peace and Psychology* 6, no. 4 (2000): 291–317.

Johnson, Leo A. "The Development of Class in Canada in the Twentieth Century." In *Capitalism and the National Question*, edited by Gary Teeple, 147–65. Toronto: University of Toronto Press, 1972.

Johnson, Leo A. "Independent Commodity Production: Models of Production or Capitalist Class Formation." *Studies in Political Economy* 6 (1981): 93–110.

Johnson, Robert, and Rianne Mahon. "NAFTA, the Redesign, and Rescaling of Canada's Welfare State." *Studies in Political Economy* 76 (2005): 7–30.

Jones, Michael Anthony. *The Australian Welfare State: Evaluating Social Policy* (4th ed.). Sydney: Allen and Unwin, 1996.

– *The Australian Welfare State: Origins, Control, and Choices.* Sydney: Allen and Unwin, 1990.

Jupp, James. "The Australian Labor Party: Platforms, Politics, and Performance." In *Forces in Australian Politics*, edited by John Wilkes, 28–77. Sydney: Angus and Robertson, 1963.

– "Their Labour and Ours." In *Australian Politics: A Reader*, edited by Henry Mayer, 231–42. Melbourne: F.W. Cheshire, 1966.

Kagarlitsky, Boris. "The Challenges for the Left: Reclaiming the State." In *Socialist Register: Global Capitalism versus Democracy*, edited by Leo Panitch and Colin Leys, 294–311. London: Merlin Press, 1999.

Kangas, Olli, Urban Lundberg, and Niels Ploug. *Three Routes to Pension Reform.* Stockholm: Institute for Future Studies, 2006.

Kautsky, Karl. "The Social Revolution." In *The Marxists,* edited by C. Wright Mills. New York: Dell. 1962.

Kautsky, Karl. *The Class Struggle.* New York: W.W. Norton, 1971.

Kealey, Gregory S., and Bryan D. Palmer. "The Working Class and Industrial Capitalist Development in Ontario to 1890." In *Canadian Economic History: Classic and Contemporary Approaches,* edited by Mel Watkins and Hugh Grant, 141–60. Ottawa: Carleton University Press, 1993.

Keating, Paul. *Address to the Victorian Fabian Society.* Fabian Newsletter, 1987.

– "Labor's Commitment to Smaller Government." *Institute of Public Affairs Review* 39, no. 3 (1985): 19–22.

– *Working Nation.* Canberra: Australian Government Publishing Service, 1994.

Kelly, David. *A Life of One's Own: Individual Rights and the Welfare State.* Washington, DC: Cato Institute, 1998.

Kelly, Paul. *The End of Certainty.* Sydney: Allan and Unwin, 1992.

– *The Hawke Ascendancy.* North Ryde: Angus and Robertson, 1985.

Kelsey, Jane. *Economic Fundamentalism.* London: Pluto Press, 1995.

Kennedy, Paul. *Preparing for the Twenty-First Century.* New York: Random House, 1993.

Kennedy, Richard. "Introduction: Against Welfare." In *Australian Welfare History: Critical Essays,* edited by Richard Kennedy, 202–21. Melbourne: Macmillan of Australia, 1982.

Kent, Tom. *A Public Purpose: An Experience of Liberal Opposition and Canadian Government.* Montreal and Kingston: McGill–Queen's University Press, 1988.

Kerr, Clark, John T. Dunlop, Frederick H. Harbison, and Charles A. Myers. *Industrialism and Industrial Man: The Problems of Labor and Management in Economic Growth.* New York: Oxford University Press, 1964.

Kewley, Thomas H. *Australia's Welfare State.* Melbourne: Macmillan of Australia, 1969.

– *Social Security in Australia 1900–72.* Sydney: Sydney University Press, 1973.

Killeen, Gordon, and Andrew James. *Annotated Canada Pension Plan and Old Age Security Act* (2nd ed.). Toronto: CCH Canadian, 2002.

Kirkwood, John. *Social Security Law and Policy.* Sydney: Law Book Company, 1986.

Kiser, Edgar, and Aaron Matthew Laing. "Have We Overestimated the Effects of Neoliberalism and Globalization?" In *The Rise of Neoliberalism and Institutional Analysis,* edited by John L. Campbell and Ove K. Pedersen, 51–68. Princeton: Princeton University Press, 2001.

Kitschelt, Herbert, Peter Lange, Gary Marks, and John Stephens. "Convergence and Divergence in Advanced Capitalist Democracies." In *Continuity and*

Change in Contemporary Capitalism, edited by Herbert Kitschelt, Peter Lange, Gary Marks, and John Stephens, 427–60. New York: Cambridge University Press, 1999.

Klassen, Thomas R., and David Forgione. "Forced Retirement: Organized Labour's Predicament." In *Time's Up! Mandatory Retirement in Canada*, edited by C.T. Gillin, David MacGregor, and Thomas R. Klassen, 74–89. Toronto: James Lorimer, 2005.

Knight, Jamie, Carla Nassar, and Paula Pettit. *Canada and Quebec Pension Plan and Employment Insurance Acts*. Toronto: Carswell, 2010.

Knowles, Stanley. *The New Party*. Toronto: Ryerson Press, 1961.

Kobrin, Stephen J. "The Architecture of Globalization: State Sovereignty in a Networked Global Economy." In *Governments, Globalization, and International Business*, edited by John H. Dunning, 146–71. New York: Oxford University Press, 1997.

Korpi, Walter. *The Democratic Class Struggle*. London: Routledge and Kegan Paul, 1983.

– "Power, Politics, and State Autonomy in the Development of Social Citizenship: Social Rights During Sickness in Eighteen OECD Countries Since 1930." *American Sociological Review* 54, no. 3 (1989): 309–28.

– *The Working Class in Welfare Capitalism*. London: Routledge and Kegan Paul, 1978.

Korpi, Walter, and Joakim Palme. "New Politics and Class Politics in the Context of Austerity and Globalization: Welfare State Regress in 18 Countries, 1975–95." *American Political Science Review* 97, no. 3 (2003): 425–46.

Kovacs, Aranko E. "The Philosophy of the Canadian Labour Movement." In *Canadian Labour in Transition*, edited by Richard Ulric Miller and Fraser Isbester, 119–43. Scarborough: Prentice-Hall, 1971.

Kruger, Arthur. M. "The Direction of Unionism in Canada." In *Canadian Labour in Transition*, edited by Richard Ulric Miller and Fraser Isbester, 85–118. Scarborough: Prentice-Hall, 1971.

Kuhnle, Stein. "The Nordic Welfare States in a European Context: Dealing with New Economy and Ideological Challenges in the 1990s." In *Welfare State Futures: An Introduction*, edited by Stephan Leibfried and Herbert Obinger, 103–19. Cambridge: Cambridge University Press, 2001.

Kymlicka, Will. *The Multicultural Welfare State*. Paper presented at the Conference York CVS, 24 November 2005.

Lam, Karen E., and Michael Walker. *The Next Step in Changing the Canada Pension Plan*. Fraser Forum, May 1997.

Lam, Newman, James Cutt, and Michael J. Prince. "The Canada Pension Plan: Retrospect and Prospect." In *Reform of Retirement Income Policy: International and Canadian Perspectives*, edited by Keith G. Banting and Robin W. Boadway, 105–34. Montreal and Kingston: McGill–Queen's University Press, 1997.

LaMarsh, Judy. *Memoirs of a Bird in a Gilded Cage.* Toronto: McClelland and Stewart, 1969.

Langille, David. "The Business Council on National Issues and the Canadian State." *Studies in Political Economy* 24 (1987): 41–85.

Langley, Paul. "In the Eye of the Perfect Storm: The Final Salary Pension Crisis and Financialisation of Anglo-American Capitalism." *New Political Economy* 9, no. 4 (2004): 539–58.

– "Pension Fund Capitalism, Pension Fund Socialism, and Dissent from Investment." In *Global Economy Contested: Power and Conflict across International Division of Labour*, edited by Marcus Taylor, 141–58. London: Routledge, 2008.

Latham, Mark. *Budget Reply Speech.* ALP News Statements, 13 May 2004. http://www.alp.org.au//media/0504/20007469.html

– *Civilising Global Capital: New Thinking for Australian Labor.* St Leonards: Allen and Unwin, 1998.

– "The Myths of the Welfare State." Institute of Public Administration Australia, Old Division. Brisbane, 14 June 2001. http://www.ipaa.org.au/_dbase_upl/Welfare%20Latham.pdf

– "The New Economy and the New Politics." In *The Enabling State: People before Bureaucracy*, edited by Mark Latham and Peter Botsman, 29–48. Annandale: Pluto Press, 2001.

– *Opportunity for All.* Address by Leader of the Opposition, Mark Latham, to the ALP National Conference, Sydney, 29 January 2004. http://www.australianpolitics.com/news/2004/01/04-01-29.shtml

Laycock, Joseph E. *The Canadian System of Old Age Pensions.* PhD diss. Chicago: University of Chicago Press, 1952.

Leacy, F.H., ed. *Historical Statistics of Canada* (2nd ed.). Ottawa: Statistics Canada, 1983.

Ledger, Anthony James Joseph. *Australian Socialism: An Historical Sketch of its Origin and Developments.* London: Macmillan, 1909.

Lemoine, Roy. "The Growth of the State in Quebec." In *The Political Economy of the State*, edited by Dimitrios Roussopoluos, 59–87. Montreal: Black Rose Books, 1973.

Levitt, Kari. *The Silent Surrender: The Multinational Corporation in Canada.* Toronto: Macmillan, 1970.

Lewis, Tom. "Marxism and Nationalism." *International Socialist Review* 13 (August–September 2000). http://isreview.org/issues/13/marxism_nationalism_part1.shtml

Liberal and National Parties of Australia. *Future Directions: It's Time for Plain Thinking*. Canberra: The Parties, 1988.

Liberal National Party of Australia. *The Coalition's Future Directions: It's Time for Plain Thinking*. Canberra: Liberal National Party, 1988.

Lindquist, Evert A., and Gilles Paquet. "Government Restructuring and the Federal Public Service: The Search for a New Cosmology." In *Government Restructuring and Career Public Service in Canada*, edited by Evert A. Lindquist, 71–111. Toronto: Institute of Public Administration of Canada, 1997.

Lipset, Seymour Martin. *Agrarian Socialism*. Berkeley: University of California Press, 1971.

Lipset, Seymour Martin, and Gary Wolfe Marks. *It Didn't Happen Here: Why Socialism Failed in the United States*. New York: W.W. Norton, 2000.

Lipton, Charles. *The Trade Movement of Canada 1827–1959*. Montreal: Canadian Social Publications, 1968.

Little, Bruce. *Fixing the Future: How Canada's Usually Fragmented Governments Worked Together to Rescue the Canadian Pension Plan*. Toronto: University of Toronto Press, 2008.

Lowy, Michael. *Fatherland or Mother Earth? Essays on the National Question*. Sterling: Pluto Press, 1998.

Lynch, Julia. *Age in the Welfare State: The Origins of Social Spending on Pensioners, Workers, and Children*. Cambridge: Cambridge University Press, 2006.

Macintyre, Stuart. "After Social Justice." In *Social Policy and Challenges of Social Change*, edited by Peter Saunders and Sheila Shaver, 1–13. Sydney: University of New South Wales, 1995.

Macleod, Alex. "Nationalism and Social Class: The Unresolved Dilemma of the Quebec Left." *Journal of Canadian Studies* 8, no. 4 (1973): 3–14.

Macpherson, Crawford Brough. *Democracy in Alberta: Social Credit and the Party System*. Toronto: University of Toronto Press, 1962.

Manow, Philip. "Comparative Institutional Advantages of Welfare State Regimes and New Coalitions in Welfare State Reform." In *The New Politics of the Welfare State*, edited by Paul Pierson, 146–64. Oxford: Oxford University Press, 2001.

Markey, Ray. "The ALP and the Emergence of a National Social Policy, 1880–1910." In *Australian Welfare History: Critical Essays*, edited by Richard Kennedy, 103–30. Melbourne: Macmillan of Australia, 1982.

– *The Making of the Labor Party in New South Wales*. Kingston: New South Wales University Press, 1988.

Marsh, Leonard. *Report on Social Security for Canada*. Toronto: University of Toronto Press, [1943] 1975.

Marshall, Thomas Humphrey. *Citizenship and Social Class and Other Essays*. Cambridge: Cambridge University Press, 1950.

– *Class, Citizenship, and Social Development.* New York: Anchor Books, 1965.

Marx, Karl, and Fredrich Engels. *The Communist Manifesto.* Translated and edited by L.M. Findlay. Toronto: Broadview, 2004 [1848].

Matthews, Trevor. "Employers' Associations, Corporatism, and the Accord: The Politics of Industrial Relations." In *State, Economy, and Public Policy in Australia,* edited by Stephen Bell and Brian Head, 194–218. New York: Oxford University Press, 1994.

Mayer, Kurt B. "Social Stratification in Two Egalitarian Societies: Australia and the United States." In *Australian Politics: A Reader,* edited by Henry Mayer, 30–56. Melbourne: F.W. Cheshire, 1966.

McBride, Stephen. *Paradigm Shift: Globalization and the Canadian State.* Halifax: Fernwood Publishing, 2005.

McBride, Stephen, and John Shields. *Dismantling a Nation.* Halifax: Fernwood Publishing, 1993.

McCarty, J.W. "The Economic Foundation of Australian Politics." In *Australian Politics: A Reader,* edited by Henry Mayer, 2–29. Canberra: F.W. Cheshire, 1967.

McDonald, Lynn. *The Party That Changed Canada: The New Democratic Party, Then and Now.* Toronto: Macmillan of Canada, 1987.

McDougall, John. *Drifting Together: The Political Economy of Canada–US Integration.* Toronto: Broadview, 2006.

McEwen, Nicola. *Nationalism and the State: Welfare and Identity in Scotland and Quebec.* Brussels: Peter Lang, 2006.

– "State Welfare Nationalism: The Territorial Impact of Welfare State Development in Scotland." *Regional and Federal Studies* 12 (2002): 6–90.

McEwen, Nicola, and Luis Moreno, eds. *The Territorial Politics of Welfare.* London: Routledge, 2005.

McKay, Ian. *Rebels, Reds, and Radicals: Rethinking Canada's Left History.* Toronto: Between the Lines, 2005.

McLaughlin, Andrew. "How Business Relates to the Hawke Government: The Captains of Industries." In *Business and Government under Labor,* edited by Brian Galligan and Gwynneth Singleton, 147–67. Melbourne: Longman Cheshire, 1991.

McMinn, Winston Gregory. *Nationalism and Federalism in Australia.* Melbourne: Oxford University Press, 1994.

McMullin, Ross. *The Light on the Hill: The Australian Labor Party 1891–1991.* Melbourne: Oxford University Press, 1991.

Mead, Lawrence M. *Beyond Entitlement: The Social Obligations of Citizenship.* New York: Free Press, 1985.

Mendes, Philip. "Australian Neoliberal Think Tanks and the Backlash against the Welfare State." *Journal of Australian Political Economy* 3 (2003): 30–56.

– *Australia's Welfare Wars Revisited.* Sydney: University of New South Wales Press, 2008.

Menzies, Robert Gordon. *Speech of Time: Selected Speeches and Writings.* London: Castellan, 1958.

Miliband, Ralph. *Marxism and Politics.* Oxford: Oxford University Press, 1977.

– "Socialist Advance in Britain." In *Socialist Register,* edited by Ralph Miliband, 103–120. London: Marlin, 1983.

– *The State in Capitalist Society.* London: Quartet Books, 1984.

Miller, David. *On Nationality.* Oxford: Oxford University Press, 1995.

Miller, Richard. "Organized Labour and Politics in Canada." In *Canadian Labour in Transition,* edited by Richard Miller and Fraser Isbester, 204–39. Scarborough: Prentice-Hall of Canada, 1971.

Miller, Richard Ulric, and Fraser Isbester, eds. *Canadian Labour in Transition.* Scarborough: Prentice-Hall, 1971.

Mintz, Jack M., and Thomas A. Wilson. "Private Provision of Retirement Income: Tax Policy Issues." In *Reform of Retirement Income Policy: International and Canadian Perspectives,* edited by Keith G. Banting and Robin W. Boadway, 209–37. Montreal and Kingston: McGill–Queen's University Press, 1997.

Mishra, Ramesh. *Globalization and the Welfare State.* Northampton: Edward Elgar, 1999.

– *The Welfare State in Capitalist Society: Policy of Retrenchment and Maintenance in Europe, North America, and Australia.* Toronto: University of Toronto Press, 1990.

Modigliani, Franco, and Arun Muralidhar. *Rethinking Pension Reform.* Cambridge: Cambridge University Press, 2004.

Moller, Stephanie, Evelyne Huber, John Stephens, David Bradley, and François Nielsen. "Determinants of Relative Poverty in Advanced Capitalist Democracies." *American Sociological Review* 68 (2003): 22–51.

Moore, John. *Australian Conciliation and Arbitration Commission: Inquiry into Principles of Wage Fixation,* vol. 11. Canberra: Australian Government Publishing Service, 1978.

Morton, Desmond, and Terry Copp. *Working People: An Illustrated History of the Canadian Labour Movement.* Ottawa: Deneau, 1980.

Moschonas, Gerassimos. *In the Name of Social Democracy: The Great Transformation, 1945 to the Present.* New York: Verso, 2002.

Munnell, Alicia H. *The Future of Social Security.* Washington, DC: Brookings Institution, 1977.

Myles, John. *Income Security and Stability during Retirement in Canada.* Statistics Canada Research Paper Series no. 36. Ottawa: Statistics Canada, 2008.

– *Old Age in the Welfare State: The Political Economy of Public Pensions.* Lawrence: University Press of Kansas, 1989.

– *The Market's Revenge: Old Age Security and Social Right.* Ottawa: Caledon Institute of Social Policy, 1995.
– "When Markets Fail: Social Welfare in Canada and the United States." In *Welfare States in Transition: National Adaptations in Global Economy*, edited by Gøsta Esping-Andersen, 116–37. London: Sage, 1996.
Myles, John, and Paul Pierson. "The Comparative Political Economy of Pension Reform." In *The New Politics of the Welfare State*, edited by Paul Pierson, 305–33. Oxford: Oxford University Press, 2001.
Myles, John, and Jill Quadagno. "The Politics of Income Security for the Elderly in North America: Founding Cleavages and Unresolved Conflict." In *Economic Security and International Justice: A Look at North America*, edited by Thedore R. Marmo, Timothy M. Smeeding, and Vernon L. Greene, 60–90. Washington, DC: Urban Institute Press, 1994.
– "Recent Trends in Public Pension Reform: A Comparative View." In *Reform of Retirement Income Policy: International and Canadian Perspectives*, edited by Keith G. Banting and Robin W. Boadway, 247–69. Kingston: School of Policy Studies, Queen's University, 1997.
Nairn, Bede B. *Civilizing Capitalism: The Beginning of the Australian Labor Party.* Melbourne: Melbourne University Press, 1989.
National Union. "A Brief History of Pensions in Canada." Pensions Background No. 2, 2007. http://www.nupge.ca/files/publications/Pensions%20 Documents/History_of_Pensions.pdf
Nemni, Monique. "Two Nationalisms, One Nation?" In *National History: A Canadian Journal of Inquiry and Opinions*, edited by Michael Behiels and Jeffrey Keshen, 60–82. Toronto: Irwin Publishing, 1999.
Nevitte, Neil, André Blais, Elisabeth Gidengil, and Richard Nadeau. *Unsteady State: The 1997 Canadian Federal Election.* Oxford: Oxford University Press, 2000.
Newman, Jocelyn. *The Challenge of Welfare Dependency in the 21st Century.* Discussion Paper. Canberra: Department of Family and Community Services, 1999.
Newman, Otto. *The Challenge of Corporatism.* London: Macmillan Press, 1981.
Nickell, Stephen, Luca Nunziata, and Wolfgang Ochel. "Unemployment in the OECD Since the 1960s: What Do We Know?" *Economic Journal* 115 (2005): 1–27.
Nordlund, Andres. "Social Security in Harsh Times: Social Security Development in Denmark, Finland, Norway, and Sweden during the 1980s and 1990s." *International Journal of Social Welfare* 9, no. 1 (2000): 31–42.
Nursey-Bray, Paul, and Carol Lee Bacchi. *Left Directions: Is There a Third Way?* Crawley: University of Western Australia Press, 2001.

Obinger, Herbert, Stephan Leibfried, and Francis G. Castles, eds. *Federalism and the Welfare State: New World and European Experience.* Cambridge: Cambridge University Press, 2005.

O'Connor, James. *The Fiscal Crisis of the State.* New York: St Martin's Press, 1973.

O'Connor, Julia S. "Welfare Expenditure and Policy Orientation in Canada, 1960–1990, in Comparative Perspective." In *Power Resources Theory and the Welfare State: A Critical Approach,* edited by Julia S. O'Connor and Gregg M. Olsen, 154–76. Toronto: University of Toronto Press, 1998.

O'Connor, Julia S., and Gregg M. Olsen, eds. *Power Resources Theory and the Welfare State: A Critical Approach.* Toronto: University of Toronto Press, 1998.

Offe, Claus. *Contradictions of the Welfare State.* Cambridge: MIT Press, 1984.

Olsen, Gregg M. "Locating the Canadian Welfare State: Family Policy and Health Care in Canada, Sweden, and the United States." In *Power Resources Theory and the Welfare State: A Critical Approach,* edited by Julia S. O'Connor and Gregg M. Olsen, 183–97. Toronto: University of Toronto Press, 1998.

– *The Politics of the Welfare State: Canada, Sweden, and the United States.* Oxford, UK: Oxford University Press, 2002.

Olson, Mancur. *The Rise and Decline of Nations: Economic Growth, Stagflation, and Social Rigidities.* New Haven: Yale University Press, 1982.

– "The Varieties of Eurosclerosis: The Rise and Decline of Nations Since 1982." In *Economic Growth in Europe Since 1945,* edited by Nicholas Crafts and Gianni Toniolo, 73–94. Cambridge: Cambridge University Press, 1996.

Orenstein, Mitchell A. "Pension Privatization in Crisis: Death or Rebirth of a Global Policy Trend." *International Social Security Review* 64, no. 3 (2011): 65–80.

– *Privatizing Pensions: The Transactional Campaign for Social Security Reform.* Princeton: Princeton University Press, 2008.

Organisation for Economic Co-operation and Development. *Ageing and Employment Policies: Live Longer, Work Longer.* Paris: 2006.

– Directorate for Education, Employment, Labour and Social Affairs. Occasional Papers. Paris: 1997.

– *World Economic Outlook* 75, 2004. http://www.oecd.org/economy/outlook/economicoutlook.htm

– "Income Distribution and Poverty in OECD Countries in the Second Half of the 1990s." *OECD Social, Employment, and Migration Working Papers* 22. Paris: 2005.

– *Innovations in Labour Market Policies: The Australian Way.* Paris: 2001.

– "Key Employment Policy Challenges Faced by OECD Countries' Labour Market and Social Policy." *Labour Market and Social Policy Occasional Papers* 31. Paris, FR: OECD Publishing, 1998.

– *Labour Force Statistics 1980–2000.* Paris: 2001.
– "Net Social Expenditure." (2nd ed.). Labor Market and Social Policy Occasional Papers no. 52. Paris: 2001.
– "New Orientations for Social Policy." *Social Policy Studies* 12. Paris: 1994.
– *OECD Economies at a Glance: Structural Indicators.* Paris: International Government Publication, 1996.
– *OECD Health Systems* 2. Paris: 1993.
– *Pensions at a Glance 2009: Retirement-Income Systems in OECD Countries.* Paris: 2009.
– *Pensions at a Glance 2011: Retirement-Income Systems in OECD and G20 Countries* (2011). http://www.oecd.org/redirect/dataoecd/32/55/47271565.pdf
– "Should We Extend the Role of Private Social Expenditure?" OECD Social, Employment, and Migration Working Papers no. 23. Paris: 2005.
– *Society at a Glance: OECD Social Indicators.* Paris: 2005.
– "The Value of Pensions Entitlement: A Model of Nine OECD Countries." OECD Social, Migration, and Migration Working Papers no. 9. Paris: 2003.
– Working Papers no. 36. Paris: 1988.

Orloff, Ann. "Gender and the Social Rights in Citizenship: The Comparative Analysis of Gender Relations and Welfare States." *American Sociological Review* 58 (1993): 303–28.

Orloff, Ann Shola, and Theda Skocpol. "Why Not Equal Protection? Explaining the Politics of Public Social Spending in Britain, 1900–1911, and the United States, 1880–1920." *American Sociological Review* 49, no. 4 (1984): 726–50.

Ozanne, Elizabeth. "Ageing Citizens: The State and Social Policy." In *Ageing and Social Policy in Australia,* edited by Allan Borowski, Sol Encel, and Elizabeth Ozanne, 233–45. Cambridge: Cambridge University Press, 1997.

Pal, Leslie A. "Civic Re-Alignment: NGOs and the Contemporary Welfare State." In *The Welfare State in Canada: Past, Present, and Future,* edited by Raymond Benjamin Blake, Penny E. Bryden, and J. Frank Strain, 84–104. Concord: Irwin, 1997.

Pal, Leslie A., and Kent Weaver. "The Politics of Pain." In *The Government Taketh Away: The Politics of Pain in the United States and Canada,* edited by Leslie A. Pal and Kent Weaver, 1–40. Washington, DC: Georgetown University Press, 2003.

Palme, Joakim. *Pension Rights in Welfare Capitalism: The Development of Old-Age Pensions in 18 OECD Countries 1930 to 1985.* Stockholm: Universitet Stockholms, 1990.

Palmer, Bryan D. *Working Class Experience: Rethinking the History of Canadian Labour, 1800–1991* (2nd ed.). Toronto: McClelland and Stewart, 1992.

Pammett, John H. "Class Voting and Class Consciousness in Canada." *Canadian Review of Sociology and Anthropology* 24, no. 2 (1987): 270–90.

Pampel, Fred C., and John B. Williamson. *Age, Class, Politics, and the Welfare State.* Cambridge: Cambridge University Press, 1989.

Panitch, Leo. "Capitalist Restructuring and Labour Strategies." *Studies in Political Economy* 24, no. 2 (1987): 131–49.

– "Dependency and Class in Canadian Political Economy." *Studies in Political Economy* 6 (1981): 7–34.

– "The Impoverishment of State Theory." *Socialism and Democracy* 13, no. 2 (1999): 21–42.

– "Rethinking the Role of the State." In *Globalization: Critical Reflections,* edited by James H. Mittleman, 81–113. Boulder: Lynn Rienner, 1996.

– "The Role and Nature of the Canadian State." In *The Canadian State: Political Economy and Political Power,* edited by Leo Panitch, 1–23. Toronto: University of Toronto Press, 1977.

– *Working Class Politics in Crisis: Essays on Labour and the State.* London: Verso, 1986.

Papillon, Martin, and Luc Turgeon. "Nationalism's Third Way? Comparing the Emergence of Citizenship Regimes in Quebec and Scotland." In *The Conditions of Diversity in Multinational Democracies,* edited by Alain G. Gagnon, Montserrat Guibernau, and François Rocher, 315–38. Montreal: Institute for Research on Public Policy, 2003.

Paquet, Gilles. "Governance and Emergent Transversal Citizenship: Toward a New Nexus of Moral Contract." In *From Subjects to Citizens: A Hundred Years of Citizenship in Australia and Canada,* edited by Pierre Boyer, Linda Cardinal, and David John Headon, 231–257. Ottawa: University of Ottawa Press. 2004.

Parkin, Andrew, and John Warhurst. "The Labor Party: Image, History and Structure." In *The Machine,* edited by Andrew Parkin and John Warhurst, 21–48. St Leonards: Allen and Unwin, 2000.

Parsons, Talcott. *The Evolution of Societies.* Englewood Cliffs: Prentice-Hall, 1977.

Peck, Jamie. *Workfare States.* New York: Guilford, 2001.

Penner, Norman. *The Canadian Left: A Critical Analysis.* Scarborough: Prentice-Hall, 1977.

Pentland, H. Clare. *Labour and Capital in Canada 1650–1860.* Toronto: James Lorimer, 1981.

Perrin, Guy. "Reflections on Fifty Years of Social Security." *International Labour Review* 99 (1969): 249–90.

Pesando, James E. *Public and Private Pensions in Canada: An Economic Analysis.* Toronto: Ontario Economic Council, University of Toronto, 1977.

– *From Tax Grab to Retirement Saving: Privatizing the CCP Premium Hike.* Toronto: C.D. Howe Institute, 1997.

Pickersgill, John Whitney. *The Mackenzie King Record.* 2 vols. Toronto: University of Toronto Press, 1960.

Pierson, Christopher. *Beyond the Welfare State? The New Political Economy of Welfare* (2nd ed.). State College: Pennsylvania State University Press, 1998.

Pierson, Paul. "Coping with Permanent Austerity: Welfare State Restructuring in Affluent Democracies." In *The New Politics of the Welfare State,* edited by Paul Pierson, 410–56. Oxford: Oxford University Press, 2001.

– *Dismantling the Welfare State?* Cambridge: Cambridge University Press, 1994.

– "The New Politics of the Welfare State." *World Politics* 48, no. 2 (1996): 143–79.

Piven, Frances Fox. *Labor Markets in Postindustrial Societies.* New York: Oxford University Press, 1992.

Pixley, Jocelyn. *Citizenship and Employment: Investigating Post-Industrial Opportunities.* Cambridge: Cambridge University Press, 1993.

– "Economic Democracy: Beyond Wage Earners' Welfare State." In *The Australian Welfare State: Key Documents and Themes,* edited by John Wilson, Jane Thomson, and Anthony McMahon, 38–60. Melbourne: Macmillan Education Australia, 1996.

Plant, Raymond. *The Neo-Liberal State.* New York: Oxford University Press, 2010.

Podger, Andrew Stuart, Judith Elizabeth Raymond, and Wayne Smithers Jackson. "The Relationship Between the Australian Social Security and Personal Income Taxation Systems: A Practical Examination." In *Social Welfare Finance: Selected Papers,* edited by Ronald Mendelsohn, 27–97. Canberra: Centre for Research on Federal Financial Relations, Australian National University, 1982.

Pontusson, Jonas. "From Comparative Public Policy to Political Economy: Putting Political Institutions in Their Place and Taking Interests Seriously." *Comparative Political Studies* 28, no. 1 (1995): 117–47.

Porter, John. *The Vertical Mosaic.* Toronto: University of Toronto Press, 1965.

Poulantzas, Nicos. *Political Power and Social Classes.* London: Verso, 1982.

– *State, Power, Socialism.* London: Verso, 1978.

Pratt, Henry J. *Gray Agendas: Interest Groups and Public Pensions in Canada, Britain, and the United States.* Ann Arbor: University of Michigan Press, 1993.

Preece, Daneil V. *Dismantling Social Europe: The Political Economy of Social Policy in European Union.* Boulder: First Forum Press, 2009.

Przeworski, Adam. *Capitalism and Social Democracy.* Cambridge: Cambridge University Press, 1985.

– "Class, Production, and Politics: A Reply to Burawoy. " In *Rational Choice Marxism,* edited by Terrel Carver and Paul Thomas, 167–89. State College: Pennsylvania State University Press, 1995.

Prince, Michael. "Federal Budgeting in the Post-Deficit Era." In *How Ottawa Spends 1998–1999*, edited by Leslie A. Pal, 151–96. Toronto: Oxford University Press, 1998.

Probert, Belinda. "Globalization, Economic Restructuring, and the State." In *State, Economy, and Public Policy in Australia*, edited by Stephen Bell and Brian Head, 98–118. Melbourne: Oxford University Press, 1994.

Provencher, Jean. *René Lévesque: Portrait of a Québécois.* Montreal: Gage, 1975.

Pulkingham, Jane, and Gordon Ternowetsky. "The Changing Landscape of Social Policy and the Canadian Welfare State." In *Remaking Canadian Social Policy: Social Security in the Late 1990s*, edited by Jane Pulkingham and Gordon Ternowetsky, 2–29. Halifax: Fernwood Publishing, 1996.

Purvis, Barrie. "Why the Accord Has Failed. Discussant I." 2002. http://archive.hrnicholls.com.au/archives/vol6/vol6-9a.php

Pusey, Michael. *Economic Rationalism in Canberra: A Nation-Building State Changes its Mind.* New York: Cambridge University Press, 1991.

Putnam, Robert D. "Who Bonds? Who Bridges? Findings from Social Capital Benchmark Survey." Presentation to the annual meeting of the American Political Science Association, Chicago, 2004.

Quadagno, Jill. *The Transformation of Old Age Security: Class Politics in the American Welfare State.* Chicago: University of Chicago Press, 1988.

Quaid, Maeve. *Workfare: Why Good Social Policy Ideas Go Bad.* Toronto: University of Toronto Press, 2002.

Quarter, Jack, Isla Carmichael, Jorge Sousa, and Susan Elgie. "Social Investment by Union-Based Pension Funds and Labour-Sponsored Investment Funds in Canada." *Industrial Relations* 55, no. 10 (2001): 92–115.

Québec. Direction des Communications Regie Des Rentes du Quebec. *For You and Your Children: Guaranteeing the Future of the Quebec Pension Plan.* 1996. http://www.rrq.gouv.qc.ca/Pages/page404.aspx?url=/SiteCollectionDocuments/www.rrq.gouv.qc/Anglais/publications/regime_rentes/rrq_livvert_en.pdf.

– *Quebec Pension Legislation.* Montreal: CCH Canadian, 1965.

Quiggin, John. "Labor Vision against Tradition." *The Drum* (2011). http://www.abc.net.au/news/2011-04-05/quiggin—labor27s-vision-against-tradition/55366

– "Social Democracy and Market Reform in Australia and New Zealand." In *Social Democracy in Neo-Liberal Times: The Left and Economic Policy Since 1980*, edited by Andrew Glyn, 109–28. New York: Oxford University Press, 2001.

Radice, Hugo. "Taking Globalization Seriously." In *Socialist Register: Globalization versus Capitalism*, edited by Leo Panitch and Colin Leys, 1–23. London: Merlin Press, 1999.

Ragin, Charles. *The Comparative Method: Moving beyond Qualitative and Quantitative Strategies*. Berkeley: University of California Press, 1987.

– "A Qualitative Comparative Analysis of Pension Systems." In *The Comparative Political Economy of the Welfare State*, edited by Thomas Janoski and Alexander M. Hicks, 320–43. Cambridge: Cambridge University Press, 1993.

Ralph, Diana. "Fighting for Canada's Social Programs." *Canadian Review of Social Policy* 34 (1994): 75–85.

Rawson, Donald William. *Labor in Vain? A Survey of the Australian Labor Party*. Croydon: Longmans, 1966.

Reform Party of Canada. *Responsible Social Reform: Renewing CPP Security for Canadians*. Reform Party of Canada, Ottawa, 1995.

Rein, Martin, and John Turner. "How Societies Mix Public and Private Spheres in Their Pension Systems." In *Rethinking the Welfare State: The Political Economy of Pension Reform*, edited by Martin Rein and Winfried Schmahl, 251–92. Northampton: Edward Elgar, 2004.

– "Public–Private Interactions: Mandatory Pension in Australia, the Netherlands, and Switzerland." *Review of Population and Social Policy* 10 (2001): 107–53.

Rhodes, Martin. "The Political Economy of Social Pacts: Competitive Corporatism and European Welfare Reform." In *The New Politics of Welfare State*, edited by Paul Pierson, 165–94. London: Oxford University Press, 2001.

Rice, James J., and Michael J. Prince. *Changing Politics of Canadian Social Policy*. Toronto: University of Toronto Press, 2000.

Richards, John. *Retooling the Welfare State: What's Right, What's Wrong, What's to Be Done?* Toronto: C.D. Howe Institute, 1997.

Riches, Graham. "Australian Responses to Unemployment: Expanding the Options for Social Security Reform in Canada." In *Remaking Canadian Social Policy: Social Security in the Late 1990s*, edited by Jane Pulkingham and Gordon Ternowetsky, 172–86. Halifax: Fernwood Publishing, 1996.

Richmond, Anthony H. "Immigration and Multiculturalism in Canada and Australia: The Contradictions and Crisis of the 1980s." *International Journal of Canadian Studies* 3 (1991): 87–106.

Rimmer, Shila. *Australian Labour Market and Macroeconomic Reforms*. Melbourne: La Trobe University Press, 1994.

Ritzer, George. *Contemporary Sociological Theory* (3rd ed.). Toronto: McGraw-Hill Ryerson, 1992.

Rix, Sara E. "Old Age Income Security in Australia." *AARP Public Institute*, 2005. http://assets.aarp.org/rgcenter/econ/fs108_ss_aus.pdf

Robinson, Ian, and Richard Simeon. *State, Society, and the Development of Canadian Federalism*. Toronto: University of Toronto Press, 1990.

Robson, William B.P. "The Future of Pension Policy: Individual Responsibility and State Support." *A BNAC Policy Statement on Pension Reform.* 1–13. Washington, DC: British–North American Committee (BNAC), 1997.

– *Putting Some Gold in the Golden Years: Fixing the Canada Pension Plan.* Toronto: C.D. Howe Institute, 1996.

Rosenman, Linda. "Restructuring Australian Retirement Income: Implications of Changing Work and Retirement Patterns." *International Social Security Review* 49, no. 4 (1996): 5–24.

Rosenman, Linda, and Jeni Warburton. "Retirement Policy, Retirement Incomes and Women." In *Ageing and Social Policy in Australia,* edited by Allan Borowski, Sol Encel, and Elizabeth Ozanne, 157–72. Cambridge: Cambridge University Press, 1997.

Ross, Robert J.S., and Kent C. Trachte. *Global Capitalism: The New Leviathan.* Albany: SUNY Press, 1990.

Rothstein, Bo. "Labour Market Institutions and Working Class Strength." In *Power Resources Theory and the Welfare State: A Critical Approach,* edited by Julia S. O'Connor and Gregg M. Olsen, 283–306. Toronto: University of Toronto Press, 1998.

– "Social Capital in the Social Democratic Welfare State." *Politics and Society* 4 (2001): 207–41.

– "The Universal Welfare State as a Social Dilemma." In *Restructuring the Welfare State: Political Institutions and Policy Change,* edited by Bo Rothstein and Sven Steinmo, 206–224. New York: Palgrave Macmillan, 2002.

Rothstein, Bo, and Sven Steinmo. "Restructuring Politics: Institutional Analysis and the Challenges of Modern Welfare States." In *Restructuring the Welfare State: Political Institutions and Policy Change,* edited by Bo Rothstein and Sven Steinmo, 1–19. New York: Palgrave Macmillan, 2002.

Salter, Liora, and Rich Salter. "Displacing the Welfare State." In *Understanding Canada: Building on the New Canadian Political Economy,* edited by Wallace Clement, 311–34. Montreal and Kingston: McGill–Queen's University Press, 1997.

Saunders, Peter. *The Ends and Means of Welfare: Coping with Economic and Social Change in Australia.* Cambridge: Cambridge University Press, 2002.

– *Welfare and Inequality: National and International Perspectives on the Australian Welfare State.* Cambridge: Cambridge University Press, 1994.

Sawer, Marian. "Inventing the Nation through the Ballot Box." In *From Subjects to Citizens: A Hundred Years of Citizenship in Australia and Canada,* edited by Pierre Boyer, Linda Cardinal, and David John Headon, 61–78. Ottawa: University of Ottawa Press, 2004.

Sax, Sidney. *Ageing and Public Policy in Australia.* Sydney: Allen and Unwin, 1993.

Sayers, Anthony M. "Regionalism, Political Parties, and Parliamentary Politics in Canada and Australia." In *Regionalism and Party Politics in Canada*, edited by Lisa Young and Keith Archer, 209–19. Toronto: Oxford University Press, 2002.

Scarbrough, Elinor. "West European Welfare States: The Old Politics of Retrenchment." *European Journal of Political Research* 38 (2000): 225–59.

Schedvin, Boris. "Staples and Regions of Pax Britannica." *Economic History Review* 4 (1990): 533–59.

Scheiwe, Dan. *Was Comparability Overstated for Political Advantage? An International Comparison of AAS 25: Financial Reporting by Superannuation Plans.* (Working paper, 1998–2002), 1998. http://eprints.qut.edu.au/859

– *Why Australia's Pension System Is Not a Good International Model.* Pension Institute. Discussion Paper 12.PI.9912, 1999. http://www.pensions-institute.org/workingpapers/wp199912.pdf

Schmitter, Philippe C. "Still the Century of Corporatism." *Review of Politics* 36 (1974): 85–131.

Schwartz, Herman. "Internationalization and two Liberal Welfare States: Australia and New Zealand." In *Welfare and Work in the Open Economy*, edited by Fritz W. Scharpe and Vivien. A. Schmidt, 69–121. London: Oxford University Press, 2000.

Segal, Hugh. *Beyond Greed: A Traditional Conservative Confronts Neoconservative Excess.* Toronto: Stoddart, 1997.

Shaver, Sheila. "Australian Welfare Reform: From Citizenship to Supervision." *Australian Journal of Social Issues* 36, no. 4 (2001): 277–93.

– "Consideration of Mere Logic: The Australian Age Pension and the Politics of Means Testing." In *States, Labor Markets, and the Future of Old Age Policy*, edited by John Myles and Jill Quadagno, 105–23. Philadelphia: Temple University Press, 1991.

– *Universality and Selectivity in Income Support: An Assessment of the Issues.* Sydney: Ashgate, 1997.

Sherry, Nick. "Australia's Policy Response to the Global Financial Crisis." Address to the Institute of Actuaries of Australia Biennial Convention, Sydney, 21 April 2009. http://ministers.treasury.gov.au/DisplayDocs.aspx?doc=speeches/2009/012.htm&pageID=005&min=njs&Year=&DocType=

Shields, John, and B. Mitchell Evans. *Shrinking the State: Globalization and Public Administration Reform.* Halifax: Fernwood Publishing, 2002.

Shragge, Eric, ed. "Workfare: An Overview." In *Workfare: Ideology for a New Underclass*, edited by Eric Shragge, 17–34. Toronto: University of Toronto Press, Higher Education Division, 1997.

Simeon, Richard. "Studying Public Policy." *Canadian Journal of Political Science* 9, no. 3 (December 1976): 548–80.

Skocpol, Theda. “Bringing the State Back In.” In *Bringing the State Back In*, edited by Peter B. Evans, Dietrich Rueschemeyer, and Theda Skocpol, 3–38 Cambridge: Cambridge University Press, 1985.

– *Protecting Soldiers and Mothers: The Political Origins of Social Security in the United States*. Cambridge: Belknap Press of Harvard University Press, 1995.

Skocpol, Theda, and Edwin Amenta. “States and Social Policies.” *Annual Review of Sociology* 12 (1986): 131–57.

Smardon, Bruce. “The Federal Welfare State and the Politics of Retrenchment in Canada.” *Journal of Canadian Studies* 34, no. 2 (Summer 1991): 122–41.

Smith, David E. “Canadian Political Parties and National Integration.” In *Canadian Political Parties in Transition* (2nd ed.), edited by A. Brian Tanguay and Alain G Gagnon, 362–84. Toronto: Nelson Canada, 1996.

– “Indices of Citizenship.” In *From Subjects to Citizens: A Hundred Years of Citizenship in Australia and Canada*, edited by Pierre Boyer, Linda Cardinal, and David Headon, 19–30. 2004. Ottawa: University of Ottawa Press.

Smith, Rodney, and Michael Wearing. “Do Australians Want the Welfare State?” *Politics* 22, no. 2 (1987): 55–65.

Smyth, Paul. “Australian Social Policy in an International Context.” In *Social Policy in Australia: Understanding for Action*, edited by Alison McClelland and Paul Smyth, 121–43. Melbourne: Oxford University Press, 2006.

Social Welfare Policy Secretariat. *Alternative Strategies to Meet the Income Needs of the Aged*. Canberra: Australian Government Publishing Service, 1982.

Soskice, David. “Divergent Production Regimes: Coordinated and Uncoordinated Market Economies in the 1980s and 1990s.” In *Continuity and Change in Contemporary Capitalism*, edited by Herbert Kitschelt, Peter Lange, Gary Marks, and John Stephens, 101–34. Cambridge: Cambridge University Press, 1999.

Spies-Butcher, Ben. “Labor, Neo-Liberalism, and the Welfare State.” *Solidarity Magazine*. (2009). http://www.solidarity.net.au/mag/back/2009/17/labor-neo-liberalism-and-the-welfare-state

Stanford, Jim. *Paper Boom: Why Real Prosperity Requires a New Approach to Canada's Economy*. Toronto: Canadian Centre for Alternatives, James Lorimer, 1999.

Stephens, John. “The Scandinavian Welfare States.” In *Welfare States in Transition: National Adaptations in Global Economy*, edited by Gøsta Esping-Andersen, 32–65. London: Sage, 1996.

– *The Transformation from Capitalism to Socialism*. Champaign: University of Illinois Press, 1979.

Stevens, Bron, and Pat Weller, eds. *The Australian Labor Party and Federal Politics: A Documentary Survey*. Melbourne: Melbourne University Press, 1976.

Stevenson, Garth. “Political Decentralization: A Critique of Provincialism.”

In *Canada What's Left? A New Social Contract Pro and Con*, edited by John Richard and Donald C. Kerr, 141–6. Edmonton: NeWest Publishers, 1986.

Strange, Susan. *The Retreat of the State.* Cambridge: Cambridge University Press, 1996.

Streeck, Wolfgang. "Neo-Corporatist Industrial Relations and the Economic Crisis in West Germany." In *Order and Conflict in Contemporary Capitalism*, edited by John H. Goldthorpe, 291–314. New York: Oxford University Press, 1984.

Stilwell, Frank. "Works, Wages, Welfare." In *Understanding the Australian Welfare State: Key Documents and Themes*, edited by Anthony McMahon, Jane Thomson, and Christopher Williams, 23–38. Croydon: Tertiary Press, 2000.

Stursberg, Peter. *Lester Pearson and the Dream of Unity.* Toronto: Doubleday Canada, 1978.

Swank, Duane. *Global Capital, Political Institutions, and Policy Change in Developed Welfare States.* London: Cambridge University Press, 2002.

– "Political Institutions and Welfare State Restructuring: The Impact of Institutions on Social Policy Changes in Developed Democracies." In *The New Politics of the Welfare State*, edited by Paul Pierson, 197–233. London: Oxford University Press, 2001.

Swank, Duane, and Alexander Hicks. "The Determinants and Redistributive Impacts of Welfare State Spending in the Advanced Capitalist Democracies, 1969–1980." In *Political Economy in Western Democracies*, edited by Norman J. Vig and Steven E. Schier, 115–39. New York: Holmes and Meier, 1985.

Swartz, Donald. "The Politics of Reform: Conflict and Accommodation in Canadian Health Policy." In *The Canadian State: Political Economy and Political Power*, edited by Leo Panitch, 311–42. Toronto: University of Toronto Press, 1977.

Tamagno, Edward. *Occupational Pension Plans in Canada: Trend, Coverage, and Income of Seniors.* Ottawa: Caledon Institute of Social Policy, 2006.

Tamir, Yael. *Liberal Nationalism.* Princeton: Princeton University Press, 1993.

Taylor, Charles. *Reconciling the Solitudes.* Montreal and Kingston: McGill–Queen's University Press, 1993.

Teeple, Gary. *Globalization and the Decline of Social Reform.* Toronto: Garamond Press, 1995.

Teipe, Emily J. *America's First Veterans and the Revolutionary War Pensions.* Lewiston: Edwin Mellen Press, 2002.

Therborn, Göran. "Karl Marx Returning: The Welfare State and Neo-Marxist, Corporatist, and State Theories." *International Political Science Review* 7, no. 2 (1986): 131–64.

– "Social Democracy in One Country." *Dissent* (Fall 2000): 59–65.

– *When, How, and Why Does a State Become a Welfare State?* Nijmegen: Institute for Political Science, Catholic University, 1983.

Thomas, Norman C. "Public Policy and the Resurgence of Conservatism in Three Anglo-American Democracies." In *The Resurgence of Conservatism in Anglo-American Democracies*, edited by Barry Cooper, Allan Kornberg, and William Mishler, 96–136. Durham: Duke University Press, 1988.

Tilly, Charles. "Globalization Threatens Labor's Rights." *International Labour and Working Class History* 47 (1995): 1–23.

Timonen, Virpi. *Ageing Societies: A Comparative Introduction.* Maidenhead: McGraw-Hill Open University Press, 2008.

– *Restructuring the Welfare State: Globalisation and Social Policy Reform in Finland and Sweden.* Cheltenham. Edward Elgar, 2003.

Titmuss, Richard M. *Essays on the Welfare State.* London: Allen and Unwin, 1976.

Torfing, Jacob. *Politics, Regulation, and the Modern Welfare State.* New York: St Martin's Press, 1998.

Townson, Monica. *Pensions under Attack.* Ottawa: Canadian Centre for Policy Alternatives, 2001.

Trades and Labour Congress of Canada. *The Trades and Labour Congress of Canada: An Historical Review, 1870–1955.* Ottawa: Trades and Labour Congress, 1955.

Tsokhas, Kosmas. *A Class Apart? Business and Australian Politics 1960–1980.* Melbourne: Oxford University Press, 1984.

Turner, John A., and David M. Rajnes. "Can Private Pension Systems Fill the Gap?" *Ageing International* 22, no. 2 (1995): 38–43.

UN Department of Economic and Social Affairs. *World Public Sector: Globalization and the State.* New York: 2001.

Vidlund, Mika. *Old Age Pension Reforms in the EU-15 Countries at the Time of Retrenchment.* Working Paper. Finnish Centre for Pensions, 2006. https://www.utu.fi/fi/yksikot/soc/yksikot/sosiaalitieteet/topsos/julkaisut/Documents/vidlund_mika.pdf

Wahl, Asbjorn. *The Rise and Fall of the Welfare State.* London: Pluto Press, 2011.

Wallace, Ruth A., and Alison Wolf. *Contemporary Sociological Theory: Expanding the Classical Tradition.* Belmont: Wadsworth, 1999.

Walter, James. *Tunnel Vision: The Failure of Political Imagination.* St Leonards: Allen and Unwin, 1996.

Wanna, John. "Can the State Manage the Macroeconomy?" In *State, Economy, and Public Policy*, edited by Stephen Bell and Brian Head, 225–49. New York: Oxford University Press, 1994.

Watts, Robert William. "The Origins of the Australian Welfare State." In *Australian Welfare History: Critical Essays*, edited by Richard Kennedy, 225–55. Melbourne: Macmillan of Australia, 1982.

Watts, Ronald L. "Federalism and Diversity in Canada." In *Autonomy and Ethnicity: Negotiating Competing Claims in Multi-Ethnic States*, edited by Yash Ghai, 29–52. Cambridge: Cambridge University Press, 2000.

Weaver, Kent. "Cutting old Age Pensions." In *The Government Taketh Away: The Politics of Pain in the United States and Canada*, edited by Leslie A. Pal and Kent Weaver, 41–65. Washington, DC: Georgetown University Press, 2003.

– "Whose Money Is It Anyhow? Governance and Social Investment in Collective Investment Funds." In *Rethinking the Welfare State: The Political Economy of Pension Reform*, edited by Martin Rein and Winfried Schmahl, 294–315. Northampton: Edward Elgar, 2004.

Weaver, Kent, and Paul D. Pierson. "Imposing Losses in Pension Policy." In *Do Institutions Matter? Government Capabilities in the United States and Abroad*, edited by Kent Weaver and Bert A. Rockman, 110–50. Washington, DC: Brookings Institution, 1993.

Weiss, Linda. *The Myth of the Powerless State*. Ithaca: Cornell University Press, 1998.

Whitaker, Reg. "Neo-Conservatism and the State." In *Socialist Register*, edited by Ralph Miliband, Leo Panitch, and John Saville, 1–31. London: Merlin Press, 1987.

– *A Sovereign Idea*. Montreal and Kingston: McGill–Queen's University Press, 1992.

Whiteford, Peter. "Reforming Pensions: The Australian Experience." In *Rethinking the Welfare State: The Political Economy of Pension Reform*, edited by Martin Rein and Winfried Schmahl, 83–100. Northampton: Edward Elgar, 2004.

Whitehouse, Edward. *Canada's Retirement Income Provision: An International Perspective*. Ottawa: Department of Finance, 2009. http://www.fin.gc.ca/activty/pubs/pension/ref-bib/whitehouse-eng.asp

Whitfield, Dexter. *Public Services or Corporate Welfare: Rethinking the Nation State in the Global Economy*. London: Pluto Press, 2001.

Whitlam, Edward Gough. *The Whitlam Government 1972–1975*. Pinewood: Penguin Books, 1985.

Wilensky, Harold L. *Comparative Social Policy: Theories, Methods, Findings*. Berkeley: University of California, 1985.

– *The New Corporatism, Centralization, and the Welfare State*. Beverly Hills: Sage, 1976.

– *Rich Democracies: Political Economy, Public Policy, and Performance*. Berkeley: University of California Press, 2000.

– *The Welfare State and Equality: Structural and Ideological Roots of Public Expenditures*. Berkeley: University of California Press, 1975.

Williams, Christopher. "Reinventing the Welfare State: Neo-liberalism and Beyond." In *Understanding the Australian Welfare State: Key Documents and*

Themes, edited by Anthony McMahon, Jane Thomson, and Christopher Williams, 248–62. Croydon: Tertiary Press, 2000.

Williams, Jack. *The Story of Unions in Canada.* Toronto: J.M. Dent, 1975.

Williamson, John B., and Fred C. Pampel. *Old Age Security in Comparative Perspective.* New York: Oxford University Press, 1993.

Wilson, H. Thomas. *Retreat from Governance.* Hull: Voyageur Publishing, 1989.

Winer, Stanley L., and Allan M. Maslove. "Fiscal Federalism in Australia and Canada." In *Reforming Fiscal Federalism for Global Competition: A Canada–Australia Comparison*, edited by Paul Michael Boothe, 45–68. Edmonton: University of Alberta Press, 1996.

Wolfe, David. "The Canadian State in Comparative Perspective." *Canadian Review of Sociology and Anthropology* 26, no. 1 (1989), 95–126.

Wonik, Kim. "Social Insurance Expansion and Political Regime Dynamics in Europe 1880–1945." *Social Science Quarterly* 88, no. 2 (2007): 494–514.

Woodsworth, David Edward. "Book Review/Recensions." *Canadian Journal of Social Work Education* 7, no. 1 (1981): 125–26.

Workman, Thom W. *If You're in My Way, I'm Walking: The Assaults on Working People Since 1970.* Black Points: Fernwood Publishing, 2009.

World Bank. *Averting the Old Age Crisis: A World Bank Policy Research Report.* New York: Oxford University Press, 1994.

– *Pension Reform and the Development of Pension Systems: An Evaluation of World Bank Assistance.* Washington, DC: 2006. http://ieg.worldbank.org/Data/reports/pensions_evaluation.pdf

– *Social Protection Sector Strategy: From Safety-Net to Springboard.* Washington, DC: 2001. http://www.worldbank.org/404_response.htm

Wright, Erik Olin. "A General Framework for the Analysis of Class Structure." In *The Debate on Classes*, edited by Erik Olin Wright, 3–43. London: Verso, 1990.

– "Class Analysis." In *The Debate on Classes*, edited by Erik Olin Wright, 3–43. London: Verso, 1990.

Yargin, Daniel, and Joseph Stanislaw. *The Commanding Heights: The Battle between Government and the Marketplace That Is Remaking the World.* New York: Simon and Schuster, 1998.

Young, Walter D. *The Anatomy of a Party.* Toronto: University of Toronto Press, 1969.

Ziguras, Stephen. "Australian Social Security Policy: Doing More with Less?" In *Social Security in Australia: Understanding for Action*, edited by Alison McClelland and Paul Smith, 161–77. Melbourne: Oxford University Press, 2006.

Zijderveld, Anton C. *The Waning of the Welfare State: The End of Comprehensive State Succour.* New Brunswick: Transaction Publishers, 1999.

Index

Page numbers in italics refer to tables.

Studies in Comparative Political Economy and Public Policy

1 *The Search for Political Space: Globalization, Social Movements, and the Urban Political Experience*/Warren Magnusson
2 *Oil, the State, and Federalism: The Rise and Demise of Petro-Canada as a Statist Impulse*/John Erik Fossum
3 *Defying Conventional Wisdom: Political Movements and Popular Contention against North American Free Trade*/Jeffrey M. Ayres
4 *Community, State, and Market on the North Atlantic Rim: Challenges to Modernity in the Fisheries*/Richard Apostle, Gene Barrett, Peter Holm, Svein Jentoft, Leigh Mazany, Bonnie McCay, Knut H. Mikalsen
5 *More with Less: Work Reorganization in the Canadian Mining Industry*/Bob Russell
6 *Visions for Privacy: Policy Approaches for the Digital Age*/Edited by Colin J. Bennett and Rebecca Grant
7 *New Democracies: Economic and Social Reform in Brazil, Chile, and Mexico*/Michel Duquette
8 *Poverty, Social Assistance, and the Employability of Mothers: Restructuring Welfare States*/Maureen Baker and David Tippin
9 *The Left's Dirty Job: The Politics of Industrial Restructuring in France and Spain*/W. Rand Smith
10 *Risky Business: Canada's Changing Science-Based Policy and Regulatory Regime*/Edited by G. Bruce Doern and Ted Reed
11 *Temporary Work: The Gendered Rise of a Precarious Employment Relationship*/Leah Vosko
12 *Who Cares?: Women's Work, Childcare, and Welfare State Redesign*/Jane Jenson and Mariette Sineau with Franca Bimbi, Anne-Marie Daune-Richard, Vincent Della Sala, Rianne Mahon, Bérengèr Marques-Pereira, Olivier Paye, and George Ross
13 *Canadian Forest Policy: Adapting to Change*/Edited by Michael Howlett
14 *Knowledge and Economic Conduct: The Social Foundations of the Modern Economy*/Nico Stehr
15 *Contingent Work, Disrupted Lives: Labour and Community in the New Rural Economy*/Anthony Winson and Belinda Leach
16 *The Economic Implications of Social Cohesion*/Edited by Lars Osberg
17 *Gendered States: Women, Unemployment Insurance, and the Political Economy of the Welfare State in Canada, 1945–1997*/Ann Porter
18 *Educational Regimes and Anglo-American Democracy*/Ronald Manzer
19 *Money in Their Own Name: The Feminist Voice in Poverty Debate in Canada, 1970–1995*/Wendy McKeen

20 *Collective Action and Radicalism in Brazil: Women, Urban Housing, and Rural Movements*/Michel Duquette, Maurilio Galdino, Charmain Levy, Bérengère Marques-Pereira, and Florence Raes
21 *Continentalizing Canada: The Politics and Legacy of the Macdonald Royal Commission*/Gregory J. Inwood
22 *Globalization Unplugged: Sovereignty and the Canadian State in the Twenty-First Century*/Peter Urmetzer
23 *New Institutionalism: Theory and Analysis*/Edited by André Lecours
24 *Mothers of the Nation: Women, Family, and Nationalism in Twentieth-Century Europe*/Patrizia Albanese
25 *Partisanship, Globalization, and Canadian Labour Market Policy: Four Provinces in Comparative Perspective*/Rodney Haddow and Thomas Klassen
26 *Rules, Rules, Rules, Rules: Multi-Level Regulatory Governance*/Edited by G. Bruce Doern and Robert Johnson
27 *The Illusive Tradeoff: Intellectual Property Rights, Innovation Systems, and Egypt's Pharmaceutical Industry*/Basma Abdelgafar
28 *Fair Trade Coffee: The Prospects and Pitfalls of Market-Driven Social Justice*/Gavin Fridell
29 *Deliberative Democracy for the Future: The Case of Nuclear Waste Management in Canada*/Genevieve Fuji Johnson
30 *Internationalization and Canadian Agriculture: Policy and Governing Paradigms*/Grace Skogstad
31 *Military Workfare: The Soldier and Social Citizenship in Canada*/Deborah Cowen
32 *Public Policy for Women: The State, Income Security, and Labour*/Edited by Marjorie Griffin Cohen and Jane Pulkingham
33 *Smiling Down the Line: Info-Service Work in the Global Economy*/Bob Russell
34 *Municipalities and Multiculturalism: The Politics of Immigration in Toronto and Vancouver*/Kristin R. Good
35 *Policy Paradigms, Transnationalism, and Domestic Politics*/Edited by Grace Skogstad
36 *Three Bio-Realms: Biotechnology and the Governance of Food, Health, and Life in Canada*/G. Bruce Doern and Michael J. Prince
37 *North America in Question: Regional Integration in an Era of Economic Turbulence*/Edited by Jeffrey Ayres and Laura Macdonald
38 *Comparative Public Policy in Latin America*/Edited by Jordi Díez and Susan Franceschet

39 *Wrestling with Democracy: Voting Systems as Politics in the Twentieth-Century West*/Dennis Pilon
40 *The Politics of Energy Dependency: Ukraine, Belarus, and Lithuania between Domestic Oligarchs and Russian Pressure*/Margarita M. Balmaceda
41 *Environmental Policy Change in Emerging Market Democracies: Central and Eastern Europe and Latin America Compared*/Jale Tosun
42 *Globalization and Food Sovereignty: Global and Local Change in the New Politics of Food*/Edited by Peter Andrée, Jeffrey Ayres, Michael J. Bosia, and Marie-Josée Massicotte
43 *Land, Stewardship, and Legitimacy: Endangered Species Policy in Canada and the United States*/Andrea Olive
44 *Copyfight: The Global Politics of Digital Copyright Reform*/Blayne Haggart
45 *Learning to School: Federalism and Public Schooling in Canada*/Jennifer Wallner
46 *Transforming Provincial Politics: The Political Economy of Canada's Provinces and Territories in the Neoliberal Era*/Edited by Bryan M. Evans and Charles W. Smith
47 *Comparing Quebec and Ontario: Political Economy and Public Policy at the Turn of the Millennium*/Rodney Haddow
48 *Ideas and the Pace of Change: National Pharmaceutical Insurance in Canada, Australia, and the United Kingdom*/Katherine Boothe
49 *Democratic Illusion: Deliberative Democracy in Canadian Public Policy*/Genevieve Fuji Johnson
50 *Purchase for Profit: Public-Private Partnerships and Canada's Public Health-Care System*/Heather Whiteside
51 *Beyond the Welfare State: Postwar Social Settlement and Public Pension Policy in Canada and Australia*/Sirvan Karimi

www.ingramcontent.com/pod-product-compliance
Lightning Source LLC
LaVergne TN
LVHW041112090826

844660LV00061B/725/J
9781487500412